THE

WORKS OF THOMAS MANTON, D.D.

VOL. XXII.

THE COMPLETE WORKS

OF

THOMAS MANTON, D.D.

VOLUME XXII.

CONTAINING

SERMONS ON SEVERAL TEXTS OF SCRIPTURE;

TOGETHER WITH

COPIOUS INDEXES OF SUBJECTS AND TEXTS TO
DR MANTON'S WORKS.

Sovereign Grace Pubishers, Inc.
P.O. Box 4998
Lafayette, Indiana 47903

Printed In the United States of America
By Lightning Source, Inc.

CONTENTS.

SERMONS

ON

SEVERAL TEXTS OF SCRIPTURE

SERMON UPON PROVERBS VI. 6-8.

Go to the ant, thou sluggard; consider her ways, and be wise: which having no guide, overseer, or ruler, provideth her meat in the summer, and gathereth her food in the harvest.—PROV. vi. 6-8.

MAN being fallen from God, and the primitive perfection of his nature, may be taught his duty by the meanest creatures; therefore in scripture we are often referred to the beasts of the field and fowls of the air. As, for instance, to cure our ingratitude, the prophet bids us consider the beasts: Isa. i. 3, 'The ox knoweth his owner, and the ass his master's crib; but Israel doth not know, my people doth not consider.' And to cure our distrust, Christ sends us to the ravens: Luke xii. 24, 'Consider the ravens: for they neither sow, nor reap; which neither have storehouse, nor barns; yet God feedeth them: how much more are ye better than the fowls.' And to cure our insensibility and improvidence in the season of action, and to put us on using fit remedies, we are sent to the stork and crane: Jer. viii. 7, 'The stork in the heavens knoweth her appointed times, and the turtle, and the crane, and the swallow, observe the time of their coming; but my people know not the judgment of the Lord.' These creatures know the time of coming and going, but man is stupid and senseless. Now here we are sent to school to a far more inferior creature, the ant or pismire. Certainly there is a great deal of morality in the bosom of nature, if we had the skill to find it out. There are in most of the creatures shadows both of virtues and vices; and if I may speak my mind, these are the true layman's books, and the images from whence we may learn understanding and the knowledge of God.

Here, to shame him, the sluggard is sent to the ant—'Go to the ant, thou sluggard,' &c.

In which words we have—(1.) The learner, the sluggard. (2.) The teacher, the ant. (3.) The manner of address directed, 'Go, consider her ways, and be wise. (4.) The lesson to be learned, diligence and labour, or providence and foresight. Diligence and labour, in that 'she provideth her meat, and gathereth her food.' And providence and foresight, that this is done in 'harvest and summer;' in the time when it is to be had, when there is much grain spilt or shed. (5.) The enforcement of this lesson; that the ant doth this though she hath 'no guide, overseer, and ruler.'

1. The scholar or learner is the sluggard, who is averse and back-

ward to his necessary duty, both in temporals and spirituals; and so
sins not only against the law of God, but his own nature; for a living
soul was never given us to be idle. Nature made our faculties for use.
All the world about us is in action; the sun runneth his course, the
waters flow for our use and benefit, the winds blow, the earth bringeth
forth, cattle labour for us; but the sluggard is the shame of the
creation; every creature is a witness against him to condemn his
sloth. But here the slothful are sent to the ant to learn to labour, and
make provision for futurity. And thus, to correct our stupidness and folly,
God sendeth us to the least of the dumb and unreasonable creatures.

2. The teacher is the ant, a sedulous and sagacious creature.
Wonders are spoken of them in writers, which I list not to trouble you
with; as what skill they show in framing their cells, that they may not be
drowned by wet; what order and discipline they use among themselves;
what diligence they use to get provision, not only by day, but by night,
as Ælian tells us. In the full moons of summer and harvest they
rest not. What sagacity they have in biting off the ends of the corn,
that it may not grow; how they perish not, but live in the wettest and
coldest winter. The grasshopper, that singeth away the summer, dieth
whilst they supply themselves out of the store which they have
gathered by their industry. To dilate on these things at large would
savour more of the natural historian than the divine.

3. The direction, or the manner of address; in three things—(1.)
Go; (2.) Consider her ways; (3.) Be wise.

[1.] For the first, 'Go;' as their fashion was to go to their doctors
and teachers: 1 Kings xiv. 3, 'Go to the prophet, and he shall tell thee
what shall become of the child.' In those days the party, if capable,
did not send for the prophet, but went to him. So here, 'Go to the
ant;' to shame the sluggard, as if he needed to perform that office to
the ant which they showed to their eminent prophets. But when they
come, what must they do?

[2.] 'Consider her ways.' This doctor teacheth not by words, but
by example; and therefore the sluggard is not bidden to hear, but to
see, and consider her ways; that is, see the great diligence of this
creature, and their marvellous order in passing to and fro; not cross-
ing one another, but if any be overlaboured, helping them, as your
eye will easily inform you.

[3.] 'Be wise.' Be not a spectator only, but an improver; not more
learned, or able to discourse of these things, but more wise, to cure
idleness and improvidence.

4. The lesson to be learned; which is—(1.) Labour; and (2.)
Foresight.

[1.] Labour. In the hottest times they are most busy, and endure
the trouble of it. Their industry is a pattern to us.

[2.] Their foresight. They do this in the 'summer and harvest.'
They suffer not the opportunity to pass. As we are to labour if we
would attain eternal life (Acts xxvi. 7, 'Unto which promise our
twelve tribes, instantly serving God day and night, hope to come'), so
we are also to redeem the season: Eph. v. 16, 'Redeeming the time,
because the days are evil.' Means, and mercies, and life itself, lie upon
uncertainties.

5. The amplification of this provident industry of the ant; and so it enforceth the lesson, 'Which having no guide, overseer, or ruler;' that is, the ant doth her duty by instinct, not as compelled thereunto by any that have power to check and control her. Naturalists tell us that the bees are a feminine monarchy, but the ants a democracy and commonwealth, where every one's natural industry prompts him to seek his own good, and the good of the whole.

But to the text. Three words are used; she hath no 'guide' to go before her and show her what to do; no 'overseer' to observe whether she doth it or no; no 'ruler' to punish her for idleness or miscarriage; yet she labours. All this is spoken to aggravate the sluggish improvidence of man. We have a guide, the Lord, who 'hath showed us what is good,' Micah vi. 8. We have an inspector; God is our witness as well as our guide: Prov. xv. 3, 'The eyes of the Lord are in every place, beholding the evil and the good.' We have a lord and ruler, to whom we must give an account: Rom. xiv. 12, 'Every one of us shall give an account of himself to God.' And shall we be idle and neglect our duty?

From the whole you see—

1. The argument is *a minore ad majus*, from the less to the greater, to shame us. If the creatures that want reason do for their own preservation with such diligence make preparation for time to come, how much more inexcusable are we, who are endowed with reason, and can foresee the end, and chose the means, bound to provide for the future, and forecast and foresee for those things that belong to our future happiness? And if we make not use of it to that end, we are highly culpable before God.

2. It is bound the more upon us, because this instinct of nature which prompts them to this is not their providence, but God's, who is the Creator of nature, and hath put this disposition into them. Now, hath not God put such a disposition and inclination into us much more? Surely man is made a nobler creature than the beasts, and is more fitted to his use and end; for it is said, Job xxxv. 11, 'Who teacheth us more than the beasts of the earth, and maketh us wiser than the fowls of heaven.' Beasts have instinct, but men have the gift of reason and conscience bestowed upon them, and do not only understand their own duty, but may make wise collections from what God hath put into other beings.

3. That this is binding upon us, both as to the body and soul; for we consist of both, and must make provision for the welfare of both.

[1.] That we should provide for our bodily welfare will be easily granted, and is agreeable enough with the context, which speaketh of the inconveniency of asking, and borrowing, and engaging others in suretyship; and that we should rather by our diligence and providence live by our callings, that we may not need to borrow. This application maketh the context run on smoothly. Now though it may be presumed that in these things wherein common reason and sense inviteth men to this diligence and providence, all should have a quick and tender ear, yet some idle drones there are who live without a calling, and have nothing whereby to support themselves; who are not only worse than the ant, that by labour layeth up for the time of want, but worse than the grasshopper, that have scarce a merry life for the present, but involve themselves and their friends in manifold inconveniences, living by borrowing when they have nothing to pay, which is but a specious kind of theft and robbery.   Or, if they can support themselves for the present, tempt God to forsake them in their age, when they do not employ themselves as instruments of his providence, for their own private or the public good.   They that be busy in an honest calling may have to supply their own necessities, and to give to him that needeth: Eph. iv. 28, 'Let him that stole, steal no more; but rather let him labour, working with his hands the thing which is good, that he may have to give to him that needeth.'   By stealing is meant not only downright theft, but all those fraudulent and deceitful ways whereby a man doth wrong his neighbour in his outward estate.   As a remedy, he prescribeth diligence in some good and honest calling, and then he may expect God's blessing, that he will give him a competency, not only to support him in his necessities, but also to enable him to relieve others.   But when men will not labour, they are cast upon temptations to use sinful shifts to keep them in their straits.   Therefore it is the Lord's will that every one should betake himself to some lawful calling and employment, and serve God therein with a good conscience; for God usually blesseth this conscientious diligence with such a measure of success, that they have wherewith to sustain themselves and be helpful to others.   Whereas others cannot trust in God who neglect to use the means, for he never undertook to provide for us in our sins, or that laziness, carelessness, idleness, luxury, and neglect of our affairs should not be our ruin, for then his providence would run contrary to his word: 'He becometh poor that dealeth with a slack hand; but the diligent hand maketh rich,' Prov. x. 4; and ver. 22, 'The blessing of the Lord maketh rich: and he addeth no sorrow with it;' implying that God's blessing goeth with man's industry.   So that though our great business be to press men to look after eternal life, yet as idleness is a sin, and a great part of sensuality, and disposeth for other sins, we need to read the lecture of the ant to many men to awaken them out of their sluggishness, and indulgence to the ease of the flesh in temporal affairs, that they neither live without a calling, nor without industrious diligence in their calling; that they may not tempt God's providence to provide for them, when they take no course to live by; nor become drones and unprofitable burdens of the earth, and so prove a clog and disgrace to religion, and lie also open as a prey to Satan; for the devil employeth them whom he findeth not employed by God, or who refuse to be employed by him; and so they prove a reproach to providence by their want, and a disgrace to religion by their carnal shifts, lies, and devices.

[2.] That we should provide for our soul's welfare, the lesson of the ant is also useful to us; for if diligence and providence be recommended as necessary for christians, surely the best and greatest works call for most of our care: Prov. iv. 7, 'Wisdom is the principal thing, therefore get wisdom: and with all thy getting get understanding.'   And those things which are of most absolute necessity, which must be done or we are undone for ever, must be despatched with the greatest earnestness and diligence: Luke x. 42, 'One thing is needful.'   And besides, for those that are of most profit, that conduce to eternal life, and bring a blessing upon our present affairs, these are to be most minded in their season and opportunity. Such are spiritual affairs: Mat. vi. 33, 'Seek first the kingdom of God.' Therefore the contemplation of the ant concerneth these affairs. If we must 'consider her ways, and be wise,' surely we should mind these things; for the best wisdom is to be wise to salvation. And this doth chiefly become christians; for God that giveth instinct to the creatures, and reason to all men, hath given faith to those that live in the church: 1 John v. 20, 'He hath given us an understanding, that we may know him that is true; and we are in him that is true, even in his Son Jesus Christ. This is the true God, and eternal life.' The knowledge of the true God directeth us to eternal life as our happiness. So that this life is our opportunity, our summer and harvest as to the means, the time of action, but hereafter is the time of retribution and reward. Therefore man, being born to labour, and having not only reason to guide him, but faith, and being to give an account of what he hath done in the body, he is now, while means and mercies last, to provide for the world to come. Therefore 'go to the ant, thou sluggard.' Thou careless christian, consider the manner and course of life of this poor creature, how vigilant, careful, and diligent she is in providing for the time to come, and do something proportionably for thy great hopes.

Doct. That serious diligence is required of christians in improving the present season in order to eternal life.

1. There is much work required of a christian. Christianity is not a loitering profession, but is always represented to us as a laborious thing: Phil. ii. 12, 'Work out your own salvation with fear and trembling;' John vi. 27, 'Labour not for the meat that perisheth, but for that meat which endureth to everlasting life;' 2 Peter iii. 14, 'Be diligent, that ye may be found of him in peace, without spot, and blameless.'

[1.] There is much diligence required to get into a state of grace: Luke xiii. 24, 'Strive to enter in at the strait gate; for I say unto you, many shall seek to enter in, but shall not be able.' Therefore, if we are yet unconverted, we are to bestir ourselves, and use all means that we may not come short of converting grace. If we miss it, it is long of ourselves; we forfeit it by our negligence and carelessness.

[2.] There is much diligence required to keep ourselves in a station of grace. There are many soul-endangering sins which we are apt to indulge; therefore David saw need to beg, Ps. cxix. 133, 'Order my steps in thy word, and let no iniquity have dominion over me;' and the apostle warneth converted christians, Rom. vi. 12, 'Let not sin, therefore, reign in your mortal bodies, that ye should obey it in the lusts thereof.' And there are many duties required to which we are backward and averse, at least remiss and cold; therefore we need to be exhorted, Rom. xii. 11, 'Not to be slothful in business, but fervent in spirit, serving the Lord.' We cannot be zealous enough in our pursuit after eternal happiness. If it were about riches and honours, a cold desire and dull pursuit were not amiss; but about God, and Christ, and heaven, coldness is a contempt.

[3.] There is much diligence required to get grace evidenced: 'Give diligence to make your calling and election sure,' 2 Peter i. 10. Providing comfort against the hour of death: 2 Peter iii. 14, 'Wherefore, beloved, seeing that ye look for such things, be diligent, that ye may be found of him in peace, without spot, and blameless.'

[4.] There is much diligence required to keep up assurance, as well as to get it. It is gotten with diligence, and kept with watchfulness: Heb. vi. 11, 'And we desire that every one of you do show the same diligence, to the full assurance of hope unto the end.' So far as we abate in our qualification, so far doth our assurance abate. Well, then, you see from first to last that there is much work required of a christian.

2. That the opportunity of doing this work is confined to this life; and when that is at an end, it presently ceaseth. There is no mending of errors in the other world. Now is the season, and therefore we should speedily, and without delay, set about our work: Isa. lv. 6, 'Seek ye the Lord while he may be found, call ye upon him while he is near.' There is a time of finding, which, when it cometh to an end, all opportunity is lost. The Father's season is while he waiteth; the Son's season while he offereth grace; the Holy Ghost's season while he stirreth the waters. So, on the contrary, Luke xix. 42, 'If thou hadst known, even thou, at least in this thy day, the things that belong to thy peace; but now they are hid from thine eyes.' Men know not their day and time, and so show themselves more silly and brutish than the ant. A child of God is wise in time, and the sensual and brutish worldling is wise too late; when he is in the other world, then he wisheth that he had minded God, his soul, and heaven more. What will it profit us to think of working when it is too late to work, and we are *in termino*, in our final estate?

3. We have a guide, overseer, and ruler, to whom we must render an account of what we do, which is denied to the ant.

[1.] We have a guide. Our work is such as our Creator expects from us. Surely God made not such a creature as man for nothing. He sent us into the world, and hath appointed us our business, which we are to do here; as our Lord telleth us, John vi. 38, 'I came down from heaven, not to do mine own will, but the will of him that sent me.' So none of us come into the world to live to ourselves, but to God; not to do our own will, but to finish his work; to love, serve, glorify, and obey him. Many live in the world they know not why, and they go out of the world they know not whither.

[2.] We have an inspector or overseer, who observeth how we spend our time, and what we are continually doing: Ps. cxix. 168, 'I have kept thy precepts and thy testimonies; for all thy ways are before me.' God seeth what we do daily: he observeth with what posture of heart we rise in the morning, and converse all day, and go to bed at night.

[3.] We have a ruler that will call us to an account if we neglect our duty to him, and that provision that we should make for eternity. Unless we be found of him in peace, and without spot and blameless, we cannot enter into his kingdom; for 'without holiness no man shall see the Lord.' Every man's qualification must be judged, and a strict inquiry made into our ways, what we have done in the body, whether good or evil: 2 Cor. v. 10, 'For we must all appear before the judgment-seat of Christ, that every one may receive the things done in the body, according to that he hath done, whether it be good or bad.' Now seeing we know these things, or look for these things, what preparation should we make that we may be accepted in the judgment, when we are to give an account of ourselves to our supreme Lord?

Use 1. To press us to mind our work in this our day.

1. This life is our opportunity, and when that is over, there is no more working; no praying, nor hearing, nor glorifying God upon earth: John ix. 4, 'Therefore we must double our diligence before all opportunity be lost. It must go with you for ever as you behave yourselves now.

2. Consider how swiftly time passeth away, and we know not how soon it may have an end. The present life is always *in fluxu*, in motion; like a stream or current, that runneth as fast from us as it cometh to us. That part which is past is, as it were, resigned up to death already; that which is to come is not yet ours, nor can we make any sure reckoning of it; that which we count present is usually divided between us and death. It wasteth as we are writing, thinking, speaking, or doing anything. So that we die as fast as we live: Job ix. 25, 26, 'Now are my days swifter than a post; they flee away, they see no good: they are passed away as the swift ships, as the eagle that hasteth to the prey.' He sets forth the passing of time by a post on land, who is to make quick despatch; and by a ship under sail before the wind in the water, and by an eagle in the air. Thus is set forth the fugacity of man's life. Now should any of this time be lost?

3. We have lost much time already: 1 Peter iv. 3, 'For the time past of our life may suffice us to have wrought the will of the gentiles, when we lived in lasciviousness, lust, excess of wine, revellings, banquetings, and abominable idolatries.' We lost much time in childhood, when we were not in a capacity to express any act of love and thankfulness to God; much in youth, when we followed after vain pleasures; and in our riper age, we are too careless and mindless of eternity. Now as travellers that set forth later ride the faster, so should we double our diligence, and be more hard at work for God.

4. Consider how comfortable it will be when we die that we have made preparation, known our season, done the things which God hath given us in charge, thought of this hour, and made provision for it before it come upon us. This was our Lord's plea: John xvii. 4, 'I have glorified thee on earth, I have finished the work thou gavest me to do.' This was Hezekiah's prayer: Isa. xxxviii. 3, 'And he said, Remember now, O Lord, I beseech thee, how I have walked before thee in truth, and with a perfect heart, and have done that which is good in thy sight.' This was Paul's confidence: 2 Tim. iv. 6-8, 'For I am ready to be offered up, and the time of my departure is at hand. I have fought a good fight, I have finished my course, I have kept the faith: henceforth there is laid up for me a crown of righteousness, which the Lord, the righteous judge, shall give me at that day; and not unto me only, but to all that love his appearing.' Now we should be able to comfort ourselves in like manner. The remembrance of a diligent, well-spent life will be a great cordial to us in such an hour.

5. After death we shall have the fruit and benefit of it: Rev xiv. 13, Their works follow them;' that is the reward of their works. They

enjoy the comfort and benefit of whatever they have done and suffered for Christ; in another world, they are fully satisfied.

Use 2. Is by way of inquiry.

1. To inquire what should be the reason why men should be so silly and neglectful, when they have such great things in view and pursuit, and do no more in order to the obtaining of them, which concerneth not only the carnal world, who wholly neglect these things, but also the children of God, who are so cold in them. You see sense teacheth the ants, and reason should teach men, and grace inclines the saints, but yet they are slight and overly.

The reasons are these—

[1.] They forget or consider not what God is, or how great and good a master they serve; for if they did, they would earnestly address themselves to serve and please him. How great is he ! Poor, sorry service is a contempt of his majesty : Mal. i. 14, 'Cursed be the deceiver that hath in his flock a male, and voweth and sacrificeth to the Lord a corrupt thing; for I am a great king, saith the Lord of hosts.' So also how good is he ! Who hath done so much for them : Col. i. 10, ' That ye walk worthy of the Lord, unto all pleasing;' 1 Thes. ii. 12, ' That ye would walk worthy of God, who hath called you to his kingdom and glory.' And he will do more : Heb. xi. 6, 'He is a rewarder of them that diligently seek him.' These are the considerations that may serve to cure our neglect, and show we can never do enough for God; surely never too much for him.

[2.] They do not consider the end and consequence of their work. Eternity should quicken and put life into the dullest creatures. It is hell you are avoiding, heaven that you are seeking after : Prov. xv. 24, ' The way of life is above to the wise, that they may depart from hell beneath.' Now in the case of heaven and hell, flight and speed is always necessary, or the most serious and earnest diligence that we can use : Mat. iii. 7, ' Who hath warned you to flee from the wrath to come ? ' Heb. vi. 18, ' Who have fled for refuge to take hold of the hope set before them.' Now it is not a wet winter that we provide against, but everlasting torments.

[3.] They do not count negligence and slothfulness so great and so dangerous an evil. If they do not oppose God, or break out into open sin, they think no great harm will come of it; but, Heb. ii. 3, ' How shall we escape if we neglect so great salvation.' Oh, there are millions in hell lamenting their carelessness ! And the great fault of the world is to make light of those things : Mat. xxii. 5, ' And they made light of it ;' and Mat. xxv. 30, ' Cast the unprofitable servant into outer darkness ; there shall be weeping and gnashing of teeth.' How many poor creatures knock and cry when it is in vain. They neglected their season, got not oil in their lamps while it may be had. When their lamps should have been burning, their oil was to buy; and so they perish for ever.

[4.] They are diverted by worldly business, providing for the bodily life. They are too much like ants in one thing ; all their care is what they shall eat and drink, and how they may live in pomp, and ease, and honour; and then by the cares of this world and voluptuous living, ' they bring forth no fruit to perfection,' Luke viii. 14. They have some religion, but not such as is carried on in the way of sincere and serious diligence.

[5.] There is not a sound belief of the world to come. When the apostle presseth to diligence, 2 Peter i. 5, 'And besides this, giving all diligence, add to your faith virtue,' &c. ; and ver. 10, 'Wherefore the rather, brethren, give diligence to make your calling and election sure ; for if ye do these things, ye shall never fall ;' he urgeth this argument, ver. 16, 'For we have not followed cunningly-devised fables, when we made known unto you the power and coming of our Lord Jesus Christ ;' implying that men will see a reason for their diligence if they have a sound persuasion of the truth of religion ; and if we do not with zeal and constancy seek to add to faith virtue, and to make our calling and election sure, to enter abundantly into the kingdom of heaven, we dishonour the gospel, as if it were but a fable. Sense teacheth the creatures to shun misery and seek their happiness, and reason doth much more teach man, who can foresee the good and evil to come ; but where the good lieth in the other world, there faith must interpose. Now if faith be either none or weak, so will our endeavours and pursuits be. Most men have but a weak persuasion of the world to come, and the truth of eternal life, and therefore their endeavours are so overly.

2. To seek for a remedy of this.

[1.] Live in the continual remembrance of God, who is our guide, overseer, and ruler. It is his work we do, as well as our own, for he hath appointed it, and he always looketh on to see how we do it. And will you loiter in his sight, when a very eye-servant will work while his master standeth by ? Besides, in the close of our life we must give up our account ; that should be oftener thought of : Job xxxi. 14, 'What then shall I do, when God riseth up ; and when he visiteth, what shall I answer him ?' Such an eye should we always have to God's approbation and condemnation, and entertain frequent, serious thoughts of being called to an account by God, and the inquiry that shall be made, how we have spent our time, how we have improved our talents and interests, what our ways have been. This is as the cold water cast into the boiling pot, to stop the fervours of youthful lusts : Eccles. xi. 9, 'Rejoice, O young man, in thy youth, and let thy heart cheer thee in the days of thy youth, and walk in the ways of thine heart, and in the sight of thine eyes ; but know thou, that for all these things God will bring thee to judgment.' This bindeth the whole duty of man : Eccles. xii. 13, 14, 'Fear God, and keep his commandments ; for this is the whole duty of man. For God shall bring every work into judgment,' &c. This maketh God's servants more careful to do their work in its season : 2 Cor. v. 10, 11, 'For we must all appear before the judgment-seat of Christ, that every one may receive the things done in the body, according to that he hath done, whether it be good or bad. Knowing therefore the terror of the Lord, we persuade men,' &c.

[2.] Whenever we feel a loathness and backwardness to our work, let us set about it the more earnestly ; for the more we give way to it, the more we contract an habit of idleness and sloth. It is an industrious creature that is here set before us to shame us, a creature always busy ; so should we be. Therefore when you find any sluggishness, let not the ease of the flesh overcome you, but do you overcome it. This evil

is best avoided by resistance ; and a duty recovered out of the hands
of difficulty is the sweeter, and maketh labour for the future more easy
to us ; for the more we stir up ourselves, the more we get a sedulous
disposition : Isa. lxiv. 7, 'There is none that stirreth up himself to take
hold of thee.' It may be at first you will have much ado with a backward heart; but urge it on, and you gain upon it, and what seemeth
impossible or difficult at first becometh easy afterwards. The way to
godliness is by godliness, and duty fitteth for duty.

[3.] Think oftener of heaven and hell, what we shun and what we
seek after. We are so dull and lazy because we see not the rest we
hope for, nor the torments that we fear. If both were before our eyes,
we should be other manner of christians in all holy conversation and
godliness. But what we see by faith should in some measure affect
us, as if it were before our eyes: 2 Cor. iv. 18, 'While we look not to
the things that are seen, but at the things which are not seen,' &c. ;
and 2 Peter iii. 14, 'Wherefore, beloved, seeing that ye look for such
things, be diligent, that ye may be found of him in peace, without spot
and blemish.'

[4.] Consider the great sin of negligence. Not to do good is to do
evil ; for it is an omission of necessary duties : 'Every tree that bringeth
not forth good fruit, shall be hewn down,' &c., Mat vii. 19. If you had
a servant, though he did not steal, nor answer again with contradiction,
nor drink with the drunken, &c., yet if he should sit always idle, and
not do those things you require of him, he would be counted a bad
servant : Mat. xxv. 30, 'Cast the unprofitable servant into outer darkness.' Not the thief, the drunken, but 'the unprofitable servant.' If
you hire a man to labour in the vineyard, will you be contented if he
doth not steal your fruit, though he standeth idle all the day, and neither
destroyeth the weeds, nor pruneth the vines, nor manureth the ground ?
Much more must neglect of God's service be a great sin.

[5.] To overcome worldly affections, consider not only how sure and
near, but how great our reward is. This will make us more diligent :
1 Cor. xv. 58, 'Therefore, my beloved brethren, be steadfast, unmov-
able, always abounding in the work of the Lord, forasmuch as ye
know that your labour is not in vain in the Lord ; ' that is, this will
oblige you to the utmost industry and diligence in God's service. If a
poor man will work so hard for a shilling a day, shall we be so sluggish
when we seek after the kingdom of God and eternal happiness? Alas !
what are all our labours to the glory that shall be revealed in us ?
Our reward is great in itself, and is greater according to the proportion of our labour : 1 Cor. iii. 8, 'Every man shall receive his own
reward, according to his own labour.' So Eph. vi. 8, 'Whatsoever
good thing any man doth, the same shall he receive of the Lord.'

SERMON UPON PROVERBS III. 18.

She is a tree of life to them that lay hold upon her ; and happy is every one that retaineth her.—PROV. iii. 18.

THE context is spent in an exhortation to wisdom, to get spiritual and heavenly wisdom. The argument is first generally proposed and particularly amplified. Generally proposed, ver. 13, ' Happy is the man that findeth wisdom, and the man that getteth understanding ; ' secondly, particularly amplified—

1. By the worth and excellency, ver. 14, 15, ' For the merchandise of it is better than the merchandise of silver, and the gain thereof than fine gold. She is more precious than rubies ; and all the things thou canst desire are not to be compared with her.

2. From the utility and profit, ver. 16, ' Length of days is in her right hand ; and in her left hand, riches and honour.' She is represented as a queen having both hands full of blessings, ' Length of days in her right hand ; and in her left, riches and honour.'

3. The pleasantness of wisdom, ver. 17, ' All her ways are pleasantness, and all her paths are peace.' Which is added to sweeten the difficulties in attaining or pursuing after it, or regulating our lives and actions according to the tenor of it.

4. Here is another special benefit which we have by wisdom, or the saving knowledge of God in Jesus Christ, above all hitherto mentioned before : as pleasantness and peace during our service, so eternal life and happiness as our final reward. Here it is metaphorically expressed, with allusion to the tree of life in paradise, ' She is a tree of life to them that lay hold upon her.'

In the words we have—(1.) The benefit we enjoy by wisdom ; (2.) The persons qualified.

1. The benefit is expressed metaphorically and literally ; the latter explaineth the former. It is ' a tree of life,' and ' happy is every one.' She is so a tree of life as to make them happy that get her ; as it is usual with Solomon to express any great felicity by a tree of life : Prov. xiii. 12, ' Hope deferred maketh the heart sick ; but when the desire cometh, it is a tree of life ; ' that is, the man is pleased and satisfied, as if he were fed with apples in paradise. So Prov. xi. 30, ' The fruit of the righteous is a tree of life ; and he that winneth souls is wise.' Therefore by this metaphor Solomon understandeth some great felicity, and ordinarily eternal felicity, as the latter clause mani-

festeth, 'And happy is every one.' He meaneth it of our chief happiness; that is, all and every one that so do, how despicable soever in the world, they shall not be forgotten and passed over by God.

2. The persons qualified to enjoy this happiness. They that 'lay hold on her,' or they 'that retain her.' The one expression noteth the getting of wisdom, the other the keeping of it; and they both imply the manner also, diligence in getting, and constancy in keeping.

[1.] In getting. Wisdom is not profitable to them that only see her at a distance, or lightly salute her, but to those that with singular industry seek after her, and labour to get her: Prov. iv. 7, 'Wisdom is the principal thing, therefore get wisdom; and with all thy getting get understanding.'

(1.) Get it above all things; that is, whatever you go without, be sure you be not without wisdom or saving grace: Luke x. 42, 'One thing is needful; and Mary hath chosen the better part, which shall not be taken away from her.' You may do well enough though you want worldly honour and greatness, but you cannot do well enough if you want spiritual wisdom: Mat. xvi. 26, ' But what is a man profited, if he shall gain the whole world and lose his own soul? or what shall a man give in exchange for his soul?'

(2.) Get it upon any terms, though with the loss of all other things: Mat. xiii. 45, 46, 'The kingdom of heaven is like unto a merchant-man seeking goodly pearls; who, when he had found one pearl of great price, he went and sold all and bought it.' You must get wisdom, though at the expense of all that you have gotten.

(3.) Get it by any means, with all the care and diligence that you can use: Prov. viii. 34, 'Blessed is the man that heareth me, watching daily at my gates, waiting at the posts of my doors.' Begrudge no labour and pains to get into the gospel-state.

[2.] In keeping, constancy is required. We must not be put off till we have it; and when we have it, we must not let it go, but persevere in the way that wisdom prescribeth, and obey God at the dearest rates. We must retain her, though despised, though opposed by the world: Heb. x. 39, 'For we are not of them that draw back to perdition, but of them that believe to the saving of the soul.'

To the purchasing of the soul: we do not purchase it from God, for we have it by mere gift, but we purchase it from the world; liberty to save the soul at hard terms. But if we have gotten wisdom, we must never part from her, whatever it cost us. Well, then, get this wisdom we must, with all earnestness of endeavour, with all watchfulness and care, and firmness and certainty keep it. He that doth not do both is not blessed; that is, that doth not make it his main work and business to get wisdom, and doth not hold out and overcome *temptations*.

Doct. That wisdom doth restore men to that life and happiness which they lost in Adam.

We shall explain the point.

1. By wisdom may be understood Christ, who is the wisdom of the Father, 1 Cor. i. 24, and is both the object and fountain of happiness of the saints. He is the fountain of happiness as being the procurer and author of it: Col. iii. 4, 'When Christ, who is our life, shall appear, then shall ye also appear with him in glory.' And the object of it:

John xvii. 24, 'Father, I will that those whom thou hast given me may be where I am, and behold my glory;' and is truly and properly the tree of life, whose fruit is for food and leaves for medicine: Rev. xxii. 2, 'And in the midst of the street of it, and of either side of the river, was there the tree of life, which bore twelve manner of fruits, and yielded her fruit every month: and the leaves of the tree were for the healing of the nations.' There is no inconvenience to understand it of Christ, or else of the saving knowledge of God in Christ; as one is the author, the other is the means to bring it about: John xvii. 3, 'And this is life eternal, that they may know thee the only true God, and Jesus Christ whom thou hast sent.'

2. By life is meant the life of grace, begun here by the Spirit, and perfected in heaven. By wisdom we begin the life of grace here, and hereafter shall obtain the life of glory. In the Hebrew the word for life is in the dual number, the tree of lives; of both the lives, the life of holiness and the life of happiness, of grace and of glory. How this agreeth with the metaphor here used I shall show you by and by. This life is begun in regeneration when Christ cometh to live in us by his Spirit: John iii. 3, 'Except a man be born again, he cannot see the kingdom of God.' The immediate effects of the new birth are life and likeness to God; and it is perfected in heaven: Col. iii. 3, 4, 'Our life is hid with Christ in God. When Christ, who is our life, shall appear, then shall we also appear with him in glory.' This life is safely laid up in God, through Christ, in due time to be manifested in all its glory.

3. That this life is restored to those that live under the evangelical dispensation, provided they use the means, which are to lay hold on her and retain her. These are the things we must press upon you, to apprehend and retain, that is, we must receive the faith of Christ, and live accordingly. First be engaged in a course of godliness, and then hold it on, whatever temptations we have to the contrary. And accordingly two ordinances are required in the gospel—baptism, which signifieth our entrance, and the Lord's supper which confirmeth our vows of a new life, and bringeth down more grace for the performance of them; or, as our Lord sets it forth, by the gate and the way: Mat. vii. 14, 'Strait is the gate, and narrow is the way that leadeth unto life; and few there be that find it.' The gate by which we enter is faith and repentance. The narrow way is a strict obedience, doing the will of God, and not our own. And though few mind these things, we must mind them. It is elsewhere represented by making and keeping covenant. Making covenant: Ps. xl. 5, 'Gather my saints together unto me, those that have made a covenant with me by sacrifice.' Keeping covenant: Ps. xxv. 10, 'All the paths of the Lord are mercy and truth, even to such as keep his covenant and his testimonies.' We make it by faith; we keep it by a resolved, holy, and heavenly life: Rev. xxii. 14, 'Blessed are they that do his commandments; that they may have a right to the tree of life.' They that believe, repent, and obey, they have a right to the apples of paradise, to eat of this blessed tree; as (to accommodate the notions of the text to these things) many as take hold of Christ by a lively faith, and resolve to live holily; and this resolution must be made whatever difficulties we have to fight with in the

accomplishing of it : Rev. ii. 7, ' To him that overcometh I will give
to eat of the tree of life which is in the midst of the paradise of God.'
It is promised to the conqueror who overcometh the world, and is
faithful to death.

1. Let me confirm it—(1.) By showing what the tree of life was to
Adam ; (2.) What Christ will be to us if we choose him and walk in
his ways.

[1.] What the tree of life was to Adam.   That there was such a tree
in paradise appeareth, Gen. ii. 9, ' And out of the ground made the
Lord God to grow every tree that is pleasant to the sight, and good for
food ; and the tree of life in the midst of the garden, and the tree of
knowledge of good and evil.'   For the physical use of it, whether it
might be wholesome, and a natural means to prolong life, we meddle
not with ; the mystical use is that which falleth under our consideration,
as it was a sacrament of immortality, or a sign of eternal life to man, if
he had obeyed God his Creator.   Now sacraments have a mutual respect
to privileges and duties.   As it relateth to his duty, Adam had two
things enjoined him ; the one *præcesse creaturis*, to rule over the creatures,
the other *subesse creatori*, to be subject to his Creator.   He had no need
of a caveat for the one ; he was ready enough to govern and bear
sovereignty : but for his duty to God, he had great need to be put in
mind of that ; therefore under the condition of obedience, life present
and future was promised to him.   Those were his privileges : as he had
received a natural life, *in esse*, in being ; so an eternal life, *in posse*, in
power, and so had matter and just occasion of thankfulness and obedience.   For this end served the tree of life as a token and pledge that
he had received and should continue his life at God's will and pleasure.
The tree of life sealed the continuance of his natural life during his
abode upon earth ; and eternal life, when he should be removed thence,
to enjoy the fulness of God's blessed presence for ever in heaven ; for
in all probability the life promised answereth the death threatened.
Now the death threatened is eternal, and therefore the life promised
is eternal also.   In short, it was God gave him life, and not the tree ;
working not by physical efficacy, but by sacramental representation.
It represented to Adam that God was his life and the length of his
days, as he is also to us : Deut. xxx. 20, ' That thou mayest love the
Lord thy God, and that thou mayest obey his voice, and that thou
mayest cleave unto him ; for he is thy life, and the length of thy days ;'
Job x. 12, ' Thou hast granted me life and favour, and thy visitation
hath preserved my spirit.'   Expressing thereby God's care in preserving
his natural life.   His life could not be preserved but by God's immediate power, care, and love, which Job calleth his ' visitation,' or
looking after us, as a parent overseeth his child *conditione corporis*.
Adam was mortal as other men are, and no temporal thing could
preserve him but immortal *beneficio conditoris*, by the bounty of his
Creator, and the tree of life was the sign and assurance of it.

[2.] When Adam sinned, this privilege was forfeited: Gen. iii. 22,
' And the Lord said, Behold, the man is become as one of us to know
good and evil ;' that is, he will be at his own finding and know what
is good or evil for himself, and not take my direction, but live according to his own will : ' And now, lest he put forth his hand, and take

also of the tree of life, and eat, and live for ever. Therefore the Lord sent him forth from the garden of Eden.' That expression might seem to intimate that if Adam, in a state of sin and mortality, had tasted of the tree of life, he should now, notwithstanding his fall, live for ever; but God respected not the event in that speech, but the opinion of Adam, or the use for which the tree was ordained. Possibly man might believe Satan suggesting that Adam notwithstanding his fall might be immortal still · by the use of that tree; therefore God drove him out of paradise. But the true reason is, God would not suffer Adam to make use of the token of life when he had forfeited life itself by his transgression. The tree had lost its use; it was the sign of life to Adam; therefore to prevent his sin in profaning the holy ordinances when he had no right to them, God drove him out. Thus our first parents, being separated from God, they were separated from life, for God was their life.

2. What Christ will be to us if we choose his ways, and walk in them. Take that in these propositions—

[1.] That we, that did once partake of life (which lieth in the fruition of God) in our common root and first father Adam, are now excluded by sin: Eccles. vii. 29, 'Lo, this only have I found, that God hath made man upright, but they have sought out many inventions.' In our mere natural estate we are deprived of life: Eph. ii. 1, 'And you hath he quickened who were dead in trespasses and sins.' And the longer we live in our unrenewed estate, we are the more estranged from it: Eph. iv. 18, 'Being alienated from the life of God, through the ignorance that is in them because of the blindness of their heart.' And so made incapable in a further degree: Ps. liii. 2, 'God looked down upon the children of men to see if there were any that did understand, that did seek God.' Every sin maketh the breach and distance between us and God broader and wider.

[2.] In pity to lost mankind God hath set up a new tree of life. Though we are deprived of the first tree, yet God hath planted a better, which yieldeth better fruit, to be enjoyed in a better place. This better tree is Christ: Rev. xxii. 2, 'And in the midst of the street of it, and on either side of the river was there the tree of life, which bare twelve manner of fruits, and yielded her fruit every month; and the leaves of the tree were for healing of the nations.' This tree can be no other but Christ, who by his ordinances dispenseth all manner of blessings and comfort to his people at all times. His fruit, abundance of spirituality in obedience to the doctrine of the twelve apostles: the leaves, the mere outward and civil conversation, is so excellent that it draweth others to imitation and conversion. And it is said, 1 John v. 12, 'He that hath the Son hath life; and he that hath not the Son hath not life.' His fruit is better; the fruit of the first tree was corporeal, and did only represent spiritual and heavenly things; but this fruit is the things themselves, saving grace and eternal life: Cant. ii. 3, 'I sat down under his shadow with great delight, and his fruit was sweet to my taste.' And we have this life and immortality in a better place than Adam had. Not in an earthly paradise among beasts, but in an heavenly paradise, in the immediate presence of God and his holy angels: Eph. i. 3, 'Blessed be the God and Father

of our Lord Jesus Christ, who hath blessed us with spiritual blessings in heavenly places in Christ.' Therefore heaven is called
paradise: Luke xxiii. 43, ' This day shalt thou be with me in paradise.'
And Paul was caught up into paradise, 2 Cor. xii. 4, ' Which is the
same with the third heaven,' ver. 2. Oh ! what should we do but take
hold of this tree, gather the fruit of it ? What greater thing can be
given us than Christ, and what shall we want if we have him for our
Redeemer and Saviour ?

[3.] This grace is offered to all that lay hold of him, and will not let
him go, but still cleave to him by an entire dependence and close adherence. There are two things qualify us for the grace of Christ—
thankful acceptance and close adherence ; and the heirs of promise are
described sometimes by the one, and sometimes by the other.

(1.) Acceptance : John i. 12, ' To as many as received him.' Whosoever do broken-heartedly, thankfully, and heartily take the Lord
Jesus to be their Lord and Saviour, and are resolved to seek their
happiness in God through him, are adopted into his family, and are
made heirs according to the hope of eternal life : Heb. vi. 18, ' Who
have fled for refuge, to lay hold upon the hope set before us.' They
have a heaven of glory at their lives' end. They cannot be satisfied
till they are in their city of God, till they have a right, and get some
possession of Christ and his benefits, which is mainly done by faith
and hope. We believe Christ to be that to us as the gospel sets him
forth to be ; consent he shall be such a one to us, and therefore trust
in him, and resign up ourselves to him, that he may do the works of a
saviour for us and in us. Well, then, do you heartily entertain him
in your souls for these ends ? and do you depend upon him, that he
will according to his word accomplish these ends? namely, deliver you
from the guilt, and power, and punishment of sin ; also work grace, and
preserve, and quicken, and strengthen it unto eternal life. Then we
begin to live in him : Gal. ii. 20, ' The life that I live in the flesh, I
live by the faith of the Son of God.'

(2.) Adherence. There is first choosing and then cleaving : Acts
xi. 23, ' And exhorted them all that with purpose of heart they would
cleave unto the Lord;' Cant. iii. 4, 'I found him whom my soul loveth ;
I held him, and would not let him go.' Abiding in him : John xv. 4,
' Abide in me.' There is no fear of breaking the union on his part.
His gracious presence is secured by his love and promise. All the
danger is in breaking on our part. And though Christ doth finish
the work he hath begun, yet we must use caution and watchfulness ;
not consent to quit him upon any terms. This adherence is a continuance in faith, and love, and strict obedience.

(1st.) In faith : Col. i. 23, ' If ye continue in the faith, grounded
and settled, and be not moved away from the hope of the gospel.' He
had spoken of their reconciliation with God through Christ ; now the
comfort did depend on their perseverance. It is not enough for us to
assent to the truth of the gospel, and once to embrace Christ, and
choose the good things offered by him for our portion, but still Christ
must be precious to us, and our faith firm and fixed.

(2d.) Love : Rom. viii. 35, ' Who shall separate us from the love of
Christ ? Shall tribulation, or distress, or persecution, or famine, or

nakedness, or peril, or sword ?' Cant. viii. 7, 'Many waters cannot quench love, neither can the floods drown it; if a man would give all the substance of his house, it would be utterly contemned.' Love cannot be bribed nor quenched; nothing can unclasp those mutual embraces.

(3d.) Strict obedience and holiness: Rev. xxii. 14, 'Blessed are they that do his commandments, that they may have a right to eat of the tree of life.'

[4.] And this when there are sore temptations to drive us from God: Rev. ii. 7, 'To him that overcometh will I give to eat of the tree of life which is in the midst of the paradise of God.'

Use 1. To persuade us to get and keep this wisdom, and this saving knowledge of Christ, which may produce faith, love, and obedience.

1. Consider the motives propounded, life and blessedness. These are most desirable things. All would be happy, and all would live to enjoy them ; yea, the general desire of all men is to prolong their life, though in misery; but this life is happy, and it is eternal, and recommended to us with all the advantages which the place heaven can afford us. The tree of life is gone, when paradise was defaced by the flood; but God hath provided a better life by the death of his Son, that we shall live for ever, both in body and soul, eternally in heaven. Nothing else but this deserveth to be called life. The bodily life is short ; it is a dying life or a living death. It floweth from us as fast as it cometh to us ; but this never fadeth, but endureth for ever. The bodily life is subject to pain and misery, but the heavenly, full of joy and endless glory. The bodily life is supported with meats and drinks, but there God *is* all in all. The bodily life is consistent with sin, but this life is pure and perfect : 'We shall see God as he is, and be like him,' 1 John iii. 2 ; Jude 2, 4, 'Now unto him that is able to keep you from falling, and to present you faultless before the presence of his glory with exceeding joy.' In the bodily life we have a mixture of sorrow with all our comforts, but here is full contentment and satisfaction : Ps. xvi. 11, 'In thy presence is fulness of joy, and at thy right hand are pleasures for evermore.'

2. It is a new recovery of life lost and forfeited. After our long exile from God, he hath found out a way how we may return to him again, and live in communion with him. The work of redemption Christ himself hath performed for us, without asking our consent, or imposing any conditions upon us. He took our nature, fulfilled the law, satisfied the offended lawgiver, merited grace, conquered death, the devil, and hell. But to apply the comfort of these benefits, somewhat is required of us ; for a neglected Christ will not profit us. Of how much sorer punishment shall we be thought worthy if we despise God's second dispensation ? Then to the breach of our duty will be added the slighting of our remedy : John iii. 18, 'He that believeth not is condemned already, because he hath not believed in the name of the only-begotten Son of God.' And if salvation itself cannot save us, nor life quicken us, what will become of us ? If God offereth his grace, and we will not lay hold of it and retain it, we are justly miserable.

3. Here is motive enough to recompense all the difficulties and troubles in getting and keeping Christ.

[1.] In getting. Christ is not to be had with a large wish or a cold prayer. There is much waiting and striving, and praying and meditating ere the soul is well settled, and can be brought to trample upon all things so we gain Christ. The tree in paradise was provided by God, and planted in the midst of paradise without Adam's labour: so is Jesus Christ provided for us by the mere grace of God; but before we get to him, we must conquer guilty fears, rebellious lusts, and much averseness of heart; many a bitter pang before we come to lay hold of this grace, which is troublesome to them which would sleep quietly in their sins. But if you will set yourselves in good earnest to get him, it will be worth your pains; for ' he is a tree of life to them that take hold of him,' and your first faith is rewarded with a sweet taste of this blessed fruit.

[2.] In keeping. The trouble will be recompensed: Ps. cxxvi. 5, 'They sow in tears, but they shall reap in joy.' You have your temptations to overcome; you make your way to heaven by conflict and conquest every step: ' Without are fightings, within are fears.' Now we have the wrestling life, overcoming first one difficulty and then another. We make a snare to ourselves if we look for too much satisfaction in the world: but the clearer sight we get of heaven by faith and hope, the more we are strengthened. Here we must expect our conflicts, but there our quietness and rest. Now the happiness God hath provided for his people in heaven is enough to sweeten our crosses and encourage our obedience. Surely if we kept this recompense in our view it would strike temptations dead: Rom. viii. 18, ' For I reckon that the sufferings of this present time are not worthy to be compared with the glory which shall be revealed in us.' The reward is sufficient, though we lay down our lives for Christ; for the case is, whether we will yield it as a debt to nature, or resign it to Christ, who hath promised to render it again with advantage.

4. There is wisdom in it. Surely they walk most wisely that are guided by God's counsel. Carnal men think their own way to be wisest, who spend all their time and care in attaining profit, and pleasure, and preferment in the world. There is present advantage, and they judge the way of the godly to be mere folly, who spend their strength in looking after spiritual and heavenly things, which they count to be but fancies; but a little time will discover this error. They who thought themselves to be the only wise men shall certainly be found to be mere fools, and the godly the wisest adventurers, whose wisdom shall be to them a tree of life. Oh, what poor things are present delights, which draw away the carnal, if compared with these choice satisfactions and pleasures which are to be had at God's right hand for evermore! Death will soon show that they are in an happier condition that suffer all things for an unseen world and the life to come, than the sensual and ungodly, that have their good things here: Luke xii. 20, 'Thou fool! this night thy soul shall be required of thee: then whose shall these things be which thou hast provided?' Jer. xvii. 11, ' At his end he shall be a fool.'

Use 2. To inform us that life is to be had and best preserved by

obedience and close adherence to God. Which, though it be principally meant of life eternal, which is God's gift: Rom. vi. 23, 'The gift
of God is eternal life;' assured to us by promise, if we believe in Christ,
and obey the gospel: 1 John ii. 25, 'And this is the promise that he
hath promised to us, even eternal life;' yet in its proportion it holdeth
good of life natural also. Our life and breath is in his hand: Dan. v.
23, 'And the God in whose hand thy breath is,' to take it away or continue it at his own pleasure: Ps. civ. 27, 'Thou takest away their
breath, and they die.' The sound in the pipe continueth no longer than
he that pipeth bloweth in it. Now obedience or disobedience are the
terms of communicating or withholding of it. It is said, Job xxxvi. 6,
'He preserveth not the life of the wicked.' Though it be continued by
him, yet it is not out of any respect to them. They have not a moment's
assurance of the continuance thereof. If therefore we live by him, let
us live to him and for him, and then, when he is pleased to put a period
to this natural live, we may live for ever with him.

SERMON UPON PSALM XCI. 1.

He that dwelleth in the secret place of the Most High shall abide in the shadow of the Almighty.—Ps. xci. 1.

This psalm is thought to be composed upon occasion of that great pestilence which destroyed seventy thousand in the space of three days, 2 Sam. xxiv. Whether David is the author of it is disputed; for though some of the Greek and Latin copies have a title ascribing it to David, yet the Hebrew has none. I should think it is not David's.

1. For David's psalms usually have his name prefixed, together with the occasion; which, the case being so weighty, probably here it would not have been omitted.

2. It is not likely that David, having drawn that great calamity on the people by his sin, and expressing his resentment of it with so much penitence, would make no mention of it in the contexture of this psalm, nor signify his repentance by some passage or other.

It is more likely to be composed by Gad, a prophet of those times, called David's seer, and whose ministry God made use of to offer David his choice of pestilence, war, or famine. It is probable that holy man, being no way accessary to David's sin, declareth his confidence and trust in God, for an example to other believers in like dangers. He maketh no mention of David's sin, it being both needless and undutiful to discover the nakedness of his prince, who had already manifested such an exemplary repentance. But whoever was the penman, the devil himself grants it to be the word of God, for he quotes a passage out of it: Mat. iv. 6, 'It is written, He shall give his angels charge concerning thee.'

In this verse (which is the ground of the whole psalm) there is— (1.) A qualification; (2.) A privilege.

Both are almost expressed in the same terms, to show that our privilege and our duty are near of kin. God is wont to reward grace with grace: Ps. xxxi. 24, 'Be of good courage, and he shall strengthen your heart;' and Ps. xxvii. 14, 'Wait on the Lord; be of good courage, and he shall strengthen thine heart.' So delight with delight: Isa. lviii. 13, 14, 'If thou turn away thy foot from the sabbath, from doing thy pleasure on my holy day, and call the sabbath a delight, the holy of the Lord, honourable, and shalt honour him, not doing thine own ways, nor finding thine own pleasure, nor speaking thine own words: then shalt thou delight thyself in the Lord,' &c. But here it is the duty and the fruit. What do you desire in the time of danger but to abide in the shadow of the Almighty? Do so, and you shall abide. Make him your refuge, and he will be your refuge. Dwell in God, and you shall dwell in God.

But though the qualification and privilege be expressed in like terms, yet they are not altogether the same; but as in the qualification you may observe three things, so the privilege answereth it—(1.) The act of faith; (2.) The manner of preservation; (3.) The author, or person trusted.

1. The act of faith, 'He that dwelleth;' in the privilege, 'shall abide.' He that doth dwell shall dwell.

2. The manner of preservation. It is called in the qualification, 'The secret place of the Most High;' in the privilege, 'The shadow.' The secret place: Sept.—*ἐν βοηθείᾳ τοῦ ὑψίστου,* 'He that dwells in the help of God.' God's help is secret, unknown, and unaccessible to the carnal world, who live by sense. The other term, 'shadow,' signifieth defence; for a cool shade was a great relief to travellers in that hot country: Num. xiv. 9, 'Their defence is parted from them;' margin, 'Their shadow is departed from them.' Here the Sept. *ἐν σκέπῃ,* 'In the protection.' The Chaldee addeth, 'In the shadow of the clouds of the glory of the Almighty.'

3. The author, or person trusted for preservation. In the qualification, 'Most High;' in the privilege, 'Almighty.' The one noteth his supreme authority and command, the other his invincible power.

Doct. That whosoever will trust himself in God's hands may remain secure under his protection in the midst of all dangers.

The point will be best discussed by considering these things—(1.) What it is to trust ourselves in God's hands; (2.) How it is expressed and recommended to us in this text; (3.) How necessary a duty this is for all christians.

I. What it is entirely to trust ourselves in God's hands. We shall consider the nature and the grounds of it.

1. The formality, nature, or essence of it consists in two acts—in resigning ourselves to God's will, and in resting with quietness, and depending upon him for the good we stand in need of. It is expressed in scripture by two words—(1.) Consecrating; and (2.) Committing ourselves to God.

[1.] Consecrating, or devoting or giving up ourselves to his will: Rom. xii. 1, 'I beseech you by the mercies of God, that ye present your bodies a living sacrifice, holy, acceptable to God.' There is a twofold will of God—his governing and his disposing will. We give up ourselves to obey his governing will as our ruler: Rom. vi. 13, 'Yield yourselves unto God, as those that are alive from the dead, and your members as instruments of righteousness unto God.' We give up ourselves to submit to his disposing will as our owner: 2 Sam. xv. 26, 'Behold, here I am, let him do unto me as seemeth good unto him.' The one, to do what he will have us to do; the other, to be what he will have us to be. Both are presupposed in trust, which resulteth from owning God as our God: Ps. xxxi. 14, 'I trusted in thee, O Lord; I said, Thou art my God.' Till we have given up ourselves to him, how can we trust him? And till we give up ourselves entirely

to him, to be governed and disposed of by him at his pleasure, we do
not trust him.   Therefore this is included in the fundamental article
of the covenant, in the choice of God as our God.   And so Ruth's conversion to the God of Israel is expressed : Ruth ii. 12, 'A full reward
be given thee of the God of Israel under whose wings thou art come to
trust;' that is, to whom thou hast given up thyself, whatever befall
thee.   She left her own people to obey his will and trust his providence.

[2.] The other word is committing ourselves to him ; a notion often
used, and of great significancy in this matter: as, 2 Tim. i. 12, 'For I
know whom I have believed, and I am persuaded that he is able to
keep that which I have committed unto him against that day;' 1 Peter
iv. 19, 'Wherefore, let them that suffer according to the will of God
commit the keeping of their souls to him in well-doing, as unto a
faithful creator ;' and Ps. xxxvii. 5, 'Commit thy way unto the Lord ;
trust in him, and he shall bring it to pass.'   This is when the soul
rests quietly in God by faith, as a man doth in his habitation, and we
can go on cheerfully in the duties of our general or particular calling,
knowing that while we are in God's hands we are in safe hands, come
what will come.   We are not troubled about any event, but entirely
commit it to God.

2. The grounds of this trust are two—(1.) God's nature ; (2.) His
covenant.   His nature showeth his all-sufficiency ; his covenant assureth
us of his readiness to help us.

[1.] His nature is a ground of trust ; for God is represented to us
as an infinite, eternal being, wise, powerful, and good.   As he is
infinitely wise, so he knoweth all things, what may hurt and what may
help us: Mat. vi. 32, 'Your heavenly Father knoweth that you have
need of all these things ;' 'And he knoweth how to deliver the righteous out of temptation,' 2 Peter ii. 9.   And then he is powerful, or
able, whatever difficulties arise: 2 Tim. i. 12, 'I know whom I have
believed, and I am persuaded that he is able to keep that which I have
committed unto him unto that day;' Rom. iv. 21, 'Being fully persuaded, that what he had promised he was able also to perform.'   So
he is good: Ps. cxix. 68, 'Thou art good, and doest good.'   So Ps. c. 5,
'The Lord is good, his mercy is everlasting, and his truth endures to
all generations.'   Now it is not enough that there be *notitia*, a knowledge with assent, but there must be *fiducia*, a reliance or dependence
upon these things, on the infinite wisdom, power, and goodness of God,
that he will to us show himself a God wise, good, and powerful, as he
doth to all his creatures.

[2.] His covenant or promise is a ground of trust ; for God's promises are the sacred bands which he hath put upon himself, the rule
and warrant of our faith, and the great encouragement of it.   As it is
said of Sarah, that 'she judged him faithful that had promised,' Heb.
xi. 11.   Surely God will make good his word.   Believers may be confident of it, though the event be never so unlikely : Ps. lvi. 4, 'In God
I will praise his word, in God have I put my trust, I will not fear
what flesh can do unto me.'   When we have God's word, it is enough
for the triumph of faith, though the dispensations of his providence
little answer our expectations.   Only here lieth a difficulty ; certain it

is that God's nature and his word both together are a foundation of
trust; and when his wisdom, power, and goodness is at the bottom of
the covenant, it is made thereby more firm and valid to us; for our
general security lieth in the nature of God as the particular warrant
of our faith in his promise. But when these two are severed, when we
have no particular express promise, how far may we depend upon his
nature? I answer—

(1.) Consider what trust is. Not a confidence of particular events,
but a resigning and committing ourselves to God. Then you will see
that his nature relieveth very much, though we have no express promise. Surely a powerful God can do all things that we expect from
him. He can keep and preserve us when all means fail. A wise God
knoweth what is best for us, and a good God will not forsake his children or people.

(2.) We have general promises when we have not particular; as
Heb. xii. 5; that God will not utterly forsake us; that he will not
leave us to insupportable difficulties: 1 Cor. x. 13, 'God is faithful,
who will not suffer you to be tempted above that you are able: but
will with the temptation also make a way to escape, that ye may be
able to bear it;' that 'all things shall work for good,' Rom. viii. 28.
But for disposing the particular event; on the one hand, God is so
wise and good that we need not disquiet ourselves about it; but on
the other, we must not make promises to ourselves, nor become false
prophets to ourselves, nor entertain a confidence of particular events
without God's express warrant.

(3.) We may lawfully hope for good success though there be no
promise, if there be nothing to the contrary; because God is so ready
to do good to all his creatures, especially to his people and faithful
servants, when in their distress they seek to him and humbly wait
upon him. Surely we ought not to be faithless and distrustful in particular exigencies. There is a common bounty and goodness of God
which is over all his works: Ps. cxlv. 9, 'The Lord is good to all; his
tender mercy is over all his works. This reacheth to the preservation of
the smallest worm, decketh the lilies, feedeth the ravens and fowls of
the air; therefore certainly more noble creatures, such as man is, may
expect their share in this common bounty. How much more may
God's people and children? See Mat. vi. 25, &c., 'Therefore I say
unto you, Take no thought for your life, what ye shall eat, or what ye
shall drink; nor yet for your body, what ye shall put on: is not the
life more than meat, and the body than raiment? Behold the fowls
of the air; for they sow not, neither do they reap, nor gather into
barns, yet your heavenly Father feedeth them. Are ye not much better
than they?' Will he not give to children that which he giveth to
beasts, to fowls of the air, to enemies? You would count him an
unnatural father which would feed his dogs and hawks, and let his
children die of hunger.

(4.) In case the scruple be whether any promise belong to us, see the
parables: Luke xi. 8–13, 'I say unto you, Though he will not rise and
give him because he is his friend; yet because of his importunity, he
will rise, and give him as many as he needeth. And I say unto you,
Ask, and it shall be given you; seek, and ye shall find; knock, and it

shall be opened unto you.   For every one that asketh, receiveth, &c.;
Luke xviii. 7, 8, 'And shall not God avenge his own elect, which cry
day and night unto him, though he bear long with them?   I tell you
that he will avenge them speedily.'   Thus we should raise ourselves
into a confidence and comfortable expectation in waiting on this good
God.

II. Let us see how it is expressed and recommended to us in this
text.   Here is the person trusting, the act, the encouragement to trust.

1. The person trusting is indefinitely expressed, 'He that dwelleth,'
&c.   And the indefinite expression in the case is equivalent to an universal inviting all.   There is no exception against any because of their
outward condition.   'He,' whatsoever he be, high or low, rich or poor;
for God is no accepter of persons, but is rich to all that call upon him.
Among men it is otherwise; the poor, who most need cherishing and
protection, have least share of it.   Men barter with their kindness, and
give harbour and entertainment to them from whom they may receive
it again.   It is the fashion of the world to respect great ones.   If a rich
or noble man should invite himself to our houses, we take it for a great
favour, and strain ourselves to give them suitable entertainment; the
more free they are to take any part of the provision made for them, the
more we thank them, as if obliged by a new benefit; which liberty, if
a poor man should take, we should look upon it as a bold intrusion.
It is the rich are respected, the rich are entertained in the world, whose
causes and suits are despatched, when the poor can hardly get access
and audience.   As all floods run to the sea, so do the respects of the
world to the rich and mighty.   But this is a general and common
promise, which excludeth no sorts of men.   Here is no distinction of
high and low, prince and subjects, nobles and common people; whosoever come to seek an hiding-place in God are welcome, if they come in
faith.   He doth not say, The prince or potentate that dwelleth in the
secret place of the Most High, &c., lest he should exclude meaner people;
nor doth he say, Only the poor and destitute that dwell, &c., lest the
trust of princes and persons of better condition should be cut off.   No;
the bosom of God's providence is open to receive persons of all sorts,
ages, sexes, degrees, and state of life.   He is present with all, provideth
for all, protects all, supplieth all that flee to him in their tribulation:
Ps. xxxiv. 6, 'This poor man cried, and the Lord heard him.'   Not
the mighty prince or eminent saint.   Prayers in cottages are as acceptable to him as prayers in palaces.

2. The act, 'He dwelleth in the secret place of the Most High.'   He
that expecteth the protection of the Almighty must be a person qualified for that protection; he must be one that dwelleth in God; such as
are reconciled to him by Christ Jesus, such as have taken God for their
God, such as fear him, and have chosen him for their portion, and are
resolved with an upright heart to obey him; these are the objects of
God's protection, blessing, and defence: Ps. lxxxiv. 11, 'The Lord
God is a sun and shield: the Lord will give grace and glory: no good
thing will he withhold from them that walk uprightly.'   The Lord
complaineth of some that would lean upon him and yet continue in
their sins: Micah iii. 11, 'The heads thereof judge for reward, and the
priests thereof teach for hire, and the prophets thereof divine for money:

yet will they lean upon the Lord, and say, Is not the Lord among us? none evil can come upon us.' Such God will cast off, as Paul cast off the viper that fastened upon his hand. These sleep too securely already in their sins, and God never intended to provide a pillow for them in his promises. These God meaneth to punish, not protect. These rather build castles in the air than dwell in the secret place of the Most High.

More particularly, this dwelling in God—

[1.] Noteth trust, or making God our refuge, in whom alone we seek safety, comfort, and defence. In a time of danger men seek out for a secure dwelling and safe place of retreat: Prov. xviii. 10, 11, ' The name of the Lord is a strong tower: the righteous fleeth to it, and is safe. The rich man's wealth is his strong city, and an high wall in his own conceit.' What wealth is to another, that the name of the Lord is to the righteous person; he hath no dependence but on God, from whom he expecteth safety and supply. Whither doth a man retreat from the storm, but to his house? There he seeketh shelter, and there he enjoyeth all his comforts. So doth a believer in God; there is his protection and consolation. We have a sure dwelling in reality, they in conceit.

[2.] It noteth a constant intimacy or continual trust. We do not call our tarrying in an inn for a night our dwelling, nor running to a tree or shelter in a storm, with a mind to depart thence as soon as it ceaseth. Many run to him in their distresses. No; the secret of the Most High must be our dwelling-place, or the place of our constant residence. The expression intendeth such as live in an holy familiarity with God, and have constant recourse to him: Job xxii. 21, ' Acquaint now thyself with him, and be at peace.' Most men make use of God in their straits, when they are beaten to him, and have no other place of retreat. No; it is meant of such a trust as puts us upon a constant communion with God, or an habitual converse with him, not by fits. In this Ps. xci. 9, ' Thou shalt make the Most High thy refuge, and my God thine habitation.' God cannot be well our refuge unless he be also our habitation. A refuge is a place of retreat and safety in a time of war, and an habitation is the place of our residence and abode in a time of peace. So that whatsoever our condition be, our dependence must be still on God. When things are prosperous, he must be owned as the fountain of our blessings, and all our comforts taken immediately out of his hand, acknowledging that we hold all by his mercy and bountiful providence. If we consider our forfeiture by sin, the uncertainty of these outward comforts, and the continual necessity of God's providential influence, and how apt the heart is to be enticed from God by carnal confidence, we shall soon find that trust is as necessary in prosperity as adversity. Then in adversity no man can withdraw himself from God; therefore it is best dwelling in him. *Qui a te fugit, quo fugit, nisi a te placato, ad te iratum?* He doth but forsake him as a friend to find him as an enemy. There is no way to avoid his justice but by flying to his mercy. We may escape the wrath of earthly kings and potentates; their eyes cannot see all, nor their hands reach all; but who can lie hid from him that filleth heaven and earth, that he should not see him and find him out? Jer. xxiii. 24, ' Can any hide himself in secret places, that I shall not see him, saith the Lord? Do not I

fill heaven and earth, saith the Lord ?   Our sins cannot be hidden from
his sight, nor our persons from his punishment.   There can be no
hiding-place without God, nor hiding-place against God.   None can
hide himself from him, but in him.   Mercy receiveth those whom justice
threateneth.

3. The encouragements to this trust.   They are three—

[1.] The titles and attributes given to God, 'Most High,' and 'Almighty.'

(1.) The first is 'Most High.'   There are many names given to God
in scripture, but this is most proper to the case in hand ; for all our
enemies and dangers are something under God, and at his disposal.
Whether they be men or devils, they are not exempted from the dominion and government of God's providence.   If you be in their hand,
they are in God's hands, and can do no more than he pleaseth.   Devils
are spiritual wickednesses in high places ; they are high, but God is
Most High.   So when men oppress others by their power : Eccles. v.
8, ' He that is higher than the highest regardeth, and there be higher
than they.'   Nothing on this side heaven should be feared by a believer ;
for the Lord in whom he trusts, ' is high above all,' Ps. cxiii. 4.   Could
we dwell more above with God, how would both the splendour and
terror of all worldly glory be lessened in our eyes ; how soon and easily
should we despise this little ant-hill of the world, where poor worms
creep up and down, and make a great deal of pudder about a thing of
nought !

(2.) The other title is 'Almighty.'   We need not warp, nor shrink,
nor shift: Gen. xvii. 1, 'I am God Almighty; walk before me, and be
thou perfect.'   He is able to keep off danger, to give us all manner of
happiness.   You have his promise who hath power and dominion over
all things in the world ; and if omnipotency shall be employed for your
comfort and protection, why should you be disquieted ?   His power is
above all power, and his wisdom above all wisdom, and his love will
never fail.   He can destroy what resists his will ; for he that made all
things out of nothing can easily turn them into their original nothing
again.   If we can do nothing for our own relief, he can do all things ;
one beck of his will is enough to make a world ; he can speak creatures
into being or nothing at his pleasure.

[2.] The expressions that set forth the manner of this help.   They
are two—'The secret of the Most High,' and 'The shadow of the
Almighty.'

(1.) The first word, 'The secret,' hath various acceptations.   Sometimes it is put for the knowledge of God's will : Ps. xxv. 14, 'The
secret of the Lord is with them that fear him ;' and Prov. iii. 32, 'His
secret is with the righteous.'   Sometimes it is put for his gracious
protection : Job xxix. 4, 'The secret of the Lord was upon my tabernacle.'   So Ps. xxxi. 20, 'Thou shalt hide them in the secret of thy
presence from the pride of man.'   By it is meant that special favour of
God which the world knoweth not, or his providence, that protecteth
his people and keepeth them safe, though they have nothing to trust to.
As there is a secret curse, that, like a moth, eateth out all the enjoyments of the wicked, so there is a secret and insensible blessing that
maketh godly men to prosper in the midst of all difficulties.   This
secret preservation is not discerned by carnal men; they are kept, and

none knoweth how, when, to appearance, they are not only laid in common with others, but exposed to the rage of others. Well, then, God's power, wisdom, and goodness, whereon faith doth fix itself, is a riddle and mystery to the world, which carnal reason knoweth not how to improve to any satisfaction and comfort. However, it teacheth us to depend upon the providence of God, whether there be any appearance of the benefit we look for, yea or no. If the name of the Lord be a strong tower, it is an invisible tower, only found out by faith and entered into by faith. Therefore he that would take up his dwelling-place in God must not go altogether by probabilities of sense, but govern himself by grounds and reasons of faith.

(2.) The other notion is, 'The shadow of the Almighty.' Shadow is defence, as we said before. Yea, not only defence and safety is implied in it, but that sweet refreshing of mind which they find who repose themselves under the protection of God; as it is a mighty comfort to men when they come out of the scorching heat of the sun into some shady place: Ps. lvii. 1, 'Under the shadow of thy wings will I make my refuge, until these calamities be overpast.' So Ps. xxxvi. 8, and in many other places. The allusion to chickens shrouding themselves under the dam's wing, or the outstretched wings of cherubims, &c., or else to the shadow of a tree, as Cant. ii. 3. Thus Jonah was mightily refreshed with the shadow of his gourd; and you know how passionate he was when it was blasted, see Jonah iv. 8, 9. But this is another manner of shadow. Earthly shadows may be blasted, but this is always fresh and green; here we may abide, and have many cool refreshings. There is no danger of the withering of our shadow, or our being thrust out.

[3.] It is given out as a promise, 'He that dwelleth shall abide;' which implieth two things—(1.) Leave to dwell in God; (2.) Assurance of safety and comfort.

(1.) Leave to dwell in God. There is an entrance for and admission of poor penitent believers. The throne of grace or mercy-seat standeth always open in the times of the gospel: Heb. iv. 16, 'Let us therefore come boldly to the throne of grace, that we may obtain mercy, and find grace to help in time of need.' None are rejected that come in faith, and seek all their hope and comfort in God through Christ. When times are uncertain, and we know not the bottom of the dangers that compass us about, is it not a great comfort to have a hiding-place, where we may remain secure and without fear? And is any place more secure than the heart of God? Evil may come at us in other places, but there we are safe day and night. Now we may have a room in the heart of God if we will but enter into his peace, and seek our reconciliation by Christ Jesus: 'He that cometh to me, I will in no wise cast out,' John vi. 37.

(2.) It implieth assurance of safety and comfort: 'He shall abide under the shadow of the Almighty.' We have here his word to build upon: Ps. lxii. 5, 6, 'My soul, wait thou only upon God, for my expectation is from him. He is only my rock, and my salvation, and my defence; I shall not be moved.' What should harm you when God taketh you into his protection, in whose hands are all persons and things? If he be made a friend, and his power and love engaged for

us, your souls may dwell in full ease and content: Ps. v. 3, 'I laid me
down and slept, for the Lord sustained me.' So Ps. iv. 8, 'I will lay
me down and sleep, for thou only makest me dwell in safety.' There
is ground of confidence that God is our preserver. Never shall we be
free from vexing, tormenting cares and fears till we can thus dwell in
God, and build all our hopes upon his truth, love, and power. A child
of God is not stupid and foolhardy; he hath as tender a sense of his
natural interests as others have; he doth often think of the vanity and
uncertainty of all earthly things; he has a greater reverence for all
events of providence, as he eyeth God in them; yet none are less discom-
posed, whatever falleth out in the world, because they trust God, and can
cast themselves into the arms of his providence, and depend upon his
love and promise, even then when he seemeth to be an enemy to them.
They have resigned themselves to God, and rest satisfied in the disposals
of his providence, how harsh and severe soever they seem to them.

III. How necessary a duty this is for all christians. It is necessary—

1. With respect to the honour of God; for trust is the practical acknowledgment of his being and attributes—his wisdom, goodness, and
power. Of his being. It is natural worship. *Jure venit cultos ad
sibi quisque deos:* Jonah i. 5, 'Then the mariners were afraid, and
cried every man unto his god.' Whom we take to be our god, we
trust him with our all: Ps. lxii. 8, 'Trust in him at all times, ye
people, pour out your heart before him; God is a refuge for us.' All
invocation and worship is founded in trust: Rom. x. 14, 'How shall
they call on him in whom they have not believed?' And as we acknowledge his being the proper object of our worship, so his attributes.
His wisdom: Prov. iii. 5, 6, 'Trust in the Lord with all thy heart, and
lean not to thine own understanding. In all thy ways acknowledge him,
and he shall direct thy path.' We see none is so wise to guide and
direct us as God. So we show that his power is above all power when
we can depend on him, running the hazard of the greatest terrors:
Dan. iii. 17, 18, 'If it be so, our God, whom we serve, is able to deliver
us from the burning fiery furnace; and he will deliver us out of thine
hand, O king. But if not, be it known unto thee, O king, that we will
not serve thy gods, nor worship the golden image which thou hast set up.'
On the contrary, it is a despising or lessening of God's power to be
afraid of man: Isa. li. 12, 13, 'I, even I, am he that comforteth you;
who art thou, that thou shouldst be afraid of a man that shall die, and
of the son of man which shall be made as grass? and forgettest the Lord
thy Maker, that hath stretched forth the heavens, and laid the founda-
tions of the earth?' So for goodness. You are so satisfied with the
promise and thing promised that you can forsake all other happiness
and hopes in confidence of salvation offered to you by Jesus Christ:
Heb. x. 39, 'We are not of them who draw back unto perdition, but
of them that believe to the saving of the soul.' In lesser things, it is
a great owning of God's goodness, when you have this persuasion in
your minds, and can say, I know that my good God will not forsake
me, as the apostle doth in effect: 2 Tim. iv. 17, 18, 'All men forsook me,
but the Lord stood with me, and I was delivered out of the mouth of
the lion; and the Lord shall deliver me from every evil work, and
preserve me to his heavenly kingdom.'

2. To quicken our duty; for unless we can trust God, the soul will never be faithful and true to him; but when we seek all safety and comfort from his protection, we will more study to please him. Our dependence is the great tie upon our obedience: 1 Tim. iv. 10, 'Therefore we both labour, &c., because we trust in God.' This giveth life to our service, comfort in our reproaches, support in all our trials; so that we go on readily, without disquiet of mind, in all our difficulties, upright in our dealings. Men warp and turn aside to crooked ways, unless they be persuaded that God taketh care of them, and will maintain them by honest and lawful means. The ground of uprightness is the persuasion of God's all-sufficiency: Gen. xiii. 1, 'The Lord appeared to Abraham, and said unto him, I am the Almighty God; walk before me, and be thou perfect.' On the other side, the ground of apostasy is unbelief: Heb. iii. 12, 'Take heed, lest there be in any of you an evil heart of unbelief, in departing from the living God. So it is the ground of shifts: Isa. xxviii. 15, 'We have made lies our refuge, and under falsehood have we hid ourselves.' They that cannot depend upon God fly to other means.

3. To settle and quiet our hearts and minds. He that looks no higher than the course of affairs in the world, can never have any firm peace in his own soul; but trust easeth of all fears, cares, and estuations of mind: Ps. cxii. 7, 'He shall not be afraid of evil tidings; his heart is fixed, trusting in the Lord;' Prov. xvi. 3, 'Commit thy way unto the Lord, and thy thoughts shall be established.' This allayed the storms in David's spirit: Ps. xlii. 5, 'Why art thou cast down, O my soul, and why art thou disquieted in me? hope thou in God, for I shall yet praise him for the help of his countenance.' When we can refer all to God, then we are at peace: Phil. iv. 6, 7, 'Be careful for nothing, but in everything, by prayer and supplication with thanksgiving, let your request be made known unto God. And the peace of God, which passeth all understanding, shall keep your hearts and minds through Christ Jesus.'

Use 1. To reprove those that trust something else instead of God. Every man hath some shadow under which he refresheth himself, some crutch upon which he leaneth, some satisfaction wherein his soul is pleased, or something that shall bear him up or bear him out in the course he taketh.

1. Some trust in the creature against God; as those that strengthen themselves in their sins because of their great power, wealth, and interest: Ps. lii. 7, 'Lo, this is the man that made not God his portion, but trusted in the abundance of his riches, and strengthened himself in his wickedness.' Alas! they will soon find God is too hard for them, blasting all their power and wealth, and bringing it to nothing, when once it is a fit sacrifice to his justice.

2. Some trust in the creature without God; as in wealth, and honour, and favour of men, &c.; and so God is neglected, and the sinner is laid asleep in the midst of the greatest soul-dangers. Alas! all things on this side God will prove a ruinous habitation to us: 1 Tim. vi. 17, 'Trust not in uncertain riches.' So for honour: Ps. xlix. 12, 'Man being in honour, abideth not.' God can soon lay it in the dust. How often have we seen the most shining glory go out in a snuff? The

favour of men is very variable. The prophet cried out, 2 Sam. xix.
43, 'We have ten parts in David.' But in the very next verse, 2 Sam.
xx. 1, one said, 'We have no part in David.' However, they die: 1
Kings i. 21, 'Otherwise it shall come to pass, when my lord the king
shall sleep with his fathers,' &c. In the general, Ps. cxviii. 8, 9, 'It
is better to trust in the Lord, than to put confidence in man. It is
better to trust in the Lord, than to put confidence in princes.' If you
were as careful to please God as to get men's favour, it would be better
for you than within a while you will find it to be.

3. Some trust in the creature, in a co-ordination with God; as those
in Isa. iv. 1, 'In that day shall seven women take hold of one man,
saying, We will eat our own bread, and wear our own apparel; only
let us be called by thy name, and take away our reproach.' God hath
the name, but they trust the creature indeed; or at least hope, by both
conjunctly, to make their felicity. They serve God and mammon.
They see riches will not cure a disease, prevent death, save a soul;
these things they leave to God; but wealth will do much in the world,
and therefore they trust in wealth as well as God's promises: Mark x.
24, 'How hard is it for them that trust in riches to enter into the
kingdom of God?' Alas! this is false: Luke xii. 15, 'Take heed,
and beware of covetousness; for a man's life consisteth not in the
abundance of the things which he possesseth.' This sin appeareth
when we cannot deny ourselves for God.

Use 2. To press you entirely to trust yourselves in God's hands.
Here take notice of—

1. The adventure of faith after disappointments: Luke v. 5, 'And
Simon answering, said unto him, Master, we have toiled all the night,
and have caught nothing: nevertheless, at thy word I will let down the
net.' Dig the pit, and see if God will fill it with rain.

2. The waiting of faith, though you find not success presently: Isa.
xxviii. 15, 'Because ye have said, We have made a covenant with death,
and with hell are we at agreement; when the overflowing scourge shall
pass through, it shall not come unto us: for we have made lies our
refuge, and under falsehood have we hid ourselves.' Greedy and
impatient longing must have present satisfaction.

3. The resolution of faith: Job xiii. 15, 'Though he slay me, yet
will I trust in him.'

4. The submission and resignation of faith. Make sure of heaven,
and for other things, let God order them as he pleaseth: Mat. vi. 33,
'Seek first the kingdom of God and his righteousness, and all these
things shall be added unto you.'

5. The prudence of faith. Settle your mind as to present necessities;
and for future contingencies, leave them to God's providence.

SERMON UPON JOHN XIX. 34-37.

But one of the soldiers with a spear pierced his side, and forthwith came thereout blood and water. And he that saw it bear record, and his record is true; and he knoweth that he saith true, that ye might believe. For these things were done, that the scripture should be fulfilled, a bone of him shall not be broken. And again another scripture saith, They shall look on him whom they pierced.—JOHN xix. 34-37.

I HAVE taken occasion upon these opportunities to go over the story of Christ's passion by several paragraphs. This paragraph treateth of the things which happened between the death and burial of Christ: and the main thing offered therein is that notable circumstance that happened immediately after Christ's death, the flowing of water and blood out of Christ's side.—

In the words you have—

1. The occasion of this circumstance, ver. 31–33, 'The Jews therefore, because it was the preparation, that the bodies should not remain upon the cross upon the sabbath-day (for that sabbath-day was an high day), besought Pilate that their legs might be broken, and they might be taken away. Then came the soldiers, and brake the legs of the first, and of the other that was crucified with him. But when they came to Jesus, and saw that he was dead already, they brake not his legs.'

2. The circumstance itself, 'But one of the soldiers with a spear pierced his side, and forthwith came thereout blood and water.'

3. A solemn attestation of it, ver. 36, 'For these things were done that the scriptures should be fulfilled, A bone of him shall not be broken.'

4. The ends of God's providence, which are two—the fulfilling of the prophecies of scripture, confirmed by the citations of many places.

[1.] That Christ should die without breaking of a bone, ver. 36, 'A bone of him shall not be broken.'

[2.] That yet his body should be pierced with a spear, ver. 37, 'Again another scripture saith, They shall look on him whom they have pierced.'

I shall go over these circumstances in my accustomed method, with brief observations or hints of meditation.

First, The occasion of the words, which was the niceness and scrupulosity of the Jews, that the dead bodies might not hang upon the

C

cross upon the sabbath-day, especially that high sabbath of the passover. Therefore they go to Pilate to hasten the death of the malefactors by breaking their legs; which is readily granted, and accordingly executed upon the two thieves, but not upon Christ, because he was dead already. I shall not stay on the occasion, only observe—

1. That superstition is fuller of ceremony than mercy. We find the Jews very tender in the lesser points of the law. They made no conscience of spilling innocent blood, yet by no means would put the price of blood into the treasury. They made no conscience of bringing Christ to the cross, but are zealous not to have him hang there on the great sabbath of the passover; as if God would accept their eating the typical lamb, when they had slain the Shepherd of the flock and of the church.

2. That the worst of men are usually very solicitous about external worship. The wicked Jews, that crucified the Lord of life, would not have the passover profaned with an unseemly spectacle. Every man must have somewhat of religion, or else conscience will not be quiet; and externals are very easy. We find it in our carnal people, that with much reverence observe the externals of the sacraments; though they altogether neglect the obligation of them. They are as zealous for the supper as the Jews for the decency of the passover, and yet are false and faithless in their allegiance to Christ; like madmen, tear the bond, and yet prize the seal.

3. From their going to ask leave of Pilate for the additional punishment, we learn that malefactors are not to be taken out of the hands of justice. Every degree of punishment and torment is left to the magistrate, and not to the malice of the executioner or the fury of the multitude: Deut. xxv. 2, 3, 'And it shall be, if the wicked man be worthy to be beaten, that the judge shall cause him to lie down, and to be beaten before his face, according to his fault, by a certain number. Forty stripes he may give him, and not exceed: lest if he should exceed, and beat him above these with many stripes, then thy brother should seem vile unto thee.' Therefore the judge was to be present when the malefactor was beaten, that they might not receive more or less stripes than the law awarded.

4. From Pilate's grant observe, that when once a man giveth up himself to please men, there is no end of compliance. Pilate, by the importunity of the Jews, is first drawn to scourge Christ, and then to crucify him, and now to sign an order for breaking his legs, a torment unusual, and contrary to the custom of the Romans. When we are tempted to serve men, we have need consider the issue. The first temptations are modest and plausible, but afterwards more servile and odious. It is good to break off at first, unless we mean to keep time and pace with every lust of men.

5. From Christ's being dead already, before the others crucified with him, we learn his willingness to die for us. His love made quick despatch. He could have retained his life longer, but he was willing to let it go, that everything might be finished that was necessary for our comfort and restoration.

6. We learn also from hence, the voluntariness of his death. If his legs had been broken, his death would have seemed an effect of violence

rather than willing resignation. He had said, John x. 18, 'No man taketh it from me, but I lay it down of myself : I have power to lay it down, and I have power to take it again.' It is meant of his divine power, and to notify that there was no force put upon Christ, but he would undertake it, and appear in this circumstance. In this oblation Christ would be the priest ; his legs were not broken, but he gave up the ghost. Thus I have opened the occasion.

Secondly, The circumstance itself, in the 34th verse, 'But one of the soldiers with a spear pierced his side, and forthwith came thereout water and blood.' They brake not his legs, but to make an experiment whether he were truly dead, and had any sense and feeling left, and to put some scorn upon his body, one of the soldiers, out of malice, and beyond his commission, pierced his side with a spear ; and the heart being pierced, together with the bag of water that encircleth the heart, and Christ's body not being cool, there followed a flux of water and blood.

I shall look upon this circumstance under a threefold consideration—

1. As an act of Christ's love and condescension, that he would expose his body to the malice and violence of wicked men. He might have withered and dried up the soldier's arm, as he did Jeroboam's when he stretched it out to reach the prophet ; but by this stroke Christ would have his heart and bowels opened to us, to show how full of love he was to sinners. Look, as at the beginning Adam's side was opened, and Eve was taken out of Adam's side, so is the church out of Christ's side. He suffered his side to be opened that he might open to us the gate of life. Some of the ancients compared this wound in Christ's side to the door in the side of the ark, by which all the creatures that were not to perish in the flood found entrance. By this door we have entrance into the heart of Christ, and by Christ presented to God the Father. *Patet arca cordis per foramina corporis*, saith Bernard. By the hole of his side we may espy the secret of his heart. He opened his side, that we might see his heart. He would have sinners know that he had not a drop of blood which he accounted too good for us. He would now let out the residue, that he might not keep a drop. His heart was first pierced with love, and then with a spear. It had never been pierced with a spear if it had not been first pierced with love. Christ saith, Cant. iv. 9, 'Thou hast ravished my heart, my sister, my spouse.' First *wounded with love to the church, and that brought him to* the cross, and there he was wounded and pierced with the malice of men. Other members were wounded before, and now his heart. His hands and feet were pierced with nails, and his life-blood dropped out by degrees ; but now his side is pierced, and through his side his heart, which caused the flux of water and blood.

This circumstance is useful to beget hope and thankfulness.

[1.] Hope for all wounded sinners. It is said of those converts, Acts ii. 37, 'That they were pricked in their hearts.' This is the usual case of all the saints in pangs of the new birth ; they are pricked, and wounded in heart with a sense of their sin and rebellion and unkindness to God. Now this is some ground of comfort ; Christ's own heart was wounded. The bowels of mercy were now set open by a spear, and to penitent sinners they shall never be shut more. Therefore when you are wounded, think of the wounds of Christ. These are the clefts of the rock in which a poor guilty creature may lie hid when wrath maketh inquisition for sinners. When God caused his glory to pass by, he put Moses in a cleft of the rock, Exod. xxxiii. 22 ; and the spouse is described to lie hid in 'the clefts of the rock, and the secret places of the stairs,' Cant. ii. 14 ; which certainly is meant of some secret hiding-place in time of danger, wherein God is wont to protect his people. Your hiding-place is the wounds of Christ. Here you may run for shelter. Oh, it is sweet to be found in him, by his side to get into his heart, and there to lie hid till the pursuit of wrath be over. Everything that was executed upon the person of Christ should be some advantage to faith, for it maketh up a part of his merit. The wounds of Christ are the best cure for the wounds of a sinner. The prophet saith, ' By his stripes we are healed,' Isa. liii. 5.

[2.] It yieldeth matter of thankfulness that Christ would expose his body to so many violences and indignities for man's sake. It is mangled with whips, because one prophet speaketh of stripes. It is nailed to the cross, because it is said in another, ' They pierced my hands and my feet,' Ps. xxii. 16. Wounded with a spear, because it is said again, ' They shall look upon him whom they have pierced,' Zech. xii. 10. Christ's body, though it were excellently tempered, seemeth to be assumed for no other purpose but to be harassed with sorrows and extremities. How should this increase our thankfulness ! Soldiers, to endear themselves to their country, are wont to show their wounds and scars received in public service. Christ hath wounds and marks to show : as he said to Thomas, John xx. 27, ' Reach hither thy finger, and behold my hands ; and reach hither thy hand, and thrust it into my side, and be not faithless, but believing.' In the sacrament these things are represented to faith. Christ doth, as it were, show you his marks and his wounds. Remember Christ retaineth them in his glorious body as tokens of his sufferings and combats, and this body you are to look upon by faith. Remember it, and cry out, O my dear Lord, and my God ! with Thomas ; a vehement, abrupt speech, noting an admiration of Christ's mercy. Twice in that chapter we read that he showed his wounds, ver. 20 and 27. Christ loveth to show his wounds. *Quanto vilior pro nobis factus est, tanto charior esse debet.* By how much the cheaper he was made for us, so much the dearer he ought to be to us.

Let all this endear him to your souls. When you take the cup of blessing, remember that cup was filled out of the side of Christ. When thou art drinking, thou art spiritually drinking his blood, that thou mayest indeed bless God.

2. I look upon this circumstance as a certain pledge of Christ's death. The flowing of water and blood showeth the pericardium was pierced, a bag which keepeth water about the heart. The place in which the heart is enfolded is full of a waterish matter, which by this stroke was let out ; so that it did not appear by the former passages that Christ was dead, but this was a certain evidence which made it manifest ; his heart being pierced, which is certainly mortal, if he had been living before. Now his enemies could not say he was half dead, and that his

resurrection was but a reviving out of a swoon. And this is one reason St John is so earnest in his attestation of this circumstance, because all our faith and hope is built on the truth and certainty of Christ's death. Beyond death there can be no more required. They that are thirsty of revenge can never be quiet till the party be dead. God's justice was thirsty of satisfaction, but now Christ is dead all is finished. What would you have more? The flux of water and blood is a certain seal and confirmation. Divine justice pursued Christ, and the affronts and injuries of men are not ended till the bag about the heart be pierced, and there issue out water and blood, so that all the world should have a visible testimony that Christ was really dead.

From this circumstance I shall a little speak of the certainty and the necessity of Christ's death, and the comfort thereon depending, a matter weighty and of great importance in religion : 1 Cor. xv. 3, 'I delivered unto you first of all that which I also received, how that Christ died for our sins according to the scripture.' There was a real expiration and delivery up of his soul to God, which was now showed openly and truly, and not done in show and fiction. To confirm the truth his heart is pierced, and he remained three days in the grave, under the power and dominion of it. However, Christ died, yet not whole Christ died, but only according to his human nature. Though he yielded up the ghost, that is, the natural human life, yet the hypostatical union was not dissolved. There was a separation of the soul from the body, yet both remained united with the divine nature. So that here was no dissolving of the person of Christ; and therefore he is said to raise himself. His human body, though it lay in the grave, was still a part of his person.

3. The necessity of Christ's death. I shall instance but in a double relation to the covenant—

(1.) As a surety; and (2.) As a testator. Christ was to die—

[1.] As a surety. We had deserved death, but our surety was to pay our debt. The sentence under which man lay was a sentence of death; therefore his life was laid down to redeem ours. As Paul undertook for Onesimus, Philem. 18, ' If he hath wronged thee, or oweth thee ought, put that on mine account;' so Christ for us : ' He suffered for our sin, the just for the unjust,' 1 Peter iii. 18. He died in our room and stead : 1 Tim. ii. 6, ' He gave himself a ransom for all, to be testified in due time.' He died not by any weakness of nature, but by voluntary consent. Christ had to do with several parties, and so died under several relations. He had to do with the devil and his agents, so he died as conqueror; with the Jews, and so he died as a martyr; he had to do with his Father, so he died as a surety; and as a person in covenant with the elect, so he died as a sacrifice. The devil was his enemy, God his judge, and himself his own priest. The Father issued out a process, and Christ offered up himself to be killed by the Jews.

[2.] As a testator or maker of the new testament. We could never have had the great blessings of the covenant if Christ had not died: Heb. ix. 16, ' For where a testament is, there must also of necessity be the death of the testator.' Till then the testament is not in force. Christ promised to make a new testament, therefore to die, or else he

could not make good his word. Christ is lifted up to the cross as upon
his deathbed, and there he dieth of love, and leaveth great legacies
to the church—pardon, grace, and glory ; disposeth of heaven, and all
things conducing thereunto. This testament is engrossed, and a formal instrument made of it in the gospel, sacraments, seals. The
apostles were the notaries to witness from heaven in a glorious way by
miracles on earth, by the Spirit, water, and blood, 1 John v. 6–8.
Christ, because of the duplicity of his nature, may be allowed to be a
witness to his own will. The Spirit descending like a dove, appearing
in cloven tongues of fire. And there are three which confirm this
truth in the hearts of believers—the Spirit, the water, and blood.
Ease in conscience by the blood of Christ, the work of holiness in the
heart, and the certioration of the Spirit.

Use 1. Oh, let us make use of this great comfort, Christ is dead !
The apostle beginneth his triumph thence : Rom. viii. 34, ' Who is he
that condemneth? It is Christ that died.' He died in our name and
stead, whereby we are absolved ; as the ram was taken, and Isaac let
go : Job xxxiii. 24, ' I have found a ransom.' God will not exact the
debt twice. Believers do not live as if they had a surety to die for
them, or a testator to make them such great and rich legacies. If we
would meditate on the death of Christ with comfort and profit, we must
consider these things ; for still we must consider with respect to the
covenant and the transactions of God with men.

1. The horrible deserving of sin, and the hatefulness of it to God.
We must have a redeemer, or be all lost. This redeemer must make
full satisfaction, both in respect of the infinite value of his person,
which was not the blood of an angel, but the blood of God, and the
extremity of his sufferings. The great almighty God, the author of
life, must come and die himself : Isa. xliii. 24, ' Thou hast made me
to serve with thy sins, and hast wearied me with thine iniquities.'
Jesus Christ, the eternal Son of God, must come and be put upon an
harsh service. Life itself must assume death. The Lord Almighty,
filling the whole world with his glory, hung dying upon the cross.

2. The great love of God, that, when we wanted a ransom, God gave
it us out of his own treasury. Among all the treasuries of heaven
nothing more precious and excellent than Jesus Christ. Christ must
pay for the rest. He sendeth his own Son to endure the shameful
death of the cross ; the natural Son for the adopted sons : 1 John iv.
9, 10, ' In this was manifested the love of God towards us, because
that God sent his only-begotten Son into the world, that we might live
through him. Herein is love, not that we loved God, but that he
loved us, and sent his Son to be a propitiation for our sins ; ' Rom. v.
8, ' God commendeth his love to us, that while we were sinners Christ
died for us.' This was a circumstance to set out love.

3. The unspeakable love of Jesus Christ, his meekness and patience.
How may we admire the ready mind of Christ ! Heb. x. 5–7, ' Wherefore when he cometh into the world, he saith, Sacrifice and offerings
thou wouldst not, but a body hast thou prepared me. In burnt-
offerings and sacrifices for sin thou hast had no pleasure ; then said
I, Lo, I come (in the volume of the book it is written of me) to do thy
will, O God.' If nothing but the shameful death of the cross will do,

yet it was readily agreed to. If any had cause to love his life, Christ
had; it dwelt with God in a personal union.

4. The sufficiency of this sacrifice: Heb. x. 14, ' By one offering he
hath perfected for ever them that are sanctified.' Christ hath no
more work to do, but only to look for the travail of his soul. He hath
paid the full price, made a full purchase. The vessels of honour
cannot be dashed. No satisfaction remains to be paid by ourselves;
there needeth nothing by way of satisfaction.

Use 2. Let us not be quiet till we feel Christ is dead. Great reports
without experience beget atheism: Rom. vi. 5, ' If we have been planted
together in the likeness of his death;' Gal. ii. 20, ' Who hath loved me,
and gave himself for me.' Is the heart of our corruptions wounded?
is Christ incarnate? is Christ formed in us? is Christ dying, and we
feel nothing? It availeth us nothing.

Thirdly, I look upon it as a symbol and type of his mediatory office.
Christ was in every part furnished: 1 John v. 6, ' This is he that
came by water and blood, even Jesus Christ: not by water only, but
by water and blood.' Now this water and blood are two of the witnesses: ver. 10, ' Hath this testimony within himself.' It setteth forth the
double benefit of Christ's death. He came to satisfy and to sanctify;
by water noting the force of grace upon the heart, and by blood noting
peace and ease of conscience. These flowed so distinctly as they might
be discerned. *Aqua quæ diluat, sanguis qui redimat*—Ambrose.
Water to wash, blood to redeem: an allusion to the ancient Jewish
rites. There were under the law ablutions and oblations; there was a
purification by water to take away the filth of sin, and an expiation
by blood to take away the guilt. Now water and blood, that issued
from Christ's side, prefigured both these. He came not only to justify,
but to sanctify. By a double symbol Christ would teach us that he is
the true expiation and laver, λουτρον και λυτρον. So suitably there are
two ordinances in the gospel—baptism and the Lord's supper. Out
of Christ's side, saith St Austin, came the two sacraments. Christ
came not only to disannul guilt and the curse, but to destroy sin; to
cleanse from inward corruption, as well as procure their reconciliation
with God. Of the first, the legal washings were a type; of the second,
the sacrifices.

Use 1. To rejoice in Jesus Christ, because we are complete in him.

1. There is ' a fountain open for sin and for uncleanness,' Zech. xii.
1, and it is a fountain ever springing and overflowing. When Christ
was pierced upon the cross, like a full vessel he sent out water and
blood; water to purify the church, and blood to feed it. From the
same source there flows a double fountain—*De eadem origine, aqua
et sanguis emanant.* Let us draw water hence with the buckets of
faith, and do it with joy: Isa. xii. 3, ' Therefore with joy shall ye draw
water out of the wells of salvation.' The Jews in the feast of taber-
nacles, they were to go to Siloam and draw water. He that brought
the water did it that it might be poured out before the Lord upon the
altar with wine. They did it with trumpets and hymns, and hosan-
nas often repeated. Thence Christ saith, John vii. 37, ' And in
the last day, the great day of the feast, Jesus stood and cried, saying,
If any man thirst, let him come unto me and drink.' With great

variety of melody they went to fetch water from Siloam to the temple in golden vessels. Oh, consider here is a double stream say, as it is Isa. xlv. 24, ' Surely shall one say, In the Lord have I righteousness and strength.' Enough to justify, enough to sanctify. Oh, come again and again to this fountain !

2. To teach us what to expect from Christ. Come for this double benefit. It is sad to have Christ in one quality of a mediator and not in another. Say, Lord, out of this side of thine there flowed not blood alone, but water and blood ; as they flowed together out of thy pierced side, so let them ever flow together into my wounded soul, justification and sanctification : those things which thou hast joined let me not ever put asunder. Consider it is dishonourable to Christ when these two are severed. Celsus and others reproached the church as a common sanctuary for villains and profligate persons. No ; it is a school of discipline, an hospital to cure them, not shelter them in sin. Both go together. It was convenient that, before he sanctified man in himself, he should justify him before God ; first reconciled, and then receive privileges of grace ; and after reconciled, it is again convenient they should be sanctified, lest Christ should have an ulcerous body. When Esther was chosen to be queen, she had garments given her out of Ahasuerus' wardrobe, and she was to accomplish the months of her purification.

3. Whenever we beg pardon, there is always a serious study of sanctification ; they are inseparably joined in God's dispensation : 1 Cor. i. 30, ' But of him ye are in Jesus Christ, who of God is made unto us wisdom and righteousness, and sanctification and redemption ; ' 1 Cor. vi. 11, ' And such were some of you, but ye are washed, but ye are sanctified, but ye are justified in the name of the Lord Jesus, and by the Spirit of our God.' Whosoever truly repenteth of sin doth not only seek the judicial abolition of it, but the real. A serious aim at the glory of God doth carry the soul more against the corruption of sin than the guilt of it. The abolishing of the guilt doth directly respect our profit, but the abolishing of corruption doth profit the glory of God, that we may not offend him.

SERMON UPON MATTHEW XIX. 30.

But many that are first shall be last, and the last shall be first.—
MAT. xix. 30.

THESE words are a part of Christ's answer to Peter's question, ver. 27,
'Behold, we have forsaken all and followed thee : what shall we have
therefore?' What had Peter to forsake? a cottage, a net, a fisher-boat :
a great all! But we are apt to think much of what we part with on
Christ's score, if it be but the superfluity of our estate, if we suffer a
disgraceful word or a small inconveniency, or be but browbeaten with
a frown, we are apt to inquire, 'What we shall have therefore?' as if
God were greatly indebted to us. We need not seek another pay-
master; Christ will not be behindhand with us. Christ's answer is—

1. To their particular case, as apostles, ver. 28, 'Jesus saith unto
them, Verily I say unto you, That ye which have followed me in the
regeneration, when the Son of man shall sit in the throne of his glory,
ye also shall sit upon twelve thrones, judging the twelve tribes of
Israel.' We do not enough think of the general renovation of all
things. It seemeth the number of the apostles ought to be twelve.
Therefore Matthias was chosen in the room of Judas. And that the
apostles shall have eminent honour in that day.

2. As to the general case, ver. 29, 'And every one that hath forsaken
houses, or brethren, or sisters, or father, or mother, or wife, or children,
or lands for my name's sake, shall receive an hundredfold, and shall
inherit everlasting life. None can be a loser by God, no, not in the
midst of his troubles and persecutions, but hath the comforts and
experiences of God by the way: Mark x. 29, 30, 'And Jesus answered
and said, Verily I say unto you, There is no man that hath left house,
or brethren, or sisters, or father, or mother, or wife, or children, or
lands, for my sake and the gospel's, but he shall receive an hundredfold now in this time, houses, and brethren, and sisters, and mothers,
and children, and lands with persecutions, and in the world to come
eternal life.'

3. By way of admonition, not to reckon too much of their present
fidelity to Christ, for temptations might come; others later called
might exceed them : 'Many that are first shall be last, and the last
shall be first.'

In the words observe two things are asserted—(1.) The 'first shall be last;' those in the first rank might be cast back; (2.) The 'last shall be first;' advanced to the highest place in christianity.

First, For the former proposition, 'Many that are first shall be last.' For explaining of it, observe—

1. That it doth not universally and necessarily prove so, but for the most part it will be so; not all without exception, but many that are first shall be last. Therefore: Luke xiii. 30, 'And behold, there are last which shall be first, and there are first which shall be last.' You may keep your priority and precedency to the end, if you do not grow dead, and drowsy, and sleepy. If they that began early acquit themselves with any zeal and industry suitable to their beginnings, the saying shall not prejudice them. Proverbs hold, ἐπὶ τὸ πολυ, for the generality; and this is a proverbial speech, adapted and used by our Saviour with an holy purpose, to caution his disciples against pride in what they had already done and suffered for his sake: they were too well conceited of their forsaking all to follow Christ.

2. Observe, that it is applicable not only to persons, but nations and societies and communities of men; for in Luke it is applied to the rejection of the Jews and the calling of the gentiles: Luke xiii. 29, 30, 'And they shall come from the east and from the west, and from the north and from the south, and shall sit down in the kingdom of God. And behold, there are last which shall be first; and there are first which shall be last.' Many nations, cities, and countries that have embraced the true worship and service of God may lose their crown, and suffer their candlestick to be removed to others. In a little succession of time there are strange changes and revolutions as to the state of religion among a people: Mat. xi. 23, 'And thou, Capernaum, which art exalted unto heaven, shall be brought down to hell.' The gospel is the honour of any country, city, or town; and where it is most clearly preached, that place is exalted most, and made nearest heaven; but through their unthankfulness, unfruitfulness, and contempt, this honour and glory may be taken from them, and they sunk as low in judgments as formerly exalted for privileges; and thus it may be interpreted as to the enjoyment of means, 'They that are first shall be last;' that is, they that get away the gospel from them.

3. Observe, that this firstness and lastness is to be understood with respect to matters of religion. In the world it is often verified that they who have had the precedency of others may afterwards be set far behind them: 1 Sam. ii. 7, 8, 'The Lord maketh poor, and maketh rich: he bringeth low, and lifteth up. He raiseth the poor out of the dust, and lifteth up the beggar from the dunghill, to set them among princes, and to inherit the throne of glory: for the pillars of the earth are the Lord's, and he hath set the world upon them.' That prosperity may not be without a curb, nor adversity without a cordial in the government of the world, God turneth things upside down, and the mighty and opulent are brought low, and the base and despicable raised to great riches, dignity, and honour; which should quiet our minds whenever it falleth out, because the great sovereign of the world hath so appointed it, and will take his own course without asking our leave or waiting for our consent. But here it is meant of religious matters, or things appertaining to God. First and last often shift places.

. In matters of religion it may bear a good sense, that God's latter dispensation is better than the former, and those that live under it exceed the other.

[1.] Our condition under the covenant of grace is better than that in innocency under the covenant of works; as a vessel that is soldered is strongest in the crack, or an hedge that is mended is more firmly fenced than it was before the gap or breach. Take, for an instance, Adam and Job. Job is more happy in his misery than Adam in his innocency; he was victorious on the dunghill, when the other was defeated on the throne; he gave no ear to the counsel of his wife: Job ii. 10, 'Curse God, and die,' when the woman seduced Adam. He despised the assaults of Satan, when the other suffered himself to be worsted at the first temptation; he preserved his righteousness in the midst of his sorrows, when the other lost his innocency in the midst of paradise, where he had all manner of delights and pleasures. So that the grace of the Redeemer doth much excel the innocency of Adam.

[2.] The last edition of the covenant doth excel the former, and they that live under the gospel of Christ are in a much better condition than those that lived under the economy of Moses. They had more of outward prosperity, but these have more of the Spirit. They were more exempted from suffering, but these are more fortified against sufferings; Christ hath not taken away the fight, but secured the victory; and though all that will live godly in Christ Jesus must suffer persecution, yet they have an hundredfold in this life, and in the world to come life everlasting: 'For many that are first shall be last, and the last first,' Mark x. 30, 31.

5. In matters of religion some may have the precedency of others; either—(1.) In reality and truth; or (2.) In appearance only; or in their own opinion; or in the opinion of others.

[1.] In reality and truth. Some may have the precedency two ways; either—(1.) As to time; (2.) As to zeal and fervency in the profession of religion.

(1.) As to time. As they began sooner, or have served God longer, so they are first. Surely this is a precedency and a privilege. The apostle saith of Andronicus and Junia, they 'were in Christ before him,' Rom. xvi. 7; Eph. i. 12, 'That we should be to the praise of his glory, who first trusted in Christ.' Those who do not retard or delay their conversion, but are converted early to God, are more obliged by his mercy to serve and honour him, because he did so soon break off the yoke of their slavery to sin and Satan, and also they take the way to honour and obey God sooner than others that yet lie in their sins. They are sooner capacitated to serve him, and therefore it is their honour and glory that they are first.

(2.) As to zeal and fervency in the profession of religion. Some are in the first rank of christians, and are more forward than others; as the apostle made boast of the forwardness of the Corinthians, and thereby stirred up other people, yet was afraid this boasting might seem a vanity and over-confidence of them: 2 Cor. ix. 2–4, 'For I know the forwardness of your mind, for which I boast of you to them of Macedonia, that Achaia was ready a year ago; and your zeal hath provoked very many. Yet have I sent the brethren, lest our boasting of you should be in vain in this behalf; that, as I said, ye may be ready : lest haply if they of Macedonia come with me, and find you unprepared, we (that we say not, you) should be ashamed in this same confident boasting.' This the apostle doth lest the rich Corinthians would be disgraced before the poor Macedonians, the business cooled again ; he was forced to quicken them. We see many in their youth are eminently zealous, willing to run all hazards with Christ ; but when their first heats are spent, grow worldly, careless, if not greatly profane, and are strangely withered and blasted in their age.

6. Those that have these advantages of being first may become last.

[1.] Some that come after them in time may exceed them in labour and christian diligence; and though the other keep up the life of grace still, yet they may be much outshined, and outstripped ; as, for instance, these apostles of our Lord who left their all, and seemed to deserve so much of him, were exceeded by Paul, who professed himself to be ' one born out of due time,' 1 Cor. xv. 8, yet laboured more abundantly than they all, ver. 10. Well, then, the first may be last; though called sooner, yet may do less service than those that were called afterwards ; so to be last doth not imply a loss of grace, but an excellency in latter converts.

[2.] As to zeal in profession and practice. Certainly it is our duty to keep up our vigour to the last, for they that ' are planted in the house of the Lord should bring forth fruit in old age,' Ps. xcii. 14. The older they grow they should be the more fruitful. Enoch kept up his communion with God throughout his whole life: Gen. v. 23, 'Enoch walked with God,' after he begat sons and daughters. And it is the commendation of Mnason of Cyprus, that he was 'an old disciple,' Acts xxi. 16 ; one that was rooted in the doctrine of the gospel, and had for a long time owned Christ. But oftentimes it falleth out that they that are longest at work do not always the most or best service.

This may fall out two ways—

(1.) By the larger measures of grace vouchsafed to the latter converts above others, of which no reason can be given but God's will. He is arbitrary in his gifts, but not in his judgments. In converting grace, as to time and degree, he acts *ut dominus*, as a free lord: Rom. ix. 16, ' It is not of him that willeth, nor of him that runneth, but of God that showeth mercy.' But in rewarding grace, he acteth *ut rector et judex :* 1 Cor. ix. 24, ' So run that you may obtain.' They that have done most, and served him longest, are most richly rewarded. But in mere donatives God will do with his own as he pleaseth. Instances in David : Ps. cxix. 98–100, ' Thou hast made me wiser than mine enemies, wiser than my teachers, wiser than the ancients.' God may furnish the younger with larger gifts of prudence, knowledge, boldness, zeal, and industrious activity. So Paul : 1 Cor. xv. 10, ' But by the grace of God I am what I am : and his grace which was bestowed on me was not in vain ; but I laboured more abundantly than they all; yet not I, but the grace of God which was in me.' Now this might affect the apostles, who being leavened with carnal conceit, dreamed of great offices in the kingdom of the Messiah, that might become others more worthy than they, richly furnished to do God and the church service.

(2.) By the fault of those that did formerly excel ; by their pride, carelessness, and security, they may be thrown back behind many, who for a time had nothing of God and goodness in them.

(1st.) For their pride; if they be conceited that they deserved more at God's hand than others. Many who, in the conceit of their own merit, were first, shall, in the course of God's dispensations, be found last : James iv. 5, 6, ' Do ye think the scripture saith in vain, The spirit that dwelleth in us lusteth to envy ? But he giveth more grace.' The envious, proud spirit is blasted : ' The spirit that dwelleth in us lusteth to envy, but he giveth more grace ; wherefore he saith, God resisteth the proud, but giveth grace to the humble.' Now, of all pride, spiritual pride is most provoking : as the pride of the legal justiciary : Luke xviii. 9, 14, ' And he spake this parable unto certain which trusted in themselves that they were righteous, and despised others. I tell you, this man went down to his house justified rather than the other : for every one that exalteth himself shall be abased, and he that humbleth himself shall be exalted.' The humble publican is preferred before the conceited pharisee. So the elder brother, who impersonateth those who grow conceited of their own profession, and envieth the grace of God to others : Luke xv. 29, ' And he answering, said to his father, Lo, these many years do I serve thee, neither transgressed I at any time thy commandment, and yet thou never gavest me a kid that I might make merry with my friends.' If any of this leaven get into the hearts of God's children, God will prefer others before them. He will have his grace magnified and adored. And we must cherish an humble sense of all that we suffer and do for him, that we are nothing and that he is all.

(2d.) Their laziness. They do not improve and grow according to their standing, and the many advantages they have by so long acquaintance with God ; but are apt to grow dead, drowsy, formal, and customary, and go on in a tract of duties without any life and vigour, Luke viii. 18. He that useth not grace shall not increase it ; whereas others' diligence shall be blessed. Some start up that have more grace in a little time than they that have been getting many years.

(3d.) It may come to pass through their security. When they have had some losses for Christ, they may think all their trials are over. A man of long standing, being secure of salvation, may grow negligent, and supposing that he hath grace, and is possessed of the love of God, there needeth not such diligence as when he was doubtful ; and if he go round in a course and tract of duty, and avoid grosser sins, it is enough, and he is now past all danger ; and so is tempted to leave his first love and zeal, Rev. ii. 4. After the first labours of regeneration, and the difficulties of reconciliation with God, are past over, and he hath gotten some peace, and confidence, and freedom from the terrors of the law, then he is in danger of security, by which means all runneth to waste in the soul, and our nakedness will soon appear. Take, for an instance, David and Joseph. The one will show us the danger of laying aside of our fear and caution, the other the benefit of a constant watchfulness and circumspection : 2 Sam. xi. 2, 3, ' And it came to pass in an eveningtide that David arose from off his bed, and walking upon the roof of the king's house ; and from the roof he saw a woman washing herself ; and the woman was very beautiful to look upon. And

David sent and inquired after the woman : and one said, Is not this Bathsheba, the daughter of Eliam, the wife of Uriah the Hittite ? ' Gen. xxxix. 7-9, ' And it came to pass after these things, that his master's wife cast her eyes upon Joseph, and she said, Lie with me. But he refused, and said unto his master's wife, My master wotteth not what is with me in the house, and he hath committed all that he hath to my hand. There is none greater in the house than I ; neither hath he kept back anything from me but thee, because thou art his wife : how then can I do this great wickedness, and sin against God ? ' The one was a young man, the other old, and well experienced in the ways of God : Joseph a single man, David had a multitude of wives ; Joseph had the advantage of secrecy, David was fain to make way to his adultery by other sins ; Joseph was solicited, David the solicitor ; yet how foully did the one fall, because secure ? The other had his heart possessed with the fear of God.

2. In appearance only. I have spoken to you of the softest interpretation of the words ; now I shall show you how they may be understood of those that are first in their own opinion only, or in the opinion of the world ; and so they that are first, that made a great blaze of profession for a while, and at length, last ; and so to be last is to be nothing. It is not meant of gradual declinings, but total apostasy, which is the end of many that are forward in outward show and profession of Christ and the gospel, do, after they have professed a religion awhile, suffer it to die away, and vanish into nothing ; a greater abuse and mischief to the church of God than if they had never professed : so they come to be least in the kingdom of heaven ; that is, to have no room nor place there, Mat. v. 19 ; and elsewhere, to reap sparingly is not to reap at all, 2 Cor. ix. 6 ; and Mat. xxi. 31, ' Publicans and harlots go into the kingdom of God before you.' It is not to be understood as if the one made haste into the kingdom of God, and the other were only slow and remiss, but did at length enter. No ; they were opposite, and averse, and never entered : ' This man went to his house justified rather than the other,' Luke xviii. 14. Not as if the pharisee was justified ; but the meaning is, not justified at all. There are many such speeches : so that many that have begun well for the present shall afterwards fall away, and be utterly excluded from the kingdom of heaven. Such as are foremost in outward shows and profession of religion are not always the best christians : Gal. iii. 3, 4, ' Are ye so foolish ? having begun in the Spirit, are ye now made perfect by the flesh ? Have you suffered so many things in vain ? if it be yet in vain.' All former profession, praying, hearing, suffering, is lost, if we by one afterchange should reproach our former practice : Gal. v. 7, ' Ye did run well ; who did hinder you ? ' They had made some progress in the ways of God ; their aftercarriage may be no way answerable to their promising beginnings ; they may not only grow remiss and lazy, but strangely perverted by the allurements of the flesh and the world. A carnal and unsound heart will either take some offence, or by some temptation or other be taken off from the profession and practice of godliness, by sensuality, error, or worldliness : John vi. 66, ' From that time many of the disciples went back, and walked no more with him.' Demas for a time made a good profession, but afterwards was blinded by the world : 2

iv. 10, 'For Demas hath forsaken us, having embraced the present world.' So the scripture taketh notice of many other blazing stars that fell from heaven like lightning. It will be so; all that are called are not elected: Mat. xx. 16, 'So the last shall be first, and first last; for many are called, but few are chosen.' Therefore we should not be contented with the beginnings of christianity only; many times there are plenty of blossoms, and yet but little fruit, and those who have had good beginnings may afterwards greatly dishonour the name of Christ by their scandal or defections from him. They may seem to be first in the kingdom of heaven, and to be the very flower of christianity, but prove afterwards the very dregs of christianity. The foolish virgins had their lamps as well as the wise, but their oil failed; they went forth to meet the bridegooom as the wise did, but they were afterwards shut out, Mat. xxv. 10. It is not enough to make the profession plausible, but to see the practice be real and the heart sound. Some in an hopeful way went far, but at last all is lost.

Use 1. See that you do not make an ill use of it.

1 It is not to discourage men from beginning betimes, or remembering their Creator in the days of their youth. No; we should believe with the first. Epenetus is called the first-fruits of Achaia, Rom. xvi. 5. Surely it is an honour to be first in the service of God. The sooner the better. The more experience of God, the more inured to his blessed yoke. All the sacrifices of the law were to be offered to God young, and in full strength. We expect eternal life, and therefore no part of our temporal life should be diverted from God. Therefore to discourage beginning early were to play the devil's game, who would fain feast upon the flower and freshness of our youth, and leave God the scraps and fragments of old age. No; begin betimes; but hold on and keep your crown.

2. Not to quench your zeal and forwardness in profession of godliness, provided it have a root: Deut. v. 29, 'Oh that there were such an heart in them, that they would fear me, and keep my commandments always, that it might be well with them, and their children after them.' And that you keep up this life and vigour, and still stir up yourselves that you may not grow dead, and drowsy, and sleepy, but acquit yourselves with a like affection in the progress as in the beginning: Heb. iii. 14, 'For we are made partakers of Christ, if we hold the beginning of our confidence steadfast unto the end.' An old disciple keepeth up his dignity still; it is not the newness of the thing affected him. No forwardness in religion is good, if you do afterwards grow remiss and lazy.

Use 2. The right use that we should make of it—

1. Is to excite men to a perseverance in a course of holiness and righteousness, that the end may answer the beginning. Do not break off the race till you come to the goal: Heb. iv. 1, 'Let us therefore fear, lest a promise being left with us of entering into his rest, any of you should seem to come short of it;' Phil. iii. 14, 'I press towards the mark for the prize of the high calling of God in Christ Jesus.' If you trust to your former righteousness, and commit iniquity, all is lost, Ezek. xxxiii. 13. No; this work must be brought to an end, that you

may not be rejected and disallowed at last, after all that you have done and suffered for Christ. They came into the vineyard at several hours, Mat. xx., but all tarried till the close of the day. Some are converted sooner, some later; but all hold out to the end. In the work of redemption Christ never gave over till all was finished, John xix. 30. So must we never give over till we can say, It is finished; or, with Paul, 2 Tim. iv. 8, ' I have fought a good fight, I have finished my course, I have kept the faith.' We have no licence to slacken our course and give over till all be finished, and then we keep our precedency to the last.

2. To press you to diligence in growth and progress, that you may still go on from strength to strength, Ps. lxxxiv. 7; for this is the way to keep up your precedency. Many do not fall off, nor make shipwreck of the faith; yet they make no progress, but are soon outstripped by those that come after; they do not provoke them to an holy emulation: Heb. x. 24, ' Let us consider one another to provoke to love and good works.' Actively we must provoke others by our example, and passively we must provoke ourselves; we must not justify and encourage that common negligence and forgetfulness of God which prevaileth in the world. Cold dealing in christianity doth so; but when zealous in the best things, we enkindle one another, and awaken one another to a greater zeal and mindfulness of God and the world to come. You should condemn the world by your seriousness, and you harden them in their impenitency by your straitness and worldliness, as if you had no other hope than· what the world can afford you.

3. To an humble sincerity, thinking meanly of yourselves, or anything that you do or have done. Surely the first are last in their own account. If you are low and poor in your own eyes, affect not to be great in the eyes of others. God will show you that it is his grace made the difference, by raising up other instruments of his glory that have not half your advantages, and yet how do they grow both in the knowledge and love of Christ. Twice Christ marvelled; at the faith of the centurion, having so little means: Mat. viii. 10, ' When Jesus heard it, he marvelled, and said unto them that followed, Verily I say unto you, I have not found so great faith, no, not in Israel;' and at the unbelief of his own countrymen, who had so great means: Mark vi. 6, ' And he marvelled at their unbelief.' And truly it is an humbling consideration to us when others have thriven in less time, and by smaller means than you have had; though low in the esteem of the world, yet outshine you in meekness, patience, and blameless conversation, and fervent prayers.

' And the last shall be first.' The last, such as are backward as to any affection to heavenly things, yea, afar off as to any profession or sense of religion; these shall in time to come show themselves more forward than others who were in Christ before them; prove glorious christians at the last: it may be so.

Now here are ' first ' and ' last.' God doth not call all his elect at once, but some sooner, some later. Andrew and Peter were first called, and then Philip. Some called young; as Timothy, 2 Tim. iii. 15. Some in elder age. Obadiah feared God from his youth, 1 Kings xviii.

SERMON UPON MATTHEW XIX. 30.   **49**

12; Lydia and the jailer in middle age, Acts xvi.; Manasseh about
sixty years of age, near on his death, 2 Chron. xxxiii. 19.

Use 3. Let us not despair of any.

1. Judge of nothing before the time. They may be called that are
afar off: John x. 16, 'Other sheep have I.' Christ knoweth the elect,
looketh upon himself engaged to bring them in. We know them not,
but Christ knoweth them.

2. As soon as you are called, mind your work: Col. i. 6, 'Which is
come unto you, as it is in all the world, and bringeth forth fruit, as it
doth also in you since the day ye have heard of it, and knew the grace
of God in truth.'

3. These last shall be first. Many late converted ones grow eminent
in grace, for these reasons—

[1.] Those that have been great sinners love much, because much
was forgiven to them: Luke vii. 47, 'Her sins, which are many, are
forgiven her; for she loved much: but to whom little is forgiven, the
same loveth little.' It was long ere they would hearken to God and
regard his offers; therefore now they bestir themselves the more.

[2.] They live in a constant admiration of grace; whereas others
may bear up themselves too much upon their own worth: James iv.
6, 'Wherefore he saith, God resisteth the proud, but giveth grace to
the humble.'

[3.] Because they recompense their long delay by their after diligence: Eph. v. 16, 'Redeeming the time;' as travellers that set out
late ride the faster: 1 Peter iv. 3, 'For the time past of our life may
suffice us to have wrought the will of the gentiles, when we walked in
lasciviousness and excess of wine, revellings, banquetings, and abominable idolatries;' 2 Sam. xix. 11, they that were last in bringing back
the king to his house, were most zealous for his interest afterwards.

[4.] They look upon themselves obliged to do as much for God as
they did for Satan: Rom. vi. 19, 'For as you have yielded your members servants to uncleanness, and to iniquity unto iniquity, even so now
yield your members servants to righteousness unto holiness.' Therefore
those that have been grievous sinners, when God toucheth their hearts,
prove eminent saints and seek to excel in righteousness and holiness.

Use 1. You that are converted late should double your diligence.
As you have been instances of the corrupt vigour of nature, so also of
the sacred power of grace: or if recovered out of some eminent fall, as
Peter, John xxi. 15, Peter had been boasting before, that if all men
forsook him, yet he would not forsake him. Now Christ puts the
question to Peter, John xxi. 15, 'Simon Peter, lovest thou me more
than these?' He expecteth not only love, but comparatively more
love; not only to check his making comparisons, but also to show that
those that are recovered by grace from grievous errors should be more
eminent in love to Christ. The renewed sense of pardoning mercy
should sharpen their affections to Christ, and we should show more
unfeigned zeal.

Use 2. Do not upbraid others with past sins, when they are afterwards more forward and earnest in the ways of God. We should not
rake in that filth which God hath covered. Many a choice instrument
of God's glory hath been recovered out of Satan's clutches.

VOL. XXII.   **D**

SERMON UPON 1. JOHN I. 7.

And the blood of Jesus Christ his Son cleanseth us from all sin.—
1 John i. 7.

In the context the apostle speaketh of communion with God. Now communion with God we cannot have till we be reconciled to him by Christ, and none can be looked upon as reconciled to him by Christ, but those that endeavour conformity to God in purity and holiness; for the manner of speech is hypothetical and continual: 'If we walk in the light, as he is in the light, we have fellowship one with another, and the blood of Jesus Christ his Son cleanseth us from all sin.'

In the words observe—

1. A privilege or benefit; to be cleansed from all sin.

2. The extent, 'From all sin.' Original, actual, small, great, omissions and commissions, past sins, present infirmities.

3. The meritorious cause of it, 'The blood of Jesus Christ.'

4. The subject to which it is applied, or the parties interested; they that 'walk in the light, as he is in the light.'

Doct. That remission of sins which is promised in the new covenant to the sanctified is procured by the blood of Jesus Christ.

I. The privilege or benefit is to be cleansed from sin. The phrase importeth both justification and sanctification. Where cleansing from sin is spoken of as a duty required of us, it always importeth sanctification: Isa. i. 16, 'Wash you, make you clean, put away the evil of your doings before mine eyes, cease to do evil.' But where it is spoken of as a mercy received from God, there it implieth sometimes both benefits; for both go together: as Eph. v. 26, 'He gave himself for it, that he might sanctify and cleanse it with the washing of water by the word.' It implieth there our whole translation from the state of sin and death to an estate of grace and life: both justification, or doing away the guilt of sin, and sanctification, or the renovation of our natures. Sometimes it implieth one benefit only or principally, which sense must be determined by the context. As, for instance, when both benefits are mentioned together, and one of them in other terms: as 1 John i. 9, 'To forgive us our sins, and cleanse us from all unrighteousness.' There cleansing intendeth sanctification, which, with pardon, is made a distinct branch of our recovery.

When this cleansing is ascribed to the blood of Christ, it principally noteth justification; when to the Spirit, sanctification. So they are distributed, 1 Cor. vi. 11, 'But ye are washed, but ye are sanctified, but ye are justified in the name of the Lord Jesus, and by the Spirit of our God.' As to give instances: Ezek. xxxvi. 25, 'I will sprinkle clean water upon you, and you shall be clean.' That water signifieth the sanctifying Spirit; and his cleansing work is sanctification. So Titus iii. 5, 'But according to his mercy, he saved us by the washing of regeneration, and the renewing of the Holy Ghost.' But when it is ascribed to the blood of Christ, it principally signifieth justification, as in the text: and Rev. i. 5, ' And washed us from our sins in his own blood;' and in many other places. Well, then, when the blood of Christ is said to be beneficial to cleanse us, it is meant of his taking off the guilt of sin, and our obligation to wrath. Sin is the whole cause of God's displeasure against us, and that which maketh us odious in his sight, as a filthy thing is to us. Therefore when we are freed from sin by the death of Christ, we are said to be cleansed: Guilt is not a quality, but a relation, or an obligation to punishment, which the law of God hath made the sinner's due, which relation and obligation ceaseth when that is done which our supreme Lord and Judge requireth. For man is bound to God no further than God will have him bound. And when the obligation is dissolved, the punishment is no more in force.

To understand this distinctly, we may, with respect to justification, consider three things in sin:—(1.) The fault; (2.) The guilt; and (3.) The punishment.

1. The fault is a criminal action. This is not taken away, either as a natural action or a faulty action, contrary to the law of God; for that is impossible. Not as a natural action; for such a fault we committed, either by omitting good, or doing evil. *Factum infectum fieri nequit ;* that which is done cannot be undone. Nor as it is a faulty action contrary to the law of God. This Christ taketh not away neither; for that were to disannul the obliging force or authority of the law. The sins we committed are sins still. Christ came not to make the law less holy, or the fault to be no fault. What shall we say then to this first thing in sin? The fault is not taken away; but it is passed by as it is the foundation of our guilt. The scripture sets it forth by the metaphor of removing it out of God's sight: Ps. ciii. 12, ' As far as the east is from the west, so far hath he removed our transgressions from us ;' that we may not be objects displeasing to him. And it is expressed, 'Thou hast cast all my sins behind thy back,' Isa. xxxviii. 17; as men cast behind their backs such things as they list not to look on, or remember. In humiliation we set them before our face; but in pardoning, God casts them behind his back. So in a like expression he is said 'to pass by the transgression of the covenant of his heritage,' Micah vii. 18. Pardon is a passing over, a seeing and not seeing the faults of his people. God quits the plea, doth not call to an account for them. It may further be represented by taking off the filthy garment wherewith the high priest was clothed when he stood before the Lord : Zech. iii. 4, ' Take away the filthy garments from him, and unto him he said, Behold, I have caused thine iniquity to pass from thee, and I will clothe thee with change of raiment.' Whilst we are clothed with filthy

garments, we are unpleasing objects in God's sight, therefore they are removed, that we may be accepted.

2. The guilt. There is a twofold guilt, *reatus culpæ* and *reatus pœnæ*; the guilt of sin and the guilt of punishment. The *reatus culpæ*, or guilt of sin, is seen by applying the law to the fact, and both to the person that hath committed it: 1 John iii. 4, 'Whosoever committeth sin transgresseth also the law, for sin is the transgression of the law.' Such a fact is sin, because the law forbiddeth it, and I am a sinner because I have done it. Now this is not taken away; my faulty act is an offence, and I am an offender, and none of us can be reputed as those that never omitted any duty, or committed any sin; for the new covenant is not set up to make us innocent, but pardonable upon certain terms. And when we come to God as our offended governor, we plead not as innocent, but as sinners, desiring that in the behalf of Christ our sins may be forgiven to us. There is also *reatus pœnæ*, or guilt of punishment, which resulteth from the sanction of the law, binding us to suffer such penalties as the law hath determined. Now this may be considered, *quoad meritum, vel quoad eventum*, according to the merit, or according to the event; according to the merit of the action, what the action in itself deserveth, which is condemnation to punishment; this Christ hath not taken away, nor ever intended to take away. Every sinful action is *in se, et merito operis*, in itself, and by the desert of the work, damnable or deserving damnation; but *quoad eventum*, as to the event and effect: ' There is no condemnation to them that are in Christ,' Rom. viii. 1. By the new covenant we are discharged from the obligation to punishment, and so are said to be cleansed, purged, pardoned. This will be more clear and plain to you by considering what is required of us in suing out our pardon. We must not deny the fault or sin, but confess it: 1 John i. 9, 'If we confess our sins, he is faithful and just to forgive us our sins, and to cleanse us from all unrighteousness.' And we must acknowledge the guilt and desert of God's righteous law: 1 Cor. xi. 31, 'If we judge ourselves, we shall not be judged of the Lord.' There must be self-accusing and self-judging. In self-accusing we confess *reatum culpæ*, the guilt of sin, our breach of the law. In self-judging we confess *reatum pœnæ*, that we deserve condemnation; without either of which there would be no due recourse to God for pardon, or that humiliation and brokenness of heart which the scripture calleth for, or else these would be performed perfunctorily and formally, if there were not a ground in the nature of the thing. For if the guilt of the fault were utterly dissolved, how can I heartily accuse myself of such and such things before the Lord? Or if the guilt of punishment were so far dissolved that my actions did not in their own nature, and by God's righteous law, deserve such condemnation and punishment, how can I broken-heartedly acknowledge myself to have deserved the greatest evil which his law threatened? So that this cleansing of us is not a vacating the action, as if it had never been done, or a denial of the fault, as if it were no fault, nor a disannulling of the desert of punishment, but a remission of the punishment itself, or a discharge from the penalty which sin hath made our due debt.

3. The punishment. Where sin is pardoned, there is a discharge

from the punishment due upon the guilt. Sin is not imputed to condemnation; nay, the man is dealt with before the tribunal of the judge as if he were pure and clean from all sin. He deserves indeed to be accursed, but the penitent, broken-hearted sinner is accepted to pardon, and shall be exempted from eternal punishment: John v. 29, 'He hath everlasting life, and shall not come into condemnation;' that is, he hath escaped eternal death and shall enjoy everlasting life.

But now for the question, whether all sins be forgiven at once; past, present, and to come? I must answer negatively; sins to come cannot properly be said to be pardoned, for till they are committed we are not guilty of them, and this would be not so much a pardon, as an indulgence and licence to sin; such as the man of sin is wont to give to his superstitious adherents, indulgences for so many years to come. Then a man once converted could no otherwise than frivolously pray, 'Forgive us our trespasses.' It would take away care of avoiding sin to come, and repentance for what is past. Daily sins displease God, and deserve death. Forgiveness of sin sometimes is spoken of with respect to the purchase: Heb. x. 14, 'For by one offering he hath perfected for ever them that are sanctified.' There needeth no more sacrifice. Sometimes with respect to the offer in the new covenant: Acts xiii. 38, 39, 'Be it known unto you therefore, men and brethren, that through this man is preached unto you the forgiveness of sins. And by him all that believe are justified from all things from which ye could not be justified by the law of Moses.' The same covenant pardoneth all; there needeth no other covenant. Sometimes it may be considered as applied as soon as we do believe: Rom. viii. 1, 'There is now no condemnation to them that are in Christ;' Eph. i. 6, 'Wherein he hath made us accepted in the beloved, in whom we have redemption through his blood, the forgiveness of sins.' By pardon we partake of a threefold benefit.

[1] The state of the person is altered: from a child of wrath he is put into a state of grace; from a child of the devil, made a child of God: John i. 12, 'But to as many as received him, to them gave he power to become the sons of God.'

[2.] There is an actual remission of all past sins till that day.

[3.] There is a right to sue out pardon for daily failings: John xiii. 10, 'Jesus saith unto him, He that is washed needeth not, save to wash his feet.' We contract new defilement every day by going up and down in a dirty world. Well, then, the certain remedy is provided, which will pardon our sins as soon as we are capable.

II. The extent of this benefit, 'All sin.' This showeth how perfect this deliverance is. If we should be freed from some sins only, and left under the guilt of others, we could never be upon sure terms. Though the self-judging sinner seeth multitudes of sins in himself, yet that will not hinder his free and full pardon; nor need it to obstruct the peaceable estate of it in his conscience. For where God forgiveth one sin, he forgiveth all: Ps. ciii. 3, 'Who pardoneth all thy sins,' Micah vii. 18, 'Thou wilt cast all their sins into the depths of the sea.' Sins are of several kinds, original, actual; of omission, commission; small, great; secret, open; past enormities, and present infirmities. Look into thy bill; what owest thou? A christian is amazed when he cometh to a serious account with God. But he needeth not be discouraged, since upon sincere and unfeigned repentance God pardoneth all that is past, and will not be severe, notwithstanding present failings and imperfections. All sins are mortal, all of them damnable : wherefore, if all sins be not pardoned, we remain in danger of the curse. Any one sin let alone is sufficient to exclude us out of heaven. Therefore, first or last, all is pardoned. Justice hath no more to seek of Christ, and we have full leave to sue out our pardon in his name.

III. The meritorious cause of it, ' The blood of Christ.'

Here let us see—(1.) What the blood of Christ doth ; (2.) Whence it hath this power to cleanse us from all our sins.

1. What the blood of Christ doth. It may be considered three ways—as shed, pleaded, sprinkled.

[1.] As shed. This is necessary by way of merit and satisfaction, to obtain for us the pardon of sins. After the entrance of sin into the world, God, that is inclined to do good to his creatures, would have it manifestly appear that he hated sin, and loved righteousness : therefore, sin being already committed, and the punishment of eternal death incurred, he would show the hatred of his justice and holiness against sin, and yet spare the sinner: Rom. iii. 25, ' Whom God hath set forth to be a propitiation through faith in his blood, to declare his righteousness for the remission of sins.' Heb. ix. 22, 'Without shedding of blood there is no remission of sins.' And in the gospel, Christ is the true sacrifice for sin, accepted by God for sinful man, that he may be cleansed and purified, or freed from the wrath and punishment which sin had made his due. Hereby is enough done to signify God's purest holiness, and his utter hatred and detestation of sin, and to declare his love of justice, and to keep up the authority of his law, and instruct the world that it is a dangerous thing to transgress it.

[2.] As pleaded—(1.) By Christ in heaven ; (2.) By us in prayer.

(1.) By Christ in heaven ; for Heb. ix. 12, ' But by his own blood he entered in once into the holy place, having obtained eternal redemption for us.' It is that which is presented to God as the full price and ransom of souls.

(2.) By us in prayer ; for the apostle saith, Heb. x. 19, 'Having therefore, brethren, boldness to enter into the holiest by the blood of Jesus.' When we beg any blessing, especially this necessary benefit, the pardon of our sins, that which supporteth our confidence of audience and acceptance with God is the blood of Christ.

[3.] As sprinkled or applied, for so we are told : Heb. xii. 24, ' You are come to Jesus the mediator of the new covenant, and to the blood of sprinkling, that speaketh better things than the blood of Abel.' It is not enough that his blood be shed, or pleaded, but it must be sprinkled. In itself it hath a cleansing power and virtue ; but being sprinkled, it doth actually cleanse and purify from sin. The sprinkling of the blood of the paschal lamb saved the house from the stroke of the destroying angel, Exod. xii. 11, Heb. xi. 28. The destroying angel passed by all those whose door-posts are sprinkled. And all the elect are said to be saved ' by the sanctification of the Spirit, and the sprinkling of the blood of Jesus,' 1 Peter i. 2. And the apostle reasoneth it : Heb. ix. 13, 14, ' For if the blood of bulls and goats, and the ashes of an heifer, sprinkling the unclean, sanctifieth to the purifying of the flesh: how much more shall the blood of Christ, who through the eternal Spirit offered himself without spot to God, purge your consciences from dead works to serve the living God.' In the type of the red heifer there was a solemn sprinkling to the purifying of the unclean, which answereth the purging of our consciences by the blood of Christ: the one purifieth the flesh, the other the conscience: the one freed from such penalties as the law imposed for legal and ceremonial offences, the other from dead works, which are pollutions before God; and so are spiritual evils, and eternal penalties, that unfit us for communion with God. Well, then, we see there must be application; therefore let us consider how it is to be applied, or the means of sprinkling, both on God's and our part.

(1.) On God's part, the means of applying are, external or internal: for the external means we have an account of them, Eph. v. 26, 'That he might sanctify and cleanse it by the washing of water through the word:' that is, by the word and sacraments; so he applieth to us the virtue of his death.

(1st.) By the preaching of the word. The great duty of the ministers of the gospel is to sprinkle the hearts of the people with the blood of Christ, by the preaching of the new covenant: not only to assure them that pardon of sins may be obtained: Acts x. 43, 'To him gave all the prophets witness, that through his name whosoever believeth on him shall receive remission of sins;' but to instruct them how it may be had; that such as repent and believe, and do what becometh either duty, shall be assuredly cleansed from sin and accepted with God. The apostle telleth us the sum and substance of his preaching was, repentance towards God, and faith in our Lord Jesus Christ, Acts xx. 21. Repentance towards God is necessary, that we may acknowledge our obligation to his law, bemoaning our former sin and misery, and devoting ourselves anew to him, that we may do his will, and walk in his ways. Faith in Jesus Christ is necessary, that those that have benefit by him may own the author of their deliverance, and put their cause into his hands, that he may reconcile them unto God. Repentance is our turning to God, as faith is a thankful owning of our Redeemer. Thus the word giveth both instruction and assurance; for it is both a doctrine, and a grant or charter.

(2d.) The sacraments are the means of this sprinkling, or applying the cleansing virtue of Christ's blood. These are two; baptism: Acts ii. 38, 'Then Peter said unto them, Repent, and be baptized every one of you in the name of Jesus, for the remission of sins;' the Lord's supper: Mat. xxvi. 28, 'For this is my blood of the new testament, which is shed for many for the remission of sins.' Both excite and assure us of the participation of this benefit by Christ. They excite as they are applied to every one; for every one that submitteth to these ordinances bindeth himself to seek after this benefit in the way wherein Christ will dispense it; and this they do assure us as they work, increase, and strengthen faith in us, and are a solemn investiture to Christ and his benefits.

(3d.) Internal; by the effectual operation of the Spirit, as the fruit of Christ's intercession. Therefore it is said, 1 John iii. 8, 'There are

three that bear witness on earth, the Spirit, the water, and the blood;
and these three agree in one. The τὸ κρινόμενον, or thing to be proved,
is that Jesus is the Son of God. The Spirit beareth witness to this,
applying the blood of Christ to the conscience, and purifying and
sanctifying them as with clean water. These are not one, as the first;
but these agree in one, as they do establish the same conclusion, as
they do concurringly establish it: neither simply nor apart; not water
apart, nor blood apart, nor Spirit apart, but they all concur; the Spirit,
by water and blood, appeasing our guilty consciences, and washing
away the guilt of sin. And it is said, 1 John v. 10, 'He that believeth
on the Son of God hath his witness in himself;' the Spirit by the
blood of Christ pacifying his conscience, and sanctifying his heart:
Rom. v. 5, 'The love of God is shed abroad in our hearts by the Holy
Ghost given unto us.' The business is, what is meant here by the
love of God? I take it for the great instance of his love, the reconciling
the world to himself by Jesus Christ; for it immediately followeth,
'For when we were yet without strength, in due time Christ died for
the ungodly.' Surely it is not taken for our love to God, but his love
to us, which was chiefly seen in that great instance. We have the
effect and feeling, the sense and comfort of it, by the Spirit.

(2.) The means of sprinkling on our part; for until we believe, the
blood of Christ produceth not its effect upon our souls: Rom. iii. 25,
'Whom God hath set forth to be a propitiation through faith in his
blood.' Faith believeth the great love of Christ in the shedding of
his blood for the expiation of our sins, and doth excite us to live in a
constant course of obedience to him who died for us: 2 Cor. v. 14, 15,
'For the love of Christ constraineth us, because we thus judge, that if
one died for all, then were all dead: and that he died for all, that
they which live should not henceforth live unto themselves, but unto
him which died for them.' All that sincerely believe in Christ, and
embrace the gospel, have their sins pardoned, are accepted with God
in Christ, and live in amity with him: Rom. viii. 1, 'There is no condemnation to them that are in Christ.' They are now actually admitted into communion with God, and the privileges of Christ's death.
But these who thus believe, how far obedience concurreth I will not
now debate; it is enough to say, that sincere believers are freed from
sin, and the direful consequences of it.

2. Whence hath the blood of Christ such a cleansing virtue? Partly
from the institution of God, and partly from its own intrinsic worth
and value.

[1.] From the institution of God: Col. i. 19, 20, 'It pleased the
Father that in him should all fulness dwell. And having made peace
through the blood of his cross by him to reconcile all things unto himself, whether they be things in earth or things in heaven.' It pleased
the Father to make use of the blood of his cross to reconcile the world
to himself. Divine institution puts a value upon things; for surely
God accepts what he hath appointed, let it be otherwise never so considerable, anything is of force unto that whereunto God hath ordained
it. God's will is the reason and cause of all things. If God will
appoint bread and wine to be the mysterious instruments of his grace,
who can contradict his will? Well, then, this is one ground of our

confidence, that Christ is not a mediator of our choosing. If we had offered God a satisfaction, or Christ had interposed of his own accord, we might have met with a like answer as Moses had : Exod. xxxii. 32, 33, 'If thou wilt, forgive their sin : and if not, blot me out of thy book. And the Lord said, Whosoever hath sinned against me, him will I blot out of my book.' But God will not refuse what he hath appointed himself.

[2.] From its own intrinsic worth and value. There is more in Christ than what an institution puts upon him.

(1.) The dignity of the person ; who is not only perfectly holy, and separate from sinners, but hath also a divine virtue and power. Both concur in Christ, who was that holy thing born of the virgin, and was also a person subsisting in the Godhead. Who had a fulness of all grace, Col. i. 19. 'And the fulness of the Godhead dwelt in him bodily,' Col. ii. 9. Not mystically, as in believers ; not symbolically, as in the sacraments ; nor typically, and by way of shadow, as in the types of the law ; but really and personally. And therefore it is said in the text, 'The blood of Jesus Christ his Son ; ' and elsewhere : 'Redeemed by the blood of God,' Acts xx. 28. If the person satisfying be an infinite person, so is his satisfaction. The scripture improveth this notion, both in opposition to the sin of Adam ; there is a πολλῷ μᾶλλον, a much more, put upon Christ : Rom. v. 15–17, ' But not as the offence, so also is the free gift ; for if through the offence of one man many were made sinners ; much more the grace of God, and the gift by grace, which is by one man, Jesus Christ, hath abounded unto many. And not as it was by one that sinned, so is the gift ; for the judgment was by one to condemnation, but the free gift is of many offences to justification. For if by one man's offence death reigned by one ; much more they which receive abundance of grace, and of the gift of righteousness, shall reign in life by one, Jesus Christ.' The value of the first Adam did merely arise from God's institution ; yet one act of the first Adam was enough to ruin millions of souls, because God instituted him to be a public head and common root to all his seed. God hath also instituted Christ, but his acts were much more of an unlimited influence, because without any institution he was really better worth than all the world. So in opposition to the ceremonies of the law, there is a πολλῷ μᾶλλον, a much more, put upon Christ : Heb. ix. 13, 14, ' For if the blood of bulls and goats, and the ashes of an heifer, sprinkling the unclean, sanctifieth to the purifying of the flesh, how much more shall the blood of Christ purge your consciences from dead works to serve the living God ? ' The rites of old were able to work that for which they were ordained, cleanse from all uncleanness, and so stand before God in his worship ; but besides, there is an infinite worth in Christ to purge the conscience from sin. His person gave a value to his suffering, so that one serveth for all. He is worth millions of us. His temporary sufferings are enough to take off the penalty of eternal punishment due for the disobedience of the whole world.

(2.) The nature of the work. It was a glorious act of obedience. Do not think God is cruel, and standeth upon a little blood. No ; he standeth upon his honour. He hath made a law, and his law must have satisfaction ; the debt of obedience must be paid : Rom. v. 19,

'As by one man's disobedience many were made sinners; so by the obedience of one shall many be made righteous;' Phil. ii. 8, 'He became obedient unto death, even the death of the cross.' The authority of the lawgiver was to be salved by obedience; and the dread of the penalty, by an obedience to the death. It standeth, the Mediator, in no less than his blood, before God will make friendship with us. The law said, 'In the day thou sinnest thou shalt die the death.' Therefore Christ must lay down his life, by a most shameful, painful, cursed death. He that is above all law taketh the yoke of obedience upon him. His suffering death for the sin of man at the command of his Father, was the highest degree of obedience that ever was performed to God. So much love showed to God and man, so much self-denial, so much humility and patience, such resignation of himself to God, as cannot be paralleled.

(3.) The grievousness of the sufferings which Christ endured. He suffered the punishment due to us, in his agonies and desertion; and so 'carried our griefs, and bear our sorrows,' Isa. liii. 4. His bloody sweat, his prayers and strong cries, his troubles of soul, show it; he was made sin, and made a curse, for us. What can be expected more? He not only bore our sins on his body on the tree, but we read also of his soul sufferings: John xii. 27, 'Now is my soul troubled, and what shall I say?' His desertion: Mat. xxvii. 46, 'My God, my God, why hast thou forsaken me?' He was forsaken for a while, that we might be received for ever. All these things give hope to penitent believers that there is a sure ground laid whereby they may be cleansed from their sins.

IV. The persons that have this benefit are such as 'walk in the light, as he is in the light.' They propound no lower pattern to themselves than the perfection and excellences of God. Here it is disputed by divines what respect this qualification hath to the benefit? Whether merely as a sign, or as a condition. The form is conditional. The generality determine that this is propounded as a sign of our communion with God. But others urge against them, that then there may be communion with God while we are in our sins; for *omne signum est posterius signato;* the sign is after the thing signified. Be it a natural sign, as the smoke of fire; or an arbitrary sign, as a tavern by a bush, or a servant by his badge and cognisance. Therefore, for some time at least, a man hath communion with God before he is holy. But this argument may be answered thus, that sanctification is the first gift. We are first sanctified, and then justified; when a man sanctified walketh in the light, it is a sign of his sanctification and justification. But they further urge that the apostle discourseth not of the evidence, but means; therefore it is best to say, It is both a sign and a condition without which we cannot have benefit by Christ's death; but the first condition is faith; next, love and holiness to continue our interest in this privilege. Those that walk in the light do in some sort resemble God, and endeavour to be more like him every day in goodness or holiness.

Use 1. For information in sundry particulars.

1. It showeth us the heinous nature of sin. A deep stain it is that could not be washed off but by the blood of Christ. All in their natural

estate are become filthy and odious to God: Ps. xiv. 3, 'They are all gone aside; they are altogether become filthy;' objects displeasing in the eye of holiness, therefore we need to be cleansed. The leper cried out, 'Unclean;' so must we.

2. It showeth us the great love of Christ: Rev. i. 5, 'Who hath loved us, and washed us in his own blood.' That he would die an accursed, shameful death, to recover us to God, our hearts should be deeply possessed with a sense of his love. There are three things set it forth to us—(1.) The way he took to cleanse us; (2.) The fulness of the benefit; (3.) The daily application.

[1.] The way he took to cleanse us. It was by his blood: 1 John iv. 10, 'Herein was love; not that we loved God, but God loved us, and sent his Son to be a propitiation for our sins.'

[2.] The fulness of the benefit: 'His blood cleanseth from all sin.' There needeth no other sacrifice, no other covenant. It is done perfectly: Heb. x. 14, 'For by one offering he hath perfected for ever them that are sanctified.'

[3.] The daily application. This fountain is always open. We sin daily, and every day we sue out our discharge in Christ's name. The best of God's children make but too much work for pardoning mercy. We contract new filth by walking up and down in a dirty, defiling world: John xiii. 10, 'He that is washed needeth not save to wash his feet.' Now where much is forgiven, there should be the more love, Luke vii. 47.

Use 2. To persuade you to make use of Christ's death for this effect. If the price be paid by Christ, and accepted by God for the ransom of souls, and the liberty proclaimed to us, surely it is our own fault if we remain yet in bonds. Either you are senseless of your spiritual condition, and so despise the fruits of Christ's death, or else you have not that esteem of the blood of Christ as you ought to have, as if he had not made full satisfaction. Both are great crimes.

1. Consider your misery by reason of sin. The Redeemer hath no work to do in stupid and senseless souls. They that know not their misery regard not their remedy. The offers of the gospel are always made to the sensible, the broken-hearted, the weary, the thirsty, the heavy laden. Many are welcome to Christ that know not themselves penitent believers; but never any welcome that knew not themselves condemned sinners: Luke xviii. 13, 14, 'And the publican, standing afar off, would not lift up so much as his eyes to heaven, but smote upon his breast, saying, God be merciful to me a sinner. I tell you this man went down to his house justified rather than the other; for every one that exalteth himself shall be abased, and he that humbleth himself shall be exalted.'

2. Be firmly persuaded of the sufficiency of what Christ hath done for man's redemption, that you may not have slight thoughts of the blood of Christ. It is that blood by which Christ entered into the holy place, having obtained eternal redemption for us, Heb. ix. 12. It is the blood of the 'everlasting covenant, which maketh us perfect in every good work,' Heb. xiii. 20, 21; that precious blood by which we are redeemed from our vain conversations, 1 Peter i. 18; that blood which purges our conscience from dead works, Heb. ix. 14.

3. Make hearty application of it. Lay the plaster upon the sore.
In the word, when you hear the offers of grace in the gospel, that God
desireth not the death of a sinner, that he is willing to save those that
believe in Jesus Christ, put in for a share: 1 Tim. i. 15, ' This is a
true and faithful saying, and worthy of all acceptation, that Jesus came
into the world to save sinners, of whom I am chief ;' Rom. viii. 31,
' What shall we say then to these things ?   If God be for us, who can
be against us ? '   Job v. 27, ' Hear it, and know it for thy good.'   Bring
it home to thine heart.   So in the Lord's supper, where we solemnly
remember his death ; there we hear of the blood of the new testament
which was shed for the remission of sins.   Now apply it: 1 Cor. x. 16,
' The cup of blessing which we bless, is it not the communion of the
blood of Christ ? the bread which we break, is it not the communion
of the body of Christ ? '

4. Labour to make your claim more sure.   Walk in the light.   The
ground of comfort is the blood of Christ ; the matter of comfort is the
covenant ; but we must look to our claim and title, or else this grace
is not brought home to us, nor we sanctified and enabled to live to
God: John xvii. 19, ' And for their sakes I sanctify myself that they
also might be sanctified through the truth ;' 1 John iii. 7, ' He that doeth
righteousness is righteous, even as he is righteous.'

SERMON UPON JOB X. 2.

*I will say unto God, Do not condemn me ; show me wherefore thou
contendest with me.*—JOB x. 2.

THESE words are spoken by Job in the bitterness of his soul, and as
one weary of his many and heavy troubles. In them take notice—

1. Of a resolution of addressing himself to God, and bringing his
complaint before him, 'I will say unto God,' &c.

2. The matter of his address ; it is double—

[1.] A deprecation of condemnation, ' Do not condemn me.'

[2.] An inquiry after the reasons of his afflictions, ' Show me wherefore thou contendest with me.'

Let me first explain the letter of the words, and then come to the
sense.

1. The deprecation ' Do not condemn me.' Do not make me or
count me wicked. So Heb. his conscience did testify of his uprightness, and therefore he desireth God would not deal with him as wicked.
It is explained ver. 7, ' Thou knowest I am not wicked.' Condemnation is the sentence of a judge. Now in a judge three things are considerable—(1.) His opinion ; (2.) His sentence ; (3.) His execution.
With respect to all three the word is used.

[1.] The opinion of a judge deeming or counting one wicked ; as to
justify is to count one righteous : Rom. viii. 33, 34, ' It is God that
justifies ; who is he that condemns?' So to condemn is to count one
wicked. This respects the inward mind, and what appeareth on evidence.
So it is said, Prov. xvii. 15, ' He that justifieth the wicked, and condemneth the just, they are both an abomination unto the Lord.' It is not
meant of judicial absolution and condemnation, but in private opinion.

[2.] The sentence passed or pronounced on the tribunal. So to
condemn is to declare one unrighteous or punishable : Deut. xxv. 1,
' If there be a controversy between men, and they come unto judgment,
that the judges may judge them, then they shall justify the righteous,
and condemn the wicked ;' that is, pass sentence upon them, pronounce
them wicked. Otherwise to declare our opinion is not always lawful.
We may *pejus timere*, fear the worst, for our caution ; but not *sim-
pliciter definire*, absolutely determine, till called to the judgment.

[3.] The execution. When they are dealt with as wicked : 1 Kings
viii. 32, ' Then hear thou in heaven, and judge thy servants, condemn-
ing the wicked, to bring his way upon his own head ; and justifying

the righteous, to give him according to his righteousness.' Like expressions there are often : as Ps. cix. 7, ' When he shall be judged, let him be condemned;' Heb. ' go out wicked, or guilty.' So Ps. cxxv. 5, 'They shall be led forth with the workers of iniquity ;' that is, as malefactors to execution. Now all these senses are intended, opinion, sentence, stroke ; chiefly the last. Do not deal with me as a wicked person, or afflict me as an evil-doer. He desires God to deal more tenderly with him, not as a judge, but a father : Jer. x. 24, 'O Lord, correct me, but in judgment ; not in anger, lest thou bring me to nothing.'

2. His inquiry after the cause of his afflictions, ' Show me wherefore thou contendest with me.' The word ' contendest ' is emphatical. It notes God's contending with man as an adversary in a suit or cause. Before he considered God as a judge ; now as an advocate pleading, not for, but against him. For providence is a kind of arguing and pleading, not by words, but deeds ; and therefore called his controversy ; as Hosea iv. 1, ' The Lord hath a controversy with the land;' and Micah vi. 2, ' The Lord hath a controversy with his people, and will plead with Israel.' This controversy is pleaded with sharp afflictions whereby God appeareth against them as their opposite party. Now Job desireth to know the reason and cause, he having feared God and eschewed evil. And yet God suffered all this misery to come upon him, as if he were condemned and executed without trial.

[1.] The sense. Before I tell you that, let me note to you that there is a mixed nature in a child of God, but a prevalency of the better part. Accordingly this scripture must be explained. There is some weakness bewrayed in these words, but more grace.

(1.) It was weakness that he mistook the present dispensation, thinking that God condemned him when he did but try him. He may sharply chastise those whom he loveth and justifieth, yet not condemn them as wicked ; rather the contrary: 1 Cor. xi. 32, ' When we are judged, we are chastened of the Lord, that we may not be condemned with the world.'

(2.) It was weakness, in that he thought there was no sufficient cause that God should condemn him ; whereas the common pollution wherein we are involved doth sufficiently justify the severest trials he can bring upon us. He hath cause enough to condemn his best servants, and those that are not wicked ; yet because they are sinners, ought to look upon themselves, in strict justice, as deserving the greatest punishments : Ps. cxxx. 3, ' If thou, Lord, shouldst mark iniquity, O Lord, who should stand ? ' Ps. cxliii. 2, ' Enter not into judgment with thy servant, for in thy sight shall no man living be justified.'

(3.) Clearly he was under some perturbation and passion ; for he considered God not only as a judge, but as a litigant party with whom he might expostulate about his quarrel and controversy: ' Show me wherefore thou contendest with me ; ' whereas an absolute submission is necessary. Partly because of his sovereignty: Job ix. 12, ' He giveth no account of his matters.' Partly because of his exact justice. God's judgments are sometimes secret, but always just : Ps. xcvii. 2, ' Clouds and darkness are round about him.' There are reasons which we see not.

(4.) Here is some taxing of his providence, as if his dealing were unjust, and God did oppress him with his great power. For so. it followeth, ver. 3, 'Is it good for thee that thou shouldst oppress, and despise the work of thine hands?'

(5.) In all such cases there is an over-valuing of our worldly comforts and conveniences, and we look more to the loss and want of these things than the use and benefit we should get by the affliction; whereas a christian should more regard the fruit of adversity than the trouble of it: Heb. xii. 11, 'No chastening for the present seemeth to be joyous, but grievous; nevertheless afterward it yieldeth the peaceable fruit of righteousness to them that are exercised thereby.' And if God awaken him to more seriousness in religion, by his smart, loss, and want, his pleasure is more than the pain, and the gain than the want and loss.

[2.] There is something good and gracious in it.

(1.) That he bringeth his complaint to God. He doth not complain of God, but to God. To murmur in our own bosoms, or to vent our discontent to others, is in effect to slander God behind his back. Therefore his resolution to go to God is commendable: 'I will say unto God,' saith Job. This is to bring our complaint before his face.

(2.) It is good that it was grievous to him to be in the state of a condemned man. Not only to be counted a sinner, but as wicked, or one that was not sincere and approved of God, because his judgments seemed to put him in that number. To be accepted with the Lord, and approved of the Lord, is a christian's all.

(3.) That he desireth to know the cause, end, and use of his afflictions. This is good and holy if it be done—

(1st.) Not to satisfy curiosity, but conscience; for sometimes we may be in the dark about the reasons of God's dealings with us; as 2 Sam. xxi. 1, 'David inquired of the Lord,' concerning the famine, that he might know his duty.

(2d.) By way of humble supplication, not by way of expostulation, as if we were innocent, and hardly dealt withal.

Doct. 1. That open and free dealing with God in our bitterness and troubles is better than to smother and stifle our griefs, or vent them in discontent to others.

So Job saith here, 'I will say unto God,' &c. Thus David telleth us that he practised this open and free dealing with success: Ps. cxix. 26, 'I declared my ways, and thou heardest me;' that is, he opened his whole case to God, conflicts, distresses, hopes, supports, sorrows, dangers, hide nothing from him; as a man will acquaint his bosom friend with all his condition, or as sick patients will tell the physician how it is with them. Now thus to do is—

1. Filial ingenuity; for the Spirit of adoption worketh most in our addresses to the throne of grace; and there it betrayeth itself in a παρρησία, a telling God our mind: Heb. iv. 16, 'Let us come boldly to the throne of grace, that we may obtain mercy, and find grace to help in time of need;' Heb. x. 19, 'Having boldness to enter into the holiest;' Eph. iii. 12, 'In whom we have boldness and access with confidence.' Laying forth our whole estate and condition before him, sins to be pardoned, doubts to be resolved, miseries to be redressed, perplexities to be helped by his counsel, our weaknesses to be confirmed

by his strength, our griefs and fears, that he may pity us and help us. Tell God of all; your temptations, passions; these you should distinctly lay open before him. Natural pride and self-love will not let us take shame upon ourselves, and guilt is shy of God; but the Spirit of adoption bringeth us to him with openness of heart.

2. There is in it candid simplicity. David's maschil, or psalm of instruction, viz. Ps. xxxii., shows us thus much; for ver. 2, he mentioneth 'guile of spirit,' which made him hang off from God. But then you find by the 5th verse, he had come to his ease sooner if he had sooner confessed his sin. We are in distress of conscience till this be done; especially when trouble of conscience cometh upon us for some great sin, which God will cause to be manifested for his glory. Till we come to a clearness and openness of mind, we keep Satan's counsel. Moses had a privy sore, which he was loath to disclose, and pleadeth other things, insufficiency, want of elocution; but carnal fear was the main; therefore God gently toucheth his privy sore: Exod. iv. 19, 'The Lord said unto Moses in Midian, Go, return into Egypt, for all the men are dead which sought thy life.' He never pleaded that; but God knew what was the inward let. It is a mighty thing sincerely to open our hearts to God.

3. It argueth a man given to prayer when all our complaints run in that channel, and if we have any grievance and burden upon us, we bring it before the Lord.

But must we pray when we have a distemper upon us, and come to God with our raving passions? I answer—

[1.] If this be known, we must get it removed; for we must lift up pure hands, without wrath and doubting, 1 Tim. ii. 8; and a pet against providence is the worse kind of wrath, for then we are angry with God himself. Now passion putteth strange fire into our censers.

[2.] If we are blinded for the present, and there be failings in our addresses to God, he will pardon them, but loveth the plainness of his people's hearts.

[3.] By praying, the distemper may be cured; for when we own God as our supreme and most holy and just judge, the tempest ceaseth, and our thoughts are appeased, and we reduced to a better frame.

Use 1. To direct us what to do when we have many estuations of mind. Go, open the case to God. The apostle giveth this direction: Phil. iv. 6, 7, 'Be careful for nothing, but in everything by prayer and supplication with thanksgiving, let your requests be made unto God. And the peace of God, which passeth all understanding, shall keep your hearts and minds through Christ Jesus.' As in an earthquake, when the imprisoned wind once gets a vent, the heaving and shaking ceaseth; such a quieting force there is in prayer.

2. It persuadeth us not only to pray, but to deal sincerely with God, and open our hearts to him. Tell him your griefs, wants, fears, temptations, what reasonings are apt to arise in your minds against his providence; let God know all. He knoweth it already, but let him know it from you. Give an account of yourself to God, but with that humility which becometh a creature subject to him, and hath given up himself to be ordered and disposed by him according to his own pleasure. Tell him how you came to reconcile his attributes and his pro-

vidence; you dare not quit the sense of your integrity, but you know not the meaning of his dispensations. Such plain dealing God liketh better than arting and parting it in prayer.

Doct. 2. From his deprecation of condemnation observe, it is grievous to a child of God to be condemned as a wicked man.

1. They are apt to fear it in great pressures, when God pursueth with multiplied and redoubled strokes; for these reasons—

[1.] Providence seemeth to mark them out for his enemies when he spendeth the arrows of his indignation upon them. Affliction is an act of judication. The apostle saith, 'We are judged when we are chastened of the Lord,' 1 Cor. xi. 32; and again, 1 Peter iv. 17, 'That judgment beginneth at the house of God.' God will prove himself impartially just in correcting the sins of his own; therefore he covereth himself with frowns, and seemeth to condemn us as an angry judge, rather than to correct us as a loving father. They are indeed acts of his holy justice, correcting and humbling them for sin. So far the best must own it: Ps. cxix. 75. 'I know, O Lord, that thy judgments are right, and that in faithfulness thou hast afflicted me.' But then the vindictive wrath, according to strict justice, must be deprecated: Ps. cxliii. 2, 'Enter not into judgment with thy servant.' And the providence must be expounded aright. We are not condemned when we are judged, but judged that we may not be condemned. The dispensation is medicinal, not vindictive; to promote our humiliation and sanctification, not to procure our ruin and destruction.

[2.] The world is apt to make this interpretation of great afflictions: Acts xxviii. 4, 'This man is a murderer, whom, though he hath escaped the sea, vengeance suffereth not to live;' and Luke xiii. the first five verses, they thought those greater sinners than others whom these dismal accidents befell, and so turn matters of warning into matters of censure. Nay, of Christ himself: Isa. liii. 4, 'He hath borne our grief, and carried our sorrows; yet we did esteem him smitten, and stricken of God, and afflicted.' As if these afflictions befell him for his own evil deserts, and out of a disaffection to him, as one pursued by God's justice. The like conceit had Job's friends of him: Job vi. 4, 'If thy children have sinned against him, and he hath cast them away for their transgression.' And in many other places. Therefore this arrow sticketh fast in their sides; by it they are pierced, and hit in their main confidence.

[3.] Conscience may have many misgivings because of afflictions: 1 Kings xvii. 18, 'O thou man of God! art thou come to call my sin to remembrance, and to slay my son?' Affliction reviveth the guilt: Job xiii. 26, 'Thou writest bitter things against me, and makest me to possess the sins of my youth.' They sat so close to his conscience that he could not get rid of them. Such suspicions and fears are revived in their hearts. It were well if it were only to humble us for the demerit. So we ought to judge ourselves as deserving condemnation. But to question the truth of God's grant, as if he did retract it, and make our pardon void by these afflictions, this should not be; or to conclude that he has a purpose to ruin us and condemn us for ever, this is downright despair.

2. This is grievous to them. Guilt affects the saints most. A rod dipped in guilt smarteth sorest upon their backs.

VOL. XXII.

E

[1.] This for the present depriveth them of the sense of God's love to them, which is their all and their happiness. Nothing cheereth them so much as the beams of his reconciled face : Ps. iv. 6, 7, 'Lord, lift up thou the light of thy countenance upon us. Thou hast put gladness in my heart more than in the time that their corn and wine increased ;' Rom. v. 11, 'We joy in God, through our Lord Jesus Christ, by whom we have received the atonement.'

[2.] It questioneth their love of God, as if all were counterfeit ; for God cannot condemn the soul that loveth him. And his providence seemeth to their consciences to speak out condemnation to humble them. Peter took it tenderly to have his love questioned: John xxi. 17, 'Master, thou knowest all things, and thou knowest that I love thee ;' as Job afterwards, ' Lord, thou knowest that I am not wicked.'

Use 2. It showeth what we should do that the wounds of an healed conscience may not bleed afresh again.

1. Interpret the dispensations of providence aright. Whatever God's dealings be with his children, it is to prevent condemnation, not to revive it upon them. If we have nothing else to weaken our faith and confidence, it is a temptation from Satan to question our estate merely upon the account of afflictions. It is his suggestion, If God did love thee, he would not follow thee with his judgments ; but that he hateth thee, and hath no delight in thee; this is from Satan. For so his instruments said to Christ: Mat. xxvii. 43, ' He trusted in God ; let him deliver him now if he will have him : for he said, I am the Son of God.' Now retort it for Satan : Nay, because God loveth me, he dealeth thus with me ; he meaneth to save my soul. Because we are children of God, therefore we are the more afflicted, that sins may be prevented, grace increased.

2. Remember the absoluteness of God's pardon. Sin pardoned is remembered no more, Jer. xxxi. 34; nor would be found, Jer. l. 20 : all sins cast into the depth of the sea. God will not recall his sentence of pardon.

3. Make your interest in Christ more certain and clear ; for certainly ' there is no condemnation to them that are in Christ,' Rom. viii. 1.

Now these things evidence that we are in Christ—

[1.] A change of nature is necessary : 2 Cor. v. 17, 'Therefore if any man be in Christ, he is a new creature: old things are passed away; behold, all things are become new.' If it be so, you may appeal to God that you are not a wicked man. A sinner indeed, but renewed and reconciled. You have obtained mercy not to be wicked.

[2.] You must walk holily, that you may have the testimony of a good conscience, which is a notable support in troubles : 2 Cor. i. 12, ' For our rejoicing is this, the testimony of our conscience, that in simplicity and godly sincerity, not with fleshly wisdom, but by the grace of God, we have had our conversation in the world, and more abundant to you-ward.'

4. There must be serious endeavours against the remainder of sin that may prevent the reign of it, for then you are not under the law, but under grace: Rom. vi. 14, ' To break the power of sin is not the work of a day ; these sad dispensations tend to it, not to infringe our justification, but promote our sanctification, that we may carry it more

cautiously, holily, and thankfully to God: Isa. xxvii. 9, 'By this shall
the iniquity of Jacob be purged, and this is all the fruit to take away
his sin;' Heb. xii. 10, 'They verily for a few days chastened us for their
own pleasure; but he for our profit, that we might be partakers of his
holiness.'

Doct. 3. That it is a good thing to inquire after the cause and reason
of our afflictions.

1. They will not else be so honourable to God; for God loveth to
be clear when he judgeth, Ps. li. 4, or to have the reason of his dispensation seen, that he may have the glory, we the shame: Jer. ii. 17,
'Hast thou not procured this unto thyself?' Micah vii. 9, 'I will bear
the indignation of the Lord, because I have sinned against him, until
he plead my cause, and execute judgment for me: he will bring me
forth to the light, and I shall behold his righteousness.'

2. Nor are our chastenings so profitable unto us till we know why he
doth contend with us. We reap a double advantage when we know
for what sin: 1 Cor. xi. 30, 'For this cause many are weak and sick
among you, and many sleep.'

[1.] That God never afflicteth but for a cause is necessary to be
known for his honour; but for what cause, that is necessary to be
known for our profit. We are apt to flatter ourselves with notions
and generals. Sin in the general is the common pack-horse, upon
which men lay all their burdens. But come to particulars, amend
them, avoid sin; there we are at a loss: Mal. iii. 7, 'Return unto me,
saith the Lord of hosts: but they said, Wherein shall we return?'
There we show that our repentance was but a notion. *Dolus latet in
universalibus*—Deceit lurks under generals. Therefore it is an advantage to know that not for sin in general, but for this sin, God afflicts
us.

[2.] We can the better judge of the greatness of that sin; for we
know causes by effects, and can the better see our folly by our smart:
Jer. ii. 19, 'Thine own wickedness shall correct thee, and thy back-
slidings shall reprove thee. Know therefore, and see that it is an evil
thing and a bitter, that thou hast forsaken the Lord thy God.' God is
fain to teach us as Gideon taught the men of Succoth, by briars and
thorns. By the evil that we suffer he showeth us the evil which we
commit, and so helpeth our faith by our sense.

3. Our sufferings else are more uncomfortable. No rod so uncomfortable as a dumb rod, when we do not know the cause and use of it,
but barely feel the stroke, and see no more. But when we see the use,
that maketh for comfort: Ps. xciv. 12, 'Blessed is the man whom thou
chastenest, O Lord, and instructest him out of thy law.' When the
rod hath a voice, and speaketh out the mind of God to us: Micah vi.
9, 'Fear the rod, and who hath appointed it.'

Use 3. It is lawful humbly to desire God to show us the reason of
his dispensations. And here I shall a little speak to the case.

1. For men who are wicked to make this request to God is to leave
the matter of repentance upon an uncertain debate: and it is all one
as if a man should break through a thorn hedge, and curiously desire
to know which thorn had pricked him. For those that are overgrown
with sin, it is enough to know that the author of all afflictions is God;

the cause is sin, and the end is repentance; that they must be new
creatures, or they are undone for ever.   To be more particular with
them is to defeat the purpose of the dispensation, and to put them upon
the leaving of one sin when God calleth for a change of state, or a
passing from death to life; and this is but like mending a hole in an
house that is ready to drop down.

2. To put this question to God when we do not search diligently
ourselves is to betray a duty by our prayers : for when you complain,
you must also search : Lam. iii. 39, 40, 'Wherefore doth a living man
complain ? a man for the punishment of his sins. Let us search and
try our ways, and turn again to the Lord.' Let us search what sins
have an hand in all that cometh upon us, and what special provocation
we are guilty of.

3. When one that for the main hath walked faithfully with God
puts the question, these two cautions must be observed—

[1.] That it be not out of the impatiency of the flesh, murmuring
against and taxing God's providence, as if he dealt hardly with them,
who for wise reasons will dispose of the temporal interests and condition
of his people according to his own pleasure, for his honour and their
profit. If there be an overvaluing of the prosperity of the flesh, we
bewray the cause, and yet do not see it. This is that God aimeth at,
but you would translate the matter to some other thing. He would
teach you that your happiness lieth not here; that patience and
humility under the sharpest trials is better than immunity from
them.

[2.] That it be not from an over-conceit of our own holiness, so that
you wonder why God should afflict you. Alas ! the sins of the regenerate are very provoking, and may occasion sore afflictions in this life :
Amos iii. 2, 'You only have I known of all the families of the earth,
therefore will I punish you for all your iniquities.' They sin against
a nearer relation than others do, even against God, who is their Father
by the new birth, which is more heinous than if a stranger did it,
1 Peter i. 17. They sin against more excellent operations of the Spirit
than others do, a principle of life within them : 1 John iii. 9, 'Whosoever is born of God doth not commit sin.' There is more unkindness
in their sins : Ezra ix. 14, 'Should we again break thy commandments ?' They know more of the sting of sin, and have drunk of the
bitter waters, Joshua xxii. 17; against more knowledge, for they know
more what the will of God is, James iv. 17. They make profession of
a strict obedience, and that by covenant, vow, and dedication. God's
quarrel against you is the quarrel of his covenant, Lev. xxvi. 25. You
dishonour God more than any others by your sins : Neh. v. 9, 'Is it
not good that ye should walk in the fear of God, because of the
heathen ?' You harden the wicked more than such sins in other men
would do : Ezek. xvi. 51, 'Neither hath Samaria committed half of
thy sins; but thou hast multiplied thine abomination more than they,
and hast justified thy sister in all thine abominations which thou hast
done.' Think of these things, and then put the question.

4. If the inquiry be humbly and dutifully made, it may be known
wherefore he contendeth with you.

[1.] Partly by the word of God : Heb. ii. 2, 'If the word spoken by angels was steadfast, and every transgression and disobedience received a just recompense of reward,' &c.

[2.] Partly by checks of conscience. What is your greatest burden in sore troubles? Gen. xlii. 21, 'We are verily guilty concerning our brother.' It was many years before, yet their trouble brought it to their remembrance: Isa. lix. 12, 'For our transgressions are multiplied before thee, and our sins testify against us; for our transgressions are with us; and as for our iniquities, we know them.'

[3.] Partly by christian friends, what they tell us of and observe in us. As Nathan to David: Ps. cxli. 5, 'Let the righteous smite me, and it shall be a kindness.'

[4.] Partly by enemies. Reproaches of enemies; they are sharp and quick-sighted; they soon spy out the faults of others. We often hear our enemies teaching our duty to us, that will not hearken to God. The staff of Egypt is a broken reed, Isa. lvi. 6, with Ezek. xxix. 6, 7.

[5.] The nature of affliction. God knoweth how to strike in the right vein. Usually one contrary by another.

[6.] By his Spirit, with due application to him: Job xxxiv. 32, 'That which I see not, teach thou me; if I have done iniquity I will do no more.'

SERMON UPON ACTS VII. 55, 56.

---

*But he, being full of the Holy Ghost, looked up steadfastly into heaven,
and saw the glory of God, and Jesus standing at the right hand
of God, and said, Behold, I see the heavens opened, and the Son
of man standing on the right hand of God.*—ACTS vii. 55, 56.

THESE words show the carriage of Stephen when the Jewish fury was
whetted against him. We read of some, Acts ii. 37, that were pricked
in heart when they were charged with crucifying the Messiah; but
these, when they are charged by Stephen with the same crime, are cut
at heart, ver. 54. This is not so kindly a work as that; that pierced
their spirits with sorrow, this embittered and inflamed them into
wrath and rage; they were cut at heart, and gnashed on him with
their teeth. Stephen, by that discerning they were resolved upon his
death, what doth he do? Expect to be defended and rescued by the
christians? There were none such in the council; and for other, their
religion warranted not violence against the magistrate. What then?
Being forsaken of all, he lifteth up his eyes to heaven to the Lord Jesus,
whose cause he pleaded, and for whose sake he incurred this hazard
and danger, 'But he,' &c.

In the words we have two things—(1.) His vision; (2.) The publication of it.

First, His vision; there three things are observable—

(1.) The inward impulsive cause, 'Being full of the Holy Ghost.'
(2.) The action consequent thereupon, 'He looked up to heaven.' (3.)
The event; where—(1st.) The act, 'He saw.' (2d.) The objects, or
things seen by him, 'The glory of God, and Jesus standing at his
right hand.'

1. The inward moving cause or power by which he was moved and
assisted, 'Being full of the Holy Ghost.' It is said before, Acts vi. 5,
that Stephen was a man full of faith and of the Holy Ghost. That
expresseth the habit, which was now excited and quickened into act;
his faith and confidence in God was heightened into courage; as a
good soldier hath always an habit of fortitude, but in the danger of
battle his valour is quickened, and a great ardour cometh upon him.
So holy men, that have always a spirit of faith, upon necessary occasions
are elevated beyond the line of their ordinary strength; as Stephen
was here by a new impulse of the Holy Ghost. This is notable, that

it is a special work of the Spirit of God to raise our minds to the sight
of heavenly things : 2 Cor. i. 22, 'Who hath also sealed us, and
given the earnest of the Spirit in our hearts ; ' Rom. viii. 23, 'Ourselves also which have the first-fruits of the Spirit, even we ourselves
groan within ourselves, waiting for the adoption, viz., the redemption
of our body.' All the lively effectual knowledge of any truth cometh
from him, especially a sight of heaven ; it is his office to make all our
knowledge of truth more quick, lively, and powerful, to affect the heart
and rule the life. And especially is the Spirit given as the earnest
and first-fruits of heaven.

2. The action on Stephen's part; he looketh up steadfastly into
heaven. All earthly help failing, he looketh higher ; turneth off his
eyes from the world and men to God, the great arbiter and disposer of
life and death. We read of Moses, ἀπέβλεπε εἰς μισθαποδοσίαν,
Heb. xi. 26, a looking off and a looking on. The word signifieth a
turning of the eye from one object to behold another. He turned away
his mind and heart from the honours, pleasures, and treasures of Egypt,
and fixed them on the rewards of godliness. The more we shut the
eye of sense, the better we shall open that of faith. If we did oftener
look from that which is present to that which is to come, from the
creature to God, from earth to heaven, we should be much wiser and
stronger than we are, and not so regard our worldly concernments as
that upon every rumour of danger our hearts should be shaken like the
leaves of the trees of the wood.

3. The event; he ' saw the glory of God, and Jesus Christ standing
at his right hand.' And in his publication of his vision, 'Behold, I see
the heavens opened.' Now here three difficulties are to be considered—

[1.] The opening of the heavens, how such a solid body should be
divided, and yet close and come together again.

[2.] The seeing of God, who is invisible: John i. 18, 'No man hath
seen God at any time ; ' and 1 Tim. vi. 16, ' He dwelleth in light, which
no mortal eye can approach unto and live.'

[3.] The seeing Christ at so great a distance. How can a mortal
eye reach so far through the house in which the council was met, the
intervening clouds and firmament? These difficulties we must remove
before we go further. To solve these doubts there are many opinions.

(1.) Some make it a mere intellectual vision, or the sight of faith.
He was so firmly persuaded of the truth of these things, as if he had
seen them with bodily eyes. So Abraham saw Christ's day, John viii.
56.

(2.) A prophetical vision, such as the prophets had by the immediate
instinct and operation of God. So Isaiah saw God on the throne, Isa.
vi. 1. Paul was rapt into the third heaven, whether in the body or
out of the body he could not tell, 2 Cor. xii. Most of the visions the
prophets had were of this nature: 1 Kings xxii. 19, 'I saw the Lord
sitting on his throne,' said Micaiah. A vision, as distinguished from a
dream, was an immediate representation of things, either to the imagination, or to the understanding of a man while he awoke. Certainly
this was one means whereby God did manifest himself to the prophets.
If to their imagination, then he did affect their minds and hearts with
certain sensible objects and species. If to their understanding, by cer-

tain ideas and representations, as did wonderfully ravish and transport them.

(3.) Others, a symbolical vision, that he saw these things by certain external shapes and corporeal images: as John Baptist saw the Spirit descending like a dove on Christ, John i. 32. So Moses is said to see God, Exod. xxiv. 11, as he saw some visible signs of his glorious presence. The rays of his majesty have been seen by creatures.

(4.) Others think his natural eye was so strengthened as to be able to pierce the clouds and see God's throne, and Christ at his right hand. Such a sight the blessed have hereafter: John xvii. 24, 'I will that they may be with me, that they may behold my glory.' And they think, by extraordinary dispensation, this was vouchsafed to Stephen; that he had such a supernatural light as to see heaven opened, and the splendour and majesty of God, and Christ at his right hand; in short, a glimpse of the beatifical vision.

Now which of these shall we choose for the opening of these words? The sight of faith cannot be denied; but withal it must be granted that it was accompanied with a glorious apparition and spiritual ecstasy; which if any will call a glimpse of the beatifical vision, there is nothing absurd in it; for it is said, 'His face shone like an angel,' Acts vi. 15; that is, there was a great splendour about him. And God, that wrought such a change in his body, might exhibit such a manifestation of himself to his mind as might come near to the beatifical vision.

But let us come more particularly to the difficulties alleged.

(1st.) The opening of heaven implieth not a change in the nature of heaven, or rupture there; for it was only seen of Stephen, not by his enemies. The miracle was not in heaven, but in his eye. A miraculous vision it was, or some remarkable manner of appearance. We read, the heavens were opened at Christ's baptism, Mat. iii. 16. But interpreters are at a stand whether they were really parted asunder, or only after some remarkable manner of appearance. So again, that the heavens were opened in Peter's trance, Acts x. 11. And that is granted by all that it was done in a vision. And why may not the like be supposed here?

(2d.) The second difficulty is about the sight of God. Certainly no man can see God in his essence; for he is a spirit, and a spirit cannot be seen with bodily eyes. Nor can he be seen in the infinite excellency of his majesty; for what is finite cannot comprehend what is infinite. But he may be seen in such a visible manifestation of his glory as he is pleased to represent to the view of the creature, both here and hereafter. Thus here he may and hath often been seen. Therefore when it is said, 'He saw the glory of God,' you must understand so far as he can be seen by an human eye; namely, by certain strictures and rays of his splendour and majesty, or such a brightness by which his divine glory is represented unto us. So Luke ii. 9, 'The angel of the Lord came upon them, and the glory of the Lord shone round about them;' that is, the splendour occasioned by the presence of an angel. So in the apparition of an angel to Peter in prison: Acts xii. 7, 'The angel of the Lord came upon him, and a light shined in the prison.' So by this manifestation which God made of himself to Stephen, thereby is represented a glorious majesty, such as is described Exod. xxiv. 17,

'The sight of the glory of the Lord was like devouring fire in the eyes of the children of Israel;' meaning thereby some representation of his splendour and majesty; only that was more for terror, this for comfort and support.

(3d.) For the third difficulty, about the seeing of Christ, this being an extraordinary miraculous vision, it hath been answered before. But mark, 'He saw Christ standing at his right hand.' Elsewhere he is described in another posture, of 'sitting on the right hand of God:' as Mark xvi. 14, 'He was received into heaven, and sat on the right hand of God.' That noteth his royal dignity; but standing as ready for the help of all that belong to him. God is said to arise when he will help his people; as Ps. lxviii. 1, 'Let God arise, let his enemies be scattered.' So he saw Jesus, God-man, standing, as in a posture of readiness to assist and help his servant.

Nothing remaineth for further explaining this text but the publication of his vision: 'And he said, Behold, I see the heavens opened, and the Son of man standing on the right hand of God.' This publication is made—

[1.] To show his own faith. The apostle saith, 2 Cor. iv. 13, 'We having the same spirit of faith, according as it is written, I have believed, therefore have I spoken: we also believe, and therefore speak;' that is, we having the same spirit of faith which is spoken of in David's psalms, where he saith, 'I believed, therefore I spake.' In sore afflictions he pleads the hopes of his preservation and deliverance. Therefore we profess Christ, and express our faith in him, notwithstanding all our afflictions, troubles, and dangers. A spirit of faith, when it cometh upon a man, it cannot be checked; but a bashful inconfidence is easily obstructed. Therefore Stephen would not conceal his vision to himself, but divulge it for the profit of others.

[2.] To show forth the dignity of his lord and master. Therefore he calleth him the Son of man, but acknowledgeth him to be at the right hand of God; to show that Christ reigneth as God incarnate in that flesh in which he was abased and contemptuously used by men: 'Crucified in the flesh, but liveth by the power of God,' 2 Cor. xiii. 4.

[3.] He testifieth and publisheth it to show them that they did in vain strive against the truth of Christ, whom they supposed to be utterly destroyed by their rulers; for he was in the highest glory, reigning with God in the heavens. Therefore nothing more vain and fruitless than the opposition which Satan and his agents make against Christ and his kingdom: 'For he is sat down at the right hand of God; from henceforth expecting till all his enemies be made his footstool,' Heb. x. 12, 13.

Doct. Nothing doth fortify us against the discouragements we meet with in Christ's service so much as the sight of heaven, and Christ's sitting at the right hand of God there.

In the prosecution of this point I shall consider—(1.) The objects represented, God, Christ, and heaven; (2.) The sight of them, how we can see such things, visions and raptures being antiquated things, at least not commonly dispensed; then (3.) You will soon see how this is the ground of christian courage.

First, The objects represented to us, God, Christ, heaven.

1. There is mentioned in the text the glory of God. A due sight of

God lesseneth all other things in our opinion and estimation of them and affection to them; and could we but see his glory, we might easily wink out the amiableness and terribleness of the creature; for what are all the fears of man and the rage of the world to God? the wrath of a poor creature, whose breath is in his nostrils, against the power of an eternal God? Ps. xl. 4, ' Blessed is the man that maketh the Lord his trust, and respecteth not the proud, and such as turn aside to lies.' The proud are those that abuse their prosperity to the oppression of others, and, turning aside to lies, seek to uphold themselves by earthly props and dependences, or those base arts by which atheistical men, that have no conscience, would maintain their greatness. Surely he that is afraid of man doth not rightly know God: Isa. li. 12, 13, ' Who art thou that art afraid of a man that shall die, and forgettest the Lord thy Maker.' Is not God able to bear us out in his work? Heb. xi. 27, Moses endured the wrath of the king, seeing him that is invisible. Could we get this sight of his invisible glory, lesser things would not startle us. Alas! when we come to set God against man, the match is altogether unequal; there is then the Creator against the creature, who is the mere product of his Maker's will, and can subsist and act no longer than he pleaseth; an eternal God against a bubble, that is soon blown up, and bursts. You may set his wisdom against their policy and wiles: ' For there is no wisdom, nor counsel, nor understanding, against the Lord,' Prov. xxi. 30. His love and goodness against their malice and cruelty. What matter is it if they frown when he smileth? His power against their weakness; they can be nothing without him, and therefore we need not fear the sword if we have not reason to fear him that beareth the sword. And lastly, his promises against their threatenings; he is not God if he be not above his creature. All the powers of the world are nothing to God.

2. The next object is Jesus Christ at his right hand. This is the second object in the text. Let us a little consider what this importeth. Properly speaking, God hath neither right hand nor left, for he is a spirit. It is a metaphor, therefore, which must be explained by the manner of earthly kings, who place those whom they highly esteem and honour on their right hand; as Solomon did his mother in a chair of state on his right hand, 2 Kings ii. 19; and also such whom they put in chief authority and trust next themselves, as the mother of Zebedee's children made suit to Christ that her two sons might sit, one at the right hand, the other at the left of Christ in his kingdom, Mat. xx. 21. She falsely imagined it to be an earthly kingdom, accompanied with worldly honour; and therefore the purport of her request was, that her two sons might have the highest places of authority and profit under Christ, and next to Christ in his kingdom. So Christ's sitting at the right hand of God noteth the esteem he hath with God, and his being exalted to the highest degree of glory, and majesty, and authority, and honour, next himself. First, let us see the things imported by it; secondly, the ends of it.

[1.] The things imported by it.

(1.) His great esteem with God, which is a ground of confidence; for we have a friend in heaven, as David had Jonathan in Saul's court, to give him notice of danger, and to prevent displeasure from breaking

out against him. Surely to have a friend in the court of heaven is a
great privilege; one who taketh up all differences between God and
us, and answereth all accusations of Satan and his instruments, and
preventeth wrath from breaking out upon us : 1 John ii. 1, ' If any
man sin, we have an advocate with the Father, Jesus Christ the righteous.'   We should not abuse it to wantonness and wilful sinning : yet
it is a comfort against failings, and also against the clamours and
reproaches of the world, that we have an advocate and witness on high:
' My witness is in heaven,' saith Job.

(2.) The glory and majesty which is put upon him, next to God,
more than any creature is capable of, by virtue of the unspeakable union
between the two natures. Crowned with glory and honour. He hath
the fulness of grace and glory given to him, to dispense to his redeemed
ones, Acts v. 31, which is a great comfort, to consider his personal
endowments as God incarnate.

(3.) The authority and power that is put upon him. It is said, 1
Peter iii. 22, that ' he is gone into the heavens, and is on the right hand
of God ; angels, authorities, and powers being made subject to him ; '
so that he hath the highest glory, the highest power.   And Eph. i. 20,
21, 'God hath set him at his right hand in the heavenly places, far above
all principality, and power, and might, and dominion, and every name
that is named, not only in this world, but in the world to come ; ' that
is, not only above earthly potentates, who are his vicegerents, but
heavenly powers, who are his messengers and instruments, whom he
employeth for the defence and comfort of the godly : Heb. i. 14, ' Are
they not all ministering spirits, sent forth to minister for them who shall
be heirs of salvation ? ' and for the terror and punishment of his enemies;
Ps. lxviii. 17, ' The chariots of the Lord are *seventy thousand, even thousands of angels.   The Lord is among them, as in Sinai, in the holy
place.'   Mark there, thousands of angels are but as his chariot con-
veying him from heaven to earth. And mark, 'The Lord is among them;'
that is, God incarnate; for he presently speaketh of his ascending up
on high, and leading captivity captive, ver. 18.   And among them in
his holy place ; that is, in heaven.   As at the giving of the law in mount
Sinai, there were then, so they still attend on the propagation of the
gospel.   Now this is a great comfort to the godly when they are
oppressed ; especially when the authorities and powers of the earth are
employed against them, as they were in the apostles' time.   So that we
cannot utterly fail while Christ sitteth on the right hand of God.

[2.] The ends for which Christ was exalted to sit at the right hand
of God are, to perform the several functions of his mediatorial office ;
therefore in such high esteem, such majesty, such authority. His offices
are three—his prophetical, sacerdotal, and regal office ; which he doth
by three solemn acts—

(1.) The effusion of his Spirit, to promote the ends of his prophetical
office, convincing the world of the truth of his doctrine, and converting
them by it.   Therefore the first news we hear of Christ after his ascension, as soon as he was warm in the mediatorial throne, was his pouring
out the Spirit, Acts ii. And presently the virtue of it appeared ; three
thousand souls were added to the church that day. And this is a pledge
of what is continually dispensed.   There is still a Spirit sent forth, to

convince the unbelieving world, and to conquer the opposing wisdom
and power of the flesh, John xvi. 8 ; as also to beget and continue life
in his people, that they may be actually put in possession of what he
hath purchased for them ; for he hath promised to accompany the dispensation of the gospel with this Spirit to the end of the world : Mat.
xxviii. 20, ' I am with you.'   Not only by his powerful providence, but
his convincing, supporting, quickening Spirit.

(2.) The second work Christ doth at the right hand of God belongeth to his priestly office ; and that is his intercession : Rom. viii. 34,
' He sitteth at the right hand of God, making intercession for us.'   As
the high priest went into the holy place with blood, so Christ is gone
to represent the merit of his sacrifice : Heb. ix. 24, ' Christ is entered
into heaven, now to appear in the presence of God for us.'   To answer
the accusations of Satan, 1 John ii. 1 ; to make reconciliation for the
sins of the people, Heb. ii. 17.   He doth interpose night and day to
prevent breaches, to preserve a mutual correspondence between us and
God, and sue out necessary grace for us in all our conflicts and temptations.   And this not only for the church in general, but every believing
soul, Heb. vii. 25, according to their particular wants, exigencies, and
straits : ' He is able to save them to the uttermost that come unto
God by him, seeing he ever liveth to make intercession for them.'

(3.) The third act respecteth his kingly office, or the actual administration of his kingdom, calling and gathering his people out of the
profane world, and appointing laws to them for their direction to true
happiness ; and then protecting and defending them by his divine
power and providence, giving success to his cause and servants, and
restraining and subduing their enemies, treading down Satan and all
his instruments under their feet, disappointing their attempts, and
bringing to nought their counsels, Ps. ii. ; but he doth most fully subdue
them at his second coming : Phil. ii. 10, ' That at the name of Jesus
every knee should bow, of things in heaven, and things on earth, and
things under the earth.'   Now this is a mighty encouragement.   Poor
creatures will be courageous in the eyes of their master, and he is ready
to support and strengthen them, and able to do it.   Therefore we
should say, as the apostle, 2 Tim. i. 12, ' I know whom I have believed,
and I am persuaded that he is able to keep that which I have committed unto him against that day.'

3. The third object is heaven.   Looking to heaven is a great ground
of christian courage : 2 Cor. iv. 17, ' Our light affliction, which is but
for a moment, worketh for us a far more exceeding and eternal weight
of glory.'   There is glory opposite to affliction ; a weight, a far more
exceeding weight, to light affliction ; eternal, to what is momentary.
Afflictions are *leves et breves*, light and short ; not in themselves (for
some may be grievous, and some very long) but comparatively, with
respect to our glorious reward, which, being infinite, maketh them light ;
and being eternal, maketh them short.   Alas ! no more than a point
to the circumference, no more than a feather against a talent of lead.
The good and evil of the present world is slight and inconsiderable, but
that of the other world truly great.   All the pleasures of sense are but
as a may-game to our reward ; all the troubles of our obedience but as
a flea-biting or the scratching of a pin to eternal torments.

[1.] The sight of them. We have no visions and raptures, but first we have the prospect of faith. A believer, by the eye of faith, may by the perspective of the promises look within the veil, and see the reality of those eternal and glorious things which lie in the other world. An object, though never so glorious, cannot be seen without eyes. Now faith is the eye of the soul, Heb. xi. 1. It is defined to be 'the substance of things hoped for, and the evidence of things not seen.' It is good to see how the light and sight of faith differeth from all other lights.

(1.) Compare it with the light of sense, that can only discern things near, and present with us, and before our eyes, as that it is comfortable to eat and drink, and sleep well; to be at liberty, and free from trouble, and to live a life of pomp and sensual pleasure and delight. The sweetness of honour, wealth, and pleasure are known easily, and known by all; this every one can see; but he that hath enslaved his reason to sense 'is blind, and cannot see afar off,' 2 Peter i. 9. The light of faith will discover there is no such danger as perishing for ever; no such worth in anything as in salvation by Christ; no such business of importance as seeking after eternal life.

(2.) Compare it with the light of reason. Reason can only guess at future contingencies, or at best see things in their causes or natural order, and that it is probable, if nothing letteth, such and such things will fall out; but faith can look through all distance of time and place, and contrary appearances, with such certainty and firm persuasion as if the thing were at hand: Heb. xi. 13, 'These all died in faith, not having received the promises, but having seen them afar off, and were persuaded of them, and embraced them;' John viii. 56, 'Abraham rejoiced to see my day; and he saw it, and was glad;' Rom. iv. 18, 'Who against hope believed in hope, that he might become the father of many nations.'

(3.) Compare it with the light of prophecy; that is a seeing: Rev. xx. 12, 'I saw the dead, small and great, stand before God,' &c. They agree in the common object, such things as are revealed by God. They agree in the same common nature, that it is a sight of things absent, or future and to come, with such certainty and clearness as if they were in being. They differ, because faith goeth upon the common revelation which God hath made of his mind to all the saints in scripture; the other upon some special vision and revelation made to certain chosen persons. The light of faith affects the heart with great joy and comfort; the other is usually with rapture and ecstasy.

(4.) Let us compare it with the light of glory, the beatifical vision, that worketh a change in body and soul: 1 John iii. 2, 'We know that, when he shall appear, we shall be like him.' This in the soul: 2 Cor. iii. 18, 'We all, beholding as in a glass the glory of the Lord, are changed into the same image, from glory to glory, even as by the Spirit of the Lord;' 1 Cor. xiii. 12, there see him face to face, as in a glass. Though not as highly affected with the light of faith, yet as truly and really. That nullifieth sin and misery; this mortifieth sin, and fortifieth us against misery. We have not such a full enjoyment of God as by the light of glory, yet by the light of faith we have some communion with him; it somewhat affecteth the heart, as if we saw

God on the throne, Christ in the midst of his holy ones, Paul with his crown of righteousness. It sets us above the clouds in affection; and as to foresight and foretaste, puts us in the midst of the glory of the world to come. Once more, this light of faith is like that sight which God hath of things, for it is the resemblance of it. There is a double knowledge in God, *scientia visionis, et scientia intelligentiæ.* God seeth all things that shall be in his own purpose and decree; knoweth all things that may be by his own all-sufficiency. Faith acts proportionably; it seeth all things that shall be in God's covenant and promises: 2 Cor. v. 1, ' We know, that if our earthly house of this tabernacle were dissolved, we have a building of God, an house not made with hands, eternal in the heavens.' It conceiveth what may be by the power of God: Dan. iii. 17, 18, 'Our God is able to deliver us;' though not sure of the event. It realiseth the blessing promised; when they have the promise, they have the pledge of the blessing.

[2.] The Spirit helpeth our sight. Naturally we are short-sighted, and there is a thick mist on eternity; these things are glorious in themselves, above our experience, remote from us, and we take up with toys and children's trifles. Our own natural wisdom bendeth us to present things: James iii. 15, ' This wisdom descendeth not from above, but is earthly &c., Prov. xxiv. 4. Reason is debased by sense, and wholly catereth for the body. Therefore true wisdom is from eyes anointed with spiritual eye-salve, as the apostle prayeth, Eph. i. 17, 18, ' That the God of our Lord Jesus Christ, the Father of glory, may give unto you the spirit of wisdom and revelation in the knowledge of him : the eyes of your understanding being enlightened,' &c.

[3.] The nearer approach to death, the clearer sight of heaven and Christ at the right hand of God, as ready to receive them. The most lively acts of faith are then usually put forth, the spirit being about to return to God. David's last words are noted, Num. xxiii. 1 ; so Joshua xxiii. 14. Usually there is then a clearer discerning of heaven, more elevated thoughts about it; it seemeth another thing than formerly. They that are nearer heaven, in the borders of it, do more vehemently long for and desire the actual possession of the glorious things.

Use. Let us oftener look within the veil. If you would have God look down upon you, you must look up to him. Faith is acted by serious thoughts. Carnal men mind earthly things; why not we heavenly ?

1. Believe that there are invisible good things to be enjoyed in another world. Here is our first work, when we hear of these great promises : 'Believest thou this?' John xi. 26. The things are glorious and certain, but our persuasions of the reality of them are too weak and feeble. That there is a world to come, and a state of invisible happiness and glory, nature guesseth at; for such a conceit hath been noted in the minds of men of all religions, not only Greeks and Romans, but barbarians, and people least civilised. This tradition hath passed from hand to hand throughout all successions of ages; and the nearer we trace it to the first originals of mankind, the more strong and pressing hath been the persuasion hereof. But still it hath borne up itself against all encounters of time, and in the midst of so many revolutions of human affairs, through which many truths are lost; yet this hath maintained itself.

and been readily received by all nations. But if it be dark to nature, the light of christianity doth more clearly discover it. Life and immortality are brought to light in the gospel, 2 Tim. i. 10. Christ, that purchased heaven for us, is gone into it himself, to give us a demonstration of the reality of it, 1 Peter i. 21. Having first left a promise of eternal life to all that believe in him, 1 John ii. 25, which promise was outwardly confirmed by divers miracles. Inwardly in the hearts of his people, by forming them for this estate, and giving them a taste of it in their own souls, 2 Cor. v. 6. Now, is the scripture false, the gospel a fable, the oracles of the prophets, the doctrine of Christ, his miracles, resurrection, and ascension, but a dream ? Were they all deceived that followed Christ upon these hopes, and took such pains in subduing the flesh, and hazarding their interests upon the hopes of another world ? Are the wisest sort of men the world ever saw fools ? Is sanctifying grace a fancy ? or the joys of the Spirit delusions or fantastical impressions ? The foretastes of the children of God a mere imposture ? And is it any way likely that all this solemnity should be used to establish a vain conceit ? Well, then, be persuaded of it, as if you saw it with your eyes.

2. Let us often raise our thoughts to the meditation of this heavenly bliss and glory. As a man is, so are his musings. Thoughts, being the genuine birth and immediate production of the soul, do discover the temper of it : Rom. viii. 5, 'They that are after the flesh do mind the things of the flesh,' &c. Those that are of an heavenly temper and frame do often exercise their minds in heavenly things ; their happiness lieth there, and their business tendeth thither. Our Lord telleth us, that where the treasure is, there the heart will be, Mat. vi. 21. If the mind were more taken up with these great things, they would breed in us a more excellent and choice spirit. But alas ! in most men, thoughts of heavenly blessedness are few and cold, when in the meantime their minds are thronged with all manner of vanity ; and therefore do they feel so little of the joys of the Spirit and the efficacy of grace, and do no more get up above the hopes and fears of the world. Certainly they do not hope for heaven that seldom cast a look that way. Where anything is strongly expected, the mind is wont to create to itself images and thoughts, whereby we preoccupy and foretaste the delight of what we expect ; for thoughts are the spies of hope sent toward the thing hoped for. If a man were adopted unto the succession of a crown, would he not please himself with the supposition of the honour and pleasure of the royal estate that he shall one day enjoy ? They that do not earnestly and warmly think of heaven and heavenly things have little expectation this way.

3. An earnest and desirous expectation. 'Looking for the blessed hope,' Titus ii. 13. Set your affections on it : Col. iii. 2, 'Set your affections on things above.' Groaning after it : 2 Cor. v. 2, 'In this we groan earnestly, desiring to be clothed upon with our house which is from heaven ;' Phil. i. 23, 'I am in a strait between two, having a desire to depart, and to be with Christ ; which is far better.' Without this, faith is a dead opinion or speculative assent ; hope but some cold ineffectual thought. Well, then, long to be at home. Heaven is opened for us ; Christ hath carried our nature, our flesh thither, and

advanced it on the Father's right hand; let us long in person to get thither.

4. So look to these things, that you may get your hearts above all earthly things: 2 Cor. iv. 18, 'While we look not at the things which are seen, but at the things which are not seen: for the things which are seen are temporal; but the things which are not seen are eternal.' The act is not simply denied as to things seen, but comparatively, that the world's honour or dishonour may have less influence upon us. In all our actions: 1 Cor. vii. 29, 31, 'The time is short: it remaineth, that both they that have wives be as though they had none; and they that weep, as though they wept not; and they that rejoice, as though they rejoiced not; and they that buy, as though they possessed not; and they that use this world, as not abusing it: for the fashion of this world passeth away.' We mourn for sin as if we mourned not. We should grow more dead to all impressions of sense. Though carnal satisfactions be near at hand, yet they are but short and inconsiderable: 'Demas loved the present world,' 2 Tim. iv. 10.

SERMON UPON 2 SAMUEL XXIV. 24.

Neither will I offer burnt-offerings unto the Lord my God of that which costs me nothing.—2 SAM. xxiv. 24.

IN the context you will find a laudable contention between a good king and a good subject. Since it was to David, and since it was for the Lord, Araunah would not sell, but give. On the other side, David, since it was for the Lord, he would not take, but buy.

A double reason may be given of David's refusal.

1. According to the law no man might offer to God anything but what was his own.

2. Because he would not serve God cost free.

You have both in the parallel place, 1 Chron. xxi. 24, 'I will not take that which is thine for the Lord, nor offer burnt-offerings without cost.' In the text it is notable that he calleth God, 'the Lord,' to note his majesty; and 'my God,' to note his own love, choice, and interest. Such a God he could not find in his heart to serve in a cheap and unworthy fashion. 'Neither will I offer,' &c.

Doct. A gracious heart will not serve God with that which costs him nothing; or counts that religion worth nothing which costs nothing.

Reasons. 1. This is the fruit of their faith. Carnal nature begrudgeth everything; and in the eye of sense all is lost that is laid out upon God. They say, with Judas, 'What needs this waste?' The same judgment that Seneca gave upon the Jewish sabbath, the same thoughts have carnal men of all the service of God: he said the Jews were a foolish people, *quia septimam ætatis partem perdunt vacando*, because they lost a full seventh part of their lives in idleness and rest. Now those that are thus minded, that think all is lost that is laid out in his service, will never do anything for God that is great and worthy; the refuse of what they have is thought good enough for him. That this opinion, that all that is done in religion for God's sake is as good as lost, hath an influence upon men's careless and perfunctory dealing in religion, appeareth by the first chapter of Malachi. The main intent of that chapter is to expostulate with them about their contempt of God, and the sorry service which they brought to him. Among other arguments, this is pleaded, that the meanest employment about him was not without its reward: Mal. i. 10, 'Who is there among you that would shut the doors for nought? neither do ye

kindle a fire on my altar for nought,' &c.   That is, the porters of the
temple did not open and shut the doors for nought; nor the priest
attend upon the burnt-offering for nought; they were all well rewarded
with tithes and oblations; they were all well provided for, by God's
own appointment and allowance.   This is God's argument, which
plainly showeth they were under the influence and dominion of this
blasphemous thought: that they should be losers by God, and therefore did not care how they served him.   But now a man that hath
faith, that is persuaded of God's being and bounty, Heb. xi. 6, he
thinketh he can never do enough for God; for he knoweth it will turn
to a good account.   Here, during the time of his patience, the superficial service he gets from us hath its reward: God giveth many
temporal blessings to those that worship him in the slightest fashion.
He suspended his judgments, you know, upon Ahab's counterfeit
humiliation, 1 Kings xxi. 29.   His providence plainly declareth that
none shall be a loser by him, nor do anything for nought; and therefore, shall we not do it well?   If anything be done sincerely, though
never so mean and inconsiderable, it hath its reward: Mat. x. 42,
'He that giveth a cup of cold water in the name of a disciple, shall in
no wise lose his reward.'   The smallness and meanness of the benefit,
help, or refreshing, done to any in Christ's name, shall not lose his
estimation and recompense, if it be done under that notion.   This,
though hardly credited by the unbelieving world, is very true: 'Verily
I say unto you,' and 'shall in no wise,' they are emphatical particles.
But now the more eminent services, which are carried on with hazard
and difficulty, and some considerable self-denial, surely they shall not
fail of their recompense : whatever we lose for Christ, we shall receive
again with infinite advantage: Mark x. 29, 30, 'Verily I say unto you,
There is no man that hath left house, and brethren, or sister, or father,
or mother, or wife, or children, or lands, for my sake and the gospel's,
but he shall receive an hundredfold now in this time, houses, and
brethren, and sisters, and mothers, and children, and lands, with persecutions, and in the world to come eternal life.'   He shall not only
have heaven at last; but here in this life, in the midst of persecution
an hundredfold.   Even in this time, the time of trials and troubles;
yea, by his troubles: in kind or value.   Not an hundred wives, or
mothers, or children, as Julian scoffed.   Now who would not serve
such a master, and serve him with his best, improve every received
ability, stand upon no cost and charges, so we may be faithful to him?
It would be no difficult thing to persuade men to it, if they were firmly
persuaded of these things; as it would be no hard thing to persuade
others to put out their money where they may have, not only ten in
the hundred, but an hundred for ten; or to sow their seed there
where the soil will certainly produce an hundredfold.   But we want
faith, and therefore draw back and struggle with our shoulders when
we are to do anything for God that will occasion trouble or cost.
That faith hath a great influence upon the costly and self-denying
services of the saints, is evident by the instance of Abel: Heb. xi. 4,
'By faith Abel offered a better sacrifice than Cain,' πλείονα θυσίαν,
the first, the fat, the best, the tenth.   Cain, that doubted of the world
to come, bringeth it hand over head.   So also the instance of Abraham:

Heb. xi. 17, 'By faith Abraham, when he was tried, offered up Isaac; and he that received the promises offered up his only-begotten son.' Here is a son, an only son, a son on whom the promises were fixed, and this son to fall under the weight of his own father's hands: an act that occasioned not only a conflict between his obedience and his natural affection, but a kind of riddle between his obedience and his faith. How should he offer Isaac, and yet believe that in Isaac's seed all the nations should be blessed? But faith is a strange grace; it trusts God wonderfully, and can reconcile all contradictions; it can see Isaac offered, and yet kept still, and a father of many children; gain in loss, and life in death; something in nothing. Well, then, a sound believer will not grudge at trials; when he is put upon the most difficult cases, he saith, 'Shall I serve God with what costeth me nought?' No, God shall have the best: if he will have Isaac, let Isaac go.

2. Their love to God inclineth them to this disposition of heart. Love is liberal and open-hearted; it standeth upon no labour, cost, or difficulty. Fear serveth God with a kind of reserve; it is a force put upon us, and therefore doth no more than needs must. But love is sensible that our obligation is far beyond our ability to recompense, and hath such a delight in God's service, it can never do enough for him; it counts nothing too good or too much, but all is short and too little. Love would still do more. There is a compulsion in fear, and there is a compulsion in love; for love constraineth, 2 Cor. v. 14. But how do these differ? The compulsion that is in fear is slavish, and mighty unwelcome to the soul, easily works off. That is bad ground that bringeth forth nothing except it be forced; and usually such ground, at the best, brings forth but sparingly. But love is a willing compulsion. *Amor non cogitur, sed cogit*—love is not forced, but forceth. Natural conscience worketh by fear, faith by love, Gal. v. 6. Love consecrateth and devoteth all that a man hath to the will and pleasure of him whom he loveth. *Quis legem det amanti? Amor major lex sibi ipsi est.* There needs no urging of laws. Love is a greater law to itself. No presenting of terrors where there is a strong self-inclination and propendency. It hath in its bosom as deep an engagement and obligation to please God as you can lay upon it. So that let a man's love be gained to Christ, and then he will stick at nothing. What love will do we may see in other cases; as in Jacob's love to Rachel: Gen. xxix. 20, 'And Jacob served seven years for Rachel, and they seemed to him but a few days, for the love he had to her.' So in Shechem's love to Dinah: Gen. xxxiv. 19, 'The young man deferred not to do the thing, for the delight which he had in Jacob's daughter.' Circumcision was an hated thing to them, as well as painful in itself. Well, now, so it is in religion. Where love is wanting, all that is done seemeth too much; but where love prevaileth, let it be never so difficult, it seems light and easy: Acts xx. 24, 'None of these things move me.' Where there is love there will be self-denial; it submitteth to duties against the bent and hair. Where there is love there will be labour; it is not a slothful and idle affection: 2 Thes. i. 3, 'Your work of faith, and labour of love.' Well, then, if you had a greater love to God, he would have the best of your hearts, the best of your labours, the best of your estates, and the best

of your time and strength, and you would count nothing too dear to give to him or for him; for the voice of love is, 'Shall I serve God with what costs me nought?' It is very notable that a little is accepted if it hath the stamp of love upon it. The lover's mite cast into the treasury is more worth than ten times so much outward obedience from another man. But then this is the genius of love, to do its best. He that loveth much cannot satisfy himself with a little, but still seeketh how it may more glorify and please God, and that at an higher rate: Ps. lxxi. 14, 'I will glorify him yet more and more.'

3. They have a deep sense of God's majesty and excellency, and therefore dare not put him off with anything that is vile, cheap, and unworthy. No; he shall have the best, the choice, the flower of their time, strength, love, affection. If we had an higher sense of God's majesty and greatness, we would be more careful of his worship; for he is not a God to be slighted or dallied with, or put off with a little religiousness by the by. As his spiritual nature calleth for spiritual service, so his glorious majesty calleth for eminent service, and bindeth this thought upon us, that he should not be served without cost. It is a sign we have lessening thoughts of him, if we think that any slight sorry performance, that costs us little time, little care, little preparation, done with little life and affection, will serve the turn. God pleadeth his majesty against this abuse: Mal. i. 14, 'Cursed be the deceiver, which hath in his flock a male, and voweth, and sacrificeth to the Lord a corrupt thing: for I am a great king, saith the Lord of hosts.' A king of so great majesty calleth for other manner of service than usually we bestow upon him. Common stuff will serve for an ordinary house. In a palace for a king, most costly furniture is requisite and becoming. Superficial dealing in his work is an affront of his greatness, and showeth that we have mean thoughts of him, and a want of reverence; when we put him off with the refuse, or bring common dispositions into his presence, and serve him carelessly and sorrily, thinking if the work be done it is no matter how, so we may once get it over. But he that knows God, what an high glorious God he is, dareth not be so sinfully bold and familiar with him : 'I will not serve God with what costs me nought.'

4. A cheap course of religion, such as costs little or nothing, will never be accepted with God; for it is contrary to his prescription. Our first lesson in Christ's school is self-denial, to prepare us for our after-service and obedience to him: Mat. xvi. 24, 'If any man will come after me, let him deny himself, and take up his cross, and follow me.' We promise ourselves too much when we promise ourselves nothing but pleasure and contentment, as if we could go to heaven without blows and conflicts. This self-denial is not to be exercised only in little things, or in few things. No; we must sell all for the pearl of great price, Mat. xiii. 46. And selling all for the pearl of great price is required in times of peace as well as in times of persecution. None must enter upon the profession of christianity, but they must sit down and count the charges, Luke xiv. 28. And shall we think, after all this, that we shall go to heaven without cost? Surely this is new christianity, which Christ never taught, and the scriptures

SERMON UPON 2 SAMUEL XXIV. 24.

own not ; a christianity of our own making, and therefore will not be accepted of God.

5. A cheap course of religion will yield us no comfort, nor sensible evidence of our sincerity. There are two reasons couched in one, but yet such as have a near affinity the one with the other.

[1.] There will be a sensible evidence of our sincerity. You will easily grant that it is necessary to a sound and sincere heart that we prefer Christ in our choice and esteem before the world and the flesh, and that we believe a world to come, and take heavenly things for our portion, treasure, and happiness. Now, how shall we know that we believe a world to come, if we venture nothing upon it, do nothing but what other men do, or but what we would do if there were no such hope offered to us ? How shall we know that we prefer Christ before the world, if we can deny no worldly thing for Christ's sake ; so that a man is still doubtful, and cannot tell what to say and judge of his spiritual estate and condition before God ? Heretofore, when God used extraordinary dispensations, he put his people upon special trials, that their sincerity might be more sensibly evidenced to them : Heb. xi. 17, ' By faith Abraham, when he was tried, offered up Isaac,' &c., πειρα- ζόμενος. God saw fit to put such an eminent believer as Abraham was upon such an extraordinary and eminent trial. So the young man, when he came full of self-confidence to Christ, he puts him upon a special trial : Mark x. 21, ' Go thy way, and sell what thou hast, and give to the poor.' Doth the Lord wholly discontinue, think you, this kind of dispensations ? No : Heb. x. 33, ' Partly whilst ye were made a gazing-stock, both by reproaches and afflictions ; and partly, whilst ye became companions of them that were so used.' Are not believers now put upon divers trials ? James i. 2. Should they not ' count it all joy while they fall into divers temptations,' as having an happy occasion to discover their sincerity towards God ? You are ignorant of the scriptures, and what belongeth to the usual discipline of your heavenly Father, if you conceit otherwise. Now, why doth God try us, or put his people upon sundry trials ? Doth not he know our thoughts afar off. And is he not acquainted with us, and the sincerity of our affections towards him, before we are put upon such a sensible proof ? Yes, verily ; he trieth, *non ut ipse hominem inveniat, sed ut homo se inveniat*—Augustine. Not that he may know more of man than he knew before, but that man may know more of himself than he knew before. He knoweth us already ; but he trieth us, that we may know ourselves. Indeed it is said, Gen. xxii. 12, ' Now I know that thou fearest God, since thou hast not withheld thy son, thine only son, from me.' All interpreters grant that it is *humanitus dictum,* and they expound it thus : Now there is a document ; now there is an apparent and sensible proof ; now I know, what not till now, Lord. Was Abraham's mind unknown to thee before ? Could not God tell long ago whether Abraham feared him, yea or no ? Yes ; he that knew all things knew that he feared him : yet know it he would not, that is, not approve it, till he had thus experienced it. And that was for Abraham's comfort and satisfaction. All this is for our learning, brethren. We know not that we love God more than other things till we are tried ; and tried we are not to the purpose till we are tried

in our Isaac ; in things nearest and dearest to us, and can be at some
cost for God. It is a nice case ; before a thing is liable to great uncertainty of debate ; therefore that is an happy occasion to a gracious
heart, to be put upon some exercise of self-denial: ' I will not serve
God with what costs me nought.'

[2.] God doth not so openly own men, nor pour out such a large
measure of the comforts of his Spirit upon his people, when they serve
him without cost, as he doth when they are called to deny themselves,
and all that is dear and precious to them in the world, for his sake. In
the Revelation there are many promises diversified under the notion
of ' eating of the tree of life,' Rev. ii. 7. 'Having the white stone, with
the name,' Rev. ii. 17 ; ' Of being fed with hidden manna ; ' but still
' to him that overcometh,' chapters ii. iii. They are more feasted with
comforts, and have a more liberal allowance of spiritual joys and delights
than others have ; those that have passed the pikes, and have counted
nothing dear to them, so they might keep their innocency, and approve
their faithfulness to God. Sufferers have more of the comfortable and
supporting operations of the Spirit than others have ; and in sharp trials,
when put to live by faith, and having nothing to encourage them but
their bare love to God, they enjoy usually more of the sensible comforts
of his Spirit than others do. Whereas those who are not exposed to
such difficulties, though they be sincere for the main, yet are kept more
in the doubtful, humbling way, have less of the joys of the Spirit, and
are more put to it to interpret their qualification, and make out any
hope by Christ.

Cautions for the understanding of this truth.

1. When we speak of costs in religion, be sure you do not allow so
much as a private whisper in your souls of merit; for the costliest services deserve nothing at God's hands. If we do never so much, suffer
never so much for him, ' we are but unprofitable servants,' Luke xvii.
10. Yet all our comfort and happiness is a free gift, or mere grace to
us. When David had offered many cart-loads of gold and silver, he
admireth grace, and acknowledgeth that he had but paid God out of
his own exchequer : 1 Chron. xxix. 14, ' Who am I, and what is my
people, that we should be able to offer so willingly after this sort ? for
all things come of thee, and of thine own have we given thee.' He
putteth away the glory of what was done from himself and people, that
both will and ability might entirely be ascribed to God. So Rev. iii.
10, ' Because thou hast kept the word of my patience, I also will keep
thee from the hour of temptation.' If we do never so much, and suffer
never so much, the crown of life is a gift.

2. See that you do not draw needless trials and inconveniences upon
yourselves ; for that is not zeal, but rashness and folly. Suffering for
well-doing is a duty that doth not bind, as negative precepts do, at all
times and in all cases ; nor are the children of God tied to it, as they
are to some other positive duties. We are to ' watch unto prayer,' 1
Peter iv. 7 ; redeem all opportunities for it. But this is only binding
when the will of the Lord is so, 1 Peter ii. 17 ; and that is when by his
providence he puts us under the power of persecutors, and they put us
to a necessity either of suffering or sinning. Then, when the flesh is
ready to say, Favour thyself, you must say, ' I will not serve the Lord

with what costs me nothing.' With courage and cheerfulness we must choose suffering rather than sinning. The apostle saith, James i. 2, 'Count it all joy when ye fall into divers temptations.' He saith, when we fall into them; not, when we draw them upon ourselves. It was Tertullian's error to say, Afflictions are to be sought and desired. No; they are only to be submitted unto when sent by God. We are not to desire troubles, but bear them and improve them when he layeth them upon us. Christ hath taught us to pray, 'Lead us not into temptation;' and it is but a fond presumption to cast ourselves upon it. Philastrius and Theodoret speak of some that would compel men to kill them, out of an affectation of martyrdom. This was a mad ambition, not a true zeal. And no less fond are they that seek out crosses and troubles, rather than wait for them, and by their own violence bring a just hatred upon themselves, and run headlong into dangers without necessity. If a man set fire on his own house, he is liable to the law; if it be fired by accident, he is pitied and relieved. We are not to seek the cross, or make it, but bear it, and take it up; not to fill the cup ourselves, but drink it off when our Father puts it into our hands.

3. Take heed that you only displease the flesh in a lawful way. Do not step out of the road of your duty for this, and think that the Lord is pleased with barbarous austerities; as Baal's priests gashed themselves, 1 Kings xviii. 29. And the pharisees and papists have their self-disciplinings. And Origen, who was too allegorical in plain texts, was too literal when he castrated himself, because Christ speaketh of making ourselves 'eunuchs for the kingdom of heaven,' Mat. xix. 12, intending only thereby the gift of continency, or a power over our natural affections. Exterior mortifications and dolorous impressions on the body are a piece of apocryphal bastard religion, highly prized by the world, who are given to please the flesh. If they must displease it, they affect to do it in an outward way. But as much as these things are esteemed by men, they are abhorred by God. Christ is a lover of human nature, and he hath put no such severe penance upon us. It is more acceptable to him to mortify a lust than to mangle a member of the body.

4. See that you place not too much of religion in outward things, in external pomp and gaudiness, and then put this zealous gloss upon it, 'I will not serve God with what costs me nothing.' It is easy to exceed in externals, and such things as make a fair show in the world; but the majesty and spirit of religion is lost in the pomp of self-pleasing appearances. Aquinas disputeth the question whether a *nimium*, anything superfluous in religion. He grants it in externals. A man cannot love God too much, or trust in him too much; but he may exceed in outward observances, *connaturale est nobis per sensibilia duci*. And though not too much in absolute quantity, yet too much in proportion, *non proportionatur ad debitum finem istius luctus*. 'The king's daughter is all glorious within,' Ps. xlv. 15, in faith, love, patience, sobriety. By gifts and graces is the true church known, rather than by a splendid appearance; and holiness becometh his house rather than gold and costly furniture, Ps. xliii. 5.

5. When some outward advantages do accompany religion, they

must not be foolishly thrown away upon the pretence of self-denial, but acknowledged as favours from God, as reputation, countenance, maintenance, favour of men, &c. Yet the heart must be watched narrowly when duty and interest meet together. They must not be foolishly thrown away upon the pretence of a more self-denying serving of God: this was the pretence of the false teachers, to gain credit and entrance, 2 Cor. xi. from the 7th to the 12th. And if it be real, it is foolish; for it is God's allowance both in his word and providence. Not but that a man may *cedere jure suo*, for the glory of God, the credit of the gospel, and give no offence: 1 Cor. ix. 18, 'What is my reward then? Verily, that, when I preach the gospel, I may make the gospel of Christ without charge, that I abuse not my power in the gospel.' Paul did what he could that the Corinthians might have ἀδάπανον εὐαγγέλιον; they would be prejudiced else; and Paul was fain to deny his own right to gratify them. But the heart must be watched when duty and interest meet together, that we do not make a market of religion, and a design of our profession, or a trade to live by; as we do when we look more to the secular encouragement than our duty. Their religion beareth their charges; they do not bear the charges of it. And these do rather say, I will not serve God for nothing, than, 'I will not serve God with what costs me nothing.'

6. Be not unreasonable in taxing yourselves with such a course of duty as is beyond ability and opportunity; for this is to make a snare for your own souls, and to entangle yourselves in some by-laws of your own making. And God accepts man according to what he hath, not according to what he hath not. A gracious heart may err on this hand, and think it never doeth enough. Conscience may be urging more; but even that little which we do is accepted. God is well pleased with it, because love is ill pleased with it, because it is no more nor better. Little is accepted for much when love offereth it. He taketh as much delight in the children's willingness as the more aged's strength. The main thing God looketh after is the willing mind: 2 Cor. viii. 12, 'If there be first a willing mind, it is accepted according to what a man hath, and not according to that he hath not;' and 1 Chron. xxix. 9, 'The people rejoiced, for that they offered willingly, because with perfect heart they offered willingly to the Lord.' Therefore, though we are to keep the heart liberal and open to God, and, when we have done our best, still to be willing to do more: Ps. lxxi. 14, 'I will praise him yet more and more;' yet this duty must be acted and exercised as strength and health will permit. In short, in performance of duties, the two measures are the strength and weakness of body and soul; as much as the health of the soul is more than the strength of body, our chief care must be for the soul, that the health of the soul be not lost, but still kept in good plight. That measure will show when we do too little; the other measure when the outward exercise is too much, when the health of the body is impaired or overwrought by it.

Use 1. It informeth us of the reasonableness and necessity of self-denial.

1. The reasonableness of it; for a man's heart, that is touched with any sense of religion, cannot be satisfied with a cheap course of duty. Natural light will tell us that no slight thing will become the God

whom we serve, and the glory and blessedness which we expect. Our religion were not a religion if it did not bind us to our duty, and not retrench the comforts and interests of the animal life, to preserve the spiritual in life and vigour; neither were christianity such a noble, glorious, and high institution if it did not draw us off from things earthly to things heavenly, and make them willing to quit the one for the other.

2. The necessity of it. They mistake religion that carry it on in such a way that it puts them to no cost. Wherever it is in vigour and power, it will put us to some expense. If it be otherwise, either men neglect many necessary duties, as self-examination, meditation, secret and earnest prayer, constant waiting upon God, mortifying their lusts and passions, which are all contrary to the ease of the flesh, or honouring God with their substance, Prov. iii. 4, seasonable reproof, owning his truth and stricter ways, notwithstanding troubles, persecutions, and disgraces, which are contrary to the interests and profits of the flesh; or else, secondly, they do what they do in a slight and overly fashion; and painted fire needeth no fuel. There is no trouble in a careless profession; there needs not much ado to keep it up. Where men leave the soul to the stream, and do, as Solomon saith of himself, Eccles. ii. 10, 'Whatsoever mine eyes desired, I kept not from them; I withheld not myself from any joy;' they leave their senses without guard, their affections without a bridle, and are carried on as they are impelled by their own lusts; and then varnish over all with a little profession, and talk of God, and Christ, or hearing. They may give religion a slight glance, and suffer it to have a turn among other things. Indeed such a religion puts them to no self-denial. But this is a false christianity of our own making. Here is no striving to enter in at the strait gate, no walking in the narrow way, no working out our salvation with fear and trembling. All this may be, and no denying ourselves and hazarding the displeasure of the world.

2. It informeth us that we have no reason to be displeased or overtroubled with oppositions, reproaches, and troubles for godliness' sake. God often in his providence sendeth troubles to heighten the price of profession, that it may not be taken up in a carnal design, and that every hypocrite may not take it up to hide or feed his lusts. Now when it is our lot to live in such times, they that are sincere should not be troubled at it; for then they have an happy advantage and opportunity to make their love to God more sensible and evident, when they do not serve him without cost. It is a finer and nicer debate at other times, to discern which is greatest in our hearts, our love to Christ or to the world, our esteem of things earthly or heavenly. A tried faith is sooner discerned, and God's suffering servants have a larger allowance of comfort. It is an happy occasion of discovering our sincerity; for you are now upon your trial, and more ample communion with God, and tasting the joys of the life to come. Surely these are truths which our Lord hath commended to our consideration: Mat. v. 11, 12, 'Blessed are they which are persecuted for righteousness' sake, for theirs is the kingdom of heaven. Blessed are ye when men shall revile you, and say all manner of evil for my name's sake; rejoice, and be exceeding glad, for great is your reward in heaven.' When we suffer for a

good conscience, we are to carry this cross, not only patiently, but joyfully.

Use 2. It reproveth those that put off God with anything. A sickly lamb for a sacrifice; yea, and grudge at their sorry services : Mal. i. 13, 'What a weariness is it!' Surely they are far from religion that can deny themselves nothing, that will perform a duty when they have nothing else to do, and deal reservedly, superficially, and unfaithfully in all their work, and still complain of tediousness and weariness in God's service; that think the time long, the pains too much, the cost too burthensome; can be content with a little labour perhaps, but it must not be tired too much: 'When will the sabbath be over?' Amos iii. When will the duty be done? Or it may be they will sacrifice some of their weaker lusts, or their smaller and petty sins, which yield them no pleasure or profit, but retain their great sins, wherein their souls delight; as Saul destroyed the rascal multitude and carrion cattle of Amalek, but spared Agag and the fattest of the oxen and sheep, 1 Sam. xv. 7–9; or as John destroyed the idolatry of Baal, which his interest led him to, but not the calves at Dan and Bethel, which reason of state was against, 1 Kings x. 29, 30; or as Herod did many things, but if John will touch his Herodias, he shall smart for it, Mark vi. 17, 20. Thus do they desire and hope to gain heaven at a more easy rate than an entire resignation of all to God. They may sustain some reproach, make some small losses, but to be undone by their religion, to venture reputation, estate, and life, and all, for Christ and his gospel, this they cannot endure to hear of. They can be contented to be distasted and despised by their open enemies, but so as to make themselves whole again by their own party, yield to many corruptions, and humour them, please them, as the young prophet, 1 Kings xiii. 14, 19. Oh, this is but carnal self-denial, yea, rather carnal self-seeking.

Use 3. Of caution. Let us not rest satisfied with the cheaper part of religion. No; you must be at some cost for God. They are self-seeking hypocrites that cull out the safe, the cheap, the easy part of their duty, and leave all the rest undone. A faithful discharge of your duty may bring trouble to the flesh, but it will bring comfort to the soul.

What is the cheaper part of religion I shall instance in a few things.

1. Outward profession; especially when our interests or education lead us thereunto. Alas! this is to serve God with what costs us nothing. Though it be the profession of God's stricter ways, when we have not that constitution of heart, and do not carry on that course of life which doth become such profession; for then you are but factionists; not of Christ's religion, but of his faction. God is no προσωπόληπτος, 1 Peter i. 17, 'No respecter of persons.' Herding with a strict party, while yet our hearts are not subdued to God, is nothing worth. Religion is not to be carried on in the world so: Gal. v. 6, 'In Jesus Christ neither circumcision availeth anything, nor uncircumcision, but faith which worketh by love;' Gal. vi. 15, 'In Christ Jesus neither circumcision availeth anything, nor uncircumcision, but a new creature;' 1 Cor. vii. 19, 'Circumcision is nothing, and uncircumcision is nothing,

but the keeping of the commandments of God.' It is no great matter to be of this side or that, while carnal, if there be not an heavenly, holy, mortified heart, and a sober, grave conversation.

2. A dull speculative approbation of what is good will serve no man: Rom. ii. 18, 'And knowest his will, and approvest the things that are more excellent, being instructed out of the law,' &c. The truths of God have great evidence, and reasonable men have some aptitude to discern it. Opinions are cheap things, and may be taken up and held without any great cost. Do they sway your love and practice? There is the chief trial.

3. Minding lesser while we neglect weighty things: Mat. xxiii. 23, 'Woe unto you, scribes and pharisees, hypocrites! for ye pay tithe of mint, and anise, and cummin, and have omitted the weightier matters of the law, judgment, mercy, and faith.' Ceremony rather than substance. No; there must be a uniform conscience; not make a business about small matters and neglect weighty duties.

4. Doing that which is good when no temptation to the contrary; Exod. xxxiv. 21, 'Six days shalt thou labour, and the seventh day shalt thou rest. In harvest and earing-time shalt thou rest.' They should rest then when it was a self-denial to rest, when their profit invited them to labour. To be humble when under; but lifted up, they soon discover themselves. Some will follow a good way while it is peaceable, writhe themselves into all shapes and postures, and distinguish themselves out of a sense of their duty, that they may avoid the cross, or be at any charge for God: Gal. vi. 12, 'They constrain you to be circumcised, lest they should suffer persecution for the cross of Christ.' They cannot live without honour, ease, and plenty; and therefore turn and wind any way to shift off the cross.

5. It is an easy religion to be more in public duties than in private. We have the greatest advantage to discover more earnestness of affection in private, secret duties, where usually we are slight, and slubber over things in an unhandsome fashion. Our Lord Jesus went apart into a solitary place, early in the morning, to pray the more earnestly, Mark i. 53. There we may enjoy most sensible communion with God, can most feelingly lay forth our own case. The spouse of the church is bashful, saith Bernard, and will not communicate his loves to us in company.

6. The external part of religious duties is more easy than internal. They that have knowledge and utterance may flow in expressions. The ring of parts gratifieth natural pride, and procureth our esteem with others; therefore the exercise of gifts will not discover a christian so much as the exercise of grace, faith, hope, love, humility, sobriety, mercy, mortification. Therefore should a christian measure himself rather by these things than the pomp of gifts: 'If I speak with the tongue of angels, yet without charity, I am nothing,' 1 Cor. xiii. 1.

7. It is more easy to reprove others than to reform ourselves, and to be more earnest in opposing their sins than to subdue our own. Many please themselves in invectives against the times or censuring others. It is a false zeal that is much abroad: James i. 27, 'Pure religion, and undefiled, before God and the Father, is this, To visit the fatherless and widows in their affliction, and to keep himself unspotted from the

world.' The crafty lapwing will go up and down fluttering and crying, to draw the fowler from her own nest. We have a nest of sin of our own; we are loath it should be rifled and exposed to public view, therefore we crack against others : James iii. 1, 'My brethren, be not many masters, knowing that ye shall receive the greater condemnation.'

8. Power and dominion of the truth over hearts is a far greater evidence of our sincerity than curious speculations or highflown notions: 1 Cor. iv. 20, ' The kingdom of God is not in word, but in power ;' James ii. 17, ' Faith, if it hath not works, is dead, being alone.' Be warmed, be clothed ; or, I have faith, relieving, comforting; this is best. A doing and giving is more than a bare attendance upon God in his worship : Isa. lviii. 5, 7, ' Is it such a fast that I have chosen ? a day for a man to afflict his soul ? Is it to bow down his head, as a bulrush, and to spread sackcloth and ashes upon him ? Is it not to deal thy bread to the hungry, and that thou bring the poor that are cast out to thy house ? when thou seest the naked, that thou cover him ; and that thou hide not thyself from thine own flesh ? ' Acts of charity are much better than formalities of worship.

Use 4. To press us to this self-denying way of serving God. I shall do it by these considerations—

1. How much wicked men can deny themselves for their lusts. There is not a verier drudge in the world than a carnal man. What cost is he at to satisfy his lusts ? nothing is too good for back and belly ; he can ransack the storehouses of nature for their supply, and all seemeth little enough to gratify those pleasures and delights which he fancieth. The world and the flesh engross his whole time and strength, he beginneth betimes ; the flower and freshness of his youth and strength is employed this way ; so that if God should break in upon him, and bring him to any sense of his everlasting interest, there is nothing but the dregs of age left for God ; the flesh and the world have his health and strength. If he promise anything to his Creator, whom he should remember in the days of his youth, Eccles. xii. 1, it is only his weakness and sickness. Carnal vanities have his first-fruits, and scarce his gleanings can be reserved for God and religion. In his age, how little is he reduced ! what commands doth the devil lay upon men ! and how laborious and grievous and difficult soever they be, this is no impediment. But in religion a little thing is grievous ; all proveth too much. It is a costly thing to feed any lust ; what large offers do they make ! Micah vi. 6, 7, ' Wherewith shall I come before the Lord, and bow myself before the high God ? shall I come before him with burnt-offerings, with calves of a year old ? Will the Lord be pleased with thousands of rams, or with ten thousands of rivers of oil ? shall I give my first-born for my transgression, the fruit of my body for the sin of my soul ? ' They had rather be at any pains than quit their bosom corruptions ; are more willing to promise what is impossible or sinfully cruel than kill one lust. How can a christian but blush at this, that he began with God so late, and that the best of his days were past before he thought of God ; and when he seeth the devil's martyrs, how they venture reputation, estate, life, soul, and all, for a base pleasure, and he can do so little for God ?

2. What a change it would make in the christian world if christians

of all sorts would put this question seriously to their souls, Shall I serve God with that which cost me nothing?

[1.] In ministers. Oh, how justly may God put us out of service, who have so often served him with what cost us nought! Surely, did we oftener think of this, we would be other manner of ministers than ever we have been. When we are entering into this sacred function and office, we would think what skill and industry is required to be able to guide souls unto their eternal rest; we would be more careful to get ministerial graces; that is to say, such zeal for God, such sound belief of the things whereof we speak, that we might not seem to speak of them in jest, and for fashion's sake. Such compassion over souls, for which Christ died, that we would warn every man, instruct every man, teach every man, that we may present every man perfect in Jesus Christ, Col. i. 27, 28. We would be more careful to get ministerial abilities and sufficiencies, such a stock of knowledge, speculative and experimental, that our lips might preserve knowledge, Mal. ii. 7; that we might be able to resolve cases, to answer doubts and scruples, obviate errors, convince gainsayers; not only fodder the sheep, but hunt out the wolves. We would not come to this work raw and unfledged, as many ministers, who are for the main sincere, do; we would not think that a few natural parts, or a little slight eloquence, would serve the turn. No; saith the conscientious man, 'I will not serve God with what cost me nought.' Every time we are meditating upon a word of exhortation, or thinking of attending God's throne, we would seek to find out acceptable words, and think we hear poor souls crying to us, Good sir, study for us. Certainly we would not serve God with what costs us nought. As the psalmist saith, Ps. xlv. 1, 'My heart inditeth a good matter,' baketh a good matter. It is an allusion to the mindah, or meat-offering. We would not come with a little dough-baked stuff, some raw, crude, and indigested eructations. Yea, we would deal reproofs more freely, as John Baptist told Herod plainly, Mark vi. 18, 'It is not lawful for thee to have thy brother's wife.' The flesh will be apt to say, This will be ill taken, this will procure displeasure or danger; but conscience will reply, Let him take it how he will, 'shall I serve God with what cost me nought?' The minister's conversation would be better, such as may be an example to others, such as may keep up the full value of his testimony in the consciences of men. He would aim at that singular holiness which becometh his station; for, saith he, 'Shall I serve God with what costs me nought?'

[2.] Let magistrates mind this, and they will be possessed with another spirit than most magistrates are. He will not be a careless Gallio, nor a partial Jehu, nor a lukewarm Laodicean. He will do justice, and be useful in his place; not only when his ease permitteth him, or his credit inviteth him, or may do it without any prejudice to his interests, but when his interests are in danger. He will not leave a duty undone, because trouble followeth it; when he is to contend with nobles, as Nehemiah; when hazards and displeasing attend the discharge of his office; for, saith he, 'Shall I serve God with what cost me nought? He doth not consult with inconveniencies, but duty.

[3.] Let common christians think of this in their constant duties towards God or men. Towards God. In general, he is resolved not to stand upon the ease of the flesh or the interests of the flesh. The pleasures and delights of the flesh will make us sluggish; and the interests of the flesh cowardly and faint-hearted. And then his repentance would be more full. When he cometh to enter in by the strait gate, there is required much sorrow and grief before he can settle his peace, or his soul sit easy. Now the flesh recalcitrates, and kicketh against this kind of discipline, as the bullock at yoking is most unruly; but he holdeth his heart to it by this, 'Shall I serve God with what costs me nought?' His walking in the narrow way, his mortification more full. If he findeth any bosom lusts or tender parts, they must be renounced; the right hand must be cut off, the right eye pulled out, Mat. v. 29, 30. Many do many things, but keep their Herodias. His profession is more constant, though he suffer loss of credit, estate, esteem. He is more diligent in the discharge of his duties. He dealeth righteously with men, though it be to his loss and hurt. He is more faithful in his relations, as husband, wife, master, parent, child, servant; when it is grievous. Soberly, when the flesh would crave an indulgence. What! shall I obey every vain fancy and appetite? The main care and diligence of his life is laid out, not upon the flesh, but the spirit, that God be first and chiefly served, and not self. They leave God nothing that will not give him their best.

SERMON UPON 1 JOHN II. 20.

But ye have an unction from the Holy One, and ye know all things.—
1 John ii. 20.

In the context you have a caution against seducers, who are represented under the term of antichrists, because they took upon themselves to be sent of God, as Christ was, and yet opposed the dignity of his person and the interest of his kingdom. For their number, they are said to be many, because they swarmed everywhere; and for their prevalency they had proselyted many of the baser and looser sort of christians; but the more solid were preserved untainted. And what was their preservative we are told in the text, 'But ye have an unction,' &c.

This is mentioned—

1. Partly to show the reason of their standing; not by the sharpness of their own discerning, but the enlightening of the Holy Ghost. It is the Spirit that confirmeth us in the truth of Christ's doctrine. *Hoc non docet eruditio, sed unctio*—Bernard.

2. Partly to comfort them. So many had miscarried, and been led away by this stream of error, that the best christians might be discouraged. But they had a teacher near at hand, an oracle, as it were, in their own bosoms, sufficient means and helps within themselves to keep them from these snares.

3. Partly to quicken them to the more caution. If they should be seduced, they had no excuse, having sufficient evidence of the truth of the gospel, or that Jesus is the Messiah, and so were fortified against those that would deceive them. In all reason it might be expected they should not swallow these cheats and impostures, having such experience and assurance of the truth.

In the words we have three things—

1. The privilege, or gift imparted to them, 'Ye have an unction.'

2. The fountain, or author of it, 'From the Holy One.'

3. The effect and benefit thence resulting, 'And ye know all things.'

Doct. The saints have a special anointing from Jesus Christ, to enlighten and confirm them in the truth of the gospel.

First this must be explained—

1. What is this unction or anointing? Probably the word alludeth to the holy ointment, the composition of which is described, Exod. xxx. 25; the figure of pouring out the Holy Spirit on Christ, his church, and ministers. Or if you will more largely refer it, anointing was for

two uses—to inaugurate men into any eminent office, suppose of king, or priest, or prophet; so the holy oil was poured on Aaron and his sons; and thus Jesus Christ himself was anointed; as Acts iv. 27, 'Against thy holy child Jesus, whom thou hast anointed;' which was done at the Spirit's coming down upon him. Then was his solemn inauguration manifested, and the authority and power of his mediatory office showed forth. 'God anointed Jesus of Nazareth with the Holy Ghost, and with power,' Acts x. 38. Now as Jesus was thus anointed, so were the apostles when the Spirit was poured on them, Acts ii.; and so are all ordinary ministers of the gospel, when furnished with the gifts and graces of the Spirit suitable to their calling. So are all christians: 2 Cor. i. 21, 'Now he that stablisheth us with you in Christ, and hath anointed us, is God.' So made kings and priests unto God.

2. For the entertainment of honourable guests invited to a feast: Mat. xxvi. 7, 'A woman having an alabaster box of very precious ointment, poured it on his head as he sat at meat;' Ps. xxiii. 5, 'Thou preparest a table for me in the sight of mine enemies; thou anointest mine head with oil, my cup runneth over.' So Ps. civ. 15, 'Oil that maketh his face to shine,' and 'the oil of gladness' spoken of in scripture related to the oil used in feasts: Ps. xlv. 8, 'Anointed with the oil of gladness above his fellows.' Jesus Christ, as head, was advanced and dignified above angels and men: yet his fellows or companions have a liberal effusion or communication of grace from the Spirit at the gospel-feast; there is an abundance of grace poured on them, to the refreshing of their souls.

Well, then, what is this anointing but the testimony of the Spirit given to the truth of the gospel? Now the testimony of the Spirit is twofold—objective or subjective, internal or external.

[1.] The objective or external testimony was the coming down of the Holy Ghost upon Christ and his apostles in a wonderful and miraculous manner, together with the many signs and wonders which accompanied the preaching of the gospel, whereby assurance was given them of the truths which they were to believe, especially that Christ is the Messiah: Acts v. 31, 32, 'Him hath God exalted with his right hand to be a prince and a saviour, for to give repentance to Israel, and forgiveness of sins. And we are his witnesses of these things, and so is also the Holy Ghost whom God hath given to them that obey him;' and Heb. ii. 3, 4, 'How shall we escape, if we neglect so great salvation, which at the first began to be spoken by the Lord, and was confirmed unto us by them that heard him; God also bearing them witness, both with signs and wonders, and with divers miracles and gifts of the Holy Ghost?' If there were no more in it than so, yet from heavenly truths thus asserted and assured to them they should not lightly depart upon every suggestion and insinuation from a crafty seducer, till they could bring something with as good or better evidence than those things which they had received. Christians should continue as they were.

[2.] Internal and subjective. And here I shall take notice of a threefold work of the Holy Ghost—(1.) Illumination; (2.) Conversion; (3.) Consolation.

(1.) Illumination; as they were enlightened by the Holy Ghost in the knowledge of the gospel, and the necessary things contained therein. Besides an object sufficiently revealed and externally confirmed, there is need of a prepared faculty, or visive power. Therefore an internal efficiency is necessary: Eph. i. 17, 18, 'That the God of our Lord Jesus Christ, the Father of glory, may give unto you the spirit of wisdom and revelation, in the knowledge of him: the eyes of your understanding being enlightened, that ye may know what is the hope of his calling.' That is the work of the Spirit, to open the eyes of the mind: 2 Cor. iv. 6, 'God, who commanded the light to shine out of darkness, hath shined into our hearts, to give the light of the knowledge of the glory of God in the face of Jesus Christ;' there is *lumen internum*, inward light. Therefore when Peter had acknowledged Jesus to be the Christ, Mat. xvi. 17, 'Flesh and blood hath not revealed *it to* thee, but my Father which *is* in heaven.' Human credulity is wrought by tradition, but saving faith and knowledge by spiritual illumination. When man leadeth us into truth, man may easily lead us off again. Education may furnish us with opinions in religion, and we may sacrifice some of our weaker lusts for the opinions we have imbibed by education, for men will not easily forego their prejudices; but it is the Spirit of God that settleth and confirmeth us against all contradiction; such a difference there is between taking up religion out of inspiration and out of opinion. It is the Spirit only that giveth us a clear perception and discerning of the truth, and firm adherence to it; because it removeth the incapacity or disproportion between the things revealed and the constitution and temper of our hearts: 1 Cor. ii. 14, 'The natural man receiveth not the things of the Spirit of God: for they are foolishness unto him; neither can he know them, because they are spiritually discerned.'

(2.) The mind is not only illuminated, but the heart sanctified and converted to God, and fitted for God, and so suited to spiritual and heavenly things: 'That ye put on the new man, which after God is created in righteousness and true holiness;' Titus iii. 5, 'Not by works of righteousness which we have done, but according to his mercy he saved us by the washing of regeneration, and renewing of the Holy Ghost.' Surely the renovation of the soul and the restitution of God's *image giveth us greater advantages*, both for the perception of truth and the retention of it.

(1st.) For the perception or discerning of truth from falsehood; for there are such impressions of the holiness, righteousness, and goodness of God left upon their hearts, that nothing can be offered unto them but whereof they may be competent judges by means of those dispositions stamped upon their hearts by the Holy Ghost: 2 Cor. iii. 3, 'Ye are manifestly declared to be the epistle of Christ, ministered by us, written not with ink, but with the Spirit of the living God; not in tables of stone, but in fleshly tables of the heart.' They can better taste doctrines, being freed from the distempers and delusions of the flesh, and may more easily scent an error; for there is something in holy, believing souls which is of kin to anything of truth represented without, or carrieth a repugnancy to it if it be error: Heb. viii. 10, 'I will put my laws into their mind, and write them in their hearts,'

besides the light of nature, doctrine of your deliverance and redemption by the Son of God, and your future glorification according to his
promises.   Therefore they have an advantage above other men: Ps. xi.
3, 'The Spirit of the Lord shall make him of quick understanding in
the fear of the Lord.'   He shall scent, or smell, or breathe of nothing
but what is pious and religious ; and therefore is more acute in discerning of matters of godliness, and what is agreeable or disagreeable
thereunto.

(2d.) For retention, or holding fast the truth of christian doctrine.
A man in his corrupt estate is more apt to believe Satan than he is to
believe God ; and the scale will more easily be turned against the
truth when the flesh holdeth the balance; especially where men among
professors of the truth are, as birds in a cage, still seeking to get out.
Therefore if the understanding be not cleared, and the will inclined to
Christ, and to God the Father by him, we shall easily fall off when the
temptation cometh with any considerable strength.   Certainly a man
is held faster by the heart than by the head alone.   Conviction may
breed an awe upon the conscience, but conversion suiteth the heart to
it.   Love maketh us quick of discerning, and firm of retaining truth ;
and for retaining there is something in a renewed man that taketh part
with Christ, and strongly biasseth and inclineth him to him : 2 Thes.
ii. 10, 'They received not the love of the truth, that they might be
saved.'   Truth looketh to be entertained as truth, and preferred before
any carnal interest.   Divines, when they open the nature of faith, distinguish of *certitudo evidentiæ*, and *certitudo adhærentiæ*.   There may
be more evidence in matters of sense than in matters of faith, but not
more adherence ; the one ariseth from the clear sight of the thing, the
other from the weight and worth of it.   I have not such evidence of
the world to come as I have of the things before my eyes ; but I have
such a persuasion of the certainty, which draweth me off from things
I see with my eyes, and so leave all that I see and have for that glory
which I never saw, but expect on God's promise.

(3.) Consolation.   This oil is not only the ' oil of grace,' but the ' oil
of gladness;' and the Spirit is a comforter as well as a sanctifier.   Now
when we have not only been enlightened and converted, but comforted,
found benefit by it, surely this will be a means to establish and settle
us in the truth ; for then there is a spiritual sense, or taste and savour-
ing the things of God : Phil. i. 9, 'That your love may abound more
and more in all knowledge, and in all judgment,' ἐν αἰσθήσει, sense.
And what use is there of it ?   'That ye may approve the things that
are excellent;' or δοκιμάζειν τὰ διαφέροντα, try the things that differ,
1 Peter ii. 3.   *Optima demonstratio est à sensibus*—the best demonstration is by the senses ; to know honey by description and by taste, or a
country by a map and travel.   Others have but the notion of things
contained in the gospel ; these feel the sweetness and power of them
in their own souls, Col. i. 6.   Now when a man must be persuaded,
not only against his knowledge, and against his love and his sense, desires,
hopes, against his very heart and his nature, and all his experience,
his new nature, and all the inclinations and notions of it, surely he will
not be so easily won as one that hath no experience ; there is something within that checketh the temptation.   Arguments have little

force against the inclination of nature and constant experience. There is *communis sensus fidelium*. Well, then, this anointing is the gracious operation of the Holy Ghost, whereby we are enlightened, regenerated, comforted.

Secondly, The author or fountain of the gift, 'The Holy One;' whereby is meant Christ, often so called: Luke i. 35, 'That holy thing which shall be born of thee shall be called the Son of God;' Rev. ii. 7, 'These things saith he that is holy;' Acts iii. 14, 'But ye denied the Holy One.' He was the first anointed, and hath the fulness of all grace in himself, therefore called Messiah: Dan. ix. 24, 'To anoint the Most Holy.' And from him this anointing is derived to his people, Ps. cxxxiii. 2, like the oil on Aaron's head, that descended to the beard and the skirts of his clothing. So that this holy oil is from Christ, and from him freely and abundantly dispensed unto his people. First Christ purchased it for us; secondly conveyeth it to us; for he shed his blood for us, and then his Spirit on us: Titus iii. 6, 'Which he shed on us abundantly, through Jesus Christ our Saviour.

1. He procured it for us: Gal. iii. 13, 14, 'Christ hath redeemed us from the curse of the law, that the blessing of Abraham might come on the gentiles through Jesus Christ, that we might receive the promise of the Spirit through faith.' Compare 1 Cor. x. 4, with John iv. 14, and John vii. 38, 39; the rock struck with the rod of Moses.

2. He conveyeth it to us: John i. 16, 'Of his fulness have we received, and grace for grace.' Christ is an head of influence as well as an head of eminence. It is by virtue of his anointing that we are anointed: 'Of his fulness we receive.' We go to God for it in the name of Christ. We receive it for his sake and from him; upon the account of his merit, and from him as our head.

Thirdly, The benefit, 'And ye shall know all things.' How is this to be understood? For omnisciency and infallibility is God's prerogative. And it is said of the saints that 'we know but in part,' 1 Cor. xiii. 9.

Ans. This universal particle must be restrained to the matter in hand. Two restrictions all will grant—

1. All divine things. Not secrets of nature, mysteries of trade and policy, or skill in worldly affairs. Heathens may excel God's children in these things. No; the holy Spirit, with his gifts and graces, is not given us for these ends: 1 Cor. ii. 12, 'We have received not the spirit of the world, but the Spirit which is of God, that we may know the things which are freely given us of God.' We have this Spirit to know our privileges by the gospel and the duties which belong thereunto, what is required and what granted in the charter of the new covenant.

2. There is another restriction which all will assent unto: all divine things which are revealed unto men: for Deut. xxix. 19, 'Secret things belong unto the Lord our God; but those things which he hath revealed, to us, and our children for ever.' Hidden things, not revealed in the word are to be left unto Jehovah, to do with them as he pleaseth; but it is our care only to regard those things which concern our duty and happiness; and for events or the government of his providence, to leave it to God.

3. In things revealed we must distinguish between matters that

belong to the plentitude of knowledge, and matters necessary either to salvation or establishment in the points controverted in that age.

[1.] Matters that belong to the plentitude and fulness of knowledge, as the gift of interpretation of tongues, knowledge of words, and the art of reasoning many matters in scripture. These things depend upon wit, industry, secular learning, and the common gifts of the Spirit. There are *dona ministrantia*, and *dona sanctificantia*, ministering gifts and sanctifying gifts. The carnal may come behind in no gift; for these things are for the good of the body rather than the person that hath them : 1 Cor. i. 7, 'He came behind in no gift.' And yet they were not the best sort of christians which the gospel speaketh of. But the Spirit of holiness is given us to another purpose, to bring us safe to heaven by drawing off our hearts from the creature to God, and from sin to holiness, and from self to Christ. A carnal man may excel in one sort of gifts above the sanctified in opening the significa- tion of words and phrases, methodically disposing truths, and in framing such rational deductions and pressing such arguments as are most apt to work on the heart of man. Indeed, where both meet together, ministering gifts and sanctifying gifts, there a christian is most accom- plished ; and when grace governeth his parts and quickeneth his parts, he bringeth most honour to Christ, and doth not expose religion to con- tempt, as others do ; but everything must be regarded in its proper place.

[2.] Matters necessary. These are of two sorts ; either—

(1.) Essential to christianity, and absolutely necessary to salvation. In these things the unction prevaileth : Ps. xxv. 14, 'The secret of the Lord is with them that fear him, and he will show them his covenant.' God will not conceal from them the knowledge of his will, so far as their salvation is concerned in it, the secret of the Lord, that way wherein we ought to walk, if ever we would be accepted by him. So that in the great fundamental truths the sincere christian hath the advantage : Mat. xxiv. 24, 'Insomuch that if it were possible, they shall deceive the very elect.' When learned, subtle men are deceived, the Spirit will keep the elect right.

(2.) Necessary to escape seduction, or the cheats of those antichrists that were then gone abroad, or might afterwards break into the church, to pervert the flock of Christ. In points not absolutely necessary, a godly man is more likely to be in the right rather than the ungodly ; he is under the promise of God when, according to light received, he walketh in God's ways : John vii. 17, 'If any man will do his will, he shall know of the doctrine, whether it be of God.' He is most faithful to his end, which shineth to him all along his way : Mat. vi. 22, 'If thine eye be single, thy whole body is full of light.' Having a single eye, he is most serious and industrious in the use of means ; and God's blessing usually goeth along with diligence. And so in improvement of common helps : Prov. ii. 3, 4, 'If thou criest after knowledge, and liftest up thy voice for understanding : if thou seekest her as silver, and searchest for her as for hid treasures ; then shalt thou understand the fear of the Lord.' He hath a measure and touchstone within him, the work of grace upon his heart, by which he can try doctrines, which do most obstruct or further the work of godliness ; not which please or displease the flesh; though yet good men, in some cases, may be misled with error.

2. Why this anointing doth confirm us in the truths of the gospel.

[1.] From the Spirit, who is the anointing which we have from the Holy One. And his effects suit with the nature of God. The conceptions which we have of God may be reduced to these heads—Wisdom, power, and goodness: these are the most obvious notions. Now the regenerating Spirit giveth us the effect of all these: 2 Tim. i. 7, 'God hath not given us the spirit of fear but of power, and of love, and of a sound mind.'

(1.) Wisdom, in making wise the simple by the doctrine of the gospel, Ps. xix. 7, as teaching the way to true happiness and salvation, and enabling them to walk in it. The wise men of the world cannot but applaud this course; and the dying are all of this mind, and acknowledge their own folly in doing otherwise.

(2.) Power: Phil. iv. 13, 'I can do all things through Christ which strengtheneth me.' In overcoming those appetites and desires by which the rest of the world are mastered and captivated. To be contented with their portion; to animate them against all the terrors of the world, and subdue the delights of the flesh, that they may mind the things of another world, and so have comfort in life and death.

(3.) Goodness. It discovereth the greatest love to mankind that possibly can be conceived, both in the way and the end; redemption by Christ, and the glory prepared for believers. Love becometh the very constitution of our souls: 1 John iv. 7, 8, 'Let us love one another: for love is of God; and every one that loveth is born of God, and knoweth God. He that loveth not, knoweth not God,' &c. And moral goodness in the way we are to walk in, which is the way of holiness, without any respect to fleshly pleasure or interest, and through obedience to God: 1 Peter iv. 2, 'That he no longer should live the rest of his time in the flesh, to the lusts of men, but to the will of God.' Now the soul thus formed by the Spirit, where shall he find such a discovery of God? What profession is there that can possess us with a new spirit, and such a spirit as the christian religion doth? This begets a spirit that beareth the lively image and impress of God, where it hath its natural effects on the souls of men. Half christians go beyond others in such gifts as God giveth not to the heathen world; but especially through christians, therefore rejecteth other ways.

[2.] From the nature of this enlightening or knowledge of the truth which the Spirit worketh in us. It is not a bare conjecture, but a certain establishing knowledge: John vi. 69, 'We believe, and are sure, that thou art Christ, the Son of the living God;' John xvii. 8, 'They have known surely that I came out from thee.' So that the soul is willing to adhere to it with the loss of all. A slight perfunctory apprehension is soon shaken, either by subtlety or violence; but this is firm and strong.

[3.] Those who are anointed are sanctified and consecrated to God, and so under the care and protection of his special providence. Anointing hath the notion of consecrating, and setting apart for some holy use, for God's special service. As Christ as mediator; and so christians in their proportion, as his servants, and instruments of his

glory in the world; they are qualified for it by the gifts and graces of
his Spirit: 2 Peter ii. 9, 'Ye are a chosen generation, a royal priesthood, an holy nation, a peculiar people, that ye should show forth the
praises of him who hath called you out of darkness into light.' Now
God is very chary and tender of such: Ps. cv. 15, 'Touch not mine
anointed.' They are particularly owned by God, that none might dare
to do them the least injury. Now as it is so in God's outward government by his providence, so in his internal government by his Spirit;
God looketh after them more than others, that they may take no hurt
nor annoyance.

[4.] This anointing giveth them familiar acquaintance with God,
Christ, and the Spirit. Christ's sheep will hear his voice, and will not
hear the voice of strangers, John x. 5. They have a spirit of discerning: John xiv. 17, 'Ye know him; for he dwelleth in you, and shall be
in you.' The poor infant knoweth his mother's milk, puketh if suckled
by a strange nurse, 1 Peter ii. 2, ἄδολον γάλα. Hominem olet homo,
the man in it: 'The world heareth them,' 1 John iv. 5. Besides literal
instruction, they have the advantage of knowledge and experience.

Use 1. To persuade us to get this anointing. If we pretend to
christianity, where is our unction, the virtue and efficacy of it, for the
renewing and sanctifying of our hearts?

1. You are christians only in name if you want it; of the letter, and
not of the spirit; that take up your religion upon trust, have only the
form of it. Ignorant and profane persons, have they this choice anointing? May you not as well call a dunghill a perfume, or tainted grease
a sweet oil, as to count them to have this spiritual anointing who roll
themselves in the filth and vomit of sin, as the common rabble of
nominal christians do? If you have this anointing indeed, your whole
life will be a sweet savour or a precious odour. One dead fly, one base
lust cherished, spoileth the whole box of ointment, Eccles. x. 1.

2. If you have this unction, you have a great advantage against error
and infidelity. We live in a time wherein there are many antichrists;
now he that hath an unction from the Holy One hath an evidence always
at hand to refute what is contrary to sound doctrine; something in his
bosom that will not permit him to hearken to popery and other errors.
Disputes are long, and managed with great subtlety; and as they are
backed with violence, we may be strangely perverted and blinded by
interests; nothing will be our safety but a sound experience of the religion we do profess, of the virtue, power, comfort, and sweetness of it.
God's Spirit is the seal of any doctrine, and our anointing is our establishment: 2 Cor. i. 21, 'He which establisheth us with you in Christ,
and hath anointed us, is God.' I do not say you should not look after
other things, a sound understanding of the truth in controversy; but
there will be your best preservative, which will not easily suffer them
to change their religion.

3. If you have this unction, your own interest in Christ and eternal
life is secured to you: 2 Cor. i. 22, 'Who hath also sealed us, and given
the earnest of the Spirit in our hearts;' Eph. i. 13, 14, 'In whom also,
after that ye believed, ye were sealed with the holy Spirit of promise
which is the earnest of our inheritance.' That which is the seal of religion is the seal of those that profess it. The Spirit of sanctification

subduing our corruptions, sanctifying our natures, and enabling us to do the will of God, and causing us to live in the sweet and delightful forethoughts of the life to come. This is your seal and earnest, and this is nothing but the unction spoken of in the text. Ordinary men have a reasonable nature ; common christians, those common gifts which he giveth not to the heathen world ; but the true christians have a divine nature, or the sanctifying Spirit, as their great evidence. This is given unto none but God's children. The case is determined against you if you have not this anointing : Rom. viii. 9, 'If any man have not the Spirit of Christ, he is none of his.' But for you, if you have, 1 John iv. 13, 'Hereby know we that we dwell in him, and he in us, because he hath given us of his Spirit.' Therefore without this you can have no sound comfort ; but have it, and you carry about the matter of continual joy.

4. By having this unction we are more quickened to do what we know, and to be true to the religion which we do profess ; because the truth then lieth near our hearts, and so likely to work more effectually than what is at a great distance : 1 Thes. i. 5, 6, 'Our gospel came to you not in word only, but in power, and in the Holy Ghost, and in much assurance. And ye became followers of us, and of the Lord, having received the word in much affliction, with joy of the Holy Ghost ;' 1 Thes. ii. 13, 'We thank God without ceasing, because when ye received the word of God, ye received it not as the word of men, but as the word of God, which effectually worketh in you that believe.' This unction maketh a real change in the soul : 2 Cor. iii. 8, 'We are changed into the same image, from glory to glory, even as by the Spirit of the Lord.' If there be but a form of knowledge, there will be but a form of godliness. But where this anointing is, there we are made partakers of the divine nature, and live an holy life.

What shall we do to get this unction ? I answer—

1. Beg it of God for Christ's sake, who purchased it for you, and who is ready to give you this spiritual eye-salve : Rev. iii. 18, 'Anoint thine eyes with eye-salve, that thou mayest see.' It is his office to dispense this oil, and he will dispense it freely and liberally ; for he had this power to this end and purpose. Christ taught us to pray for the Spirit.

2. Be diligent in the use of the means of grace, whereby you get the Spirit, or further measures and degrees of it. The ministration of the Spirit : 2 Cor. iii. 8 ; the word : Acts x. 44, 'The Holy Ghost fell on all them which heard the word ;' the Lord's supper : 1 Cor. xii. 13, 'By one Spirit we are all baptized into one body.' Manna came down in the dew, so the Spirit in the doctrine which distils as the dew ; so communion with the saints in all the ordinances of Christ : Ps. cxxxiii. 2, 'It is like the precious ointment on the head, that ran down upon the beard, even Aaron's, which ran down on the skirts of his garment.' The Spirit of grace is a spirit of communion. Therefore we read of the unity of the Spirit, Eph. iv. 3. When they were of one heart and one mind, then had they most plentiful effusion of the Holy Ghost.

3. Do not grieve the Spirit : Eph. iv. 30, 'Grieve not the holy Spirit of God, whereby ye are sealed unto the day of redemption.' How is the Spirit grieved ? By some one heinous provoking transgression, or

by living in a course of known sin, pride, worldliness, or sensuality.
If we wound conscience, and be secretly false to the religion which we
do profess, or have pleasure in unrighteousness, we lie open to temptations, to error and falsehood, provoke God to withhold discerning
light, and cannot know whether we have the Spirit of God or no.
Loose and careless christians are always weak in the knowledge of the
truth.

4. Let us improve our anointing, and discover it in all companies,
temptations, exercises, businesses. Wherever you come, show forth
the fragrancy of your good ointments. In your converse with God, pray
in the Holy Ghost, Jude 20; that is, pray as one that hath an unction,
with a savoury spirit, and enlarged affections. In thy converse with
men, all thy words and actions must savour of this ointment: Prov.
xxvii. 9, 'Ointment and perfume rejoice the heart; so doth the sweetness of a man's friend by hearty counsel.' In your temptations to
sluggish negligence in the spiritual life: Heb. ii. 3, 'How shall we
escape, if we neglect so great salvation?' If to downright unbelief,
there is somewhat written upon his heart that is contrary, a sense of
God and heaven there that cannot be blotted out. If by a seducer
without, it is not the regenerate, well-grounded, and experienced christians, but the loose and superficial sort, that are in most danger, like
light chaff. They that know the truth, and are made free by the truth,
the word of God will abide in them. Disciples indeed will not start
from Christ, though those in name and title often did: John viii. 31,
32, 'If ye continue in my word, then are ye my disciples indeed; and
ye shall know the truth, and the truth shall make you free.'

5. Do not abuse or make an ill use of this teaching which you have
by the anointing.

[1.] Not to rashness and self-confidence. We may be apt to do so.
Though the anointing teacheth us all things, yet three things are still
necessary—(1.) Scripture, or an outward word; for that is still God's
instrument to beget and increase faith and obedience: John xvii. 20,
'Neither pray I for these alone, but for them also which shall believe
on me through their word.' There is but one gospel, and no other to
be expected: Gal. i. 7, 8, 'Which is not another; but there be some
that trouble you, and would pervert the gospel of Christ: but though
we, or an angel from heaven, preach any other gospel unto you than that
which we have preached unto you, let him be accursed.' The Spirit is
never given to detract anything from the authority of the word. (2.)
Ministers and teachers: Eph. iv. 11, 'And he gave some apostles, and
some pastors and teachers.' These are instituted by Christ, so appointed
by the Spirit: Acts xx. 28, 'Take heed to yourselves, and to the flock
over the which the Holy Ghost hath made you overseers.' The Spirit
would never contradict himself. (3.) The Spirit himself: 1 Cor. iii.
7, 'So neither is he that planteth anything, nor he that watereth,' &c.
The spirit must breathe on his own graces, and assist the soul in the
exercise of them. It is our advantage that he is at hand to excite our
faith, that there is a preparation already.

[2.] Do not abuse it to pride and boasting that we have the Spirit,
and contemning those who excel us in useful knowledge: Jude 19,
'These be they who separate themselves, sensual, having not the

Spirit.' Those men have not most of the Spirit who boast most of it:
1 Cor. viii. 2, ' If a man think he knoweth anything, he knoweth nothing
yet as he ought to know.' This anointing is given us to see our sinful-
ness, and need of Christ and his grace, and the excellency of the life to
come. There are several ages: 1 John ii. 13, 14, ' I write unto you,
fathers, because ye have known him that is from the beginning. I
write unto you, young men, because ye have overcome the wicked one,'
&c., Heb. xii. 13, 14. Some have senses exercised more than others ; all
have not a full measure of knowledge at first. Babes, young men,
fathers ; some truths harder, some easier.

[3.] Not to security, as if infallible. Though he that hath this anointing be not so easily carried into error, and do not so obstinately continue
in it, for it is impossible for him to live in a gross error as well as in a
gross sin, yet they may err in lesser things, which may occasion much
trouble to the church. Yea, they may be led into some dangerous
error for a while, especially when they have grieved the Spirit, and
blotted that character of gospel-truth which was impressed upon their
souls ; therefore must live in a constant dependence, and holy jealousy of
themselves: 1 Cor. x. 12, ' Let him that thinketh he standeth take heed
lest he fall.'

[4.] Not to idleness and laziness ; for still we must cry for knowledge, and dig for understanding as for choice silver, Prov. ii. 3, 4, 5.
And it is the character of the good man, Ps. i. 2, ' His delight is in the
law of the Lord, and in his law doth he meditate day and night.' It is
a vile abuse of this heavenly privilege to make the Spirit a patron of
negligence, and indulging the ease of the flesh ; as if a good wit in
secular learning should never study. So as if meditation were needless
because they have the Spirit. Avoid these things, handle the matter
as the new nature directs, and it will be a great help to you.

SERMON UPON HEBREWS XII. 24.

And to the blood of sprinkling, that speaketh better things than that of Abel.—HEB. xii. 24.

In the context, the privileges of our being brought into a gospel state are reckoned up. Among other things, these two are of principal regard—That we are acquainted with the true Mediator, and the true ransom which he hath paid for our souls. (1.) The true Mediator; in the former part of the verse, 'And to Jesus, the mediator of the new covenant.' (2.) The true ransom ; that is in the text, 'And to the blood of sprinkling,' &c. In which words the blood of Christ is set forth by two things—

1. By the application of it, 'The blood of sprinkling.'
2. By the virtue and efficacy of it, 'Which speaketh better things than the blood of Abel.'

The worth and value of it is set forth by a comparison, where take notice—(1.) Of the things compared, Christ's blood and Abel's blood. (2.) Wherein they agree ; they both speak. (3.) The preference of Christ's blood ; κρείττονα, the blood of Christ speaketh better things.

The doctrines are two—

1. Those who have entered into the gospel state have the blood of Christ applied to their hearts and consciences.
2. The blood of Christ applied to the penitent believer's heart and conscience is of great value and efficacy with God.

The first point is grounded upon that term, 'The blood of sprinkling.' The second upon the other branch, 'That it speaketh better things.'

For the first, we read in scripture of blood shed and blood sprinkled. (1.) Of blood shed : Heb. ix. 22, 'Without the shedding of blood there is no remission.' Therefore Christ's blood was shed for the remission of sins. There can be no propitiation for sin without the expiation of it. The expiation of sin is by suffering the punishment due *to* it. Now the punishment was suffered when Christ was made sin for us : 2 Cor. v. 21, 'He hath made him to be sin for us who knew no sin, that we might be made the righteousness of God in him.' A curse for us : Gal. iii. 13, 'Christ hath redeemed us from the curse of the law, being made a curse for us.' (2.) We are to speak of blood sprinkled, that is, actually applied, for all believers are sprinkled with it. Blood shed hath a cleansing power and virtue, but blood sprinkled doth actually cleanse and purify from sin, when this is applied to us in particular. The 'blood of sprinkling' is not only spoken of in the text, but in many other places: 1 Peter i. 2, 'Through the sanctification of the Spirit unto obedience, and sprinkling of the blood of Jesus.' This sprinkling relateth unto the law customs, wherein, after the shedding of the blood of the sacrifice, it was sprinkled. A threefold sprinkling I shall take notice of—

1. The first was the sprinkling of the door-posts with the blood of the paschal lamb, to save the house from the stroke of the revenging angel: Heb. xi. 28, 'Through faith he kept the passover, and the sprinkling of blood, lest he that destroyed the first-born should touch them;' with Exod. xii. 22, 'Ye shall take a bunch of hyssop, and dip it in the blood that is in the bason, and strike the lintel and the two side-posts with the blood that is in the bason,' which was a type of our deliverance by Christ. Blood sprinkled was a mark of preservation; and the scripture often sets out the heart by a door, which, being opened, giveth entrance to God. Christ hath borne all that wrath which was due for their breach of the law, that so deserved wrath might pass over all his redeemed ones, to whom his blood is applied; as the destroying angel passed by all those whose door-posts were sprinkled with the blood of the paschal lamb.

2. Another solemn sprinkling that I shall take notice of was when God entered into covenant with the people of the Jews; and the blood of the sacrifice, called there 'the blood of the covenant,' was to be sprinkled half upon the altar and half upon the people, Exod. xxiv. 8. You have the story of it there at large. There was an altar built to represent God, the first and chief party in the covenant. The *altera pars paciscens* were the people represented by twelve pillars, according to the twelve tribes, Exod. xxxiv. 4. Now the words of the law were to be read, and the people were to promise obedience, and God would promise to be their God; for the covenant between God and his Israel was to be established by mutual and willing consent. Well, then, to ratify it, blood was to be sprinkled upon the altar and upon the people, that is, upon the twelve stones which were set to represent the people, or upon the people themselves, to show that God took an obligation to bless, they to obey. Now the new administration of the covenant is also ratified by the blood of sprinkling. God accepted the blood of Christ, and is satisfied with it, and ready to give out grace; and we, by the sprinkling of the same blood, are comforted and enabled to serve him. This many think is the chief sprinkling alluded unto by the apostle, for the former part of the verse speaketh of Jesus the mediator of the new covenant, and then of the blood of sprinkling, by which God is reconciled to us and we to God. We must all be sprinkled with Christ's blood before we can be admitted into covenant with him; and being once sprinkled, it doth powerfully draw down mercy on the penitent believer. In short, Christ by his blood confirmeth the new covenant. One thing I cannot omit, that presently upon that sprinkling the nobles saw the God of Israel in his majestic appearance, and did eat and drink in his presence, Exod. xxiv. 10, 11. They saw the glory and presence of God in a clear and heavenly appearance, which is a sign of the favour of God towards them that keep his covenant; as, on the contrary, a dark or cloudy

heaven is a sign of God's displeasure. This did not hurt them nor affright them; and their eating and drinking is a token of our joyful communion with God, being reconciled to him by Christ. When the altar is sprinkled, and the people sprinkled, when the atonement is made, and the atonement is received and owned, that is matter of rejoicing: Rom. v. 11, 'We joy in God through Christ, by whom we have received the atonement.' Then it is a blessed time, a time of holy rejoicing; then we may eat before him, and he will not lay his hand upon us, neither affright nor hurt us.

3. There was another solemn sprinkling, that is spoken of by the apostle, Heb. ix. 13, 14, 'For if the blood of bulls and goats, and the ashes of an heifer sprinkling the unclean, sanctifieth to the purifying of the flesh; how much more shall the blood of Christ, who through the eternal Spirit offered himself without spot to God, purge your consciences from dead works to serve the living God?' To the type of the red heifer spoken of Num. xix. There was a solemn sprinkling there for the purifying of the unclean, to which answereth the purging of our consciences by the blood of Christ; the one sanctifieth the flesh, the other the conscience; the one freed from such penalties as were by the law imposed upon souls for legal and ceremonial offences, the other from dead works, which pollute us before God; and so from spiritual evils and eternal penalties, and consequently that fit us for communion with God.

But from all these sprinklings this we find, that it noteth approbation.

Now in this first point consider—(1.) The persons; those that are entered into the gospel estate. (2.) The manner of application; how it is applied. (3.) The subject to which it is applied; their hearts and consciences. (4.) The certainty of the effect.

[1.] The persons. The apostle speaketh of such as are come to the new Jerusalem, to God the judge of all, to Jesus the mediator of the new covenant, and to the blood of sprinkling; that is, such as are entered into the gospel estate. Now the way of entering into the gospel estate is by faith and repentance: Acts xx. 21, 'Repentance towards God, and faith in our Lord Jesus Christ.' That was the sum of his preaching to Jew and gentile, to bring them to enter into the gospel estate. Repentance towards God, because we had revolted from our duty to him. And then faith in our Lord Jesus Christ is necessary, that those that have benefit by Christ should own the author of their deliverance, and put their cause into his hands, that he may reconcile them unto God. Repentance that we may acknowledge our obligation to his law, bemoaning our former misery, and devoting ourselves anew to God, to do his will and walk in his ways. Well, then, repentance is our consent of returning to God, as faith is our thankful owning of our Redeemer. It is Christ's business to bring us back again to God, from whom we have fallen and strayed. Our great end in entering into the gospel estate is that we may put ourselves into a posture and capacity of pleasing and enjoying God; and this is God's end in our pardon and reconciliation, and in offering us the benefits of the gospel. And therefore there must be a relenting towards God and a serious owning of Christ, or an hearty consent to his conduct, to be brought home to God by him, and so fully recover our lapsed condition. So Mark i. 14, 15, 'Jesus came into Galilee, preaching the gospel, and saying, The time is fulfilled, and the kingdom of God is at hand : repent ye, and believe the gospel.' When the gospel estate, or the kingdom of the Messiah, was to be set up, this is the way of entering into it, 'Repent and believe.' Which repentance, properly and distinctly taken, looketh towards God the Father, and faith towards Christ as mediator. To God we return, from whom we were gone astray by sin ; and to Christ, the means and way of our returning, without whom we cannot be reconciled to our heavenly Father, nor perform any acceptable service to him. Now surely wherever these two are, faith working by love, and repentance mortifying our sinful lusts, that in newness of life we may glorify God, there men unquestionably are entered into the gospel state, and are capable of the privileges thereof.

[2.] How is the blood of Christ sprinkled or applied to us ? Many ways.

(1.) On God's part by the Spirit, as the fruit of Christ's intercession. Therefore it is said : 1 John v. 8, 'There are three that bear witness on earth, the Spirit, the water, and the blood, these three agree in one.' The τὸ κρινόμενον, or thing to be proved there, is, that Jesus is the Son of God. Now the Spirit beareth witness to this, applying the blood of Christ to the conscience, and purifying and sanctifying them as with clean water. These are not one, as the three first ; but these agree in one ; partly as they establish the same conclusion ; partly as they do concurrently establish it; not singly and apart; not water apart, nor blood apart, nor the Spirit apart; but they all concur; the Spirit by water and blood appeasing our guilty consciences, and washing away the filth of sin, either comforting, or sanctifying, or regenerating us. So again : Rom. v. 5, 'The love of God is shed abroad in our hearts by the Holy Ghost which is given to us.' The business is what is meant there by the love of God ? I take it for the great instance of his love in reconciling the world to himself by Christ ; for it immediately follows, 'For when we were yet without strength, in due time Christ died for the ungodly.' Surely it is not taken for our love to God, but his love to us, which was chiefly seen in that great instance ; this is shed abroad in our hearts ; we have the effect, the feeling, and sense of the comfort of it by the Spirit.

(2.) By faith on our part ; for till we believe, the blood of Christ produceth not its effect in our souls : Rom. iii. 25, 'Whom God hath set forth to be a propitiation through faith in his blood.' Faith, believing the great love of Jesus Christ in shedding his blood for us, for the expiation of our sins, doth comfort us, and excite us to live in a constant course of new obedience to him who died for us : Rom. v. 1, 'Being justified by faith, we have peace with God, through our Lord Jesus Christ.' All that sincerely embrace the gospel are freely accepted with God in Christ; have their sins pardoned, live in a sweet amity with God. In short, Christ, as the means of expiation of sin and reconciliation with God, is only appliable to a man by faith. We enjoy this reconciliation by faith. God doth not actually admit any to the privileges of Christ's death till they do believe.

(3.) As a middle between both, it is sprinkled or applied by the ordinances of the gospel ; as the preaching of the word, and the sacraments.

(1st.) In the preaching of the word. As it is the great duty of the ministers of the gospel to sprinkle the hearts of the people with the blood of Christ, so to discover God's love and the virtue of his death, as to excite the hearers more earnestly to apply Christ, and take him home to themselves for their comfort and salvation. As Philip preached Jesus to the eunuch, so that he ravished his heart with him, and he could no longer be held from him : Acts viii. 36, ' As they went on their way, they came unto a certain water : and the eunuch said, See, here is water ; what doth hinder me to be baptized? And Philip said, If thou believest with all thine heart, thou mayest. And he answered and said, I believe that Jesus Christ is the Son of God.' The apostle telleth the Galatians that in the gospel Christ is evidently set forth and crucified among them, Gal. iii. 1, when he is represented with such perspicuity and plainness, and with such power and liveliness, as if painted out before their eyes ; and Col. i. 27, ' Christ in you the hope of glory, warning every man, teaching every man ;' Gal. iv. 19, ' My little children, of whom I travail in birth, till Christ be formed in you.' To have Christ so applied as that his virtue may be felt.

(2d.) By the sacraments. They are a means on God's part, and an help on yours, for the applying of Christ, or sprinkling his blood on your consciences. Baptism is the laver of regeneration, or a means to make way for the renewing of the Holy Ghost, shed on us abundantly through Jesus Christ our Lord, Titus iii. 5, 6. The blood of Christ is the fountain of all the grace communicated to us by the Spirit, though the water of baptism have an immediate respect to regeneration by the Spirit. In the Lord's supper, οὐχὶ κοινωνιά, 1 Cor. x. 16, ' The cup of blessing, which we bless, is it not the communion of the blood of Christ ? ' There we come to apply it. In short, all the ordinances are helps instituted by God to make way for the participation of Christ.

(3d.) The subject to which it is applied, the hearts and consciences of penitent believers. Under the law, the flesh was cleansed by the sprinklings there, but now the heart and conscience : Heb. x. 22, ' Having our hearts sprinkled from an evil conscience, and our bodies washed as with pure water.' That is, from that inward impurity and corruption whereof every man's conscience is judge and witness. Conscience is the most quick, lively, and sensible power of a man's soul ; so that when the heart is said to be sprinkled from an evil conscience, it is meant of a conscience unquiet by reason of sin, when a poor sinner, being sensible of sin, maketh hearty application of the blood of Christ for remission and pardon, and in all the disquiets of his soul runneth to the blood of Christ, as the only fountain which God hath opened for uncleanness : 1 John i. 7, ' If we walk in the light, as he is in the light, we have fellowship one with another, and the blood of Jesus Christ his Son cleanseth us from all sin.' Once more : Heb. ix. 14, ' Purge your consciences from dead works, that you may serve the living God.' The poor soul that is conscious to its own disobedience, and sensible of having displeased God by sin, is grievously afraid of him, shy of coming into his presence, till the blood of Christ be sprinkled and applied to it ; that freeth the soul thus conscious of sin from the guilt, impurity, and other sad consequences of it, whereupon it begins to have peace with God, and fitness for communion with him.

(4.) The certainty of the effect to all that come under the gospel. It must needs be so, for they are partakers of Christ; Heb. iii. 14, with the 6th verse. How are men affected at the first receiving of christianity with great hope and confidence in Jesus Christ, that he will do their work for them: to be partakers of Christ is to have his benefits applied to us. More particularly, they are justified and sanctified in his name, and by his Spirit: 1 Cor. vi. 11, 'Such were some of you: but ye are washed, but ye are sanctified, but ye are justified in the name of the Lord Jesus, and by the Spirit of our God.' We are assured that, if we are capable, if we have a conscience sensible of sin, and appealing to the throne of grace, and plead this blood, God will make us feel the fruits of it : 1 John i. 9, 'If we confess our sins, he is faithful and just to forgive us our sins, and to cleanse us from all unrighteousness.' When with brokenness of heart, as feeling the weight and power of sin, we bemoan ourselves to God, he hath left his faithfulness and justice at pledge with us that the stormy conscience shall be quieted, the filthy soul shall be washed and prepared for communion with God. But those who, being senseless of sin, are careless of the remedy, these feel no great effects of Christ's death in their own souls.

Use. Have you been sensibly acquainted with the power and virtue of Christ's death? Hath his blood been sprinkled upon your hearts and consciences?

1. Consider it is said: 1 John v. 10, 'He that believeth hath the testimony in himself.' What testimony was that? Look back to the 8th verse. The Spirit, by the blood of Christ pacifying his conscience, sanctifying his heart. Christianity is not only a matter to be believed, but felt. There is experience and spiritual sense, which serveth as a back and confirmation to faith, as a whet and incitement to love. Many hear of a mighty Christ, but feel nothing; these are without their testimony of religion, so in danger of atheism.

2. Consider how uncomfortable it will be for you if you only should be a stranger in Israel ; if the price be paid by Christ, and accepted by God for the ransom of our souls, and the liberty be proclaimed to us, and we through our own default and non-performance of the conditions, should remain yet in bonds: John viii. 32, 'Ye shall know the truth, and the truth shall make you free.' If he came to heal us, and we still remain, not only weak, but sick unto death, how uncomfortable will this be? Shall we receive this grace in vain, the offers and tenders of reconciliation and peace? 2 Cor. vi. 1, 'God was in Christ reconciling the world to himself.' It is that he speaketh of there.

3. Learn that it is a disparagement to Jesus Christ that you should so long profess his name, and not feel his blood applied to your hearts and consciences ; that you should rest in talk and notions, and find no more of his virtue and power, either in converting an hard heart, or in comforting a dejected spirit, or in sanctifying and cleansing a filthy soul: 'The kingdom of God standeth not in word, but in power,' 1 Cor. iv. 20. What! hath the gospel neither quieted thy conscience

nor changed thy heart? Hast thou neither effects nor sense; neither sanctification nor comfort?

4. You disparage the gospel, as if it were but a literal instruction, even as the law is to fallen man. No; there is a mighty spirit goeth along with it, to apply the truths of it to the soul: Gal. iii. 2, 'This only would I learn of you, Received ye the Spirit by the works of the law or the hearing of faith?' That is, by the doctrine of justification, by the works of the law, or by faith. He appealeth to their conscience and experience, that God giveth his Spirit to all that are reconciled to him. By the doctrine of the gospel saving grace is conveyed. The hearing of the law worketh conviction of sin, terror of conscience; but it doth not give you that Spirit that breedeth comfort and enableth you to holiness. It is by the hearing of faith, and from Christ, that we receive grace for grace.

5. If Christ's blood be not sprinkled upon you, it argueth some great fault in you. Either a senselessness of your spiritual condition; for till men be convinced of sin and misery there is no need of the blood of sprinkling, or careless despising of the fruits of Christ's death, and filling our hearts with the tumults of worldly business, that we cannot listen to the peace Christ's blood speaketh to our souls; or indulgence of some secret lusts, which darken all in our souls; or contenting ourselves with a literal christianity, resting in a traditional knowledge of gospel truths, or bare rational reflections upon them, and so sucking at our own bottle, and neglecting the Spirit, who is wont by the ordinances to apply Christ to our souls.

And how shall we know that Christ's blood is sprinkled on our souls?

I answer—The immediate fruit of his purging the conscience is serving the true and living God, Heb. ix. 14; that is the end of it. Under the law, a man, if he worshipped in his uncleanness, and before he was legally purged, defiled the tabernacle and sanctuary of God, and that soul was to be cut off. We cannot have free access with confidence and boldness to the throne of grace, nor serve the Lord with any expectation to receive mercies and blessings from him, till the blood of sprinkling hath been upon them. There are degrees of cleansing, so also of serving God. When we are fully cleansed from all sin, then we shall have full communion with God, and serve him more perfectly in the temple of heaven; but so far as Christ hath washed us in his blood, so far is he acting the part of a spiritual priest: Rev. i. 5, 6, 'And from Jesus Christ, who is the faithful witness, and the first-begotten of the dead, and the prince of the kings of the earth, and him that loved us, and washed us from our sins in his own blood, and hath made us kings and priests unto God and his Father,' &c. Peace maketh way for liberty of commerce; trading is revived again.

Doct. 2. That the blood of Christ applied to the penitent believer's heart is of great value and efficacy with God.

1. I shall explain it in the notions of the text.

2. Give the reasons why.

1. The value and efficacy of Christ's blood is set forth by a comparison with Abel's blood. It will be good a little to examine it—(1.) Wherein these two bloods agree; (2.) Wherein they differ.

[1.] They agree in these things—

(1.) That as Abel's blood was shed, so Christ's. Abel's blood, being shed, speaketh; so Christ's. Of Abel's blood it is said, Gen. iv. 10, 'What hast thou done? the voice of thy brother's blood crieth unto me from the ground.' Christ's blood hath a voice; it was not shed in vain; it pleadeth before the throne of grace on our behalf. Christ's intercession is not vocal, but real. The presenting of his blood before the throne of grace is enough; for that speaketh to God in our behalf. As the high priest under the law appeared before the mercy-seat with the blood of the sacrifices, we do not read of anything he spake: 'So Jesus with his own blood is not entered into the holy place made with hands, which are the figures of the true; but into heaven itself, now to appear before God for us,' Heb. ix. 24.

(2.) Both bloods speak; in the conscience of the sinner, and unto God. Abel's blood did speak in Cain's conscience, so that he was filled with terror and unrest; so that he went about trembling, saying, 'Mine iniquity is greater than can be forgiven,' Gen. iv. 13. Words of despair. And it spake to God; for he saith, 'Thy brother's blood crieth unto me.' And it is 'bloods' in the Hebrew, as if every drop of it had a voice to call for vengeance on Cain. So Christ's blood speaketh in the consciences of them to whom it is applied; it speaketh pardon, peace, comfort. It quieteth the soul as much as the other terrified Cain's conscience: Rom. v. 1, 'Being justified by faith, we have peace with God, through our Lord Jesus Christ.' And it speaketh to God, for he is pacified, reconciled by it: Heb. xiii. 20, 'The God of peace brought again from the dead our Lord Jesus Christ, that great shepherd of the sheep, through the blood of the everlasting covenant.' As having done his work, having pacified God for us. He was before an angry, an offended God with us, but now, by the blood of the everlasting covenant, he is propitiated and become the God of peace; by this blood our surety is enlarged, our bond cancelled, our peace is restored.

(3.) They both speak loud, and cry, so that God heareth. In Abel it is true, God is very tender of his Abels, of righteous persons; the injuries done to them he deeply resenteth: Ps. cxvi. 15, 'Precious in the sight of the Lord is the death of his saints;' Ps. lxxii. 14, 'He shall redeem their soul from deceit and violence; and precious shall their blood be in his sight;' that is, he so considereth it, and it is rated at so high a price by God, that he will not put it up. The cry of their blood is soon heard in heaven. Now the blood of the Son of God is far more precious; surely the cry of it will be heard in heaven: 1 Peter i. 19, 'With the precious blood of the Son of God, as of a lamb without spot and blemish.' If this blood be offered for the sin of man, it will be heard; it crieth loud in God's ears; for it is very precious, and will be esteemed there, however it is slighted in the world, counted κοινὸν, a common thing, Heb. x. 29. His blood *tot habet linguas pro nobis loquentes, quot pro nobis vulnera accepit;* every drop is precious.

(4.) It is a continual cry. Abel's blood did not cry once, but continually; for it is said, Heb. xi. 4, 'By it, being dead, he yet speaketh.' As he was the protomartyr, and Cain on the other side the patriarch of unbelievers: Jude 11, 'These go in the way of Cain;' but for Abel,

see Mat. xxiii. 35, 'That upon you may come all the righteous blood
shed upon the earth, from the blood of righteous Abel, to the blood of
Zacharias,' &c. Abel was the first we read of that offered lamb's blood
for sacrifice, professing thereby to seek his righteousness in the blood
of the Messiah; and for this sacrifice he was made a martyr, the first
of the order that suffered for the righteousness of faith. His blood
crieth with the rest of the martyrs, to avenge his innocency. The
carnal seed cannot endure such, but in all ages persecute them: Rev.
vi. 9, 10, 'And when he had opened the fifth seal, I saw under the
altar the souls of them that were slain for the word of God, and for
the testimony which they held. And they cried with a loud voice, saying, How long, O Lord, holy and true, dost thou not judge and avenge
our blood on them that dwell on the earth?' So Christ's blood as
yet speaketh, as if it were shed afresh: Heb. xiii. 8, 'Jesus Christ is
the same yesterday, and to-day, and for ever.' The virtue of it is
everlasting. The cry of this blood God daily heareth; it still speaketh
to him, to pacify his wrath and to pardon us; and it speaks in our
conscience, to cleanse it, and make it quiet within us; the efficacy and
virtue of it is everlasting, to all those who are made partakers of it.

[2.] The difference: 'It speaketh better things.' The one crieth
for mercy, the other for judgment. There is a difference in the end
of the cry. To understand this, we must look upon Christ under a
twofold notion—as a martyr and as a mediator.

(1.) As a martyr. So his blood speaketh as Abel's did, the same
things: 1 Thes. ii. 14, 15, 'They killed the Lord Jesus, therefore
wrath is come upon them to the uttermost.' As Cain's murder did so
much offend God that it moved him to avenge it; so Christ's blood
did so far offend God, that he punished them and their children, who
had said, Mat. xxvii. 25, 'His blood be upon us, and upon our children.'
They defied God's justice, and therein by their own mouth pronounced
their own doom, and wrath is come upon them ever since. But mark,
even here Christ prayed for them: Luke xxiii. 34, 'Then said Jesus,
Father, forgive them; for they know not what they do.' That prayer
fetched in many. Their nation was not destroyed till they rejected
the gospel, of which they had the refusal and morning market, and
had killed the Lord Jesus and persecuted the apostles, forbidding them
to preach, and so filled up the measure of their sins.

(2.) As mediator. So it speaketh better things, is presented before
God, not to desire vengeance on the murderous Jews, as Abel's blood
against Cain, but to obtain pardon and favour for believers and penitent
sinners. Abel's blood cried against Cain that shed it, but Christ's cried
for men, whose sins did cause it to be shed. Though we by our sins
did make the Lord to serve and die also, yet doth not his blood speak
against us, but for us. Our sins call for vengeance and condemnation,
but Christ's blood for pardon and reconciliation. This blood, as suffered
for the sin of man, and offered unto God, is so pleasing, so precious,
so highly accepted, that God for and in consideration of it is effectually
moved to pardon for evermore all that humbly seek benefit by it. In
short, this blood spake then when it was shed, and still speaketh
effectually before the eternal judge, as it is pleaded by Christ in his
intercession, by us in our prayers.

2. Why? Whence cometh the blood of Christ to have such a virtue and efficacy? I answer—

[1.] Partly from the institution of God.

[2.] From its own intrinsic worth and value, which lieth—(1.) Partly in the dignity of his person; (2.) The nature of the work. It was the highest degree of obedience that ever was performed to God. There was in it so much love to God, so much love to man, so much self-denial, humility, patience, such a resignation of himself to God, as could never be paralleled; and therefore was most powerful to move God to mercy, who is so inclined to show mercy of his own accord.

[3.] This blood was shed with the greatest pain, and willingly, out of love to man. The sufferings were most intense; he was made a curse for us, Gal. iii. 13. They were attended with desertion, penal disturbance, and all that the law put upon sinners, either of loss or sense: Isa. liii. 4, 5, 'He hath borne our griefs and carried our sorrows, yet we did esteem him stricken, smitten of God, and afflicted. But he was wounded for our transgressions, he was bruised for our iniquities, the chastisement of our peace was upon him, and with his stripes we are healed.' His soul was heavy to death, Mat. xxvi. 38; he was deserted: Mat. xxvii. 46, 'My God, my God, why hast thou forsaken me?' So that as it sufficiently demonstrated God's displeasure against sin, so it was very pleasing and highly accepted of God. He omitted nothing that divine justice required.

Use 1. For information.

First, To show us the nature of Christ's intercession. On the one side it will not be enough to say that his merit and sufferings continue to deserve such things at the hand of God as we stand in need of, as if the pleading were only figurative and metaphorical; that as the blood of Abel pleaded against Cain, so the blood of Christ pleads for us to God. No; there is somewhat more in Christ's intercession and acting the part of an advocate for us. On the other side, it cannot be thought that he intercedeth with such gestures and verbal expressions as men use with men, or as he himself did in the days of his flesh, when 'he offered up prayers, with strong cries and tears,' Heb. v. 7, which did become the state of his humiliation, but not glorification. He intercedeth *non voce sed miseratione.* These are the two extremes; but what is the true notion of it?

There is in it—(1.) A presenting of himself before God; (2.) A declaration of his will; (3.) An entering of his plea; (4.) A recommending of our suits.

[1.] His intercession may be conceived to consist in his appearing in heaven in our name, where the Son of God in our nature presenteth himself as ready to answer for such and such sinners. His very being there in our nature speaketh his purpose; for there he is as one that hath made satisfaction for our offences, and performed his sacrifice without the camp, now gone within the veil, to bring blood to the mercy-seat: Heb. ix. 12, 'By his own blood he entered in once into the holy place, having obtained eternal redemption for us.'

[2.] It may be supposed also to include a declared willingness and desire in our behalf to have such requests granted, such sins pardoned. The declaring of his will is a part of his intercession: John xvii 24,

'Father, I will that they also whom thou hast given me may be with
me where I am.' The like may be conceived in heaven. So Aquinas
—*Interpellat pro nobis primo humanitatem quam pro nobis assumpsit
representando; item animæ suæ sanctissimæ desiderium, quod de salute
nostra habuit, exprimendo.* He intercedes for us partly by presenting
there his human nature, which he assumed for our sakes, and also by
declaring the desire of his holy soul for our welfare. But is there not
more? Certain it is that a proper and formal prayer is not contrary
to the human nature of Christ in that glorious estate in which now it
is, neither as hypostatically united to the Godhead, nor as glorified.
Not to the first, for that he had *in via;* yet he offered prayers with
tears and strong cries. Not to the second, for Christ's human nature,
though glorified, is still a creature inferior to God, and therefore
capable of prayer. Indeed, when he was in the form of a servant,
there was more subjection than now in heaven, but still he prayeth.
Therefore—

[3.] There is an holy, reverend, though inconceivable, act of adoration of the sovereign majesty of God, whereby the Mediator, now at
the Father's right hand, doth in all his appearing for us, as being the
head of the body, adore the power, sovereignty, goodness, and wisdom
of God, with respect to the covenant of redemption, and his having
merited the benefits due to him thereby, namely, the pardon of our sins,
our comfort and peace, the enlargement, safety, and success of his own
kingdom: Ps. ii. 8, 'Ask of me, and I will give thee the heathen for
thine inheritance.' By virtue of his paid ransom he may call for
those blessings which are necessary for those who come to God by him
His saying to the disciples oftener than once, 'I will pray the Father
for you,' John xiv. 16, implieth some address to God, even in respect
to particular persons and particular cases; an entering of his plea, or
a suing out of his own right in their behalf.

[4.] His presenting our prayers and supplications, which we make
in the behalf of ourselves to God, after he hath set us a-work by his
own Spirit: Rev. viii. 3, 'Another angel came and stood at the altar,
having a golden censer, and there was given unto him much incense,
that he should offer it with the prayers of all saints upon the golden
altar, which was before the throne;' and Heb. viii. 2, λειτουργος ἁγίων,
'A minister of holy things.' By his Spirit he furnisheth us with sighs
and groans, and then presenteth them to his Father perfumed by his
own merit.

Secondly, To instruct us what use to make of this 'blood of
sprinkling.'

1. When we are confessing of sin, or reflecting upon sin, and arraign-
ing ourselves, as it were, at the bar of our judge, remember, though these
sins deserve ill, and speak much ill against us, yet the 'blood of
sprinkling' speaks better things. There is hope, and comfort, and
peace, and pardon there. Plead Christ's satisfaction to God's justice.
Say, Our Lord Jesus Christ did take our sinful debts upon him, and
undertake to satisfy for them; and I know he made full satisfaction.
I renounce all other hope of pardon, and rest my soul upon his precious blood. If he be not able to save me, I am contented to perish;
but he is able to save to the utmost all that come to God by him.

Let this be in your thoughts when God makes you feel the terrors of his justice by an involuntary impression, or you are in a broken-hearted manner moaning for sin.

2. Remember it when you hear the offers of grace in the gospel; that God desires not the death of sinners: John v. 24, 'He that hears my word, and believes on me, hath everlasting life, and shall not come into condemnation, but is passed from death to life.' Surely this is true; for 'the blood of Christ speaks better things than the blood of Abel.' It is exacted of you to sprinkle it on your consciences. Christ shed it that it might be sprinkled.

3. Remember it in the Lord's supper, as often as that is celebrated, and you hear it repeated, 'Behold the blood of the covenant which was shed for the remission of sins!' then say, Surely it is so; for 'the blood of Christ speaketh better things than the blood of Abel.'

4. Remember it in your prayers, when you come to God for pardon or any blessing, that you may come with the more confidence: you have the blood of Christ to speak for you. Christ pleads it in heaven, and you must plead it on earth: Heb. x. 19, 'Having boldness to enter into the holiest by the blood of Jesus.' That bespeaks welcome and audience. Present unto God his Son's blood, and sue for the benefit of it.

5. Remember it in your last agonies. When you are summoned into God's presence, when every moment you look to come immediately before him: Let me with confidence go to him, and say, I have been a sinner; but the blood of Christ speaks better things, and I expect the full fruit of it; that it shall indeed cleanse me from all sin: 1 John i. 7, 'The blood of his Son Jesus Christ cleanses from all sin.'

Use 2. If the blood of Christ speaketh better things than the blood of Abel, it exhorteth us to many duties.

First, To enter ourselves into the gospel state, and to qualify ourselves to receive this benefit. The apostle saith, 'Ye are come to the blood of sprinkling.' Who are come? Penitent believers. The more you exercise faith and repentance—towards God, repentance; towards Christ, faith—or come to God by him, Heb. xi. 15, the more experience you will have of the virtue and efficacy of Christ's blood. Because these two are intermixed in the soul's return to God, and it would be too long to speak of the whole nature of them, I shall give you a few considerations.

1. Know yourselves to be sinners, condemned by the law. Till this be there is no work either for repentance or faith; for what need of turning to God till we know that we are turned from him? And the Redeemer hath nothing to do for stupid and senseless souls, that know not their misery, and regard not their remedy. There is a great deal of difference between our condition and our qualification. Our condition, when Christ cometh to bring us to God, is sinful and miserable; our qualification is lively faith. The being of faith is enough, though we have not the knowledge of it; but the being in misery is not enough; that must be known and lamented. It is enough for our safety that we have faith, though we know it not; but it is not enough that we are in misery, though we know it not. The covenant of God runneth thus: He that believeth shall be saved; not, He that knoweth

he believeth shall be saved; for many have faith though they doubt of their sincerity. Ay! but it is not enough that I am a sinner; but I must know myself a sinner, be deeply sensible that I am a sinner; for the offers of the gospel are made to the sensible, the broken-hearted, the weary and heavy-laden. A man never thinketh of returning to God, doth not lie humbly at the feet of grace, cannot be thankful for a redeemer, till he knoweth his misery and bewaileth it. Many have been welcome to Christ, that knew not themselves penitent believers, but never were any welcome that knew not themselves condemned sinners. Therefore there the work beginneth. The first awakening of the soul is by a sense of our misery and lostness; and this sense must be often renewed, for without Christ we are still in hazard to perish for ever, because of the continual failings in our duty.

2. A resolved will and purpose to devote ourselves to the Lord, to please him, and enjoy him: 1 Chron. xxii. 19, 'Now set your hearts to seek the Lord;' Acts xxvi. 20, 'He exhorted them that they should repent and turn to the Lord, and do works meet for repentance;' Heb. x. 22, 'Let us draw near with a true heart, in full assurance of faith.' The heart is bent and set towards the Lord, put into a fitness and capacity of pleasing and enjoying him, which we have lost by our folly and sin. By the fall we lost the favour of God and the image of God, and so were unfit both for service and fruition. The penitent soul findeth both.

3. It is Christ only taketh away sin, reconcileth us unto his Father, puts us into a capacity to please and enjoy God. Through him we may turn to God, and perform service and obedience acceptable unto eternal life: John xiv. 6, 'I am the way, the truth, and the life: no man cometh unto the Father but by me;' 1 Peter iii. 18, 'For Christ also hath once suffered for sins, the just for the unjust, that he might bring us to God;' Heb. ix. 14, 'How much more shall the blood of Christ, who through the eternal Spirit offered himself without spot to God, purge your conscience from dead works to serve the living God?' 1 Peter ii. 24, 'Who himself bear our sins in his own body on the tree, that we, being dead to sin, should live unto righteousness.' He died to weaken the love of sin in our hearts, and to advance the life and power of grace and righteousness. We usually make use of Jesus Christ for re- conciliation with God, but not so often for service and obedience. No; we do by Christ come to God, that we may walk before him in all new- ness of life. In short, when we turn from the creature to God, from self to Christ, from sin to holiness, we come under the gospel state; and true gospel faith is a faith that beginneth in brokenness of heart: Mat. ix. 13, 'I came not to call the righteous, but sinners to repentance.' And it is carried with an earnest appetite to the gospel: Heb. vi. 18, 'That we might have a strong consolation, who have fled for refuge to lay hold upon the hope set before us.' Thus are the heirs of promise described. And then it endeth in newness of life: Rom. vii. 6, 'But now we are delivered from the law, that being dead wherein we were held; that we should serve in newness of spirit, and not in the oldness of the letter;' for Christ died, not only to free us from that sin and misery whereunto we had brought ourselves, Gal. iii. 13, but 'we are married to him, that we may bring forth fruit unto God,' Rom. vii. 4.

Secondly, The next work is to sprinkle your hearts with this precious blood; for it is the blood of sprinkling that speaketh better things than the blood of Abel; and Christ shed it that it might be sprinkled, that it may not run a-wasting. The sprinkling or applying of it to ourselves in particular is by the Spirit on God's part, and by faith on our part, and by the ordinances as a middle thing between both, as a means on God's part to convey the Spirit, and an help on our part to excite and increase faith. Therefore this sprinkling must be interpreted with respect to the Spirit, faith, and the ordinances, as the word and sacraments.

1. Our duty with respect to the Spirit in this sprinkling is when we content not ourselves with a literal and exterior christianity, with being christians in the letter rather than the spirit, Rom. ii. 29, but look after the virtue, power, and life of the truths which we do believe, when, together with the doctrine of Christ, we receive the sanctifying and comforting Spirit : christianity is a thing without us, and at a distance, till that be done. The great bane of the christian world is that they satisfy themselves with notions, and do not wait for the power; and talk of Christ, rather than feel him, and taste that the Lord is gracious. Therefore our business is earnestly to wait for the stirring of the waters, and to seek after that life and peace which is the fruit of Christ's death; for the gospel is 'the ministration of the Spirit unto life,' 2 Cor. iii. 8. Here we get a taste : 1 Peter ii. 3, 'If so be that ye have tasted that the Lord is gracious.' We feel the power, know him and the power of his resurrection, Phil. iii. 10 ; when Christ is formed in us, when we are changed into his image, have a living principle in our own souls. Therefore our duty is to beg for this Spirit, to seek and wait for this Spirit, till the Lord Jesus pour it on us.

2. With respect to faith. Our duty is to be firmly persuaded of the sufficiency of all that Christ hath done and endured for man's redemption, and to apply it to ourselves. This blood is fully expiatory of sin, and a full ransom given to divine justice for all our wrongs. The blood of bulls and goats could not satisfy divine justice, nor expiate sin, nor purge the conscience, nor remove the curse ; but when the Son of God shall come, and die an accursed death, and shed his blood for us, there is enough done to repair God in point of honour, that he may be no loser by it, to signify God's purest holiness, to express his utter hatred and detestation of sin, to declare his love of justice, and to keep up the authority of his law ; enough to teach all the world that it is a dangerous thing to transgress it. Now this must be tried, and applied to the soul, that we may be able to say, 'He is the propitiation for our sins,' 1 John ii. 2 ; that we may build upon the foundation which God hath laid in Sion. By this faith he cometh to dwell and work in our hearts : Gal. iii. 29, 'If ye be Christ's, then are ye Abraham's seed, and heirs according to the promise;' Eph. iii. 17, 'That Christ may dwell in your hearts by faith.'

3. With respect to the ordinances, the word and sacraments.

[1.] The word. When you hear the offers of grace in the gospel, that God desireth not the death of a sinner, that he is willing to save all those that believe in the Lord Jesus Christ, or come to God by him, and to pardon and bless them ; let all this excite you to sprinkle it on

your own conscience. These blessings are held forth to me: 1 Tim.
i. 15, 'This is a faithful saying, and worthy of all acceptation, that Christ
Jesus came into the world to save sinners, of whom I am chief.' Here
God calleth upon me to put in for my share: Rom. viii. 31, 'What
shall we then say to these things?' Job v. 27, 'Know thou it for thy
good.' Bring it home to thine own heart.

[2.] Sacraments. By baptism we put on Christ, Gal. iii. 27. The
Lord's supper: 1 Cor. x. 16, 'The cup of blessing which we bless, is it
not the communion of the blood of Christ? The bread which we break,
is it not the communion of the body of Christ?' In the Lord's supper we
solemnly remember the death of Christ, as the price given for the life
of our souls; we come to behold him as the Lamb of God taking away
sin. There we hear of the blood of the new testament, which was shed
for the remission of sins. Say, Surely it is so, for 'the blood of Christ
speaketh better things than the blood of Abel.' You take it and drink
it for your own comfort; there it is brought nigher to you, and if you
do not delude yourselves, in quieting your consciences with an outward
form, you may go away with much comfort. Christ representeth it to
God in his intercession, and we represent it to God in our prayers and
desires, beseeching him to be reconciled to us for Christ's sake. By
these means is the blood of Christ sprinkled and applied to us, and we
receive more of the Spirit, and our faith is increased and strengthened.

Thirdly, Observe the fruits that accrue to you by this crying blood.

1. A comfortable sense of your pardon and discharge. When it is
so, then is the redemption applied: 'In whom we have redemption
through his blood, even the forgiveness of sins,' Eph. i. 7; Rom. v
9, 'Being justified by his blood, we shall be saved from wrath through
him;' as the sprinkled door-posts were from the destroying angel.

2. The sanctification of his Spirit: 1 Peter i. 2, 'Elect according to
the foreknowledge of God the Father, through sanctification of the Spirit
unto obedience and sprinkling of the blood of Jesus Christ.' The
power of the Spirit goeth along with the application of Christ; where
the one is the other is, and where the one is not the other is not.

3. Nearness and communion with God: Eph. ii. 13, 'Ye were afar
off, but now are made near by the blood of Christ.' Two things kept
us off from God. The rigour of divine justice; when we go to a God
offended, and appeased by no satisfaction; and the terror of our consciences, or our own guilty fear. But God is now propitiated; the
grand scruple is satisfied: Micah vi. 6–8, 'Wherewith shall I come
before the Lord, and bow myself before the high God? shall I come
before him with burnt-offerings, with calves of a year old? Will the
Lord be pleased with thousands of rams, or ten thousands of rivers of
oil? shall I give my first-born for my transgression, the fruit of my
body for the sin of my soul? He hath showed thee, O man, what is
good; and what doth the Lord require of thee, but to do justly, and to
love mercy, and to walk humbly with thy God?'

4. Ready access in prayer, with assurance of welcome and audience.
In the name of the Lord Jesus, we may present our persons and sacrifices and prayers to God: Heb. x. 19, 'Having therefore, brethren,
boldness to enter into the holiest by the blood of Jesus.' When you come
for any blessing, you may come with the more confidence; you have

the blood of Christ to speak for you. Christ pleadeth it in heaven, and you must plead it on earth ; present to him his Son's blood as the ground of your request.

Use 3. Of caution. Let us take heed of the slighting of the blood of Christ, and counting it a common thing, Heb. x. 29, κοινὸν. So we count it when we think it hath no expiating or purging power, no better than the blood of bulls and goats, or the blood of an ordinary man, yea, of a malefactor. But who are so vile to think so ?

1. It is done most grossly by all wicked apostates, who, for the fear and love of the world, cast off the truth. These seem formally to renounce their interest in Christ, and prefer every base thing before him : Heb. xii. 15, 'Looking diligently lest any man fail of the grace of God ; lest any root of bitterness springing up trouble you, and thereby many be defiled.'

2. It is done by those who despise the benefits purchased thereby, the favour of God, the image of God. They that slight anything purchased by Christ's blood slight the blood of Christ itself. Our respect to the blood is judged by our respect to the benefits. He that despiseth the favour of God doth not make it his business to get it and keep it, but preferreth every paltry vanity and poor corruptible thing before it ; hath no esteem of Christ's merit and God's design, who sent his Son to procure it for us. So whosoever doth not esteem the image of God, which standeth in righteousness and true holiness, doth not esteem the blood of Christ : 'Knowing that ye were not redeemed with corruptible things, as silver and gold, from your vain conversation received by tradition from your fathers ; but with the precious blood of Christ, as of a lamb without blemish and without spot,' 1 Peter i. 18, 19. It argueth lessening thoughts of Christ's blood, as if it were shed for trifles.

3. Those who lessen the virtue, merit, and efficacy of this blood by their distrustful thoughts. We cannot think high enough of this sacred and precious blood. It is that blood by which Christ, 'entering into the holy place, obtained eternal redemption for us,' Heb. ix. 12 ; that 'blood which purgeth the conscience from dead works to serve the living God,' ver. 14 ; that blood that washeth away all stains, 1 John i. 7 ; that blood which is the blood of the new testament, the ground of the everlasting covenant, Heb. xii. 24, wherein God promiseth remission of sin, eternal life, and all needful grace, upon condition of repentance and faith in Christ. Upon this blood the covenant is grounded, and all the promises of it made firm, unalterable, and effectual. Let us, therefore, with strong confidence trust to the efficacy thereof, and be encouraged thereby to wait upon God for grace, mercy, reconciliation, pardon, and finally eternal salvation. It is surely a great fault to think diminishingly of Christ's love and mercy.

4. Those who converse with the seals of the new covenant without preparation : 1 Cor. xi. 29, 'He that eateth and drinketh unworthily, eateth and drinketh damnation to himself, not discerning the Lord's body ;' μὴ διακρίνων, not putting a difference. There is a discerning speculatively and a discerning practically. The discerning speculatively is when we are able to discourse of the meaning of these mystical rites ; practically, when we are suitably affected ; not discerning when we carry ourselves as if it were common meat and common food. Tho

impressions of reverence, delight, holy awe, discover our practical discerning. To stamp upon the king's picture or coin in contempt is a contumely to the king. The injuries done to man, or killing a man, is aggravated because man is the image of God, Gen. ix. 6, James iii. 9.

Use 4. Direction to us what to do when troubled with the terror of sin. There is a cry attributed to our sins; the cry of our sins is gone up over our heads unto heaven. Sometimes they clamour in our consciences. Oh! remember the cry of Christ's blood; that speaks aloud in heaven, let it also speak in our consciences. Inanimate things speak by our thoughts; Abel's blood by Cain's despairing fears, so Christ's blood by the joy of our faith. Remember the apostle's challenge and triumph : Rom. viii. 33, 34, ' Who shall lay anything to the charge of God's elect? It is God that justifieth ; who is he that condemneth? It is Christ that died, yea rather, that is risen again, who is even at the right hand of God, who also maketh intercession for us.' And Paul's boast : Gal. vi. 14, ' God forbid that I should glory, save in the cross of our Lord Jesus Christ, by whom the world is crucified unto me, and I unto the world.' If you have felt the virtue of it, you will remember it.

A

FUNERAL SERMON

PREACHED UPON THE DEATH OF THE REVEREND AND
EXCELLENT DIVINE

DR THOMAS MANTON,

WHO DECEASED OCTOBER 18, 1677.

BY

WILLIAM BATES, D.D.

FUNERAL SERMON.

And so shall we ever be with the Lord.—1 Thes. iv. 17, the last clause.

The words are a consolation, brought by the apostle from the third heaven, where he was, by extraordinary privilege, raised, and saw and understood how great an happiness it is to be with Christ. And they are addressed to believers, to moderate and allay their sorrows for the death of those saints, who, by their conjunction in blood or friendship, were most dear to them. Thus he speaks in the thirteenth verse, 'I would not have you be ignorant, brethren, concerning them which are asleep, that ye sorrow not as others which have no hope.' The heathens, that were strangers to a future state, and thought that, after a short course through the world, mankind would be lost for ever in the dead sea, might with some pretence abandon themselves to the extremity of their passions; but christians, to whom life and immortality are revealed by the gospel, who believed 'that as Jesus died and rose again, so all that sleep in Jesus,' that persevere in faith and holiness to the end, 'God will bring with him,' are forbid, upon the most weighty reasons, to indulge their grief in excess. The union between Christ and believers is inviolable; and from thence it follows, they shall be partakers with him in his glory. The soul immediately after death shall be with Christ. While the body reposes in the grave, it is in his presence who is life and light, and has a vital, joyful rest in communion with him. And in the appointed time the bodies of the saints, those happy spoils, shall be rescued from the dark prison of the grave, and be sharers with their souls in immortal glory.

This consummate happiness of the saints the apostle assures from highest the authority, 'The word of the Lord;' and describes his glorious appearance so as to make the strongest impression on our minds: 'For the Lord himself shall descend from heaven with a shout, with the voice of an archangel, and with the trump of God; and the dead in Christ shall rise first. Then we which are alive, and remain, shall be caught up together with them in the clouds, to meet the Lord in the air: and so shall we ever be with the Lord.' Then death, the last enemy, so fearful and feared by men, shall be destroyed; and the captive prince of the world, with all the powers of darkness, and all other rebellious sinners that obstinately joined with him, shall be brought in chains before his dreadful tribunal; and after the great act of the universal judgment shall be completed, then all the saints shall make their triumphant entry with the captain of their salvation into his kingdom, and 'shall ever be with the Lord.'

The general proposition from the words is this : The saints after the resurrection shall be completely and eternally happy in the presence of Christ.

To make this supernatural blessedness more easy and intelligible to us, the scripture describes it by sensible representations; for whilst the soul is clothed with flesh, fancy has such a dominion that we can conceive of nothing but by comparisons and images taken from material things. It is therefore set forth by a feast and a kingdom, to signify the joy and glory of that state. But to prevent all gross conceits, it tells us that the bodies of the saints shall be spiritual; not capable of hunger and thirst, nor consequently of any refreshment that is caused by the satisfaction of those appetites. The objects of the most noble senses, seeing and hearing, the pleasure of which is mixed with reason, and not common to the brutes, are more frequently made use of to reconcile that glorious state to the proportion of our minds. Thus sometimes the blessed are represented placed 'on thrones, with crowns on their heads;' sometimes 'clothed in white, with palms in their hands;' sometimes singing songs of triumph to 'him that sits on the throne,' and to their Saviour. But the reality of this blessedness infinitely exceeds all those faint metaphors. Heaven is lessened by comparisons from earthly things. The apostle who was dignified with the revelation of the successes that shall happen to the church till time shall be no more, tells us, 'it does not appear what we shall be in eternity.' 'The things that God has prepared for those that love him' are far more above the highest ascent of our thoughts than the marriage-feast of a great prince exceeds in splendour and magnificence the imagination of one that has always lived in an obscure village, and never saw any ornaments of state, nor tasted wine in his life. We can think of those things but according to the poverty of our understandings. But so much we know that is able to sweeten all the bitterness, and render insipid all the sweetness of this world.

This will appear by considering, that whatever is requisite to constitute the perfect blessedness of man is fully enjoyed in the divine presence.

First, An exemption from all evils is the first condition of perfect blessedness. The sentence of wise Solon is true in another sense than he intended.

—— Dicique beatus
Ante obitum nemo, supremaque funera debet.

No man can be named happy whilst in this valley of tears. But upon the entrance into heaven, all those evils that by their number, variety, or weight disquiet and oppress us, are at an end.

Sin, of all evils the most hateful, shall be abolished, and all temptations that surround us and endanger our innocence will cease. Here the best men lament the weakness of the flesh, and sometimes the violent assaults of spiritual enemies. St Paul himself breaks forth into a mournful complaint, 'O wretched man that I am! who shall deliver me from this body of death?' And, when harassed with the buffetings of Satan, renews his most earnest addresses to God to be freed from them. Here our purity is not absolute ; we must be always cleansing ourselves from the relics of that deep defilement that cleaves to our nature. Here our peace is preserved with the sword in our hand, by a continual warfare against Satan and the world. But in heaven no ignorance darkens the mind, no passions rebel against the sanctified will, no inherent pollution remains. The church is 'without spot or wrinkle, or any such thing.' And all temptations 'that war against the soul' shall then cease. The tempter was cast out of heaven, and none of his poisoned arrows can reach that purified company. Glorious liberty ! here ardently desired, but fully enjoyed by the sons of God above.

And as sin, so all the penal consequences of it are quite taken away. The present life is an incurable disease, and sometimes attended with that sharp sense that death is desired as a remedy and accepted as a benefit. And though the saints have reviving cordials, yet their joys are mixed with sorrows, nay, caused by sorrows. The tears of repentance are their sweetest refreshment. Here the living stones are cut and wounded, and made fit by sufferings for a temple unto God in the new Jerusalem. But as in the building of Solomon's temple the noise of a hammer was not heard, for all the parts were framed before with that exact design and correspondence that they firmly combined together ; they were hewn in another place, and nothing remained but the putting them one upon another in the temple, and then, as sacred, they were inviolable ; so God, the architect, having prepared the saints here by many cutting afflictions, places them in the eternal building, where no voice of sorrow is heard. Of the innumerable company above, is there any eye that weeps, any breast that sighs, any tongue that complains, or appearance of grief ? The heavenly state is called 'life,' as only worthy of that title. There is no infirmity of body, no poverty, no disgrace, treachery of friends, no persecution of enemies : 'There is no more death, nor sorrow, nor crying, nor shall there be any more pain ; for former things are passed away,' Rev. xxi. 4. 'God will wipe away all tears from the eyes of his people.' Their salvation is complete in all degrees. Pure joy is the privilege of heaven, unmixed sorrows the punishment of hell.

A concurrence of all positive excellences is requisite to blessedness, and these are to be considered with respect to the entire man.

I. The body shall be awaked out of its dead sleep, and quickened into a glorious immortal life. The soul and body are the essential parts of man ; and though the inequality be great in their operations that respect holiness, yet their concourse is necessary. Good actions are designed by the counsel and resolution of the Spirit, but performed by the ministry of the flesh. Every grace expresses itself in visible actions by the body. In the sorrows of repentance it supplies tears; in fastings its appetites are restrained ; in thanksgivings the tongue breaks forth into the joyful praises of God. All the victories over sensible pleasure and pain are obtained by the soul in conjunction with the body. Now it is most becoming the divine goodness not to deal so differently that the soul should be everlastingly happy, and the body lost in forgetfulness ; the one glorified in heaven, the other remain in the dust. From their first setting out in the world to the grave, they ran the same race, and shall enjoy the same reward. Here the body is the comfort of the soul in obedience and sufferings, hereafter in fruition. When the crown of purity or palm of martyrdom shall be given by the great Judge in the view of all, they shall both partake in the honour. Of this we have an earnest in the resurrection of Christ in his true body, who 'is the first-fruits of them that sleep,' 1 Cor. xv. 21; ' He shall change our vile bodies, that they may be fashioned like to his glorious body, according to the working of his power, whereby he is able to subdue all things to himself,' Phil. iii. 21. A substantial, unfading glory will shine in them infinitely above the perishing pride of this world, that is but in appearance, like the false colours painted on the feathers of a dove by the reflection of the light, which presently vanish when it changeth its posture, or the light is withdrawn. Indeed, what can be more glorious than to be conformed to the humanity of Christ, the seat of all beauty and perfection? This conformity shall be the work of his own hands. And when omnipotence interposes, nothing is difficult. The raising the body to an unchangeable state of glory is as easy to the divine power as the forming it at first in the womb; as the sun labours no more in the mines in the forming gold and silver, the most precious and durable metals, than in the production of a poor short-lived flower.

II. The soul shall be made perfect in all its faculties.

1. The understanding shall clearly see the most excellent objects: 'Now we know but in part,' 1 Cor. xiii. The naked beauty of divine things is veiled, and of impossible discovery; and the weakness of the mind is not proportionable to their dazzling brightness. But when that which is perfect is come, ' then that which is in part shall be done away.' In that enlightened state the glorious manifestation of the objects shall as much exceed the clearest revealing of them here, as the sun in its full lustre one beam of light strained through a crevice in the wall. And the understanding shall be prepared to take a full view of them. Therefore the apostle compares the several periods of the church, in respect of the degrees of knowledge, to the several ages of this life: ' When I was a child, I spake as a child, I understood as a child, I thought as a child; but when I became a man, I put away childish things.' In children the organs, either from an excess of moisture or their smallness, are indisposed for the vigorous exercise of the mind; some strictures of reason appear, a presaging sign what will be, but mixed with much obscurity; but when the organs are come to their just proportion and temperament, the soul displays its strength and activity.

All things of a supernatural order shall then be clearly discovered. The contrivance of our salvation, the ways of conducting us to blessedness, which are objects of a sublime nature, will afford an exquisite pleasure to the understanding. All the secrets of our redemption shall be unsealed. The great mystery of godliness, the incarnation of the eternal Son, and his according justice with mercy, shall then be apparent. The divine counsels in governing the world are now only visible in their wonderful effects, either of mercy or justice, and those most dreadful; but the reasons of them are past finding out. But what our Saviour said to Peter, ' What I do thou knowest not now, but shalt know hereafter,' is applicable to these impenetrable dispensations. All the original fountains of wisdom, as clear as deep, shall then be opened. We shall then see the beauty of providence in disposing temporal things in order to our eternal felicity. We now see, as it were, the rough part and knots of that curious embroidery, but then the whole work shall be unfolded, the sweetness of the colours and proportion of the figures appear. There we shall be able to expound the perplexing riddle, how 'out of the eater came meat, and out of the strong came sweetness;' for 'we shall know as we are known.'

We shall see God. Our Saviour tells us, 'This is life eternal, to know thee the only true God, and Jesus Christ whom thou hast sent.' The beginning and perfection of our happiness consists in this knowledge. The Deity is spiritual and invisible to the eye of the body, infinite and incomprehensible to the soul. But we shall then so clearly understand the divine perfections, that our present knowledge, compared to that, is but as the seeing a dark resemblance in a glass to the clear view of a person in the native beauty of his face. God is most gloriously present in heaven; for according to the degrees of excellence in the work, such are the impressions and discoveries of the virtues of the cause. Now all sensible things in the low order of nature are but weak resultances from his perfections in comparison of their illustrious effects in the divine world. The glories of the place and of the inhabitants, the angels and saints, clearly express his majesty, goodness, and power. But in a transcendent manner he exhibits himself in the glorified Mediator. He is styled 'the brightness of his Father's glory, and the express image of his person;' not only for his equal perfections in respect of the unity of their nature, but to signify that God in the person of the incarnate Mediator is so fully represented to us, that by the sight of him we see God himself in his unchangeable excellences. This appears by the following words, that 'having purged us from our sins, he sat down on the right hand of the majesty on high;' for they respect the Son of God as united to the human nature, in which he performed the office of the priesthood, and took possession of his glorious kingdom. During his humble state, the divine virtues, wisdom, goodness, holiness, power, were so visible in his person, life, revelations, and miraculous works, that when Philip so longed for the sight of the Father, as the only consummate blessedness, 'Show us the Father, and it suffices,' he told him, 'He that has seen me has seen the Father also.' But how brightly do they appear in his triumphant exaltation! It was his prayer on earth, 'Father, I will that they also whom thou hast given me be with me where I am, that they may behold my glory.' Inestimable felicity! Whether we consider him in the respect of an object that incomparably transcends all the created glory of heaven, or in the relation of our head, on a double account; partly because he was debased into the form of a servant, and suffered all indignities and cruelties of sinners for us, has received the recompense of his meritorious sufferings, the triumph of his victory, 'being glorified with the Father with the glory he had before the world was;' and partly because every member shall be conformed to him in his glory: 'We shall be like him, for we shall see him as he is.' And all felicity and glory is comprised in that promise. The sight of the face of Moses when radiant had no transforming efficacy, for the light of it was not in him as its source but by derivation. But God is light essentially, and the sight of his perfections will be productive of his likeness in us, so far as it may be in a restrained subject. When our Saviour was upon the holy mount, and one vanishing beam of glory appeared in his transfiguration, Peter was so transported at the sight that he forgot the world and himself. How ravishing, then, will the sight of him be in his triumphant majesty, when we shall be transfigured ourselves !

2. As we shall behold God's face, know his most amiable excellences, so they shall love him as perfectly as they know him. To the illustrations of the mind there are correspondent impressions on the heart. In the present state our love is imperfect, and as fire out of its sphere, dies away by our neglect to feed it with proper materials, enamouring considerations of God. But it is not so in heaven ; there the divine sun attracts every eye with the light of its beauty, and inflames every heart with the heat of his love. The continual presence of God is in different respects the cause and effect of our love to him ; for there is no more powerful attractive to love him than to see him ; and love keeps the thoughts undivided from him. ‘God is love,’ and will kindle in us a pure affection that eternity shall never lessen.

Our affections, that are now scattered on many things, wherein some small reflections of his goodness appear, shall join in one full current in heaven, where God is all in all. We shall then understand the riches of his love, that God, who is infinitely happy in himself, should make man for such a glory, and such a glory for man ; and that when for his rebellion he was justly expelled from paradise, and under a sentence of eternal death, God should please to restore him to his favour, and to give him a better state than was forfeited. We shall then understand our infinite obligations to the Son of God who descended from the heaven of heavens to our earth, and, which is more, from the majesty wherein he there reigned, from the glory wherein he was visible to the angelical minds, and became man for men, redemption for the lost, to purchase immortal life for those who were dead to that blessed life. In short, then God will express his love to us in the highest degrees that a finite creature is capable to receive from love itself, and we shall love him with all the strength of our glorified powers.

3. Complete satisfaction flows from union with God by knowledge and love : ‘ In his presence is fulness of joy, and at his right hand are pleasures for ever.’ The causes and excellences of the heavenly life are in those words expressed. The causes are the influxive presence of God, the revelation of his attractive perfections, the beholding his face, the declaration of his peculiar favour. This our blessed Lord himself had a respect to, as the complete reward of his sufferings : ‘ Thou shalt make me full of joy with thy countenance.’ And his right hand his bounty, that dispenses, and his power that secures, that felicity. The excellences of this state are fulness of joy, and that without diminution or end.

When the soul opens its eyes to the clear discoveries of the first truth, and its breast to the dear and intimate embraces of the supreme good, beyond which nothing remains to be known, nothing to be enjoyed, what a deluge of the purest pleasures will overflow it ! We cannot ascend in our thoughts so high as to conceive the excess of joy that attends those operations of the glorified soul upon its proper object. But something we may conjecture.

[1.] Those who are possessed with a noble passion for knowledge, how do they despise all lower pleasures in comparison of it! how do they forget themselves, neglect the body, and retire into the mind, the highest part of man, and nearest to God! The bare apprehension of such things that by their internal nature have no attractive influence upon the affections is pleasant to the understanding. As the appearance of light, though not attended with any other visible beauties, refreshes the eye after long darkness; so the clear discovery of truths, how abstract soever, that were before unknown, is grateful to the intellective faculty. Thus some have been strangely transported with the pleasures of a mathematical demonstration, when the evidence, not the importance of the thing, was so ravishing; for what is more dry and barren of delight than the speculation of figures and numbers? Solon, when near his end, and some of his friends that visited him were speaking softly of a point of philosophy, by a sound of wisdom was awakened from the sleep of death that was just seizing on him, and opening his eyes, and raising his head to give attention, being asked the reason of it, answered, That when I understand what you are discoursing of, I may die.[1] Such was his delight in knowledge, that a little of it made his agony insensible. But here are many imperfections that lessen this intellectual pleasure, which shall cease in heaven. Here the acquisition of knowledge is often with the expense of health; the flower of the spirits, necessary for natural operations, is wasted by intense thoughts. How often are the learned sickly! As the flint when it is struck gives not a spark without consuming itself, so knowledge is obtained by studies that waste our faint, sensitive faculties. But then our knowledge shall be a free emanation from the spring of truth, without our labour and pains. Here we learn by circuit, and discern by comparing things; our ignorance is dispelled by a gradual succession of light; but then universal knowledge shall be infused in a moment. Here, after all our labour and toil, how little knowledge do we gain! Every question is a labyrinth, out of which the nimblest and most searching minds cannot extricate themselves. How many specious errors impose upon our understandings! We look on things by false lights, through deceiving spectacles. But then our knowledge shall be certain and complete. There is no forbidden tree in the celestial paradise, as no inordinate affection. But suppose that all things in the compass of the world were known, yet still there would be emptiness and anguish in the mind; for the most comprehensive knowledge of things that are insufficient to make us happy cannot afford true satisfaction. But then we shall see God in all his excellences, the supreme object and end, the only felicity of the soul. How will the sight of his glory, personally shining in our Redeemer, in the first moment quench our extreme thirst, and fill us with joy and admiration! It is not as the naked conception of treasures, that only makes rich in ideas; but that divine sight gives a real interest in him.

[1] Ut cum istud quicquid est de quo disputatis percepero, moriar.—VAL. MAX.

The angels are so ravished with the beauties and wonders of his face that they never divert a moment from the contemplation of it.

[2.] The pure love of the saints to God is then fully satisfied. Love, considered as an affection of friendship, is always attended with two desires—to be assured of reciprocal love, and to enjoy the conversation of the person beloved, the testimony of his esteem and good-will. This kind of affection[1] seems to be inconsistent with that infinite distance that is between God and the creature. But though it is disproportionable to the divine majesty, it is proportionable to his goodness. Accordingly our Saviour promises, ' He. that loves me shall be loved of my Father, and I will love him, and will manifest myself unto him.' And to confirm our belief of this astonishing condescension, repeats it, ' If a man love me, my Father will love him, and we will come to him, and make our abode with him.' In the present state, the signs of God's special favour are exhibited to his friends. Now he bestows on them the honour of being his sons, the graces and comforts of his Spirit, the precious earnests of his love, and 'seal of their redemption.' But in eminency of degrees, the effects of his love are incomparably more glorious in heaven. Here the saints are adopted, there crowned. There he opens all the bright treasure of his wisdom, the riches of his goodness, the beauties of his holiness, the glories of his power, and by the intimate application of his presence, makes his love most sensible to them. Oh the mutual delights between God and glorified souls! God looks on them with an engaged eye, as his own by many dear titles, and is well-pleased in his own goodness to them, and ravished with the reflex of his own excellences shining in them : ' As the bridegroom rejoices over the bride' (it is the language of divine love), ' so their God rejoices over them.' And what a blessed rest do they find in the complete fruition of their beloved ! All their desires quietly expire in his bosom. What triumphs of joy follow ! Can we frame a fuller conception of happiness than to be perfectly loved by infinite goodness, and perfectly to love him?

The supreme joy of the saints is for the felicity and glory of God himself; for as the holy soul feels no more powerful motive to love God than because he is most worthy of it, as he is God, a being of infinite excellences, and therefore to be loved above the dearest persons and things, even itself, so the highest joy it partakes of is from this consideration, that God is infinitely blessed and glorious. For in this the supreme desire of love is accomplished, that the most beloved object is perfectly honoured and pleased. In heaven the love of the saints to God is in its highest perfection, and they see his glory in the most perfect manner, which causes a transcendent joy to them. And this is one reason why the saints, though shining with unequal degrees of glory, are equally content. For their most ardent love being set on God, that he is pleased to glorify himself by such various communications of his goodness, is full satisfaction to their desires. Besides, in those different degrees of glory every one is so content with his own[2] that there is no possible desire of being but what he is.

[1] Aristotle.
[2] Sic itaque habebit donum aliud alio minus, ut hic quoque donum habeat ne velit amplius.—AUG.

4. The full joy of heaven shall continue without diminution or end.

First, The number of possessors cannot lessen it. The divine presence is an unwasted spring of pleasure, equally full and open to all, and abundantly sufficient to satisfy the immensity of their desires. Envy reigns in this world, because earthly things are so imperfect in their nature, and so peculiar in their possession, that they cannot suffice, nor be enjoyed by all. But in heaven none is touched with that low, base passion; for God contains all that is precious and desirable in the highest degrees of perfection, and all partake of the influence of his universal goodness without intercepting one another. In the kingdom above there is no cause for the elder brother to repine at the Father's bounty to the younger, nor for the younger to supplant the elder to obtain the birthright. The heirs of God are all raised to sovereign glory. Every one enjoys him as entirely and fully as if solely his felicity. God is a good, as indivisible as infinite, and not diminished by the most liberal communications of himself. We may illustrate this by comparing the price of our redemption and the reward. The death of Christ is an universal benefit to all the saints, yet it is so applied to every believer for his perfect redemption, as if our Saviour in all his agonies and sufferings had no other in his eye and heart; as if all his prayers, his tears, his blood, were offered up to his Father only for that person. The common respect of it the apostle declares in those admirable words, that signify such an excess of God's love to us, 'He that spared not his own Son, but delivered him up for us all, how shall he not with him also freely give us all things?' But to imagine that[1] the propriety of every believer is thereby prejudiced, is not only false, but extremely injurious to the merit and dignity, and to the infinite love of Christ. Therefore the same apostle tells us, 'The life which I now live in the flesh, I live by the faith of the Son of God, who loved me, and gave himself for me;' as if he were the sole object of Christ's love, the end and reward of his sufferings. And this appropriating of it to himself is no prejudice to the rights of all others. St John describes himself by that truly glorious title, 'The disciple whom Jesus loved.' Could he speak this of himself without the injury and indignation of the other disciples? Certainly he might; for if we consider that incomprehensible love of Christ, expressed to them all at his last supper, after Judas was gone forth, 'As the Father hath loved me, so have I loved you,' we may easily understand that every one of them might justly believe that he was singularly beloved of Christ. They were all received in the heart, though (with John) they did not all lean on the breast of their divine master. Thus in heaven God is the universal treasure of all the saints, and the peculiar portion of every one. [2]As by his essence he equally fills the whole world, and every part of it, and by his providence equally regards all and every particular creature; so in heaven he dispenses the riches of his love to all, that they cannot desire more, if every one of them were (if

[1] Et totum se dedit universis et totum singulis. Ac per hoc quicquid passione sua Salvator præstitit, sicut totum ei debent universi, sic singuli; nisi quod prope hoc plus singuli quam universi, quod totum acceperunt singuli quantum universi.—SALVIAN.
[2] Si audiat multitudo silens, non inter se particulatim comminunt sonos, tauquam cibos: sed omne quod sonat et omnibus totum est et singulis totum.—AUGUST. in Epist. ad Volusian.

I may so express it) the only-begotten of the Only-begotten himself,
the sole heir of all the merits of his Son.   Every saint may, with the
inflamed spouse, break forth in that triumph of love, 'My beloved is
mine, and I am his.'   Nay, the great number of the glorified saints is
so far from lessening their joy, that it unspeakably increases it: 'The
innumerable company of angels, and the general assembly of the
church of the First-born,' next to the happiness of enjoying God, are
a chief part of heaven.   An unfeigned ardent affection unites that pure
society.   Our love is now kindled, either from a relation in nature, or
some visible excellences that render a person worthy of our choice and
friendship; but in heaven the reasons are greater, and the degrees of
love incomparably more fervent.   All carnal alliances and respects
cease in that supernatural state.   The apostle tells us, 'If I have
known Christ after the flesh, I know him so no more.'   By the resurrection and ascension of Christ he was transported into another world,
and had communion with him as an heavenly king, without low
regards to the temporal privilege of conversing with him on earth.
The spiritual relation is more near and permanent than the strictest
band of nature.   The saints have all relation to the same heavenly
Father, and to Jesus Christ the Prince of peace, and head of that
happy fraternity.   The principal motive of love here is for the inherent
excellences of a person.   Wisdom, goodness, holiness, are mighty
attractives, and produce a more worthy affection, a more intimate con-
federacy of souls, than propinquity in nature.   David declares that
'all his delight was in the excellent.'   But there are allays of this
noble love here.   For—

[1.] There are relics of frailty in the best men on earth, some
blemishes that render them less amiable when discovered.   Here their
graces are mixed infirmities, and but ascending to glory.   Accordingly
our love to them must be regular and serene; not clouded with error,
mistaking defects for amiable qualities.   But in heaven the image
of God is complete, by the union of all the glorious virtues requisite
to its perfection.   Every saint there exactly agrees with the first
exemplar, is transformed according to the primitive beauty of holiness.
No spot or wrinkle remains, or any such thing, that may cast the least
aspect of deformity upon them.

[2.] In the present state, the least part of the saint's worth is visible;
as the earth is fruitful in plants and flowers, but its riches are in the
mines of precious metals, the veins of marble hidden in its bosom.
True grace appears in sensible actions, but its glory is within.   The
sincerity of aims, the purity of affections, the impresses of the Spirit
on the heart, the interior beauties of holiness, are only seen by God.
Besides, such is the humility of eminent saints, that the more they
abound in spiritual treasures, the less they show; as the heavenly
bodies, when in nearest conjunction with the sun, and fullest of light,
make the least appearance to our sight.   But all their excellences
shall then be in view: 'The glory of God shall be revealed in them.'
And how attractive is the divine likeness to an holy eye!   How will
it ravish the saints to behold an immortal loveliness shining in one
another!   Their love is mutual and reflexive, proportionable to the
cause of it.   An equal, constant flame is preserved by pure materials.

Every one is perfectly amiable, and perfectly enamoured with all. Now can we frame a fuller conception of happiness than such a state of love, wherein whatever is pleasant in friendship is in perfection, and whatever is distasteful by men's folly and weakness is abolished. The psalmist breaks out in a rapture, 'Behold, how good and pleasant it is for brethren to dwell together in unity!' Love is the beauty and strength of societies, the pleasure of life. How excellent is the joy of the blessed, when the prayer of Christ shall be accomplished, that they all may be one! 'As thou, Father, art in me, and I in thee, that they also may be one in us.' God is absolutely one in his glorious nature and will, and therefore unalterably happy; and their inviolable union in love is a ray of the essential unity between the sacred persons. There are no divisions of heart and tongues, as in this Babel, but the most perfect and sweetest concord, an eternal agreement in tempers and inclinations. There are no envious comparisons; for love, that affectively transforms one into another, causes the glory of every saint to redound to the joy of all. Every one takes his share in the felicity of all, and adds to it. Such is the power of that celestial fire wherein they all burn, that it melts, and mixes souls in such an entire union, that, by complaisance and an intimate joy, the blessedness of all is, as it were, proper to every one; as if every one were placed in the hearts of all, and all in the heart of every one. If in the church of the first-born christians, in the earthly Jerusalem, the band of charity was so strict that it is said, 'the multitude of believers were of one heart and one soul;' how much more intimate and inseparable is the union of the saints in Jerusalem above, where every one loves another as himself!

It is recorded of Alexander, that entering with Hephæstion, his favourite, into the pavilion of Darius' mother, then his prisoner, she bowed to the favourite, as having a greater appearance of majesty, thinking him to be Alexander; but advised of her error, she humbly begged his pardon; to whom the generous king replied,[1] 'You did not err, mother, for this is also Alexander.' Such was their affection, that whoever was taken of them, the other was taken in him; the less ascending in the greater, without degrading the greater in the less. This is a copy of the holy love of the blessed; but with the same difference as between the description of a star with a coal and its beauty in its proper aspect. And where all is love, all is delight. Oh, how do they enjoy and triumph in the happiness of one another! With what an unimaginable tenderness do they embrace! What reciprocations of endearments are between them! Oh their ravishing conversation and sweet intercourse! for their presence together in heaven is not a silent show. In the transfiguration Moses and Elias talked with Christ. With what excellent discourses do they entertain one another! If David felt such inward pleasure from the sense of God's favours that he could not restrain the expression of it, but invites the saints, 'Come and hear, all ye that fear the Lord, and I will tell you what he has done for my soul;' certainly in heaven, the blessed with overflowing affections recount the divine benefits, the admirable methods

---

[1] Non errâsti, mater, nam hic Alexander est.—CURT. l. 8.

whereby the life of grace was begun, preserved, and carried on in the midst of temptations; the continual succession of mercies in the time of their hopes, and the consummation of all in the time of their enjoyment. How joyfully do they concur in their thanksgivings to God for the goodness of creation, in making them reasonable creatures, capable to know, love, and enjoy him when they might have been of the lowest order in the whole sphere of beings; for his compassionate care and providence over them in this world. But especially for his sovereign mercy in electing them to be vessels of honour; for his powerful grace in rescuing them from the cruel and ignominious bondage of sin; for his most free love, that justified them from all their guilt by the death of his only Son, and glorified them with himself. They are never weary in this delightful exercise, but continually bless him for his mercy that endures for ever. We may judge by the saints here, when they are in a fit disposition to praise God, what fervours they feel in their united praises of him in heaven. The psalmist in an ecstasy calls to all the parts of the world to join with him: 'The Lord reigns, let the heavens rejoice, and the earth be glad: let the sea roar, let the fields be joyful, and all that dwell therein.' He desires that nature should be elevated above itself, that the dead parts be inspired with life, the insensible feel motions of joy, and those that want a voice break forth in praises to adorn the divine triumph. With what life and alacrity will the saints in their blessed communion celebrate the object of their love and praises! The seraphims about the throne cried to one another, to express their zeal and joy in celebrating his eternal purity and power, and the glory of his goodness. Oh the unspeakable pleasure of this concert, when every soul is harmonious, and contributes his part to the full music of heaven! Oh, could we hear but some echo of those songs wherewith the heaven of heavens resounds, some remains of those voices wherewith the saints above triumph in the praises, in the solemn adoration of the King of spirits, how would it inflame our desires to be joined with them! 'Blessed are those that are in thy house, they always praise thee.'

[3.] The fulness of joy in heaven is undecaying, for the causes of it are always equal; and those are, the beatific object revealed, and the uninterrupted contemplation of it.

Whilst we are here below, the sun of righteousness, as to our perception and sense, has ascensions and declinations, accesses and recesses; and our earth is not so purified but some vapours arise that intercept his cheerful, refreshing light. From hence there are alternate successions of spiritual comforts and sorrows, of doubts and filial confidence in the saints. It is a rare favour of heaven when an humble believer in his whole course is so circumspect as not to provoke God to appear displeased against him; when a christian (as those tutelar angels spoken of in the gospel) always beholds the face of his heavenly Father, and converses with him with an holy liberty. And what a torment the hiding of God's face is to a deserted soul, only they know who feel it. External troubles are many times attended with more consolations to the spirit than afflictions to sense; but to love God with a transcendent affection, and to fear he is our enemy, no punishment exceeds or is equal to it. As his loving-kindness in their esteem is better than life, so his displeasure is worse than death. How do they wrestle with God by prayers and tears, and offer, as it were, a holy violence to the king of heaven, to recover their first serenity of mind, the lost peace of heart! How passionately do they cry out, with Job in the book of his patience, Job xxix. 2–4 'Oh that I were as in months past, as in the days when God preserved me: when his candle shined upon my head, and when by his light I walked through darkness: as I was in the days of my youth, when the secret of God was upon my tabernacle.' And sometimes God delays the revealing himself even to his dearest children; not that he does not see their necessities and hear their prayers, or is so hard that till their extremities he is not moved with compassion, but for wise and holy reasons; either that they may not return to folly, if by any presumptuous sin they forfeited their peace; or if they have been careful to please him, yet he may deprive them of spiritual comforts for a time, to keep them humble, and that with an obedient resignation to his sovereign pleasure they may wait for his reviving presence. And then joy returns greater than before. For thus God usually renders with interest what he suspended only for trial. But the saints above are for ever enlightened with the vital splendour and dear regards of his countenance, always enjoy his beamy smiles. A continual effusion of glory illustrates heaven and all its blessed inhabitants.

And their contemplation of God is fixed. If the object, though extraordinary glorious, were transient, or the eye so weak that it could only see it but by glances, the height of joy would not be perpetual; but the mind is prepared with supernatural vigour to see the brightness of God's face, and by the most attentive application always converses with that blessed object, so that the joy of heaven is never intermitted for a moment. They always see, and love, and rejoice, and praise him.

It is possible a carnal suspicion may arise in some, as if the uniform perpetual vision of the same glory might lose its perfect delightfulness; for those who seek for happiness in the vanity of the creatures are always desirous of change, and have their judgments so corrupted, that while they languish with a secret desire after an unchangeable good, yet they conceive no good as desirable that is not changed.

But to correct this gross error of fancy, let us a little inquire into the causes of dissatisfaction, that make the constant fruition of the same thing here to be tedious.

(1.) Sensible things are of such a limited goodness, that not any of them can supply all our present wants, so that it is necessary to leave one for another. And the most of them are remedies of our diseased appetites, and, if not temperately used, are destructive evils. Eating and drinking are to extinguish hunger and thirst, but continued beyond just measure become nauseous.

Besides the insufficiency of their objects, the senses themselves cannot be satisfied all at once. The ear cannot attend to delightful sounds, and the eye cannot be intent on beautiful colours at the same time. The satisfaction of one sense defeats another of enjoying its proper good; therefore the same object is not constantly pleasant, but the heart is distempered from as many causes as there are desires unaccomplished.

Add further, all things under the sun afford only a superficial delight, and miserably deceive the expectations raised of them; and many times there is a mixture of some evil in them that is more offensive than the good is delightful. The honey is attended with a sting, so that often those things we sigh after through vehement desire, when they are obtained, we sigh for grief. Now all these causes of dissatisfaction cease in heaven; for[1] God is an infinite good, and whatever is truly desirable and precious is in him in all degrees of perfection. And in his presence all the powers of the soul are drawn out in their most pleasant exercise, and always enjoy their entire happiness. The fruition of him exceeds our most raised hopes, as much as he is more glorious in himself than in any borrowed representations. God will be to us incomparably above what we can ask or think. The compass of our thoughts, the depth of our desires, are imperfect measures of his perfections. As he is a pure good in himself, so he is prevalent over all evil. It is evident, therefore, that nothing can allay the joys of saints when they are in God's presence.

(2.) Novelty is not requisite to ingratiate every good, and make it perfectly delightful. [2]God is infinitely happy, to whom no good was ever new. It is indeed the sauce that gives a delicious taste to inferior things; for men relish only what is eminent, and the good things of this world are so truly mean, that they are fain to borrow a show of greatness by comparison with a worse estate preceding. But an infinite good produces always the same pure, equal, complete joy, because it arises from its intrinsic perfection, that wants no foil to commend it. The psalmist breaks forth, 'Whom have I in heaven but thee?' This is no vanishing rapture, but a constant joyful height of affection. God, the essential happiness of the saints, is always perfectly lovely and delightly to them.

(3.) The glorified saints, in every period of their happy state, have as lively a perception of it as in the beginning. To make this evident, we must consider that the pleasure of novelty springs from a quick sense of the opposite terms between our condition in the want of some desired good and after our obtaining it. Now the mind is more intense on the advantage, and more strongly affected at first. One newly freed from the torments of a sharp disease feels a greater pleasure than from a constant tenor of health. Those who are raised from a low state to an eminent dignity are transported with their first change; but in tract of time the remembrance of their mean condition is so weakened and spent, that it is like the shadow of a dream, and proportionably their joy is lessened. Honours, like perfumes, by custom are less sensible to those that carry them. But the saints above always consider and feel the excellent difference between their suffering and triumphant state. They never lose that ravishing part of felicity, the vivid sense of past evils. Their reflections are always as strong on the misery from whence

---

[1] Vitæ nos tædium tenet, timor mortis natat omne consilium, nec implere nos ulla fœlicitas potest. Causa autem est, quod non pervenimus ad illud bonum immensum et insuperabile, ubi necesse est consistat nobis voluntas nostra, quia ultra summum non est locus.—SEN. Ep. 74.

[2] Εἰ ἡ φύσις ἁπλῆ εἴη ἡ αὐτὴ πρᾶξις ἡδίστη ἔσται. Διὸ ὁ Θεὸς ἀεὶ μίαν καὶ ἁπλῆν χαίρει ἡδονήν.—ARIST. ETH. lib. vii. c. ult.

they were raised to the pitch of happiness as in their first glorious translation.   In what an ecstasy of wonder and pleasure will they be, from the fresh memory of what they were, and the joyful sense of what they are!   I was (says the admiring soul) poor, blind, and naked; but, O miraculous and happy alteration ! I am full of light, enriched with the treasures of heaven, adorned with divine glory.   I was under the tyrannous power of Satan, but he is bruised under my feet.   I was sentenced to an everlasting separation from the presence of God, my only life and joy; but now am possessed of my supreme good.   Oh, how transporting is the comparison of these wide and contrary extremes ! How beautiful and pleasant is the day of eternity after such a dark, tempestuous night !   How does the remembrance of such evils produce a more lively and feeling fruition of such happiness !   How strangely and mightily does salvation with eternal glory affect the soul ! This gives a sprightly accent to their everlasting hallelujahs.   This preserves an affectionate heat in their thanksgiving to their victorious deliverer. And thus their happiness is always the same, and always new.   Their pleasure is continued in its perfection.

Lastly, The blessedness of the saints is without end; this makes heaven to be itself.   There is no satiety of the present, no solicitude for the future.   Were there a possibility or the least suspicion of losing that happy state, it would cast an aspersion of bitterness upon all their delights; they could not enjoy one moment's repose.   But the more excellent their happiness is, the more stinging would their fear be of parting with it.   But 'the inheritance reserved in heaven is immortal, undefiled, and fades not away;' and the tenure of their possession is infinitely firm by the divine power, the true support of their everlasting duration: 'With God is the fountain of life.'   They enjoy a better immortality than the tree of life could have preserved in Adam.   The revolutions of the heavens and ages are under their feet, and cannot in the least alter or determine their happiness.   After the passing of millions of years, still an entire eternity remains of their enjoying God. O most desirable state ! where blessedness and eternity are inseparably united.   O joyful harmony! when the full chorus of heaven shall sing, 'This God is our God for ever and ever.'   This adds an infinite weight to their glory.   This redoubles their unspeakable joys with infinite sweetness and security.   They repose themselves in the complete fruition of their happiness.   God reigns in the saints, and they live in him for ever.

From what has been discoursed we should—

1. Consider the woful folly of men in refusing such an happiness, that, by the admirable favour of God, is offered to their choice.   Can there be an expectation or desire or capacity in man of enjoying an happiness beyond what is infinite and eternal ?   O blind and wretched world ! so careless of everlasting felicity ! Who can behold without compassion and indignation men vainly seeking for happiness where it is not to be found, and after innumerable disappointments, fly to an impossibility, and neglect their sovereign and final blessedness ? Astonishing madness, that God and heaven should be despised in comparison of painted trifles ! This adds the greatest contumely to their impiety.   What powerful charm obstructs their true judging of things?

What spirit of error possesses them? Alas! eternal 'things are unseen,' not of conspicuous moment, and therefore in the carnal balance are esteemed light against temporal things present to the sense: 'It does not appear what we shall be.' The veil of the visible heavens covers the sanctuary, where Jesus, our high priest, is entered, and stops the inquiring eye.

But have we not assurance by the most infallible principles of faith that the Son of God came down from heaven to live with us and die for us, and that he rose again to confirm our belief in his 'exceeding great and precious promises' concerning this happiness in the future state? And do not the most evident principles of reason and universal experience prove that this world cannot afford true happiness to us? How wretchedly do we forfeit the prerogative of the reasonable nature by neglecting our last and blessed end! If the mind be darkened that it does not see the amiable excellences of God, and the will so depraved that it does not feel their ravishing power, the man ceases to be a man, and becomes like the beasts that perish; as a blind eye is no longer an eye, being absolutely useless to that end for which it was made. And though in this present state men are stupid and unconcerned, yet hereafter their misery will awaken them, discover what is that supreme good wherein their perfection and felicity consists. When their folly shall be exposed before God, angels, and saints, in what extreme confusion will they appear before that glorious and immense theatre! Our Saviour told the unbelieving Jews, 'There shall be weeping and gnashing of teeth, when ye shall see Abraham, and Isaac, and Jacob. and all the prophets in the kingdom of God, and you yourselves turned out.' They shall be tortured with the desire of happiness without possible satisfaction. It is most just that those who err without excuse should repent without remedy.

2. Let us be excited seriously to apply ourselves in the use of effectual means for the obtaining this happiness. Indeed the original cause of it is the pure, rich mercy of God; the meritorious is the most precious obedience of our Saviour, by whom we obtain plenteous redemption. His abasement is the cause of our exaltation. The wounds he received in his body, the character of ignominy, and footsteps of death, are the fountains of our glory: 'Eternal life is the gift of God through Jesus Christ our Lord.' But the gospel declares, 'that without holiness no man shall see God.' An holy change of our natures, and perseverance in the course of universal obedience, are indispensably requisite in order to our obtaining heaven: 'Those who by patient continuance in well-doing seek for glory, honour, and immortality, shall partake of eternal life.' Now, were there no other reason of this constitution but the sovereign will of God, it were sufficient. But the foundation of it is laid in the nature of the things themselves. Therefore our Saviour does not simply declare that an unregenerate person shall not see the kingdom of God, but with the greatest emphasis, *cannot*, to signify an absolute impossibility of it. Beside the legal bar that excludes unsanctified persons from the beatific vision of God, there is a moral incapacity. Suppose that justice should allow omnipotence to translate such a sinner to heaven, would the place make him happy? Can two incongruous natures

delight in one another? The happiness of sense is by an impression of pleasure from a suitable object. The happiness of intellectual beings arises from an entire conformity of dispositions. So that unless God recede from his holiness, which is absolutely impossible, or man be purified and changed into his likeness, there can be no sweet communion between them. Our Saviour assigns this reason of the necessity of regeneration in order to our admission into heaven: ' That which is born of the flesh is flesh, and that which is born of the Spirit is spirit.' According to the quality of the principle, such is what proceeds from it. The flesh is a corrupt principle, and accordingly the natural man is wholly carnal in his propensions, operations, and end. The disease is turned into his constitution. He is dead to the spiritual life, to the actions and enjoyments that are proper to it. Nay, there is in him a surviving principle of enmity to that life; not only a mortal coldness to God, but a stiff aversion from him, a perpetual resistance and impatience of the divine presence that would disturb his voluptuous enjoyments. The exercises of heaven would be as the torments of hell to him, while in the midst of those pure joys his inward inclinations vehemently run into the lowest lees of sensuality. And therefore till this contrariety, so deep and predominant in an unholy person, be removed, it is utterly impossible he should enjoy God with satisfaction. Holiness alone prepares men for the possession of celestial happiness that is against the corruption and above the perfection of mere nature.

' Let us then, having such a joy set before us, lay aside every weight, and the sin which doth so easily beset us, and run with patience the race that is set before us, looking to Jesus, the author and finisher of our faith.' Methinks the sight of worldly men, so active and vigilant to prosecute their low designs, should quicken us to seek with the greater diligence and alacrity 'the kingdom of heaven, and the righteousness thereof.' A carnal wretch, urged by the sting of a brutish desire, with what impatience does he pursue ' the pleasure of sin, which is but for a season !' An ambitious person, with what an intemperate height of passion does he chase a feather ! A covetous man, how greedily does he prosecute the advantages of the present world that pass away, and the lusts thereof! Ah ! how do they upbraid our indifferent desires, or dull delays, and cold endeavours, when such an high prize is set before us ! Who is able to conceive the excess of pleasure the soul feels when it first enters through the beautiful gate of paradise, and sees before it that incomprehensible glory, and hears a voice from him that sits upon the throne, 'Enter into thy Master's joy,' for ever to be happy with him? The serious belief of this will draw forth all our active powers in the service of God. The feeding by lively thoughts on this supernatural food will add new vigour and lustre to our graces, and make our victory easy over the world. If we believe indeed that our bodies shall be spiritual, and our souls divine in their perfections, it will make us resolute to subdue the rebel flesh and rescue the captived spirit from all entanglements of iniquity : ' Having the promise of such an excellent reward, let us always abound in the work of the Lord.'

3. The lively hope of this blessedness is powerful to support us under the greatest troubles can befall us in this our mortal condition.

Here we are tossed upon the alternate waves of time, but hereafter we shall arrive at the port, the blessed bosom of our Saviour, and enjoy a peaceful calm : ' And so we shall ever be with the Lord.' Words of infinite sweetness ! This is the song of our prosperity and charm of our adversity : ' We shall ever be with the Lord.' Well might the apostle add immediately after, 'Therefore comfort one another with these words.'

More particularly, they are a lenitive to moderate our sorrows upon the departure of our dearest friends who die in the Lord ; for they ascend from this valley of tears to the happy land of the living. What father is so deserted of reason as to bear impatiently the parting with his son, that goes over a narrow part of the sea to a rich and pleasant country, and receives the investiture and peaceable possession of a kingdom? Nay, by how much the stronger his love is, so much the more transporting is his joy ; especially if he expects shortly to be with him, to see him on the throne, in the state of a king, and to partake of his happiness. If, then, it be impossible to nature to be grieved at the felicity of one that is loved, according to what principle of nature or faith do believers so uncomfortably lament the death of friends, of whom they have assurance that, after their leaving our earth, they enter into an everlasting kingdom, to receive a crown of glory from Christ himself? Our Saviour tells the disciples, ' If ye loved me, ye would rejoice because I said I go to my Father,' to sit down at his right hand in majesty. A pure affection directly terminates in the happiness and exaltation of the person that is loved. I am not speaking against the exercise of tender affections on the loss of our dear friends, and the pensive feeling of God's hand in it, which is a natural and necessary duty. There is a great difference between stupidity and patience ; but violent passion or unremitting sorrow is most unbecoming the blessed hope assured to us in the gospel.

Chrysostom, treating of this argument, and reflecting upon the custom of those times, wherein at funeral solemnities a train of mourning women attended the corpse, tearing their hair and face, and crying out with all the expressions of desperate sorrow, breaks forth, ' Ah, christian faith and religion ! that was triumphant over thine enemies in so many battles and victories by the blood and death of the martyrs, how art thou contradicted by the practice of these who profess thee in words ! Is this not to be sorrowful as those that have no hope ? Are these the affections, the expressions of one that believes the blessedness of immortal life ? What will the heathens say ? How will they be induced to believe the promises of Christ to his servants of a glorious kingdom, when those who are so in title, behave themselves as if they had no stendfast faith in them ? '

4. The hopes of this blessed state is able to free us from the fear of death. This last enemy gives a hot alarm to mankind, both as it deprives them of all that is pleasant here, and for the terrible consequences that attend it. To the eye of sense, a dead body is a spectacle of fearful appearance. He that a little before heard and discoursed, and with a cheerful air conversed and enjoyed the world, now is dead, and all his senses in him ; the eyes are dead to light, and the ears to sounds, the tongue to words, the heart to feel any affections, and the

countenance to discover them; nothing remains but silence, horror, and corruption. Besides, 'after death comes judgment,' and a state of unrelenting torments to the wicked. But a true believer, that has been obedient to his Saviour, sees things by another light than that of sense, and has living hopes in his dying agonies. He knows that death to the saints is but a sleep; and while the body rests in the grave, the soul is, as it were, all act, continually exercising its most noble faculties on the best objects. Does the soul sleep in that all-enlightened world, that sees with open face the infinite beauty of God? that hears and bears a part in the hymns of the angels and saints encircling his throne? that drinks of the rivers of pleasure that flow from his presence? that freely and joyfully converses with all the celestial courtiers, the princes of that kingdom, the favourites of God? Then it truly lives. This reconciles death to a christian, who has nothing more in his wishes than to be with Christ, and knows that diseases and pains, the forerunners of it, are but as breaking down the walls of this earthly dark prison, that the soul may take its flight to the happy region, and for ever enjoy the liberty of the sons of God. And for his body, that shall be reunited to the soul in glory. Methinks God speaks to a dying believer as he did to Jacob when he was to descend to Egypt, ' Fear not to go down into the grave; I will go down with thee, and I will bring thee up again.' The same almighty voice that gave being to the world shall awake those who sleep in the dust, and reform them according to the example of Christ's glorified body. Oh, how should we long for that triumphant day, and with most ardent aspirings pray, ' Thy kingdom come in its full power and glory?'

I shall now come to speak of the mournful subject, the cause of my appearing here at this time, the deceased reverend and excellent divine, Dr Thomas Manton, a name worthy of precious and eternal memory. And I shall consider him both in the quality of his office, as he was an ambassador of Christ, declaring his mind and representing his authority, and in the holiness of his person, showing forth the graces and virtues of his divine Master.

God had furnished him with a rare union of those parts that are requisite to form an excellent minister of his word. A clear judgment, rich fancy, strong memory, and happy elocution met in him, and were excellently improved by his diligent study.

The preaching of the word is the principal part of the minister's duty, most essential to his calling, and most necessary to the church. For this end chiefly the several orders in the ministerial office were instituted (Eph. iv.); and upon our Saviour's triumphant ascent and reception into heaven, an abundant effusion of the Spirit in graces and abilities descended upon men. Now, in the performing this work he was of that conspicuous eminence that none could detract from him but from ignorance or envy.

He was endowed with extraordinary knowledge in the scriptures, those holy oracles from whence all spiritual light is derived; and in his preaching gave such a perspicuous account of the order and dependence of divine truths, and with that felicity applied the scriptures to confirm them, that every subject by his management was cultivated and improved. His discourses were so clear and convincing, that none, without offering voluntary violence to conscience, could resist their evidence. And from hence they were effectual, not only to inspire a sudden shame, and raise a short commotion in the affections, but to make a lasting change in the life. For in the human soul, such is the composition of its faculties, that till the understanding be rectified in its apprehensions and estimations, the will is never induced to make an entire, firm choice of what is necessary for the obtaining perfect happiness. A sincere, persevering conversion is effected by weighty reasons, that sink and settle in the heart.

His doctrine was uncorrupt and pure, ' The truth according to godliness.' He was far from a guilty, vile intention to prostitute that sacred ordinance for the acquiring any private secular advantage. Neither did he entertain his hearers with impertinent subtleties, empty notions, intricate disputes, dry and barren without productive virtue; but as one that always had before his eyes the great end of the ministry, the glory of God and the salvation of men, his sermons were directed to open their eyes, that they might see their wretched condition as sinners, to hasten their flight from the wrath to come, to make them humbly, thankfully, and entirely receive Christ as their prince and all-sufficient saviour, and to ' build up the converted in their most holy faith, and more excellent love,' that is ' the fulfilling of the law.' In short, to make true christians eminent in knowledge and universal obedience.

As the matter of his sermons was designed for the good of souls, so his way of expression was proper to that end. Words are the vehicle of the heavenly light. As the divine wisdom was incarnate to reveal the eternal counsels of God to the world, so spiritual wisdom in the mind must be clothed with words to make it sensible to others. And in this he had a singular talent. His style was not exquisitely studied, not consisting of harmonious periods, but far distant from vulgar meanness. His expression was natural and free, clear and eloquent, quick and powerful, without any spice of folly, and always suitable to the simplicity and majesty of divine truths. His sermons afforded substantial food with delight, so that a fastidious mind could not disrelish them. He abhorred a vain ostentation of wit in handling sacred things, so venerable and grave, and of eternal consequence. Indeed, what is more unbecoming a minister of Christ than to waste the spirits of his brain, as a spider does his bowels, to spin a web only to catch flies, to get vain applause by foolishly pleasing the ignorant? And what cruelty is it to the souls of men! It is recorded as an instance of Nero's savage temper (Suetonius), that in a general famine, when many perished by hunger, he ordered a ship should come from Egypt (the granary of Italy) laden with sand for the use of wrestlers. In such extremity to provide only for delight, that there might be spectacles on the theatre, when the city of Rome was a spectacle of such misery as to melt the heart of any but a Nero, was most barbarous cruelty. But it is cruelty of a heavier imputation for a minister to prepare his sermons to please the foolish curiosity of fancy with flashy conceits; nay, such light vanities that would scarce be endured in a scene, whiles hungry souls languish for want of solid nourishment.

His fervour and earnestness in preaching was such as might soften and make pliant the most stubborn, obdurate spirits. I am not speaking of one whose talent was only in voice, that labours in the pulpit as if the end of preaching were for the exercise of the body, and not for the profit of souls; [1] but this man of God was inflamed with an holy zeal, and from thence such ardent expressions broke forth as were capable to procure attention and consent in his hearers. He spake as one that had a living faith within him of divine truths. From this union of zeal with his knowledge he was excellently qualified to convince and convert souls. The sound of words only strikes the ear, but the mind reasons with the mind, and the heart speaks to the heart.

His unparalleled assiduity in preaching declared him very sensible of those dear and strong obligations that lie upon ministers to be very diligent in that blessed work. What a powerful motive our Saviour urged upon St Peter! John xxi. 'As thou lovest me, feed my sheep, feed my lambs.' And can any feed too much when none can love enough? Can any pains be sufficient for the salvation of souls, for which the Son of God did not esteem his blood too costly a price? Is not incessant, unwearied industry requisite to advance the work of grace in them to perfection? In this the work of a minister has its peculiar disadvantage. That whereas an artificer, how curious and difficult soever his work be, yet has this encouragement, that what is begun with art and care he finds in the same state wherein it was left; a painter, that designs an exact piece, draws many lines, often touches it with his pencil to give it life and beauty, and though unfinished, it is not spoiled by his intermission; a sculptor, that carves a statue, though his labour be hard from the resistance of the matter, yet his work remains firm and durable; but the heart of man is of a strange temper, hard as marble, not easily receptive of heavenly impressions, yet fluid as water. Those impressions are easily defaced in it; it is exposed to so many temptations that induce an oblivion of eternal things, that without frequent excitations to quicken and confirm its holy purposes, it grows careless, and all the labour is lost that was spent on it. This faithful minister 'abounded in the work of the Lord;' and, which is truly admirable, though so frequent in preaching, yet was always superior to others, and equal to himself. In his last time, when declining to death, yet he would not leave his beloved work, the vigour of his mind supporting the weakness of his body. I remember when, oppressed with an obstinate hoarseness, a friend desiring him to spare himself, he rejected the advice with indignation.

He was no fomenter of faction, but studious of the public tranquillity. He knew what a blessing peace is, and wisely foresaw the pernicious consequences that attend divisions. By peace, the bond of mutual harmony, the weakest things are preserved and prosper; but where discord reigns, the strongest are near to ruin. The heavenly consent in the primitive church was a principal cause of its miraculous increase and flourishing; but after dissensions prevailed amongst christians, that was destroyed in a short time which was built by the divine union and heroic patience of the primitive christians, and the glorious begin-

---

[1] Si sudare aliter non potes, est aliud.

nings that promised the reformation of all Europe were more obstructed
by the dissensions of some employed in that blessed work, than by all
the power and subtlety, the arms and artifices of Rome itself.   How
afflictive is the consideration of our divided church!   Sweet peace!
whither art thou fled?   Blessed Saviour! who didst by thy precious
blood reconcile heaven and earth, sent down thy Spirit to inspire us
with that wisdom that is pure and peaceable, that those who agree in
the same principles of faith, in the same substantial parts of worship,
in asserting the same indispensable necessity of holiness, may receive
one another in love.   I am affectionately engaged in a matter that so
nearly touches all those that value the Protestant interest.

Briefly, Consider him as a christian; his life was answerable to his
doctrine.   It is applicable to some ministers, what is observed of the
carbuncle, by its colour, lustre, and fiery sparklings, it seems to be
actually a fire, but it has only the name and appearance of it.   Thus
some in the pulpit seem to be all on fire with zeal, yet their hearts
are as cold as a stone, without holy affections, and their lives are
unworthy their divine ministration.   But this servant of God was like
a fruitful tree, that produces in its branches what it contains in the
root; his inward grace was made visible in a conversation becoming
the gospel of Christ.

His resolute contempt of the world secured him from being wrought
on by those motives that tempt low spirits from their duty.   He would
not rashly throw himself into troubles, nor, *spreta conscientia*, avoid
them.   His generous constancy of mind in resisting the current of
popular humour declared his loyalty to his divine Master.   His charity
was eminent in procuring supplies for others when in mean circumstances himself.   But he had great experience of God's fatherly provision,
to which his filial confidence was correspondent.

His conversation in his family was holy and exemplary, every day
instructing them from the scriptures in their duty.

I shall finish my character of him with observing his humility.   He
was deeply affected with the sense of his frailties and unworthiness.
He considered the infinite purity of God, the perfection of his law, the
rule of our duty, and by that humbling light discovered his manifold
defects.   He expressed his thoughts to me a little before his death: If
the holy prophets were under strong impressions of fear upon the
extraordinary discovery of the divine presence, how shall we poor
creatures appear before that holy and dread majesty?   Isaiah, after his
glorious vision of God, reflecting upon himself, as not retired from the
commerce and corruption of the world, breaks forth, 'Woe is me, for
I am undone! because I am a man of unclean lips, and I dwell in
the midst of a people of unclean lips; for mine eyes have seen the
King, the Lord of hosts.'   It is infinitely terrible to appear 'before
God, the judge of all,' without the protection of 'the blood of the
sprinkling, that speaks better things than the blood of Abel.'   This
alone relieved him, and supported his hopes.   Though his labours were
abundant, yet he knew that the work of God, passing through our
hands, is so blemished, that, without an appeal to pardoning mercy and
grace, we cannot stand in judgment.   This was the subject of his last
public sermon.

He languished many months, but presuming he should be too strong for his infirmity, neglected it, till at last it became insuperable and mortal. Many pathetical aggravations heighten our great and dear loss; that such a faithful minister of Christ should be taken away, whose preaching was so powerful to repair the woful ruins of godliness and virtue in a degenerate age; whose prudent, pacific spirit rendered him so useful in these divided times, when professors of the same religion are alienated from one another, as if they had been baptized with the waters of strife; that before our tears had dried up for the loss of other worthy ministers, the fountain of sorrow should be opened again by this afflicting stroke. But it becomes us to receive the dispensations of heaven with humble and quiet submission, to reflect upon our sins with an holy grief, that provoke God to remove such an excellent instrument of his glory from us. Let us pray to the Lord of the harvest, that he will send forth faithful labourers into it. Oh that surviving ministers might be animated with a zeal more pure and fervent in their divine work, and that people would be wise, while a price is put it into their hands to improve it for their eternal advantage! The neglected gospel will at last be a terrible witness against the disobedient, to justify and aggravate their condemnation.

INDEX.

INDEX.

Ambition, the true, is spiritual ambition, xiv. 446.

Amen is either an affectionate desire or a great asseveration, i. 111.

Signifies either So let it be, or So it shall be, i. 253.

Signaculum fidei, et votum desiderii nostri, v. 375 ; should be to our praises as well as our prayers, *ib.*

Amiss, we pray, when our ends and aims are not right in prayer, iv. 338 ; when we ask blessings for the use and encouragement of our lusts, 339 ; when our prayers are framed out of a carnal intention they are seldom successful ; we miss when we ask amiss, 341.

Amphilochius, Bishop of Iconium, his argument with Theodosius the Great against toleration of the Arians, x. 259.

Ancients (Ps. cxix. 100), may either mean men of former times, or aged men of the same time, viii. 15 ; preferably the latter, *ib.*

Angels serve God readily, i. 148 ; cheerfully, *ib.* ; constantly, *ib.* ; faithfully, not picking and choosing, 149.

Everywhere in scripture shown to be the first instruments of God's providence, i. 284 ; not ministers of conversion and sanctification, *ib.* ; question as to special guardian angels, *ib.*

Their visible ministry extraordinary, but their invisible ordinary and perpetual, i. 285 ; this invisible ministry matter of faith, 286.

Why they did not come to Christ till the devil had departed, i. 324 ; to show that Christ had no help but his own when he grappled with Satan, *ib.* ; to show that the going of the one is the coming of the other, *ib.* ; why they ministered to him after his temptation, *ib.* ; to put honour on him, who is their head and lord, *ib.* ; for his consolation, inward and outward, 325.

God maketh use of their ministry in supporting and comforting his afflicted servants, i. 333 ; delight in the preaching of the gospel, 334 ; in the holy conversation of the godly, *ib.* ; fight against the devil, and defend the godly in their extreme dangers, *ib.* ; why God uses their ministry, *ib.* ; to manifest unto them the greatness and glory of his work in recovering mankind, *ib.* ; to maintain a society and communion between all the parts of the family of God, 335 ; to preserve his people from many dangers and casualties which fall not within the foresight of men, *ib.* ; many blessings and benefits conveyed through their ministry, 336 ; their office at death and judgment, *ib.*

Whether good or bad, often called in scripture thrones, i. 435 ; owe their being to Christ, 436 ; when created, 437 ; subject to Christ 438 ; why their creation so particularly and expressly ascribed to Christ, 439 ; to show his glory and majesty, *ib.* ; to obviate the Gnostic errors, *ib.* ; to show his right to their ministry, 440.

Christ did not die for, nor is their head as he is of the church, i. 462.

Romish worship of, is idolatry, iii. 99.

Acknowledged Christ, but men would not, iii. 249.

And archangels, God hath, always ready to defend a good cause, v. 245.

Originally created in holiness and happiness, v. 190 ; fallen through sin, 191 ; cannot tell how sin got access to them, 192 ; their number great, 193 ; time of their fall, *ib.* ; their punishment, 196.

In the election of, is shown grace, but not mercy, v. 195.

Ministry of, v. 246 ; certain that they had a great care about the people of God in ancient times, *ib.* ; not wholly ceased, though not so visible and sensible now, *ib.* ; children of God the proper object of, *ib.* ; all the children of God, without exception, 247 ; all angels so employed, *ib.*; not certain that each child of God has a special angel, *ib.*; yet all have all, 248; continues from the first conception till the entrance into glory, *ib.*; ever administered according to God's pleasure, 249; order amongst both good and bad, 251.

Angels, are they to be judged at the day of judgment? x. 29; the bad, but apparently not the good, *ib.*

The holy, contemplate and admire the mystery of redemption, xviii. 203; the person of the Redeemer, 204; the way of redemption, *ib.*; the grace vouchsafed to sinful men, *ib.*; the mission of the Spirit, 205; the gracious providences of God in leading on the church to their eternal happiness, *ib.*; the final glorious estate of the saints, *ib.*; desire to look into these things, not out of curiosity, 206; nor from total ignorance of the mystery before it was brought about, 207; because they have such a deep sense of the worth of these things that they desire to know more, *ib.*; delight in the mystery of redemption because of the glory of God discovered therein, 208; and the good of men promoted thereby, *ib.*

Anger and sorrow, God's command reacheth, ii. 336.

Groweth not by degrees like other passions, therefore the best cure is deliberation, iv. 137; is the worst thing we can bring to a religious controversy, 138; is often justified when it is not justifiable, 139; sometimes lawful, 140; sometimes necessary, *ib.*; when the principle is right, 141; when it has a right object, *ib.*; when the manner is right, *ib.*; sinful when hasty and undeliberate, *ib.*; immoderate, 142; causeless, *ib.*; without a good end, 143; nothing more makes room for Satan, *ib.*; much woundeth our own peace, *ib.*; disparageth christianity, *ib.*

Different from hatred, viii. 332.

Animal and spiritual life distinguished and described, xv. 47.

Anointing the sick with oil in the name of the Lord, not a standing ordinance in the church, iv. 448; even in the apostles' time it was not absolutely necessary, *ib.*; was not promiscuously used, 449; ceased when the miraculous gift ceased, *ib.*; Popish, or extreme unction, a mere hypocritical pageantry, 450.

Of Christ signifieth the nature of his offices as king, priest, and prophet, v. 160; and the authority on which it is founded, 161.

Of Christ, was not typical, but real, x. 167; implieth the giving of power and authority, 168; the bestowing on him of the Holy Ghost, who might make the human nature fit for the work, *ib.*; was to the office of mediator in general, particularly to be king, priest, and prophet of the church, *ib.*

Answers to prayer, importance of observing, vi. 252.

To prayer, God's children are earnest for, ix. 46; because they dare not take God's name in vain, *ib.*; not looking for, proceedeth from an ill course, 47; heedlessness, *ib.*; a touch of atheism, *ib.*; distrust, which is akin to atheism, *ib.*; some disesteem of God's favour and acceptance, *ib.*; if we do not look after, our loss is exceeding great, 48; we lose our labour in prayer, *ib.*; lose excitements to love and obedience, *ib.*; lose encouragements to pray again, *ib.*; lose the benefit of sensible communion with God, *ib.*; God loseth honour, and praise, and thanksgiving, *ib.*; how God grants, 50; extraordinarily, as in ancient times, *ib.*; ordinarily, either by granting the mercy prayed for, *ib.*; or by giving spiritual manifestations to the soul, *ib.*; or by commutation or exchange, giving another thing that is as good or better, 51.

Ant, the, a pattern of diligence, xxii. 3.

Anthony the Hermit, his study in the desert, xiii. 395.

ANTICHRIST, EIGHTEEN SERMONS ON, iii. 1.

Antichrist, the head patron of the great apostasy, iii. 28 ; revelation of, 31 ; names or titles of, *ib.* ; man of sin, *ib.* ; son of perdition, 32 ; not a single person, but a society or succession of men, *ib.*

Opposite to Christ, chiefly in respect of pride, iii. 37 ; exalteth himself above all human persons, 39 ; and above all that is reverenced, *ib.* ; usurps divine honours, 40 ; shows himself that he is God, 42 ; every tittle of this description fulfilled in the Bishop of Rome, 44 ; his manifestation stayed by the Roman Empire, 49 ; this taken out of the way about A.D. 600, 50 ; grew to its monstrous excess and height in Boniface III., 56.

Doctrine of, profitable, and very necessary to be preached and known, iii. 46.

Sets up his kingdom by Satan's agency and influence, iii. 66 ; by pretence of miracles, *ib.* ; sophistical reasonings, 67 ; fawning or threatening, preferment or persecution, *ib.*

Antichristian state, subjects of, are drawn into it with all deceivableness of unrighteousness, iii. 76 ; their misery, those that perish, *ib.* ; the reason of this shown, they received not the love of the truth, 77, 79.

State, called Babylon for idolatry, Sodom for filthiness, and Egypt for ignorance and darkness, v. 254.

Antigonus' advice to the governor of a rebellious city, xii. 60.

Antinomianism, refutation of, xi. 158 ; it is an unjust illation from the doctrine of free justification, *ib.* ; it is absurd, and contrary to the doctrine of grace, *ib.* ; it is wicked and blasphemous, 160 ; caution against, 161.

Antinomians, doctrine of the, as to grace giving freedom from the moral law, xvi. 46.

Apostasies from God in heathenism, and from Christ in Romanism, are of the kingdom of the devil, which is to be destroyed, xviii. 32.

Apostasy, temptations to, errors, scandals, persecutions, ii. 88.

General, before Christ's coming to judgment, iii. 26 ; is any defection from him to whom we owe and have performed subjection, *ib.* ; that foretold, not civil, but of the visible church from the Lord of the church, *ib.* ; will consist in undermining his authority, 27 ; and corrupting and destroying the interests of his kingdom, *ib.* ; is notable and discernible, and its head is Antichrist, 28 ; Popery this apostasy, 29.

The covenant of grace a comfort against fears of, iii. 384.

Danger and mischievous effects of, vi. 315 ; more dishonourable to God than a simple refusal, *ib.* ; falling off after a taste of the sweetness and practice of godliness a worse condition than to have never begun, 316.

Apostate, Luther confesses that he is from the devil's service, iii. 178.

Apostles, even in their private and familiar letters, very spiritual, v. 99.

Their words the rule of faith, v. 322.

Their proficiency in Christ's school, x. 220 ; had sufficient means to convince the world of the certainty of Christ's doctrine, 221.

Appeal from God's justice to his mercy, a scarcely warrantable expression, iii. 271.

Appearance, outward, divine things not to be judged by, iii. 227 ; anything of Christ not to be cast away because it is despised or discountenanced, *ib.*; because it is an afflicted way, *ib.*; because poor men are of that way, 228; because we may seem to hazard our burden by closing with it, *ib.*

Appearance, Christ's, in the world, and state of life among men, was not only very mean, but very miserable, iii. 249.

Application of grace to believers, wisdom and prudence of God in, ii. 262; in the way he taketh to convert souls to himself, *ib.*; in taking the likely course to gain the heart of man, *ib.*; in the effect itself, 263.

And appropriation of Christ, the comfort in, and love to, Christ, ii. 297.

Apprehending, Christ's, of us, implieth that any motion towards that which is spiritually good proceedeth first and wholly from Christ, xx. 85; implieth a subordinate operation on our part, 86; the infusion of a life which tends towards God and heaven, *ib.*; is followed up by his keeping us in his own hand, 87; should be answered by an exact, resolved, diligent pursuit of eternal life, *ib.*

Approbation evidenced by imitation, v. 169.

Of men, how far to be minded or made a motive by us, xviii. 120.

Appropriation of Christ and dedication to his service mutually dependent, i. 491.

Approving of ourselves to God in all our actions our great interest, vi. 229; for this we need good counsel and direction, *ib.*; this we can only get from God in his word, 230; this counsel sufficient and full to all our necessities, *ib.*

Arguments, those that cannot be moved by, God teacheth by blows, vii. 133.

Aristotle's opinions as to a first cause in creation, xiii. 411, 412.

On the worship of the ancients (Ethics, lib. viii. c. 8), xiii. 437.

Ark, the, a type of Christ, xiv. 203.

Arm of the Lord, revelation of, is the inward manifestation of the gospel by the Spirit, iii. 193, 204. See *Gospel.*

Arminian doctrine of merit, *de congruo* and *de condigno*, answered, ix. 486.

Armour, the christian's, pieces of, i. 228.

Christian, and the use of it, xi. 298.

Articles of faith, ministers not to prescribe, but explain, iv. 17.

Of the christian religion, the devils assent to, iv. 241.

Ascension of Christ, x. 270; the time, when he had finished his work and instructed his disciples, *ib.*; the place, Mount Olivet, whence he had gone to his cross and to his crown, *ib.*; to the third heaven, 271; the witnesses, the eleven apostles, *ib.*; while he was blessing them, *ib.*; on a cloud, *ib.*; as a conqueror, triumphing over his enemies, and giving gifts to his friends, *ib.*; his reception by the angels, 272; his welcome by God, *ib.*; end of, 273; that we may look upon him as in a greater capacity to do us good, *ib.*; to prepare a place for us, *ib.*; to represent his satisfaction, 274; fruits and benefits of, 275.

Ashamed, men are, when they should be bold, and bold and confident when they should be ashamed, vi. 495.

Asking, God giveth nothing without, iv. 41; yieldeth a remedy for the greatest wants, *ib.*

Assembly (συναγωγη), not for worship, but for deciding ecclesiastical matters, iv. 186.

Assent, speculative, may be without faith, ii. 303.

To the articles of religion doth not infer true faith, iv. 240.

A part of faith, but not all, iv. 349; must be firm, *ib.*; and cordial, 350.

Degrees of, conjecture, opinion, weak faith, stronger faith, and the full assurance of understanding, vi. 401.

Assurance, why so few of God's children have, v. 19 ; possible that God's power may work in us, and we not be sensible of it, *ib.* ; sometimes through carelessness, sometimes through peevishness, God's children not sensible of the power that worketh in them, *ib.* ; God doth not call all in a like violent and sensible manner, *ib.* ; this different dispensation God useth according to his own pleasure, *ib.* ; though a different dispensation used in the calling, yet there is enough to distinguish the uncalled from the called. *ib.*

It is a ground of sure confidence that a christian shall have heaven at last, that he hath it for the present, xii. 431 ; it is not only we think or hope, but we know, 432 ; our assurance of salvation is not equal to that we have of the promises of the gospel, 433 ; it is a common privilege, *ib.* ; it fortifies the soul against all the difficulties of the present life, yea, against death itself, 434 ; it is a twofold confidence, of the thing and of the person, *ib.* ; of the thing itself all true christians have, and should have, a certain knowledge, *ib.* ; why and wherefore, 435 ; reasons why we should attend upon the work of assurance, 439 ; the force and virtue of this work, 440.

Directions to those who want, xiv. 27.

A believer's, God's word and oath the immutable grounds of, xvi. 294 ; the power and certainty of God's word, *ib.* ; reasons why God gives his oath over and above his word, 295 ; the advantages we have by God's oath, 303 ; application, 305 ; objections answered, 310 ; the fruit of this assurance is strong consolation, 314 ; what is meant by ' strong consolation,' *ib.* ; how this ariseth from assurance, 316 ; how it is dispensed on God's part, and how far required on ours, 318 ; exhortation to look after this consolation, 325 ; how to get it, 328 ; how to keep it, 333.

Of good estate before God, his children may have, xx. 76 ; when grace is in some degree of eminency, *ib.* ; when their evidences are not blotted by frequent sins, *ib.* ; when they have the spirit of adoption in a more eminent degree, 77 ; when they have a more abundant sense of the love of God, *ib.* ; when the change wrought in them by grace is most sensible, *ib.* ; yet they cannot look upon themselves as out of all danger, and past all care and holy solicitude, 79 ; because there is no period put to our duty but life, *ib.* ; because all through their life they are imperfect, *ib.* ; nature of, is to exclude the fear which hath torment, but not the fear of caution and diligence, 80 ; gotten with diligence and kept with watchfulness, 81 ; in order to, we need diligence, *ib.* ; caution and watchfulness, 82 ; self-denial, 83.

Graces really and soundly exercised beget assurance of our condition before God, xxi. 155 ; graces thus really, constantly, and self-denyingly exercised leave a suitable impression on the conscience, 161.

Atheism not so bad as blasphemy, iv. 84.

Contemplation of creation an antidote to, xiii. 398.

Atheistical men deride reliance upon God in distress, vii. 39 ; and obedience to his precepts, 40.

Atheists are of all men most credulous, xii. 220.

Atonement required by the holiness of God's nature, i. ; 496 ; the honour of his governing justice, *ib.* ; to keep up the authority of his law, 497 ; to make sin odious, and obedience more acceptable to us, 498 ; to commend the love of God to us, *ib.* ; to give us hope, *ib.* ; proofs

meet with, 217 ; be established in the peace of God. and never break this peace to obtain outward peace, *ib.* ; when troubles surprise you, consider how unbeseeming it is to take offence at God's providence, *ib.* ; consider that the hurt Satan intendeth you is not to hurt your bodies, but your souls, *ib.* ; consider how short is the prosperity of the wicked, *ib.*

Bad times, to be good in, requires much holiness and heavenly-mindedness, viii. 312 ; faith, or foresight of things to come, 313 ; zeal and love to God, *ib.* ; caution, *ib.* ; sincerity, 314 ; a fixed resolution, *ib.* ; a true sight of the worth of spiritual things above carnal, *ib.*

Balaam a notable instance of a natural conscience, i. 135.

Balaam's counsel did more hurt than his curse, xviii. 45.

BAPTISM, HOW OUGHT WE TO IMPROVE ? v. 459.

Baptism, our initiation into the service of God. doth not only imply work, but fight, i. 260.

    Implies a dedication and giving up ourselves to the Father, the Son, and the Holy Ghost, according to their personal relations, ii. 104 ; a badge and a bond, 107,

    Implieth a renunciation of sins, v. 313.

    A perpetual bond upon us, obliging us to repentance and holy life, v. 469 ; improvement of, the best preparation for the Lord's supper, *ib.* ; if not improved, will be a witness to solicit vengeance against us, *ib.* ; how to improve, *ib.* ; personally and solemnly own the covenant made with God in infancy, 470 ; often renew the sense of obligation, *ib.* ; use frequent self-reflection, *ib.* ; use it as a great help in all temptation, 471.

    Signifieth Christ's death for sin, and our death to sin, xi. 171 ; also Christ's resurrection and our newness of life, 172 ; strongly obligeth us to walk in newness of life, 173 ; is representing, 175 ; sealing, 177 ; obliging, *ib.*

    An engagement upon christians to abhor carnal living, xii. 47.

    A solemn vow and profession to look after the benefits of Christ's death and mortify the deeds of the body, xiii. 194.

    The use and respect of, with reference to remission of sin, xxi. 280.

Baptismal vow, wilful sin a renouncing of, viii. 393.

Baptist, his message to Christ not for his own satisfaction, but his disciples', ii. 79.

    Obstacles to the success of his preaching, iii. 195 ; the levity and rashness of the people, 196 ; evil influence of the scribes and pharisees, *ib.* ; offence at John's boldness, *ib.*

Basil the Great, reply to Modestus when threatened with banishment, xiii. 8.

Beasts, their tractableness to man contrasted with man's disobedience to God, iv. 291 ; art and skill to subdue, a relic and argument of our old superiority, 292.

Beauty not always a sign of excellency, xiv. 423 ; a gift of God, but not to be rested in or abused to feed pride, 424.

Beginning, a title of Christ (Col. i. 18), means that he is the root and the beginning of the renewed state, i. 454.

Belief of the truth, not a cold assent, but such a lively faith as brings us under the power of it, iii. 107 ; consists of fiducial assent and obediential confidence, 116.

Believer, sad condition of, under God's corrective discipline, though he do not vacate his justified state, ii. 234.

Believers, why so few, iii. 198 ; ignorance, *ib.* ; easy slightness, *ib.* ; careless
    security, 199 ; light esteem of Christ, 200 ; presumptuous conceit
    that we have entertained Christ already, *ib.* ; hardness of heart, 201 ;
    self-confidence, *ib.* ; carnal fears, 202 ; carnal reasonings from our sins,
    ib. ; carnal apprehensions of Christ, *ib.* ; fewness of, no disgrace to the
    gospel, 203.
True, cannot wholly fall away, iii. 359.
Are the seed of Christ, iii. 388 ; by reason of the gift of the Father,
    389 ; by purchase, *ib.* ; because begotten by his power and efficacy,
    390 ; by his image formed in them, *ib.*
Are friends of God, iv. 258 ; as they are perfectly reconciled unto
    him in Christ, *ib.* ; all dispensations and duties that pass between
    them are passed in a friendly way, *ib.* ; communication of goods, *ib.* ;
    communication of secrets, 259 ; conformity and correspondency of
    will and affection, *ib.* ; mutual delight and complacency, *ib.* ; the
    special favour and respect God beareth them, 260.
Given to Christ as subjects of his kingdom, x. 206, 318 ; as scholars in
    his school, 208, 319 ; as children of his family, *ib.* ; as the wife of his
    bosom, 209, 319 ; as members of his body, 209, 320 ; given to him
    in charge, 210 ; those thus given are the elect and none other, *ib.* ;
    he undertook for them to die for them, and that they should be con-
    verted, justified, sanctified, guided to glory, and that not one of them
    should miscarry, 212 ; the Father did not save by his own power, but
    committed to the Son, partly in majesty, *ib.* ; in justice, 213 ; in
    love and mercy, *ib.*
Commensurableness of the distinct propriety of the three persons of the God-
    head in, x. 256 ; all of them and none other are elected by the Father,
    all of them and none other are redeemed by the Son, all of them and
    none other are sanctified by the Spirit, *ib.* ; follows from the unity of
    essence, *ib.* ; from the unity and agreement in will and design, 257 ;
    denied by the Arminians in doctrine, and by common people in
    practice, *ib.*
Private, the honour put upon them, xi. 16.
Their condition better than if Adam had not fallen, xi. 58.
Reckoned sufferers with Christ, xiii. 191 ; what their being crucified
    with Christ implieth, 192.
The merits of Christ's obedience and death are applied and made bene-
    ficial to penitent, xviii. 218 ; and working, *ib.*
Believing, is that which gives most honour to God, i. 85.
    A holy obstinacy in, viii. 269 ; the less sensible evidence there is of the
        object of faith, the greater and stronger is the faith, if we believe
        it upon God's word, 270.
    In Christ, implies a lively sense of our own misery and the wrath of
        God due for sin, xi, 19 ; its explicit act is when a soul thus humbled
        casts itself upon Christ for grace, mercy, and salvation, 20 ; must be
        wrought by the word, 21.
    With the heart, implieth not a dead faith, but operative, xviii. 244.
Benefactor, God is a, to all men in the way of creation and providence, vii. 394;
        to his people in the way of grace and recovery by Christ, 395.
Benefits, memory of former, an encouragement to ask anew, x. 129.
Bernard's note on Martha's complaining of Mary, xiv. 71.
    Reply to the devil when tempted to vaingloriousness, xiii. 125.
Bible, nothing but a book of precedents, v. 168.
    Not only for novices and young christians, but for all, viii. 78.

decree and purpose of God, 387; accomplished notwithstanding
Isaac's reluctance, *ib.*; Esau not actually rejected till he had himself
rejected the blessing, 388; wherein lay the strength of Isaac's faith
in blessing Jacob and Esau concerning things to come, 389; lessons
from hence, 391.

Blessings, there is a difference not only between the blessings of the wicked
and the godly, but between those of the godly themselves, xiv. 399.
    Prayer gets, but thankfulness keeps, xviii. 38.

Blindness, spiritual, caution against, iii. 93; take heed of sinning against light,
    ib.; take heed of hypocrisy in the profession of the truth, *ib.*; take
    heed of pride and carnal self-sufficiency, 94.
    Spiritual, natural to us, vi. 167; worse than bodily, 168; God alone
    can remove, *ib.*; though in part cured, we need that God should open
    our eyes to the last, 170.

Blood of Christ, the only sufficient ransom for lost sinners, ii. 295.

'*Blood* of sprinkling' (Heb. xii. 24), the persons to whom it is applied,
    xxii. 108; the manner of application, 109; the subject to which it is
    applied, 110; the certainty of the effect, 111; the value and efficacy
    of it, 112; reasons why, 115.

Boasting, what lawful and what unlawful for a christian, iv. 63.
    A usual sin of the tongue, iv. 284.

Bodies of the saints, honour put upon, i. 475; they are members of Christ,
    and temples of the Holy Ghost, *ib.*
    What care we should take how we employ, xi. 254; the senses, *ib.*; the
    tongue, 255.

Bodily presence of Christ, withdrawal of from the world, x. 278; that he
    might try the world, and yet in a way suitable to his glorious estate,
    ib.; that way might be made for his spiritual presence, *ib.*; confuta-
    tion of the Lutherans, 279.

Body, God in covenant with, as well as with the soul, i. 157.
    Resurrection of the saints is incorruptible, ii. 465; glorious, *ib.*; spiri-
    tual, *ib.*
    Plainly seen to have some indirect operation upon the soul, iii. 304.
    Of sin, means the whole stock and mass of corruption, xi. 193; must
    not only have its face scratched, but must be destroyed, 194; serious
    reflection on the death of Christ the true way of subduing, 197.
    Why called vile, xx. 169; in respect of its original, *ib.*; sustentation
    and supports, 170; the many miseries to which it is obnoxious, *ib.*;
    often made the instrument of sin, *ib.*; vile in death, *ib.*; more so
    after death, *ib.*; its future condition, 171.

'*Born* of God,' what it is to be, xxi. 63.

Bottle in the smoke, the suffering believer compared to, vii. 372; it is dry,
    and wrinkled, and shrunk, so his bodily strength decays, 373; it is
    blacked and smutched, so his beauty is wasted as well as his strength,
    374; it is contemned and cast aside as useless, so he loses his esteem
    and regard among men, *ib.*

Bounty, God's common, easier to believe than his special love, i. 157.
    Of God, general, dispensed liberally, but not specially, iv. 38.
    And mercy of God an encouragement in asking spiritual gifts, vii. 186.

Brazen serpent, a type of salvation by Christ, xvii. 454; its history, 455;
    the typical use of it, 456; the resemblance between Christ and it,
    458; the super-excellency of Christ above this and all other types and
    shadows of him, 460; the lesson in faith to be derived from, 461.

Bread, petition for daily, why put first of those that relate to ourselves, i. 149.

Bread, in the sacraments, Romish adoration of, is idolatry, iii. 100.
Brethren, a word implying love and equality, xii. 28.

 Christ, having taken our nature, accepts and acknowledges us as his, xviii. 435; may we call him our brother? 436; brotherhood only reckoned to the sanctified, 438.
Brotherhood of Christ, a real privilege to us, x. 73; a comfort against a sense of our own unworthiness, *ib.*
Burden, believers in this mortal body are burdened with a heavy load of sin and affliction, xii. 469; why affliction is a burden, *ib.*; why sin, 470; it shows our folly that we are so loath to leave this world and prepare for a better, 471; the saints, being burthened, do in a holy manner groan and long for a better life, *ib.*; that this desire is not unnatural, *ib.*; nor the result of discontent or desperation, 472; the holiness of these groans and desires, *ib.*
Burial, in holy or consecrated places not necessary, xiv. 416; in places of worship, as it is very unhealthy and unseemly, so very modern, *ib.*; the decent burial of the saints agreeable to the word of God, 417.

Cæsar's virtues more amiable than Cato's, xii. 277.
Cain, the devil's patriarch, the first root of the seed of the serpent, v. 269.
 The first-fruits of the reprobate, the patriarch of unbelievers (Tertullian), x. 90, xiii. 435.
Calamities, the greatest, to be undergone rather than the smallest sin committed, vi. 223; the greatest nothing in comparison with desertions of God and terrors of conscience, *ib.*; meek suffering of, conduceth much to God's glory, *ib.*
 Of the faithful, not incompatible with the divine justice, viii. 447; God has an absolute dominion over us and our comforts, and may give and take them away according to his pleasure, *ib.*; intending to bestow eternal blessings upon them, he will take a liberty in disposing of outward things, *ib.*; it is fit, before they go to heaven, that they should be tried, 448; afflictions have their profit and use, and conduce to their good, 449; good men are but in part good, and it is fit their carnal part should be chastised, *ib.*
 In all, we should look to God, xix. 5; because nothing falleth out without his particular providence, 6; cross issues and punishments, as well as benefits and prosperous successes, come from him, *ib.*; a great advantage to patience under, when we can consider God not as an angry judge, but a gracious father, 7; not inconsistent with adoption, 9.
CALL, CHRIST'S, NO EXCUSE AGAINST A SPEEDY OBEYING, ii. 121.
Calling, effectual, God the author of, iii. 112; none else hath authority, *ib.*; or power, 113; is by the gospel, 114; is to faith, holiness, and salvation, 115; its glory, 118; all who are elected thus called, 119.
 Of a soul to God is a new begetting and regeneration, iv. 117.
 All that the saints have and enjoy is from God, v. 15; gives us a warrant that we may possess our privileges in Christ without intrusion and usurpation, *ib.*; gives us encouragement, *ib.*; in calling, God worketh in a way suitable to his nature and ours, strongly and sweetly, *ib.*; is from self to Christ, from sin to holiness, from misery to happiness, 16; is but election put in act, 18.
 Effectual, notes and marks of, v. 21; the preparations made for it, *ib.*; the instrument or means, the word, 22; the formal means or correspondent act of the creature to the call of God, 23; the concomitant

wisdom but folly, *ib.* ; that devilish which serveth envy and strife, 309.

Carnal men send out their thoughts to forestall and fore-enjoy their content-ments ere they obtain them, iv. 387 ; their confidence of future events, *ib.*

Men make a scorn of a holy life, vii. 41 ; seriousness in religion they count mopishness and melancholy, *ib.* ; self-denial, humorous folly, *ib.* ; zeal in a good cause, distemper and excess, *ib.* ; holy singularity, factiousness, *ib.* ; fervour of devotion, imposture and enthusiasm, *ib.* ; serious speaking of God and heavenly things, canting. 42 ; faith in a future eternal state, fond credulity, *ib.* ; humility and forgiveness, simplicity or stupidness, *ib.* ; exact walking, scrupulosity and per-verseness, *ib.* ; reasons, *ib.*

And spiritual draw contrary conclusions from the same principles, vii. 404.

Men do not, and cannot, please God, xi. 478 ; it is man's duty and happiness to please God, *ib* ; should be our work and scope, 473 ; no easy matter to make it so, *ib.* ; good actions of, do not please God, 481 ; there is a defect in their state, *ib.* ; a defect in the root of the actions, *ib.* ; a defect in the manner, *ib.* ; a defect in the end, *ib.* ; why they think so meanly of the people of God, 490.

Men are fools ; proved from scripture and their own course of life, xiii. 114.

Men may for a time be raised to extraordinary quickness in duties of worship, xiii. 462.

Men are incapable of anything well-pleasing to God, xiv. 90 ; the grounds we have to press men to the use of means although they themselves are distasteful to God, 99.

Men, God useth to give many temporal good things to, xviii. 298 ; be-cause all his creatures shall have some taste of his bounty, *ib.* ; that he may reward some good in them, *ib.* ; to show that these are not the chief good things by which his special love is manifested to us, 299 ; misery of, before death, 302 ; at death, 303 ; after death, 304.

Men may be deeply affected with the christian doctrine, even to great agonies of conscience, and yet finally miscarry, xviii. 359.

Things, man naturally addicted to, more than spiritual, and to worldly vanities rather than heavenly enjoyments, to the creature rather than to God, xviii. 468.

Carnalists, proud, who scorn the simplicity of the word, reproof of, viii. 342.

Casual and fortuitous things do certainly and infallibly fall out by God's providence and heavenly government, ii. 320.

Catechising, want of, a cause of decay of godliness, v. 435.

Cause of his people, God should be desired to plead when they have to do with unjust and wicked adversaries, ix. 135 ; he pleads as a judge. 137 ; his pleading not verbal or vocal, but real and active, 138 ; the effect is the clearing of his people, and convincing of their adversaries, 139 ; necessity of this pleading, 140 ; because the people of God are often in such a condition that none will plead their cause unless God plead it, *ib.* ; though we have a good cause and hopeful instruments, yet we cannot plead it with any effect till God show himself from heaven, 141.

Causes, second, God does not leave, to their power and force, as if he were only an idle spectator in the world, i. 151 ; not to be confided in, 159.

Second, a mutual dependence and subordination between all, iv. 472.

Celsus' objection against Origen, that faith introduced error into the world and cast out science, answered, xiii. 371.

Censurers usually have their own measure returned into their bosoms, iv. 271.

Censuring, wrong when we do it out of pride and conceit, iv. 272 ; when we do it as vaunting over their infirmities and frailties, *ib.* ; when the censure is unmerciful, 273 ; when we infringe christian liberty, and condemn others for things merely indifferent, *ib.* ; when we do not consider what may stand with charity as well as what will agree with truth, *ib.* ; when we do it to set off ourselves, *ib.*

Chance, what is, to men, is providence to God, ii. 317.

Change, godly men wait for, on others it cometh unexpected, iv. 391.

Charity and doing good with our estates a fruit of faith, ii. 150.

To the poor must be performed as worship, out of respect to God, iv. 176; and unspotted life must go together, 177.

A sign and argument of the forgiveness of our sins, but not a cause, iv. 473.

Excess of, is a betrayal of the faith, vi. 291.

Works of, done out of faith and love to God, of great weight and consequence, x. 65 ; a command of God requireth, *ib.* ; the trial of our love to Christ, 66 ; the great question interrogated by Christ at the great day of accounts, *ib.*

Use of faith in the duties of, xiii. 357.

Is that love wherewith we love God for himself, and our neighbour for God's sake, xviii. 135.

Excellency and necessity of, above all other gifts, xviii. 306 ; nature and properties of, *ib.* ; with or without, we are something or nothing in religion, 312.

And purity true notes of a believer, xxi. 82.

Chastisements are not in anger when they make us better, vii. 259.

Chief end of man as a subject for meditation, xvii. 306.

Child-bearing, though bringing forth children be according to the course of nature, yet God hath a great hand in it, xiv. 275 ; faith the best midwife, 276.

Child of God hath all the divine perfections in some measure in his soul, i. 188.

CHILDREN OF WISDOM, WISDOM JUSTIFIED BY, ii. 93.

Children, can never merit of their parents (Aristotle), xii. 33.

Of God, the privilege of being, assured to us by a double testimony, that of the Holy Ghost and of a renewed conscience, xii. 125 ; marks in scripture whereby we may determine our sonship, 127 ; the Spirit and our consciences concur to produce the same conclusion, 129; the necessity of this conjunction, *ib.* ; directions to ensure this twofold testimony, *ib.*

Of God, why they act in a manner different from others, xiii. 452 ; wherein lies the difference between the worship of, and that of nominal professors, 453.

Of believing parents partakers in the privileges of the covenant for their parents' sake, xiv. 205.

Of believers, though born in sin and under the curse, are endowed with special privileges, xiv. 406.

Of believers, how far a blessing may be looked for on, xv. 465; reasons, 468 ; how this can be reconciled with experience, 469 ; to whom the promise is most eminently fulfilled, *ib.* ; advice to parents, 470 ; advice to children, 471.

CHRIST'S TEMPTATION AND TRANSFIGURATION, i. 255.
CHRIST'S ETERNAL EXISTENCE AND THE DIGNITY OF HIS PERSON, i. 413.
CHRIST'S PERSON, DIGNITY OF, i. 413.
CHRIST'S CALL, NO EXCUSE AGAINST A SPEEDY OBEYING, ii. 121.
Christ's death set forth as a ransom and as a mediatorial sacrifice, i. 366 ;
    necessity of, 367 ; the sins and guilty fears of men need such a
    remedy, *ib.* ; the glory of God requires it, *ib.*
  Indwelling in his people, xi. 66 ; not essentially, for so he is everywhere,
    ib. ; nor personally, for that would involve a personal union, *ib.* ;
    but mystically, with respect to some peculiar operations which he
    worketh in them and not in others, *ib.* ; benefits of, *ib.* ; if Christ be
    not in us, the devil is, *ib.* ; where Christ is all the Trinity are, *ib.* ;
    where the Trinity are there is a blessing, 67 ; it is a pledge we shall
    have more, *ib.*
  Death, exhortation to improve, xii. 79 ; a lively and effectual pattern of
    our dying to sin, 80 ; an act of self-denial, *ib.* ; an act of pain and
    sorrow, *ib.* ; a price paid, *ib.*
  Death set forth by the notions of a ransom and a sacrifice, xiii. 180.
  Death, the end of, xiii. 195 ; a pattern to christians of dying unto
    sin, 196.
  Innocency and purity, xiii. 305.
  Second coming, it is the duty of God's children to look and long for,
    xvi. 208 ; reasons why, 209 ; objections answered, 214 ; the glory
    of it, 218 ; the preparation, *ib.* ; the appearance itself, 220 ; the con-
    sequences, 224 ; why the appearance of Christ will be so glorious,
    226 ; comfort and advice, 228.
  Victory in our nature over Satan, matter of great praise and thankful-
    ness to God, xviii. 16.
  Coming into the world for our redemption sometimes represented as an
    act of obedience to God, sometimes of love to us, xix. 180.
  Desertion by his father. See *Desertion.*
Christian, is a sacrifice to God, ii. 223 ; as separated from common use, *ib.* ;
    and dedicated to God, *ib.*
  Has God's law for his rule, God's Spirit for his guide, the promises for
    his encouragement, God's glory for his end, vi. 13.
  Life, all christians may have the approbation of God, the testimony of
    their own consciences, and the witness of the consciences of others,
    xiii. 104 ; the approbation of God should be chiefly sought after, but
    the others must not be disregarded, 106 ; how far the testimony of
    the consciences of others is to be regarded, 108.
CHRISTIANS, DISCOURSES TENDING TO PROMOTE PEACE AND HOLINESS
    AMONG, ii. 1.
Christians to be like a die in the hand of providence, content whether they be
    cast high or low, i. 77.
  Kings in respect of power and privileges, i. 95.
  Have to pray for the pardon of their sins, i. 176.
  Must expect not only to be tempted, but to be often tempted, i. 307 ;
    the best may be tempted to the most execrable sins, *ib.*
  Weak, are more swayed by fear, advanced by the love of God, ii. 66.
  Should be a transcript of their religion, ii. 109.
  The best, are those who have their corruptions most mortified, ii. 211 ;
    should now improve their christianity to get power and strength
    against sin, 212.
  Real, comparatively few, but absolutely many, iii. 13

greatest tribulations, 168 ; there is a special allowance of comfort for
God's children in their afflictions, *ib.* ; our comforts carry proportion
with our sorrows, *ib.* ; the heart the proper seat of spiritual comfort, *ib.* ;
is of God when it is allowed by him and warranted by him, 169 ; when
the matter is provided by him, 170 ; when it is wrought in us by him,
ib. ; God challengeth as his own right to comfort the heart of men, 171 ;
his Spirit alone can comfort the heart, *ib.* ; he is ready to comfort
poor afflicted creatures that humbly submit to him, 172 ; his comforts
come with authority, *ib.* ; are full and strong, *ib.* ; follows holiness as
heat doth fire, 173 ; a singular way of, beside the word, not to be
expected, *ib.* ; to be sought in the use of God's ordinances, 174 ; end
why God giveth us, to fortify us against the enemies of our salvation,
ib. ; hath a latitude in it, including support, peace, and joy, 176.

Comfort apt to divorce from duty, iv. 8.

Sometimes put for the object or thing comfortable, as deliverance and
temporal blessings, pardon of sins, &c., vii. 304 ; sometimes subjec-
tively, for the strengthening of the mind when it is apt to be weakened by doubts, fears, and sorrows, 305 ; by patience we are kept
from murmuring, by comfort from fainting, *ib.* ; peace is a fuller
degree of, *ib.* ; joy the fullest, 306 ; though not absolutely necessary
to salvation, yet conduces much to the well-being of a christian, *ib.* ;
follows holiness, as heat doth fire, *ib.* ; is a pledge of more to ensue,
ib. ; is to be asked of God, for it is his proper gift, *ib.* ; conveyed
through his word, 307 ; received on our part by prayer, 308 ; is all
from mercy, and tender mercy, 310.

Comforts, under temptation, i. 217 ; Christ hath overcome all his enemies, and
we are interested in his victory, *ib.* ; he hath a tender sense and knowledge of our estate, 218 ; he is engaged in the battle, and fights with
us, *ib.* ; he will reward us when we have done, *ib.* ; even before the
battle, the believer may be sure of victory, 219.

Worldly, a glut and fulness of, much more dangerous than hunger, i. 274.

We cannot have perpetual, i. 411.

When God has laid in a great store of, against sufferings, usually there
is a time of expense to lay them out again, iii. 62.

Carnal, God hath many ways to blast, iv. 405.

In affliction, all others are nothing to those which we have from the
word of God, vii. 28 ; they are divine, 29 ; strong, *ib.* ; full in measure, *ib.* ; full in matter, 30 ; reviving, 31 ; are applied by the Spirit
and received by faith, 35.

When God's children ask, they also beg grace to receive them acceptably,
viii. 416.

The word holds out, to us in affliction, ix. 23 ; the privileges of the
afflicted, *ib.* ; the blessedness of another world, *ib.* ; what is acceptable
to God, *ib.* ; notable precepts that ease the heart, *ib.* ; many promises
of God's being with us, and strengthening us, and giving us a gracious issue out of all our troubles, *ib.* ; bindeth faith, which fixeth the
heart, 24 ; afflictions do rather increase than diminish, *ib.*

Never prized but in their season, x. 309 ; in great troubles, *ib.* ; in the
hour of temptation and hard conflict with doubt and corruption,
ib. ; in times of great danger and defection, through terror and persecution, 310 ; in times of disheartening because of the difficulties of
religion, *ib.* ; in the hour of death, *ib.*

oming of Christ, patient waiting for, what it is, ii. 246 ; looking, 247 ; longing,
ib. ; inseparable from love to God, 249 ; its influence on the spiritual

operative, *ib.* ; we shall obey the commandments *as* God's commandments, *ib.*

Commandments, God's, it is the property of a gracious soul to delight in, ix. 20 ; because of the proportion and suitableness of the object to the grace in his heart, *ib.* ; because of possession of it and communion with it, *ib.* ; because of precedent love to it, *ib.* ; effects of this delight, 21 ; enlargement of heart, *ib.* ; a thirst for more of it, *ib.* ; makes the operation to the object more perfect than it would be, 22.

To keep, is a laborious thing, and requireth great diligence, ix. 204 ; requireth spirit and courage, *ib.* ; much self-denial and submission, 205.

Keeping of, is legal or evangelical, ix. 223.

What it is to keep the, xxi. 201 ; how this is a gospel conscience, 205 ; reasons why this constitutes a good and quiet conscience, 206.

Commands of God, legal and evangelical, vi. 337.

COMMENTARY, PRACTICAL, ON THE EPISTLE OF JAMES, iv. 1.

COMMENTARY, PRACTICAL, ON THE EPISTLE OF JUDE, v. 1.

Common work of grace may go far as to faith, ix. 324 ; as to hope, 327 ; as to love, 328 ; is not likely to hold out, *ib.* ; even if it do not fall out, is not enough to qualify for heaven and everlasting happiness, 329.

Communion with God lieth in fruition and familiarity, i. 16.

An hour's, with God, better than all the world, i. 117.

With God breedeth some assimilation to him, i. 349.

With God, conformity the ground of, iv. 371.

Of saints, excellency of, vii. 285.

With the death of Christ signifieth, by way of privilege, that we are partakers of the benefits of his death, xi. 163 ; by way of duty, that we are bound to renounce sin, *ib.* ; the sacraments are a solemn means of, 164 ; union with Christ the ground of, *ib.* ; this union and communion signified and sealed by the sacraments, 165 ; the sacraments chiefly relate to our communion with Christ's death, 166 ; shown by the interpretation of both in scripture. *ib.* ; and by the rites used in both, 167 ; by the nature of the case, 168.

With the church no small privilege, xiv. 398 ; should be earnestly sought both for ourselves and our children, 399.

With Christ, the nature and character of, xxi. 219 ; why a privilege peculiar to those who keep his commandments, 224.

Companions of them that fear the Lord, in what sense we are to be, vii. 176 ; we must join with them in the profession of the same faith and obedience to God, *ib.* ; must often meet together to join in the same worship, 177 ; must love them and prize them, and converse with them intimately for mutual edification, *ib.* ; must own them in all conditions, and take part and lot with them, *ib.* ; to this companionship our relation enforceth us, 178 ; the new nature welcometh us, 179 ; gratitude to Christ maketh us prize all that belong to him, *ib.* ; profit and utility redounding, *ib.*

Company, we are sooner made evil by evil, than good by good, i. 342.

In heaven, part of the blessedness of those who die in the Lord, ii. 468.

Ill, a man that keepeth, is like him that walketh in the sun, tanned insensibly, iv. 178.

And fellowship of his people, Christ taketh great delight in, xi. 98.

Complaint to God the best resource when we fail in our efforts to do good to a people, iii. 193.

Confidence, false, which keeps men from God and Christ, ii. 50 ; imaginary happiness and counterfeit righteousness, *ib.*

False, reasons of, ix. 378 ; self-love, *ib.* ; an overly sense of duty, *ib.* ; want of self-examination, *ib.* ; building upon false evidences, *ib.*

And comfort arise from a good conscience, or from sanctification as well as justification, ix. 453 ; the review of a well-spent life a great comfort in death, *ib.*

Towards God, what it is, xxi. 185 ; the nature of the privilege, 186 ; the influence of a good conscience upon communion with God, 188.

Conflict, the day of the church's, is mixed, and yieldeth great variety of providences, xv. 415 ; reasons of this mixture of providences, 416.

Conflicts and trials of christians, God will give a happy end to, that he may be known to be pitiful and merciful, i. 326 ; and faithful, *ib.*

Eminent, those who come out of, are usually delivered by God in a glorious manner, i. 332.

Conformity to Christ, the grounds of the conformity of believers are God's foreknowledge and predestination, xii. 301 ; the reason of this conformity, that 'he might be the first-born among many brethren,' 302 ; exhortation to look after conformity to Christ, 308.

Conquest of Christ, benefits we have by, iii. 468 ; banishment of distracting fears, *ib.* ; encouragement to the spiritual conflict, 469 ; joy unspeakable and glorious, *ib.* ; hopes of glory, *ib.* ; great comfort in his exaltation, 470 ; is a token, earnest, and pledge of our victory, *ib.* ; what he did in, he did for our sakes, *ib.* ; usefulness and serviceableness of all that befalls us, *ib.*

Conscience, natural, usually smites more for sins of commission than of omission, i. 14 ; yet omissions argue as great contempt of God's authority, 15 ; and as much hatred of God, *ib.* ; and are as much an argument of unregeneracy, *ib.*

One of God's books of record, i. 170.

A good, is entire and universal ; of hypocrites, partial, ii. 13.

The force of, usually felt after the fact, more than before or in the fact, ii. 179.

Hath a sense of eternal life and death, ii. 364.

Peace of, founded on Christ's satisfaction, but only found in his service, iv. 126.

Is a rule, a witness, and a judge, iv. 154 ; how to be used in these offices, 155.

God alone can give laws to, iv. 384.

To keep a good conscience, and to be faithful with God, though our temporal interests be endangered thereby, requires a lively faith concerning the world to come, vii. 157 ; a sincere love to Christ, 158 ; a well-grounded resolution in the truth, *ib.* ; a contempt of the world, 159 ; a sound belief of God's providence, *ib.*

To smother and stifle the checks of, doth but increase our misery, xii. 106.

The testimony of, that we are the children of God, xii. 125 ; a secret spy within us, that observeth all our thoughts and actions, *ib.* ; called 'the candle of the Lord' (Prov. xx. 27), 126 ; the legal conscience condemneth, but the evangelical conscience acquitteth, *ib.* ; by nature is blind, partial, stupid, but by grace is pure, tender, pliant, *ib.*

A good or a bad, the beginning of heaven or hell, xii. 465.

In the guilty, an evidence of the certainty of eternal punishment, xiii. 49.

ing, 56 ; disobedience, *ib.* ; weakness of faith, *ib.* ; want of love, or coldness of love, *ib.* ; want of patience, or tarrying God's season till the promise bring forth, 57 ; we must not only continue, but continue instant, 58 ; because it is not enough to keep up the duty, unless we keep up the affections that must accompany the duty, *ib.* ; a seeming repulse or denial should make us more vehement, *ib.* ; God's dearest children are not admitted at the first knock, *ib.* ; we must not only continue praying when Christ seemeth to neglect us, but when he giveth a contrary answer, *ib.* ; whether God answereth or no, it is the duty of faith to answer itself, 59.

Controversies about trifles, great evil of, v. 117.

Religious, cautions as to conducting, v. 262.

The word to be made the judge of all, x. 460.

Of the present age, importance of a clear and satisfactory knowledge in, xi. 123 ; rules regarding, *ib.*

Controversy, every private christian not bound to study, vi. 293.

Conversation, what kind of, honoureth religion, ii. 107 ; such as is carried on with diligence and seriousness, *ib.* ; such as is governed by the respects of the other world, 108 ; such as is characterised by exact purity and holiness, 109.

Is generally either profane and sinful, vi. 126 ; or idle and vain, *ib.* ; or tattling, *ib.* ; or worldly, *ib.*

Should be edifying, xviii. 392 ; because our tongue is our glory, *ib.* ; because holy conference and edifying discourse is a means of spiritual improvement, *ib.* ; because it is a great comfort and quickening to confer together of holy things, *ib.* ; because the well-ordering of our words is a great point of christianity, 393 ; in order to, we must get a good stock of sound scriptural knowledge, 394.

Converse and conference of godly persons comfortable and pleasant, and much excelleth the merriest meetings of the carnal, vii. 287.

Conversion, God keeps, in his own hand, i. 79.

In the work of, God doeth all ; after, he still concurreth, i. 138 ; and that not only in the general, but in every act from the beginning of the spiritual life to the end, 139.

How described in scripture, i. 141 ; enlightening the mind, *ib.* ; opening the heart, *ib.* ; regeneration, *ib.* ; resurrection, *ib.* ; creation, 142 ; not in power of man to convert himself, *ib.* ; objections answered, 143.

In producing, God works according to man's nature and the principles thereof, i. 144 ; and to men's particular characters and tempers, *ib.* ; almighty power goes along with persuasion, 145 ; this power secret, but prevailing, *ib.*

Of a sinner more pleasing to God than his destruction, i. 388.

More hard to continue in, than to convert ourselves at first, iii. 179.

Of a soul, how difficult, iii. 207 ; obstacles to, *ib.* ; Satan, *ib.* ; the perverseness of man's heart, *ib.*

Beginning of, not in man's power, iv. 369.

Of a sinner properly God's work, yet ascribed to men as the ministers and instruments of it, iv. 473, 478.

Evident in fruit if not in feeling, v. 20.

So described in scripture as to inuicate the helplessness of man, v. 479.

Causes of putting off, vii. 144 ; unbelief, *ib.* ; security, *ib.* ; averseness of heart from God, *ib.* ; love of the world and of present delights and contentments, 145 ; heinousness of putting off, *ib.* ; it is flat

Covenant, new, exacts perfect, but accepts sincere, obedience, vii. 319.

New, quickening and enlivening grace promised in, ix. 94; both generally and particularly, *ib.*; encouragement to pray for grace, 95.

A manifest abuse of, to imagine that it countenanceth any licentiousness or liberty in sin, xi. 300; shown from God's design in setting it up, *ib.*; from its tenor and constitution, 301.

New, is a law, xi. 398; man, being God's creature, is his subject, and standeth related to him as his rightful governor, and therefore is to receive what laws he is pleased to impose upon him, *ib.*; man, as a reasonable and free agent, is bound voluntarily to yield up himself in subjection to his proper Lord, *ib.*; man, being bound to obey the will of God, needeth a law from God to constitute his duty, and direct him in it, *ib.*; the gospel, which is both our rule and charter, is the law which in Christ's name is given to the world, 399; agreeth with human laws in the promulgation of it with full authority, 400; in obligation and force, *ib.*; in having a sanction, *ib.*; in the sanction supposing an exercise of government according to law, 401; differs from ordinary human laws in that man in these laws barely enjoins authoritatively, but God condescends to reason, persuade, and beseech, 402; in that the law of God binds the conscience and the immortal souls of men, *ib.*

Of works, what it is, xvi. 438; all are by nature under this covenant, *ib.*; this is that which natural conscience sticks to, 439; this covenant, rightly understood, is the most ready way to convince justiciaries, and to prepare men for Christ, *ib.*

God's, with his people, xviii. 75; made to show the freeness of his grace, *ib.*; and the sureness of his mercy, 76; to leave the greater bond and obligation upon us, *ib.*; to make us more willing to serve him, entering upon his service by choice, 77; to put an honour upon his creatures, *ib.*; that both parties might be engaged to each other by mutual consent, *ib.*; none can be made with God without the interposing of a sacrifice, 78.

Legal, tenor of, xviii. 237; life promised to perfect obedience, a curse threatened to disobedience, 238.

God's people not only keep covenant with him, but the covenant keepeth them, xviii. 351; seal of, 352; those in covenant with him are his, *ib.*; by eternal election, *ib.*; by effectual calling, 353; by entering into covenant with him, *ib.*; he knoweth them, *ib.*; as elected, called in covenant, *ib.*; taketh notice of them with love, delight, approbation, 354; communicates to them saving benefits, *ib.*; their obligation to depart from all iniquity, 355.

Covenants, two, agree in their author, viii. 371; in the moving cause, which in both was the grace of God, 372; in the parties, God and man in both, *ib.*; in that God giveth sufficiency of strength to the parties with whom he made them to fulfil the conditions thereof, *ib.*; in that in both God kept up his sovereignty, and did not by his condescension part with anything of his dominion over men, 373; in both there is a mutual obligation on both parties, *ib.*; the conditions in both were suitable to the ends and scope appointed, *ib.*; differ in the ends, that of the first being to preserve and continue man in the happiness in which it found him; of the second, to restore him to the happiness which he had lost, 374; as to God, the glory of his creating bounty was the end of the first, the glory of his redeeming grace of

the second, *ib.* ; in their nature, the first stood more by commands
and less by promises, the second more by promises and less by commands, 375 ; in the terms ; unsinning obedience the condition of the
first, pardon offered in the second, 376.

Covenanting with God pressed, viii. 90 ; God's laws holy, just, and good,
therefore we should not be backward to swear to him, *ib.* ; we are
obliged by God's command, *ib.* ; actual consent and resolution quickens
our sense of duty, *ib.* ; profitable to choose the strictest engagements,
91 ; necessity of, because of our laziness, *ib.* ; fickleness, *ib.* See
Oath and *Resolution.*

Covetousness sold Christ, and envy delivered him ; these two sins still enemies
to the christian profession, iv. 303.

And carnality compared, v. 272.

A base affection, that will put a man upon the basest and most unworthy practices, iv. 336.

Bringeth God's curse upon our estates, iv. 404.

Is an inordinate desire of having more wealth than the Lord alloweth in
the fair course of his providence, vi. 379 ; and a delight in worldly
things as our chiefest good, *ib.* ; its causes, 380 ; distrust of God's
providence, and discontent with God's allowance, *ib.* ; shown by
greedy getting, 381 ; and unworthy detention, 382 ; a great hin-
drance to compliance with God's testimonies, 383.

Scripture always representeth as an odious and detestable thing, xix.
192.

Creation distinguished from emanation, i. 436.

Should be nothing in our esteem, so far as it would be something
separate from God, or in co-ordination with God, i. 276.

And providence, God's greatness and majesty seen in, i. 403.

Is either out of nothing, or *ex inhabili materia*, ii. 387.

New, is more than a moral change, ii. 386 ; or a temporary change, *ib.* ;
or a change of outward form, *ib.* ; or a partial change, *ib.* ; belongeth
to God, *ib.* ; far surpasseth that which maketh us creatures only, 387 ;
God's way of concurrence to, *ib.* ; the mediation of Christ concerned
in with respect to his merit, 388 ; and in regard of efficacy, 389 ;
necessity of, *ib.* ; because of the badness of our former estate, *ib.* ;
from the nature of God's work, 390 ; with respect to Christ, 391 ;
with respect to the use which it serveth, *ib.* ; in order to present
communion with God, *ib.* ; to service and obedience to God, 392 ; to
future enjoyment of God, *ib.* ; known by a new mind, a new heart,
and a new life, 394.

The new, doth carry a great correspondence with the old, iii. 183.

As a well-tuned instrument, but man maketh the music, iv. 294.

The morning of, xii. 180.

A work of omnipotency, xiii. 242.

Consideration of, a necessary exercise for the children of God, xiii. 389 ;
discovers much of the essence and attributes of God, his goodness,
power, and wisdom, *ib.* ; a wonderful advantage to faith in giving us
hope and consolation in distress, 391 ; puts us in mind of our duty,
ib. ; motives to quicken us to this necessary work of reflecting on
creation, 392 ; directions how to improve it to comfort and profit,
397 ; special occasions when we should propose to ourselves thoughts
of creation, 398 ; proper objects of meditation on God's several and
special excellences, 400 ; the ends of the creation, 404 ; the fruits of
solemn and serious thoughts on creation, 406 ; the truths and won-

ders of, understood by faith, and not by reason, 409 ; the world framed in an accurate, orderly, and perfect manner, 415 ; wherein this order and beauty consists, 416 ; objection answered, whence come all those disorders that are in the world ! 420 ; the wisdom and majesty of God discovered in the order of causes and admirable contrivance of the world, 422 ; shows how pleasing order and method are to God, 424 ; discovers the odiousness of sin, that disjointed the frame of nature, 426 ; the instrument in creation was 'the word of God,' 429 ; meaning of the term, 430 ; *quest.*, whether all things were created in the twinkling of an eye by God's will and pleasure, or were done by distinct days, as the history in Genesis seemeth to intimate ! 431 ; the matter or term from which the world was made, 433.

Creation, opinions of the ancients concerning, xiii. 412.

Creature, God defrauded by over-delight in, i. 238.

> Greatest glory of, to serve the will and set forth the praise of the Creator, i. 438.
>
> In what sense nothing, ii. 321 ; in comparison with God, 322 ; in exclusion of God, *ib.* ; in opposition to God, *ib.* ; the true apprehension of this mightily useful for the spiritual life, 323.
>
> Cannot yield us any comfort without God's gift or grant, iii. 167.
>
> Vanity of, matter of sense and plain experience, vii. 455 ; should be observed and improved by faith, 456 ; should moderate our desires, 457 ; our sorrows and fears, 458 ; our delights, *ib.* ; stability of the word of God often opposed to, *ib.*
>
> Meaning of the word in relation to waiting for the manifestation of the sons of God, xii. 148 ; how the creature waiteth, *ib.* ; for what, 149.
>
> In what sense made subject to vanity, xii. 157 ; by order of its natural estate, 158 ; in regard of the vanity of corruption, 159 ; in regard of its final dissolution and last change, *ib.* ; in regard of its end and use, *ib.* ; the way in which the creature came into the present state, negatively and positively expressed, 161 ; by man as a sinner, 162 ; by the will and power of the Creator, *ib.* ; reasons why the innocent creature is punished for man's sin, 163 ; the creature still an instrument of sin, 164 ; in the curse on the creature man is punished, *ib.* ; how far the creature shall be made partaker of the same glory with God's children, 167.
>
> The new, produced by the Spirit, and cannot subsist without his continual presence, xix. 399.

Creatures are sanctified to us when we enjoy God in them, i. 153.

> All, put us in mind of God, vii. 82.
>
> Men as, are some way encouraged to ask of God the grace of the new creature, vii. 271 ; man is God's immediate workmanship, *ib.* ; the making of man now is the work of God, as well as the making of the first man was, 272 ; man was created to serve God, 273 ; men are now strangely disabled to serve and please him, *ib.* ; must be new made and born again before we can know or do the will of God, 274 ; when we seek this grace, or any degree of it, it is a proper argument to urge that we are God's creatures, 275 ; it is asking another gift, because we have received one already, *ib.* ; God beareth much affection to man as he is his creature, *ib.* ; creation implieth some hope, because God forsaketh none but those who first forsake

him, 276 ; there is encouragement to faith from the resemblance between creation and regeneration, 277 ; the manner of pleading thus some preparatory work of grace, *ib.*

Credulity, uncharitable, leads to detraction, ii, 277.

Cross, how to be taken up daily, ii. 116.

Romish worship of, is idolatry, iii. 100.

The inheritance of the Church (*Ecclesia est hæres crucis*—Luther), iv. 75.

We never advance more in christianity than under, vi. 223.

What it is to take up the, xvii. 3 ; how daily, 5 ; reasons why followers of Christ must prepare their shoulders for, 6 ; it is not enough to bear, but we must take it, 9.

Crosses, christians should look for, ix. 127 ; be prepared for, *ib.* ; bear with patience when they come, 128.

Crying sins, what so called, iv. 409.

CURE DISTRACTIONS IN HOLY DUTIES, HOW WE MAY, v. 441.

Curse, upon the impenitent and obstinate sinner, vi. 200 ; the knowledge of this duty doth but the more irritate corruption, 201 ; the exaction of duty doth either terrify or stupefy the conscience, *ib.* ; is upon all that he hath, *ib.* ; and all that he doeth, *ib.* ; he is bound over, body and soul, to everlasting torment, *ib.*

Every man is by nature under, x. 89 ; there is no way to come out from, but in closing with Christ, *ib.* ; there must be an unfeigned love to him, else the curse doth remain, *ib.* ; this love must be expressed by sincere obedience, 90 ; God's, is very dreadful, *ib.* ; we know not how soon God may carry it out, and cut us off from the possibility of grace, 91 ; is ratified at the last day by Christ's sentence, *ib.* ; shall be presently executed, *ib.* ; motives to come to Christ for removal of, *ib.*

Daily bread, why we are taught to pray for, i. 165 ; that we may pray daily, *ib.* ; that there may be family prayer, *ib.* ; to make way for our gratitude, *ib.* ; to show us every day that we should renew our dependence on God, 166 ; that we may not burden ourselves with overmuch thoughtfulness, *ib.* ; to teach us that worldly things are to be sought in a moderate proportion, *ib.* ; to make us think of the uncertainty of our lives, *ib.* ; to awaken us after heavenly things, *ib.*

Danger, secure hearts cannot endure to think of ; believers do, but more of Christ, iii. 200.

Of life, God's children may be in, from day to day, viii. 116 ; why God permits this, 117 ; to check security, *ib.* ; to wean us from creature confidences and dependency, *ib.* ; to check worldliness, *ib.* ; that they may value eternal life the more, 118 ; to try their affections to him and his word, 119 ; to show his power in their preservation, *ib.* ; and in overruling all that befalls them for the increase and benefit of his church and people, *ib.*

No kind of, should make us warp and turn aside from the directions of God's word, viii. 124 ; a christian should be above all temporal accidents, *ib.* ; God can preserve us, *ib.* ; we renounced all at our first coming to Christ, *ib.* ; our sufferings shall be abundantly recompensed and made up in the world to come, 125 ; constancy is necessary, *ib.*

Of a nation doth not lie in outward probabilities so much as in the

himself, must give place to mercy, much more ought externals of human institution, 11.

183 ; to be sought of God, 184 ; especially to be sought when we begin to decline, 185 ; in unsettled times, 186.

ESTATE, BLESSED, OF THEM THAT DIE IN THE LORD, ii. 455.

Esteem, christians should not religiously value others for external and carnal advantages, xiii. 220 ; not to deny civil regard and honour to the wicked and carnal, but render that respect which is due to their rank and quality, *ib.* ; the cause of God must not be abandoned because those of the other side have more outward advantages, 221.

Of Christ, how Christ must be esteemed, speculatively and practically, xiv. 463 ; reasons why Christ must be so esteemed that his worst may be better to us than the world's best, 465.

ETERNAL EXISTENCE, CHRIST'S, i. 413.

Eternal punishment may, without injustice, be inflicted for sin of short continuance, v. 288.

As God is, so is his word, vii. 391.

Life not a chimera, vii. 405 ; not upon impossible terms, *ib.* ; not upon a defective conveyance, *ib.*

Life everywhere propounded in scripture as the great encouragement of our endeavours either in subduing sin or perfecting holiness, xii. 83 ; reasons proving that the life promised as the reward of mortification is eternal life, 83 ; the expediency of the promise of eternal life as the fruit of the mortification of sin, 86 ; the nature of this life, its personal benefit and happiness, *ib.* ; a threefold use of the reward of eternal life in the work of mortification, 87 ; the sufficiency and powerfulness of the motive, because of its certainty and excellence, 88 ; compared with life natural and spiritual, 89.

Life must be expected in the way of God's promise, xii. 198 ; its expectation is certain and desirous, 199.

Life, the qualifications of those who shall enjoy this blessed estate, xii. 436 ; different persuasions in point of certainty as to interest in, 438 ; reasons why we should attend upon the work of assuring ourselves the possession of eternal life, 439 ; the virtue and force of this assurance, 440 ; exhortation to belief in the promised glory, 442 ; the necessity of this belief, *ib.* ; it constituteth a main difference between the animal and spiritual life, 443 ; it is little credited in the world, *ib.* ; evidence of this, 444 ; how faith in the gospel worketh us to the other world, 446 ; how we should rouse up our faith, and more firmly believe the promised glory, 447 ; next to a sound belief of it there must be an earnest expectation of it, *ib.* ; we should diligently prepare and seek after it in the way of holiness, 448 ; clear up our interest in it, 449 ; and improve it to the vanquishing of temptations, *ib.*

Punishments and rewards, their end is that every man may receive according to his deserts, xiii. 81 ; the distinction of persons, *ib.* ; as there are different persons, so there are different recompenses, 82 ; the notions by which these different states are expressed, 83 ; they are alike eternal, 85 ; how it can stand with the justice of God to cast men into everlasting torment, *ib.* ; the sentence certain, speedy, and unavoidable, 87 ; executed upon the wicked first, 88.

Life, the right and interest of believers in, proved from scripture and by reason, xiv. 40 ; persuasions to faith on this ground and motive, 42 ; directions how to exercise and act faith in order to eternal life, 43 ; the love and grace of God in providing such an estate, 46 ; a comfort to God's children against want, trouble, and death, *ib.*

prayer, x. 111 ; spiritual reverence of God, 112 ; confidence in God, and a disclaiming of all sublunary confidences, *ib.* ; taking off the heart from the world, and from carnal desires, *ib.*

Fainting, of the soul is when comfort is quite gone, vii. 354 ; arises from the tediousness of present sorrows and pressures, 355 ; or from a fervent and strong desire, *ib.* ; either causeth great trouble and dejection of spirit, or defection and falling off from God, *ib.* ; considerations to preserve us from, 356.

It is a great infirmity and weakness if a christian should faint in a time of trouble, xii. 227 ; reasons why, *ib.* ; weariness and fainting compared, *ib.* ; in this weakness, if left to ourselves, we should fail but for the help of the Holy Spirit, 228 ; they who rouse themselves up and use all means are in a nearer capacity to receive this help than others, 229 ; exhortations against fainting under troubles, 230.

FAITH, SAVING, EXCELLENCY OF, ii. 140.

FAITH, LIFE OF, A TREATISE ON THE, xv. 45.

Faith, begotten in the word, exercised in prayer, i. 30.

Its nature is to appropriate and apply, i. 55.

Hope, love, and zeal, lead christians to desire Christ's second coming, i. 115 ; also their experiences, 116.

Three things in, assent, acceptance, dependence, i. 390.

Convinces us of the worth and truth of the things promised by God through Christ, ii. 141 ; what that is by which the just do live, 142 ; it looketh mainly to heaven, *ib.* ; the sure ground which it goeth upon is God's promise through Jesus Christ, 143 ; its nature is trust and confidence, 145 ; its immediate fruit and effect is a forsaking all other hopes and happiness for Christ's sake for the blessedness which he offereth, 146.

Doth not merit salvation as a reward, ii. 153 ; is assent, consent, and affiance, 154 ; is a believing in Christ, 155 ; the prime benefits which it respecteth are reconciliation with God, and the everlasting fruition of him in glory, 156 ; immediate acts and effects of, 158.

And repentance, in what they agree, ii. 194 ; in what they differ, 195 ; reasons why these are required in order to pardon, 196.

A firm and cordial assent to truth, ii. 349 ; a consent to receive Christ as offered, 350 ; trust in him for the blessings he hath procured for us and promised to us, 351.

Why required that we may receive benefit by Christ, ii. 353 ; in respect of God, that our hearts may be possessed with a full apprehension of his grace, *ib.* ; with respect to Christ, because it alone can apprehend the whole dispensation of grace by him, 354 ; because till we believe in him, we can have no comfort or use of all his offices, *ib.* ; with respect to that holiness and obedience which God expecteth from the creature, 355 ; with respect to our comfort, *ib.* ; confutation of presumptions regarding, 356.

Alone is but as sight, with love as taste, iii. 81.

Though the gift of God, yet we must labour for, iii. 215 ; to see our own weakness, *ib.* ; to manifest our obedience to God, and meet him in his own way, *ib.* ; to manifest our desires after it, 216 ; because, although we may not get faith by using the means, we shall not without using them, *ib.* ; likely that God will meet us in his own way, *ib.* ; his usual way to meet those that seek him, *ib.*

Is to a godly, as reason is to a natural man, iii. 226.

VOL. XXII.

O

as it works upon the promises, begets love and hope ; it works upon the threatenings, begets fears, 195 ; what this godly fear is, 196 ; the difference between servile and filial fear, 197 ; as the fear of Noah was the fruit of his faith, so his preparing the ark was the fruit of his fear, 201 ; this act considered in several regards; *ib.*; the ark a type of Christ, 203 ; as Noah was buried alive in the ark, so are we 'buried with Christ in baptism,' 204 ; wicked children of believing parents are partakers in the temporal blessings of the covenant for their fathers' sakes, 205; encouragements to godly parents concerning their children, *ib.*; since children are beloved of God for their parents' sakes, this should serve to shame and terrify those born of godly parents who are not so themselves, 206 ; how the faith of Noah condemned the world, 207 ; the advantages derived from the example of the godly, 208 ; christians should walk so that they may condemn the world, not by their censures, but by their lives, 212 ; directions, *ib.* ; motives, 213 ; whether all that were drowned in the flood were eternally lost, 216.

Faith, wherever it is, bringeth forth true obedience, xiv. 227 ; the ground of this obedience is the call of God, which usually consists of a command and a promise, *ib.* ; this call is of grace, 228 ; when God calls us to grace, we are not only to leave sin and the world, but all things that are dear to us, 229 ; when we give up ourselves to Christ, God would have us sit down and count the charges, 230 ; faith may sometimes make a halt and grow weary, but it rouseth itself up again, 231, 423 ; it constantly adheres to God, though it doth not presently find what it believes and expects, 231 ; how we shall know that we are called of God, 232 ; how we should behave ourselves in our calling, that we may manifest the obedience of faith, 237.

It is not enough that we live by faith, we must also die by faith, xiv. 281 ; reasons why, *ib.* ; what it is to die in faith, 284 ; reasons why they that would die in faith must live in faith, 290.

Is contented with the promises though it cannot have actual possession, xiv. 293 ; the advantage of the promises to, *ib.* ; there is not only a work of faith upon the promise, but upon the heart of the believer, 295 ; is an act of apprehension, 298 ; it apprehends the blessings as real, *ib.* ; it pondereth the worth of them, *ib.*, there is actual expectation, 299 ; that there is assent and persuasion proved from scripture, *ib.* ; this persuasion rests on God's truth and power, 300 ; is an act of the will as well as of the understanding, 302 ; the affection that is exercised in embracing the promises is joy, 303 ; this joy is manifested partly by the lively act of it in meditation, partly by the solid effects of it in our conversation, 303 ; the need there is of the power of the Spirit in the whole business of faith, 305 ; the difference between faith and other things, *ib.*

The trial of Abraham's faith, xiv. 353 ; the greatness of it, *ib.* ; his behaviour under it, 354.

In difficult cases, we must do our duty, and refer the event and success to the power of God, xiv. 369.

Spieth light at a little hole, xiv. 420.

Teaches men openly to renounce all worldly honours, advancements, and preferments, when God calls us from them, or when we cannot enjoy them with a good conscience, xiv. 431 ; how far the honours and glories of the world are to be renounced, *ib.* ; how faith operates in this renunciation, 434 ; use of this doctrine, 439 ; sundry considera-

his children must consider him as an exact and impartial judge of all
their actions, *ib.*; the strictness and justice of his judgment, 92; his
final sentence a matter of terror, 93; the execution, in case of failure
in our duty, terrible beyond expression, *ib.*; the wrath of God the
greatest evil that can befall us, *ib.*; different kinds of fear distinguished, 96; reasons why true fear of the Lord should have an
influence upon us, 97; the means how this fear cometh to be raised
in us, *ib.*

Fear that sanctifieth, and that only awakeneth for a time, distinction between, xviii. 360.

Holy, is of two kinds—of reverence, xviii. 411; of caution, 412.

Fears, carnal, hinder the soul from closing with the mercy that is in Christ, iii.
202; of God's anger, *ib.*; of being too bold with the promises, *ib.*;
of the sin of presumption, *ib.*

And cares relieved by consideration of God's faithfulness, vii. 298.

Fearlessness in owning the testimonies and ways of God before any sort of
people in the world, incumbent on us, vi. 491; holy boldness in
confession a special gift of God, *ib.*; a duty contained in our first dedication and resignation of ourselves to Christ, *ib.*; confirmed in us by
faith, 492; love to God, *ib.*; fear of God, *ib.*; a deep sense of the
world to come, 493.

Felicity, temporal, christians are not to reckon on, i. 333.

Fervency in prayer arises from a broken-hearted sense of our wants, and a
desire of the blessing we need, i. 37.

Filthiness, all sin is, iv. 148; but chiefly covetousness, lust, anger, and malice, *ib.*

'*Finished,* it is,' in what sense said, xix. 31; all the scripture prophecies
which spake of Christ's death and sufferings were now accomplished,
ib.; the substance of the types was accomplished, 33; all was finished
that was necessary to make him a fit pattern of patience to us, *ib.*;
all was fulfilled which God determined to be done for the expiation
of sin, 35.

First-born from the dead, a title of Christ, i. 455.

First-fruits of the Spirit, what they are, xii. 186; what use they serve, 187;
they that have received the first-fruits of the Spirit groan and wait for
a better estate than they now enjoy, 188; they are more apprehensive
of the misery of this life than others are or can be, 190; more
sensible of sin as a burden, 191; they are confirmed in the belief of
the certainty of this better estate, 192; do in part know the excellency of it, *ib.*; are prepared and fitted for it, *ib.*; and their right
and title to it is assured, 193; none but those who have the first-
fruits of the Spirit will hope for eternal life, 194.

Of faith, in what they consist, xiii. 330.

'*First* shall be last,' not universally and necessarily, but for the most part,
xxii. 42; not only persons, but nations and communities, *ib.*; is to
be understood with respect to matters of religion, *ib.*; and last may
be first, 48.

Flesh, confidence in, what it is, ii. 46; trusting in external privileges and
performances, *ib.*; this confidence natural to men, 49; why a good
christian should have none, 51.

Lust of, means the inordinate motions of corrupt nature, ii. 285; derived
to us from Adam in his apostasy, 287; prompts to do those things
which are most acceptable to sense, or agreeable to worldly or carnal
ends, *ib.*; still remains in the christian, though not in full force,

288 ; is importunate to be pleased, 289 ; lusts of, different in different men, 292.

Flesh and spirit, mean corrupt nature and the new nature, xi. 392 ; both
serve, to those who are influenced by them, as a guiding and inciting
principle, *ib.* ; those who are under the prevalency of the one principle
cannot wholly obey and follow the other, *ib.* ; every christian hath
these two principles in himself, the one by nature, the other by grace,
393 ; though both be in the children of God, yet the Spirit is in
predominancy, *ib.* ; the prevalency of the principle is known, not
only by the bent and habit of the will, but by the settled course of
the life, *ib.*

Or spirit, all men are after the one or the other, xi. 438 ; there is a
twofold original, 439 ; producing a twofold principle, *ib.* ; supported
and assisted by contrary powers, *ib.* ; under a distinct covenant, *ib.* ;
issuing into two places or eternal states, heaven and hell, 440.

Things of, are either things manifestly evil, as all vices and sins, xi.
441 ; or things good in their own nature, but immoderately affected,
ib. ; minding of, what? 443.

What is meant by, xii. 37 ; what it is to live after, *ib.* ; what is the
death threatened to those who so live, 39 ; its consistency with the
justice, wisdom, and goodness of God, 40 ; the certainty of its accomplishment, 44 ; the folly of those who would reconcile God and the
flesh, 46 ; dissuasives from living a fleshly life, *ib.* ; means to come
out of this estate and course of sin, 49.

Knowing Christ after the, not the respect he looked for while on earth,
but by faith, in the spirit, xiii. 222 ; there is a knowing Christ after
the flesh since his ascension into heaven, 224 ; by a naked profession
of his name without conformity to his laws, *ib.* ; by acts of sensitive
affection in reading or meditating on the story of Christ's sufferings,
or when you hear his passion laid open in a rhetorical manner, 225 ;
by expressing our respect more in pomp and pageantry than serious
devotion, or a hearty obedience to his laws, or worshipping him in
spirit and in truth, 226 ; by herding with a stricter party whilst yet
our hearts are unsubdued to God, 227 ; reasons why this knowing
Christ after the flesh will do us no good as to the salvation of our
souls, *ib.* ; reproof of those who please themselves with this deceit of
the heart, 228.

FOLLOWERS OF CHRIST, FAITHFUL, MUST EXPECT TROUBLE, ii. 113.

Fool, none like the sinner, that ventureth his soul at every cast, and runneth
blindfold upon the greatest hazard, iv. 300.

Forbearance towards erring brethren enforced by lowliness, meekness, long-
suffering, and love, ii. 71 ; considerations to press to, 77.

Brotherly, to be exercised towards those who hold the foundation, x.
331.

Forgiving our debtors not a meritorious cause of God's forgiving us, i. 182 ;
nor a pattern or rule to him, 183 ; it doth not import priority of
order, as if our acts had the precedency of God's, *ib.* ; it doth not
import an exact equality, but some kind of resemblance, 184 ; it is a
condition or moral qualification which is found in persons pardoned,
ib. ; it is a sign or note of a pardoned sinner, *ib.* ; it is a necessary
effect of pardoning mercy shed abroad in our hearts, *ib.* ; it is a duty
incumbent on them that are pardoned, *ib.* ; it is an argument breed-
ing confidence in God's pardoning mercy, 185 ; consists in forbearing

224   INDEX.

Glory already given by Christ to his people, though they have it not yet in possession, xi. 61.

Of Christ in the excellency of his person, xi. 102 ; the charity of his human nature, *ib.* ; the beholding of, is our happiness in heaven, 103.

Life of, an object of faith, xi. 216 ; grounds of believing, 217 ; the infinite love of God, *ib.* ; the everlasting merit of Christ, *ib.* ; the almighty power of the sanctifying Spirit both to change the soul and raise the body, *ib.* ; the immutable covenant or promises of the gospel, 218 ; the unquestionable right of those who are dead with Christ, *ib.*

Of God, should be the main aim of a christian in all his actions and thoughts, xiii. 121 ; love of Christ the root and principle of this, 122 ; how nearly the glory of God and the good of the church are conjoined, *ib.* ; whether in every action a christian is always bound to consider the glory of God, 123 ; actions likely to be misinterpreted and tend to our dishonour, yet, if the glory of God call for them, they must not be omitted, 125 ; the interest God hath in us by creation, preservation, redemption, and dedication, obligeth us to live to his glory, 126 ; we are above all creatures fitted for this, 127 ; all our relations are disposed of for this end, 129 ; all our gifts and abilities, 130 ; we must take care not only, negatively, that God be not dishonoured, but, positively, that he be honoured and glorified in all states and conditions, businesses and employments, 131 ; motives to induce a more earnest regard of the glory of God, 133 ; means to this end, 134.

Of God, how far we are to intend the, in every action of our lives, xv. 280.

Hope of eternal, should be ever cherished in us, xix. 142 ; because it is a special act of the new nature, *ib.* ; because the great end why the scriptures were written was to beget and cherish this hope in us, *ib.* ; because the keeping up of this hope is the distinguishing character between the temporary and the sincere convert, 143 ; because it is our great support against difficulties, *ib.* ; most needed when we come to die, *ib.*

Put upon the saints is relative and adherent, xix. 491 ; inherent and internal, 492 ; circumstantial, *ib.*

Gnostics, so called from their knowledge, were the impurest heretics, iii. 431. Feigned the world was made by angels, xiii. 432.

Goats, the wicked compared to, by reason of their unruliness and uncleanness, x. 44.

God a father, and that both by creation and covenant, i. 28.

To be praised in every address to him, i. 243.

Apprehended as a holy and happy being, and his communication of himself to a reasonable creature is either in a way of holiness or a way of happiness, ii. 267.

All, and the creature nothing, a notion which the scripture much delighteth in, ii. 321.

The Father, whatever was done by Christ as Mediator, or whatever was done to Christ, is attributed to his counsel and appointment, iii. 316 ; he designed the person, *ib.* ; qualified him for his office, *ib.* ; inflicted his sufferings, 317 ; exacted his obedience, *ib.*

To be glorified for his mercy and goodness, iii. 321 ; in appointing Christ as Saviour, *ib.* ; in fitting him to bear sin, *ib.* ; in loving him for it, *ib.* ; in rewarding him for it, *ib.* ; he alone to be glorified, 322.

God cannot be tempted of evil, iv. 86 ; apparent exceptions not real, 87.

So to be feared as also to be trusted, so trusted as also to be feared, vii. 281.

His goodness, that he will be all things to his people, viii. 173.

And Christ, what may be known concerning, x. 153 ; that there is a God, *ib.* ; evidenced by his works of creation, *ib.* ; of providence, 154 ; from the common consent of all nations, *ib.* ; from our own consciences, *ib.* ; from several experiences, *ib.* ; that God is but one, 156 ; that God is one in three persons, 158 ; that God, who is one in three persons, is the only true God, 161 ; concerning Christ, he is sent, *ib.* ; this implieth his divine original, *ib.* ; his distinct subsistence, 162 ; his incarnation, 163 ; the quality of his office, *ib.* ; the authority of his office, 164 ; that he is Jesus, a saviour, 165 ; that he is Christ, an anointed saviour, 167.

Being a creator, is also an owner, xii. 29 ; his being an owner qualifieth him for being a ruler, *ib.* ; his power and right in us cannot be alienated by our sin, 30 ; nor made away by his bestowal of gifts on the creature, 31 ; this right so inherent in God that he cannot communicate it to another, *ib.*

A searcher of the hearts of men, xii. 243 ; in what sense he is said to know the mind of the spirit in prayer, 251.

The patron of human societies and the refuge of the oppressed, xii. 323 ; he is with and for his children, *ib.* ; his providence either external or internal, 324.

The nature and providence of, an evidence of the certainty of eternal rewards and punishments, xiii. 47.

A threefold justice of, distinguished, xiii. 73.

His essence and attributes may be discovered in creation, xiii. 389.

Method and order pleasing to, xiii. 424.

What it is to please God, xiv. 48 ; what it is to come to God, 49 ; what it is to walk with God, 52 ; the necessity of pleasing God, 62 ; impossible without faith, 73.

Belief in the being of, the first point of faith, xiv. 125 ; the advantage to the spiritual life derived from meditation on this truth, *ib.* ; the existence of God proved by reference to conscience, 127 ; the consent of all nations, 129 ; the book of creation, *ib.* ; providence, 131 ; and several experiences, 132 ; we should charge this truth upon our hearts to check whispering and suspicion against the being and glory of God, 133 ; reproof of those that either wish down or live down this supreme principle, 134 ; cautions against such opinions and practices as strike at the being of God, 135 ; religious libertinism, *ib.* ; denying particular providences, 136 ; denying the immortality of the soul, 137 ; Popery, *ib.* ; expectation of light beyond scripture, *ib.* ; hypocrisy, epicurism, and scoffing, 138 ; directions for times of strong temptation, 139 ; certain seasons when this principle is most liable to be assaulted, 140 ; direction to us in our addresses to God to avoid customariness, irreverence, and deadness, and to beget confidence, 142 ; how we may keep our hearts in prayer under a sense of God's being, so as to conceive of him aright, 144.

Is not ashamed to be called their God, meaning of the phrase, xiv. 338 ; what it is to have God for our God, 342 ; who they are that have God for their God, 344 ; this doctrine should be improved by us to contentment with our portion, comfort in distress, and dependence on God for future supplies, 346 ; but especially to a hope and expecta-

Goel (kinsman-redeemer) suiteth with no person so well as Christ, ii. 293 ; meaning of the term, 294.

Golden rule applies not only to actions, but to words and thoughts, ii. 373.

Good, must be done *well*, i. 148.

And evil, by what measure we are to determine, i. 379 ; not by our fancies and conceits, but by the wisdom of God, *ib.* ; with respect to the chief good, 380 ; not always the good of the flesh, or of outward prosperity, *ib.* ; a particular must give way to a general, 381 ; not to be determined by sense, but faith, *ib.*

Delight of doing, much greater than the cost, ii. 35.

All from above, yet there are pipes and conveyances through which it comes, iv. 110 ; thought that all is from above prevents glorying in ourselves, 111 ; vaunting over others, *ib.* ; envy of those who have received more than ourselves, *ib.*

Chiefest, Augustine reckoneth two hundred and eighty-eight opinions of, iv. 122.

Not enough to do, but must do with labour, care, and diligence, v. 97.

God is, primitively and originally, the creature but derivatively, vii. 108 ; the chiefest, and other things only in subordination, *ib.* ; infinitely, *ib.* ; eternally, 109.

God doeth, to his servants, vii. 193 ; from the inclination of his own nature, *ib.* ; the obligation of his promise, 194 ; the preparation of his people, *ib.* ; persuasion of this truth one of the first things in religion, *ib.* ; arguments, 195 ; he doeth good to his enemies, therefore much more to his servants, *ib.* ; evil men give good gifts to their children, much more he to his, *ib.* ; he never giveth his people any discouragement, or just cause to complain of him, *ib.* ; if he doth not give them the good things of this world, he giveth them better things in lieu of them, 196 ; the evil things of this world he turneth to good, *ib.* ; he doth give them so much of the good things of the world as is convenient for them, *ib.* ; his doing them good is chiefly in the world to come, *ib.*

And evil, by what measure to be determined, vii. 252 ; not our fancies and conceits, but the wisdom of God, *ib.* ; its respect to the chief good or true happiness, 253 ; not always the good of the flesh, or of outward prosperity, 254 ; a particular good must give way to a general good, and our personal benefit to the advancement of Christ's kingdom, *ib.* ; not to be determined by present feeling, but by the judgment of faith, 255.

For christians, is not always the good of the flesh, or of prosperity, viii. 254 ; God knoweth what is good for us better than we do ourselves, *ib.* ; that which is not good in its nature may be in its fruit, 255 ; good is not to be determined by feeling, but faith, *ib.* ; that may be good for the glory of God which is not for our personal benefit, 257.

That which is our chiefest, and last end, is our god, and occupies the place of God, viii. 390.

And evil, a monstrous conceit to deny the distinction between, viii. 457.

Some do, by chance, ix. 270 ; some by force, 271 ; some out of craft and design, 272 ; the man of God by choice, *ib.*

In some sense no mere man is good, xvi. 423 ; in what sense men may be said to be good, *ib.* ; in what sense not, 424 ; the goodness of God explained, 428.

Man is one that seeketh after the chief good, and adhereth constantly to God in Jesus Christ as his only felicity, xviii. 466 ; and chooseth the

against being ashamed of, *ib.* ; short continuance of the world's glory, *ib.* ; God the fountain of honour, *ib.* ; shame argues insincerity, *ib.* ; the eternal recompense, 495 ; the world's judgment not to be stood upon, *ib.*

Gospel covenant, stability of, vii. 401; emblem of, in the immutable constancy of the heavens, 402. See *Heavens*, fit emblems, &c.

Excellency of the doctrine of, in certainty and clearness, x. 199.

Doctrine of, is the pattern and mould according to which the new creation is framed, xi. 318.

Is a law, xi. 395 ; a law of the Spirit, *ib.* ; of the Spirit of life, 396 ; of the Spirit of life in Christ Jesus, *ib.* ; is both our rule and our charter, 399. See *Covenant*, new.

Righteousness, what it is, xii. 461 ; carrieth the notion of a garment, 462.

Called the ' word of reconciliation' and the 'ministry of reconciliation' (2 Cor. v. 18, 19), xiii. 282.

What is said in, to whom, and by whom, xv. 52.

The earliest, xvii. 241.

As a subject for meditation, xvii. 331.

What it doth to produce goodness in the world, xix. 261 ; by its laws and precepts, *ib.* ; by the discoveries it maketh, 262 ; the examples it propoundeth for our imitation, 263 ; the rewards and encouragements which it offers, 264 ; Spirit's co-operation with, 265.

Gospeller, carnal, dealt with, x. 63.

Government, civil, is of God, but the special form not determined by him, v. 239.

God's moral, is by laws, vii. 415 ; natural, is that order into which, by his positive decree, he hath necessitated and disposed all creatures for the benefit of the world, *ib.* ; is ordinary, 416 ; or extraordinary, *ib.* ; no creature can decline or avoid, *ib.* ; celestial bodies are his servants, *ib.* ; angels are his ministers and hosts, 417 ; winds, seas, and storms, *ib.* ; sickness and disease, *ib.*

Of God is not for the ruler's benefit, but the subjects' welfare, xi. 335.

Of the world, God's way of, both external and internal, xii. 8.

God's governing power consists in legislation and judgment, xii. 30.

God's, seen in rewarding, xviii. 418 ; in punishing, *ib.* ; in all acts of judicature, God is no respecter of persons, 419.

Church, is directive rather than authoritative, xix. 429 ; must be meekly submitted to, *ib.* ; civil, 438 ; economical, *ib.*

Grace, increase of, produces increased sense of want, i. 37.

A diffusive, spreading thing, i. 79.

And mercy, distinction between, i. 161.

Revealed and offered in the most comprehensive terms, that none may be excluded, or have just cause to exclude themselves, i. 494.

The more it is tried and exercised, the more it is evidenced to be right and sincere, i. 331 ; strengthened by trial, *ib.*

Sanctifying, inseparable from pardoning, i. 424.

Sanctifying and renewing, to be got from Christ, i. 443.

Exhibits not only the goodness, but also the wisdom and prudence of God, ii. 257.

General, must in some way be made particular, else it cannot profit us, ii. 305.

Every act of, hath a necessary dependence upon that work of Christ which is most suitable to it, iii. 353.

Grace, in the covenant of, Christ sustains several relations, iii. 385; the testator or author of the covenant, *ib.*; the mediator of the covenant, *ib.*; the surety of the covenant, 386; the prime federate, *ib.*; union with Christ entitles to benefit from his actings in all these relations, 386.

Has influence on every faculty, and especially on the understanding, iii. 423.

Exercise of, must not be interrupted till it is full and perfect, iv. 35; they that have true, will not be satisfied with little, 36.

Always, after a taste, longeth for more, iv. 129.

Its glory not obvious to the senses, but inward and hidden, iv. 191.

We have not a right apprehension of, till we can see it yieldeth us more than the world can yield us, iv. 351; those that would have, must take the right way to obtain, *ib.*

Not impossible, or without passions and affections, iv. 468.

True, differences between, and false, or formality, v. 37; restraining, is only an awe upon the conscience, inclining men to forbear sin, though they do not hate it, *ib.*; common, may be in them that fall away and depart from God, 38; characteristics of in Heb. vi. 4, 5, *ib.*

Immediately wrought by the Holy Spirit, yet our thoughts in believing must not stay till we ascend and come up to God the Father, v. 41; because all beginneth with the Father, *ib.*; whatever is done by Christ is done with respect to the Father's love, *ib.*; a great support and comfort to faith to consider of the Father in the act of believing, *ib.*; in the Father's love are many circumstances which are very engaging to the soul, which are not to be found in the other divine persons, 42.

Directing, necessity of, v. 51; from the blindness of our minds, 52; the forgetfulness of our memories, *ib.*; the obstinacy of our hearts, 53.

Importance of growth in, v. 87; where there is life there will be growth, *ib.*; if we do not grow, we go backward, *ib.*; an ill sign to be contented with a little, *ib.*; we cannot have too much, 88; according to our measure of, so will be our measure of glory, *ib.*; suiteth with our present state, *ib.*; suiteth with the bounty and munificence of God, *ib.*; a necessary piece of gratitude, 89; may learn of our Lord Jesus, *ib.*; may learn of worldly men, *ib.*; observations concerning growth in, 90; infallible signs of, when we grow more spiritual, more solid, more humble, 91.

Influence of, not the warrant of duty, but the help; not the ground or rule, but the efficient working cause, vi. 240.

Preventing, working, co-working, vi. 271.

The great work of, is to make God our last end and our chiefest good, vi. 373.

Necessity of, to bring us into a state of doing God's will, vi. 377; Pelagian system, *ib.*

Frees from the yoke of oppressing fears, and the tyranny of commanding lusts, vi. 483.

Sanctifying, to understand and keep God's law, the best gift that God has to bestow, vii. 247.

The life of, begun and carried on in a constant way of dependence upon God, vii. 433; vitality or liveliness of, not dispensed by a certain law, but according to the sovereign will and good pleasure of God, 434.

God gives habitual, called the new heart, viii. 188; and actual, *ib.*; uses of the latter, 189; to direct us in the exercise of grace formerly

officers, *ib.*; to maintain and defend his people in the exercise of these things, *ib.*

Headship, belongeth to Christ according to both his natures, i. 460; duties which this relation bindeth us to, 463.

Of Christ over his church in regard of influence is by the gift of his Spirit, i. 460.

Healing by Christ's stripes, iii. 286; implies a disease incurable by human art, *ib.* (see *Disease* and *Sin*); consists in delivering from sin, 290; its fault, 291; its stain, *ib.*; its guilt, *ib.*; its punishment, *ib.*; begun when we repent and believe, *ib.*; is carried on by degrees in sanctification, 292; completed in heaven, *ib.*; means of, his stripes, *ib.*; how to be got, 294.

Hearing of Christ, what it imports, i. 395; requires a resolute consent or resignation to his teaching and instruction, 396; this resignation must be unbounded and without reserve, 397; it must be speedy as to the great solemn acts of submission, *ib.*; must be real, practical, and obediential, 398; reasons why this prophet must be heard, *ib.*; it is the beloved Son of God that speaketh, *ib.*; the matter which he speaketh is the best that can be spoken or heard, *ib.*; danger of not hearing him, 399; questions for self-examination concerning, 400; advice to weak christians regarding, 401.

Of the word should be highly valued, iv. 131; should be ready to take all occasions of, 132; preparation necessary for, 144; chiefly the laying aside and dispossessing of evil powers, 146.

Of sincere prayer, how God manifests, vi. 249; inwardly by his Spirit, *ib.*; outwardly by his providence, 250.

Heart, never right but when it lieth under the awe of a command, i. 130.

May be overcharged when the stomach is not, i. 163.

Corruption in, makes us liable to Satan's temptations, i. 239.

Difference between one that is hard against God and soft for God, and one that is hard for God and soft against God, ii. 329.

Stablishing of, implieth firmness of faith and constancy in grace, iv. 422.

To do good, they who have, will soon find an occasion, v. 97.

God requireth, in his service, vi. 354; external profession is nothing, *ib.*; external conformity is nothing worth, *ib.*; it is the heart wherein God dwelleth, not the tongue or the brain, 355; if Christ have it not, Satan will have it, *ib.*; if we love any, we give them the heart, *ib.*; this is what all may give him, 356; the whole, *ib.*; how shall we know that we give God all the heart in an evangelical sense? 360.

Of man set between two objects; corruption inclineth it one way, and grace another, viii. 149; inclination of, to good is the fruit of grace, 150; the ground of obedience, *ib.*; not a simple approbation of the ways of God, *ib.*; not a bare desire or wish, 151; not a hypocritical will, *ib.*; when so inclined, the judgment determineth for God, *ib.*; the will is poised and swayed with love and delight, *ib.*; the bent of the will is seconded with constant endeavours, *ib.*; without this inclination obedience cannot be cheerful, 152; or uniform, *ib.*; or constant, *ib.*

A worldly frame of, may be known by the working of the thoughts, counsels, and deliberations, x. 386; by esteem of worldly things, 387; the bent and resolution of the will, *ib.*; a special sagacity and dexterity in the matters of the world, and a dulness in the things of God, *ib.*; the stream of the desires, *ib.*; grief at worldly losses and disappointments, 388; extraordinary solicitousness about outward

Hospitality not festivity and expensive entertainments, iv. 211.

House, the body of man so called, xii. 424 ; what kind of house it is, 425 ; it is an earthly-tabernacle house in regard of its composition, sustentation, and dissolution, *ib.* ; the end and issue of this house, 426 ; the state of glory called a house, 428 ; this house described, *ib.*

How ought we to Improve our Baptism, iv. 459.

How we may Cure Distractions in Holy Duties, v. 441.

Human wisdom wholly to be distrusted, xv. 216 ; if we would acknowledge God, we must make him our oracle and counsellor, 218.

Humanity, real, of Christ, shown by his praying that the cup might pass from him, iii. 341.

Humble persons most gracious, and gracious most humble, iv. 356.

Humiliation, in every part of our Lord's, there is an emission of some beams of his Godhead, i. 267 ; humbled himself to purchase our mercies, but made a discovery of divine glory to assure our faith, *ib.*

Of the Son of God was a hiding of his divine glory and majesty under the veil of our flesh, i. 432 ; and a lessening of his dignity, 433.

Must be either active or passive, iv. 357 ; better that we should bring down our hearts before God, than that God should bring down our proud looks, *ib.* ; voluntary, best and sweetest, 373.

Throughout his, Christ had the glory of his person, x. 189 ; and the glory of his office, 190 ; but this glory was veiled and concealed, *ib.*

Of Christ lieth chiefly in obscuring his Godhead, xviii. 125 ; and abatement of his dignity, *ib.* ; made less than God, *ib.* ; less than the angels, 126 ; in the human nature depressed beyond the ordinary condition of man, *ib.* ; was his own voluntary act, 127 ; was for our sake, 128 ; as our mediator, *ib.* ; as our pattern, 129 ; to teach us patience under all indignities we undergo for God's sake, 130 ; humility, 131 ; more exact obedience, *ib.* ; self-denial, *ib.* ; contempt of the world and its glory, *ib.*

Humility, exhortation to, ii. 326.

Christ taught us, as in his meanness, so in his sufferings, iii. 254.

A rich man's, is his glory, iv. 68.

Of soul, the result of the true knowlege of God and ourselves, iv. 378 ; the true way to exaltation, 379.

A humble heart can best trust in God, xxi. 406 ; reasons why, *ib.* humility in bad actions more pleasing to God than pride in good ones (Austin), 410.

Humble souls do not exercise themselves in great matters, nor in things too high for them, xxi. 426 ; how many ways this may be done, *ib.* ; this affecting of great things argueth pride, 428, 434.

Husband and wife should concur in the promotion of good, xiv. 421.

Husbands, in what respect heads of their wives, xix. 466 ; directions to, 467.

Hypocrisy and double dealing abhorrent to nature, iv. 298.

And carnal pretences, the worst sort of lies, iv. 305.

A practical blasphemy, v. 141.

Hypocrite, difference between him and the upright in seeking God, i. 67.

Note of, to be scanty in moral duties and abundant in ceremonial observances, ii. 8.

Hypocrites may put themselves forth with vigour and warmth in public duties, but are slight and careless in private addresses to God, i. 16.

Their guise, ii. 13 ; partial zeal, *ib.* ; godliness and righteousness placed in outward observances or external discipline, 14 ; more in love with ceremonies than with substance, 15 ; strain greatly at a small thing, *ib.* ; make conscience not only of externals instituted by God, but mostly of those devised by themselves, 17 ; have a conceit of their own righteousness, and a disdain of others, 18.

Hypocrites pretend to Christ, but live as if he were still in the grave, iii. 360.

Cannot always be hidden, iv. 102.

Come at length to deceive themselves, iv. 173.

Defection of, should not shake our belief of the doctrine of perseverance, x. 340.

The mortification of, external but not internal, xii. 57.

The groans of believers more than their pompous petitions, xii. 252.

Idleness and sin joined together, so idleness and destruction, iii. 199.

Idolatry, Christ's indignation against, i. 313.

Is a worshipping of a creature with divine worship, iii. 99 ; Papists guilty of, *ib.* ; worship angels, saints, the Virgin Mary, images, the cross, the bread in the sacrament, *ib.*

Of the heathens, turned the glory of God into the image of a man ; of christians, judges of God according to the model and size of their own minds and dispositions, iv. 43.

Is not only worship of false gods, but worship of the true God in a false manner, v. 252 ; the most plausible and seductive is idolatrous respect to the bodies and relics of dead saints, 253.

Idols must be renounced before our hearts can incline to God, ii. 104.

Ignorance, an obstacle to the reception of the gospel, iii. 198.

Is either necessary, through want of means, or through want of due means, iii. 428 ; or negligent, when men have means and do not use them, 429.

Set forth by the notions of darkness and blindness, xiii. 284.

From natural defect and imperfection, is no sin, xviii. 119.

How far it excuseth from sin, xix. 27.

Great danger of, to ourselves and others, xix. 384 ; pretences for remaining in, 385.

Illumination cometh from God only, ii. 75 ; given by degrees, *ib.*

By the Spirit accompanies the word, to make it effectual to us, to show us God as revealed in Christ, iii. 24.

Even common, is from the Spirit, iii. 211.

Divine, God's best servants think they can never enough beg, viii. 924.

Divine, a great gift, especially obliging to praise and thanksgiving, ix. 245 ; for every mercy we should praise God, *ib.* ; and most for the best gifts, 246 ; especially for spiritual benefits, *ib.* ; amongst these, divine illumination one of the best, 247 ; its worth appeareth in its author, 249 ; in the objects known, 250 ; in the use for which it serveth, 251 ; in the manner of knowing, 252.

Image of God in man and in Christ, difference between, i. 430.

Of God in man, iv. 295 ; his intellectual nature, *ib.* ; in the qualities of knowledge, righteousness, and true holiness, *ib.* ; in his state, a happy confluence of all inward and outward blessings, 296 ; a dissuasive from evil-speaking and slandering, *ib.* ; images not to be worshipped, yet the image of God not to be bespattered with reproaches, 297.

Of God our primitive glory and excellency, xix. 172 ; its restoration the effect of our new creation, *ib.* ; its completion in heaven the object of our hope, 173 ; involved in our being his children, *ib.* ; and dear children, 174.

Jude or Judas, called also Lebbæus and Thaddeus, all which names signify praise, v. 9 ; brother of James, therefore the Lord's cousin, 10.

JUDE, PRACTICAL COMMENTARY ON THE EPISTLE OF, v. 1.

Judging the word, is done grossly by those who deny its divine authority, or accuse it, as the Papists do, as an uncertain rule, or examine the doctrines of it by their private rule, or the writings and precepts of men, iv. 383.

Judgment, day of, why called the day of redemption, i. 114.

At the day of, there shall be a congregation, iii. 11 ; a segregation, 12 ; an aggregation, *ib.*

A great help to our christian course to think of the day of, iv. 222.

In the day of, the least circumstances of our sinful actions shall be brought forth as arguments of conviction, iv. 405 ; matter of our sin shall in hell become matter of punishment, 406.

Day of, a great day, v. 211 ; because it is the consummate act of Christ's regal office, *ib.* ; because great things are then done, 212 ; great preparations for, *ib.* ; great transactions in, 213 ; great consequences of, 215 ; should be looked for, 217 ; longed for, *ib.* ; provided for, 218.

Day of, implied in the sentence pronounced in Eden, prophesied of by Enoch, and taught ever since, v. 291.

And justice, to do, a comely property in God's children, viii. 239 ; by it we are made like to God, *ib.* ; is acceptable and pleasing to God, 240 ; fitteth for communion with God, *ib.* ; is as suitable to the new nature as fruits to their own tree, 241 ; is lovely and venerable in the eyes of the world, *ib.* ; it conduceth much to the good of human society, 242 ; a comfortable property, *ib.* ; comfort of, from peace of conscience, 243 ; from the many promises of God, both as to the world to come and this present life, *ib.*

Day of, why delayed, ix. 447 ; not from any unreadiness in Christ, *ib.* ; on the part of the good, that the number of the elect may be gathered, *ib.* ; on the part of the wicked, that they may have a time of improvement, and be left without excuse, 448.

The last, delineations of, in scripture, are partly literal and partly parabolical, x. 14 ; Christ the fittest judge, 16 ; by reason of his understanding, 17 ; his justice and righteousness, 18 ; his power, 19 ; his authority, *ib.* ; his appearance as judge shall be glorious and full of majesty, 23 ; appears from considering the dignity of his person, *ib.* ; the quality of his office, *ib.* ; the greatness of his work, 24 ; some of his foregone appearances, 25 ; his great glory will take off the scandal of the cross, and recompense him for his humiliation, 26 ; will beget reverence and fear in the hearts of those who are to be judged, 27 ; will be a comfort to his people, *ib.* ; angels to attend him, partly for a train, partly that by their ministry the work may be more speedily and powerfully despatched, 28 ; scoffing objections answered, 31.

All who have lived in the world, from the beginning to the end of time, shall be present at, x. 33 ; grown persons and infants, 34 ; the dead, and those who shall be alive at the coming of Christ, 35 ; good and bad, *ib.* ; believers and unbelievers, 36 ; men of all conditions, 39 ; not some of all sorts, but every individual person, *ib.*

Of the last day shall be according to works, x. 60 ; to glorify God's holiness, 61 ; his remunerating justice, *ib.* ; his veracity and faithfulness, *ib.* ; good works are perfectional accomplishments, *ib.* ; they are qualifications to make them capable of his remunerating justice, *ib.* ;

they are signs and tokens of their being accepted with God, 62; they
are measures according to the degrees of grace, *ib.*

Judgment, the great duty of a nation in danger of, is to give the Lord a
compromise, or make up the breach between him and them, xvi. 26;
what it is to give God a day of compromise, *ib.*; the nature of the
work, 28; the manner of it, 29; why this is the proper duty of a
people in danger, 30; serious observations to awaken us out of
security, 33.

To come, to be insisted upon in preaching, xviii. 362; makes access
into the hearts and consciences of men more easy, because of its suitableness to natural light, *ib.*; doth most befriend the great discovery of the gospel, 363; doth best solve doubts about present providences, *ib.*

Future, demonstration of, from the sufferings of the godly, xx. 209.

Judgments, spiritual, the sorest of all, ii. 275.

God's internal, are chiefly blindness of mind and hardness of heart,
iii. 86.

Of God on the wicked do exceedingly amplify his mercies towards us,
iii. 109.

The way to escape, is to mourn for them before they come, iv. 401.

God's, under the gospel, more spiritual, but not less severe, than of old;
formerly he smote with death, now with deadness, v. 169; great,
do usually follow great mercies, if great sins come between, 175.

Of righteousness, God's precepts are, and are accounted by his people,
vi. 61; because they are the judicial sentence of God concerning our
state and actions, *ib.*; because of the suitable execution that is to
follow, in this world and the next, 63.

Of God (*misliphatim*), are either laws enacted, or judgments executed
according to those laws, vii. 47.

Of God upon the wicked compared to treading them down, viii. 209;
implies a full punishment, 210; a disgraceful punishment, *ib.*; certainty of, *ib.*; he can, *ib.*; he hath, *ib.*; he will, 211; because of his
invariable justice, *ib.*; because of the suitableness between judgment
and sin, *ib.*; for the undeceiving of the world, *ib.*; to undeceive
sinners themselves, *ib.*; to check the insolency of those who abuse
their power, 212.

God's, upon others should be observed, viii. 214; the observation must
be to a good end, *ib.*; must be sure that we do not make providence
speak the language of our fancies, *ib.*; we may reason from the provocation to the judgment, but must not infer special wickedness from
affliction, *ib.*; when there are remarkable circumstances in which the
sin and the judgment meet, 215; when judgments fall upon them in
the very act of their provocation, *ib.*; when they are the authors of
their own destruction, 216; when they are brought down wonderfully, suddenly, *ib.*; when judgments are executed by unlikely means,
ib.; when such accidents bring a great deal of glory to God, *ib.*; when
God supplies the defects of men's justice, *ib.*; when the word, in the
express letter, is made good upon men, *ib.*; observation of, a mighty
cure to atheism, *ib.*; a notable curb to keep us from sin, 217.

Of God in ancient times ought to be laid to heart by us, especially when
like sins abound, viii. 232; that light upon other countries should be
made use of, because usually they go in a circuit, 233; when executed
before our eyes, must be the more considered, *ib.*; though we be well
at ease in our own persons, *ib.*; though they pursue but a few, all

should fear, *ib.* ; though they light upon enemies to us and God, their fall is not to be insulted over, 234 ; much more should we tremble at his judgments upon his own people, *ib.*

Judgments, when God's, were abroad in the earth, the church had continual thoughts of God, and her endeavours were early and earnest, xii. 275.

Judiciousness, or soundness of mind, a great blessing, vii. 203 ; its office, to distinguish and judge rightly of things that differ, that we may not mistake error for truth and evil for good, *ib.* ; to determine and resolve, 204 ; to direct as well as decree, 205 ; a great defect in most christians, 206 ; mischief arising from this defect, *ib.* ; they are apt to be misled and deceived, *ib.* ; they are fickle and irresolute, both in the profession and practice of godliness, 207 ; they easily miscarry, and make religion a burden to themselves, or else a scorn to the world, *ib.* ; makes them troublesome to others, by preposterous carriage, rash censuring, needless intermeddling, 208 ; makes them troublers of the church of God, *ib.* ; must be sought of God, 209 ; must be sought in the word, 210 ; increased by long use and exercise, 211 ; by sense and experience, *ib.* ; hindrances, 212 ; a passionate or wild addictedness to any carnal things, *ib.* ; pride, *ib.*

Jurisdiction, God hath an absolute, over us, vi. 197.

Just man is a renewed man, xviii. 388 ; a man furnished with knowledge of the things that concern his duty, *ib.* ; a mortified man, *ib.* ; a man biassed with a love to God and Christ and heaven, 389 ; his tongue as choice silver, *ib.* ; for purity, *ib.* ; for profit, 391.

Justice, severity of God's, seen in the scattering of the twelve tribes, iv. 19.

Divine, impartiality of, v. 170. See *Righteousness*.

Much of, in all God's judgments, vii. 293 ; must be from God's nature, *ib.* ; judgment never without a cause, 294 ; judgment not immediately executed when there is a cause, 295 ; judgments inflicted always short of the cause, *ib.*

An attribute that belongs to God as a governor, xx. 216 ; is legislative or judiciary, 217 ; rewarding or punishing, *ib.* ; exercised more darkly in this world, more plainly hereafter, 218.

Justification, as opposed to crimination, is the work of an advocate ; to condemnation, of a judge, ii. 94.

Of sinners, privilege of the gospel to discover a way for, iii. 416 ; can be done by no other way, doctrine, or knowledge in the world, *ib.* ; in the gospel fully and amply done, 417. See *Gospel*.

Reconcilement of Paul and James regarding ; Paul speaketh of the justifying of a sinner from the curse of his natural condition, the accusations of the law, &c., and accepting him into the favour of God, which is of grace, and not of debt ; James, of the justifying and approbation of that faith by which we are thus accepted of God, iv. 245 ; in Paul, is opposite to the condemnation of a sinner in general ; in James, opposite to the condemnation of a hypocrite in particular (Diodati), 246 ; Papists say that Paul speaketh of the first qualification, and excludeth works done before baptism ; James, of the second justification, by which a justified man is made more just, and the works he speaketh of are performed in faith, and by the help of divine grace, 261 ; confutation of this, *ib.* ; Arminians and Socinians make new obedience the instrument of justification, and that the grace of God is seen only in the acceptance of our imperfect obedience, 262 ; confutation, *ib.* ; orthodox, though they differ somewhat in words and

give their sins, *ib.* ; and assure them of his love, *ib.* ; conscience
speaketh peace and comfort, 356 ; the title to the heavenly inheritance is more clear, *ib.* ; easier access to God, 357 ; work is more easy,
because not done against the bent of the heart, *ib.* ; mercies and comforts are more sweet, because they come from God's love, and are used
to his glory, 358; because of the honour of it, 359; holiness is the
image of God upon the soul, *ib.* ; high and noble ends, 360 ; a noble
course, *ib.* ; the approbation of God, 361 ; the excellency is intrinsic,
ib. ; the honour is everlasting, 362.

Life eternal, what it is, xi. 363 ; life both in soul and body, 364 ; a good
and happy state, 365 ; endless and everlasting, 366.

Eternal, is the full fruition of eternal joys, without any possibility of
losing them, xi. 377 ; is God's free and gracious gift to the sanctified,
ib. ; the freest gift, 378 ; the richest gift, *ib.*

Believers have, notwithstanding death, xii. 15 ; this to be understood of
body and soul, *ib.* ; the righteousness of Christ the meritorious cause,
16.

Everlasting, a benefit of the new covenant, xii. 120.

But a passage to eternity, xiii. 5.

The happy condition of the godly so called, xiii. 83 ; temporal and
eternal compared, *ib.*

Natural, what it is, xiii. 203.

To come, proved from the righteousness of God, since else christians were
of all men most miserable, xix. 133 ; argued from God's wisdom, 134 ;
and holiness, *ib.* ; and justice, 135 ; and goodness, *ib.* ; from the
nature, state, and condition of man, 137 ; as God's subjects, *ib.* ; as
bound to be upright and sincere in God's service, 138 ; with respect
to man's comfort and solace in his troubles, *ib.* ; with respect to the
credit and esteem of God's servants in the world, 139 ; should support in sharp afflictions, *ib.* ; and in death, 140 ; nature saith it may
be, faith saith it shall be, 141.

The great end and business of a christian, should be to honour and
glorify Christ, xx. 179 ; is from him and should be to him, 180 ; we
are his by creation, *ib.* ; preservation, 182 ; redemption, 183 ; conquest, 184 ; actual possession, *ib.* ; resignation and voluntary consent, *ib.* ; only worth having when we can honour Christ by it, *ib.* ;
directions, 185 ; motives, 186.

Eternal, our present afflictions are as nothing in comparison of the hope
of, xx. 372.

Light gotten by the word of God is *lux manifestans;* it manifesteth itself and
all things else, viii. 352 ; *lux dirigens, ib.; lux vivificans, ib. ; lux
exhilarans,* 353.

Necessity of divine, before we can understand the things of God, x. 201.

Of faith and light of prophecy, wherein they differ and wherein they
agree, xiv. 400.

In the Lord, how christians are, xix. 245 ; noteth not so much their
perfection as the perfection of the dispensation they are under, *ib.* ;
noteth some good measure and degree of participation, *ib.* ; noteth
that they have received grace, not only for themselves, but for the
good of others, 246.

And darkness, children of, there should be a broad and sensible difference between, xix. 306 ; this difference discovered by those actions
that are proper to either state, 307 ; this distinction to be kept up on
the part of the godly, *ib.* ; the children of God are fitted and prepared

for this, 308 ; great inconveniences follow if the distinction be not maintained, *ib.*

Lights, God the father of, iv. 112 ; lessons from this title, 113.

Like for like, awarded even to God's children in this world, ii. 382.

Likeness of believers to Christ as the eternal son of God, xi. 55 ; as Mediator, *ib.*

To Christ, in what it consists, xx. 463 ; how it is the fruit of vision, 464.

Little children, christians of all ranks and ages are and should be as, xx. 381 ; the term implieth newness of birth, *ib.* ; and remission of sins, 382.

Living to God is making his glory the scope of our lives, vii. 441 ; walking so as God may own us with honour, *ib.*

To God, the duty and property of the spiritual life is to refer all our actions not to self, but to God, xiii. 210 ; self-denial required as our first lesson, 211 ; as soon as we are alive by grace, our affections, respects, and endeavours are turned into a new channel, *ib.* ; we cannot live to ourselves and God too, *ib.* ; living to God doth not note one single action, but the whole course and conduct of our lives, 213 ; love to God the great principle that draweth us off from self to God, *ib.* ; the great thing that breedeth and feedeth this love is Christ's death, 214 ; Christ's death considered as to the intention, the grace and help merited, and the obligation left on the creature to live not for themselves but unto God, *ib.* ; that we are not our own, but God's, proved by reasons, *ib.* ; the danger which will ensue if we live to ourselves and not to God, 216 ; motives to press us to this weighty duty of living to God and not to ourselves, 217 ; directions, 218.

By faith, what it is, xv. 48 ; how and why we are said to live by faith, *ib.*

Longing after holiness and subjection to God, motives to, vi. 431 ; these desires shall be granted, *ib.* ; the result of the granting of them will be only good, *ib.* ; how to awaken, 432 ; go to God, who giveth to will and to do, *ib.* ; cherish the sparks, and blow them up into a flame, *ib.* ; improve your tastes, *ib.* ; watch over other desires that would dull and blunt the edge of the spirit, 433 ; renew your desires every time you come to God, *ib.* ; consider your wants, *ib.* ; and the fulness that is in Christ, 434 ; and his readiness to give to you, *ib.*

Long-suffering, creation teacheth us a lesson in, xii. 181.

God's, an encouragement to repentance, xviii. 231 ; this forbearance showeth that he is gracious, merciful, willing to be reconciled, *ib.* ; so doth his continuance to us of forfeited mercies, *ib.* ; these mercies do not harden in their own nature, but merely by the sinner's abuse of them, 232 ; he hath provided a remedy for us by Jesus Christ, *ib.* ; affected scruples whether this be intended for us are a sin, and do not disoblige us from our duty, 233 ; he hath appointed means, *ib.* ; he warneth us against the abuse of mercies, *ib.* ; he defers punishment, *ib.*

LOOKING BACK ILL BECOMES THOSE WHO HAVE SET THEIR FACES HEAVENWARD, ii. 130.

Looking back, what it is, ii. 132 ; pretending to follow Christ, while the heart hankers after the world, 133 ; being discouraged in his service by trials and difficulties, *ib.* ; respects either mortification or vivification, *ib.* ; how ill it becometh those who have put their hand to the spiritual plough, 134 ; in respect of the covenant into which they enter, or the manner of entrance into it, *ib.* ; with respect to the duties of christianity, *ib.* ; in respect of the hurt that cometh both to themselves and to religion, 135 ; with respect to the disproportion

the love of Christ, 95 ; none have a greater charge—Christ's new
commandment, *ib.* ; directions, 96.

Love, of all graces, most needs keeping, v. 344 ; decay of, seen in a remission
of the degrees, 345 ; or an intermission of the acts and exercises, *ib.* ;
rules to prevent declining in, 346 ; to God, will put us upon looking
for Christ's second coming, 347.

Was made for God and all that is of God's side; hatred, for sin, viii. 155.

Of God to Christ as God, xi. 74 ; as mediator, *ib.* ; to the saints, 76 ;
between these two there is a disparity, 77 ; yet a likeness, 78 ; like
grounds, nearness and likeness, *ib.* ; like properties, 79 ; both are
free, *ib.*; tender and affectionate, *ib.* ; eternal, 80, 109 ; unchangeable,
80 ; fruits and effects, 81 ; communication of secrets, *ib.* ; spiritual
gifts, *ib.* ; sustentation and gracious protection, *ib.* ; acceptance of
service, 82 ; reward, *ib.* ; chiefly to be measured by his spiritual
bounty, 83 ; importance of a sense and comfortable apprehension of,
85 ; means of ensuring this, *ib.* ; comfort to those who have the
effects, but not the sense of, 86 ; evidences of concernment in, 87.

God's, in Christ, is the ground of all other favours and graces whatsoever,
xi. 136; all the goodness that is in us cometh from, *ib.* ; the love of
God in us is from his love to us, 137 ; his love to us is in us in the
effects, and in the sense and feeling, *ib.*

To Christ, preferring a public good before our own personal eternal
interest, an undoubted evidence of, xii. 2.

Of God, nothing so worthy of our love, xii. 273 ; cannot reign where
the love of the world reigneth, *ib.* ; the comfort by which we are
supported in all our distresses, *ib.* ; there are two acts in this love,
desire after and delight in God, 274.

Of God, what it is in its object, act, and properties, xii. 276 ; in the
object there is a double motive to excite us to love God, because he
is good and doeth good, *ib.* ; and this goodness is threefold, essential,
moral, and beneficial, *ib.*; the act, what it is and what it implies, 278 ;
the properties of this love, what they are and what they are not, 279 ;
why love to God is made the evidence of our interest in the privileges
of the sons of God, 281 ; love of God a sure and sensible note of
effectual calling, 283 ; exhortation to love of God, 285.

Is of invincible force, xii. 400 ; is accompanied by desire, hope, and
delight, *ib.* ; this ariseth partly from the real worth of the privilege,
and partly from their esteem and value of it, 414 ; nothing can
separate us from the fruition of this love, *ib.* ; we ought to be firmly
persuaded of this, 415 ; means whereby this persuasion is bred in
us, *ib.* ; the advantage those christians have above others who make
it their business to love God and count it their happiness to be loved
by him, 418.

Of Christ, the power which secures believers in their conflicts, and
makes them triumph over all temptations, xii. 405 ; proof from scripture and the properties of Christ's love, 407 ; it is a transcendent,
tender, and constant love, *ib.* ; it is an operative and effective love,
408.

Of God in Christ, what it is, xii. 413 ; the people of God apprehend it
a blessed and comfortable position when assured of this love, *ib.*

Of Christ, the root and principle of all sincere desires after the glory of
God, xiii. 122.

The strongest arguments and the greatest terrors inoperative without,
xiii. 139.

Lusts must be prevented by mortification, and suppressed by watchfulness, and kept by resolution from execution, v. 316.

The more they are mortified, the more sincerely will we seek after the glory of God, xiii. 136.

Foolish, xviii. 192 ; hurtful, *ib.* ; destroying our peace, *ib.* ; injurious to grace, 193 ; their tendency is ruin in this world, *ib.* ; perdition or eternal damnation, *ib.*

Luxury, a sin very natural to us, iv. 412 ; chiefly incident to the rich, *ib.* ; their abundance doth not excuse it, *ib.*

Lying, the way of, either means generally the way of sin, vi. 276 ; or particularly the sin of falsehood, 277 ; men strongly inclined to, 278 ; most inconsistent with the temper and sincerity of a child of God, *ib.*

In the ordinary acceptation of it, is speaking that which is false, with an intention to deceive, ix. 187 ; or concealing the truth which ought to be confessed, 188 ; or when our practices do not correspond with our profession, *ib.* ; to be hated and abhorred.

To God, argueth not only falsity and hypocrisy, but mischief or evil thoughts of God, xix. 279 ; to men, is assertory or promissory, 280 ; different kinds of, *ib.* ; the sporting lie, *ib.* ; the officious lie, 281 ; the pernicious lie, *ib.* ; in ordinary commerce, 282 ; in courts of justice, *ib.*

A sin most contrary to the nature of God, who is truth itself, xix. 283 ; Jesus Christ was eminent for sincerity and truth, *ib.* ; nothing maketh us more like the devil, *ib.* ; a sin most contrary to the new nature wrought in the saints, 284 ; a sin most contrary to human society, *ib.* ; a sin very hateful to God, 285 ; a sin shameful and odious in the eyes of men, *ib.*

Magistrate, his official duty regarding religion, v. 237.

Magistrates, their duty to suppress error, v. 120.

Are under Christ as Mediator, x. 131.

Must not be obeyed in things contrary to the word of God, xiv. 424 ; have not always been the best friends to Christ, 425.

Majesty of God, great and glorious, i. 403 ; in the present state we are not able to bear any extraordinary manifestation of, 406.

And composure of the scriptures, viii. 335.

Malice and ill-will lead to detraction, ii. 276.

Of the Jews, acts of, ascribed to the ordination of God, iii. 369.

Of the wicked against the children of God ariseth from envy at their interests, their esteem and respect in the world, viii. 129 ; from hatred of their holiness, *ib.*

Man, his natural condition as set forth in scripture, i. 139 ; born in sin, *ib.* ; greedy of sin, 140 ; sin the constant frame of his heart, *ib.* ; his inability to reclaim himself, *ib.*

Christ called the Son of, not to deny his Godhead, but to express the verity of his human nature, xviii. 155.

Manifestation of God's name by Christ to his people is by outward revelation and inward illumination, x. 198.

Of the saints, how the saints will be manifested, xii. 155 ; the circumstances attending their manifestation, *ib.* ; that this manifestation ought to be earnestly desired and expected by us, 156.

Mankind universally gone astray from God and the way of true happiness, iii. 296 ; all sinners by nature, 297 ; all that come to the use of rea-

son have actually sinned against God, 299 ; this departing from God
fitly represented by the straying of sheep, 301.   See *Departing.*

Man of sin, the name given by the Jews to Antiochus, iii. 31 ; applicable to
the Papacy, 32.

MAN'S IMPOTENCY TO HELP HIMSELF OUT OF HIS MISERY, v. 473.

MANTON'S, DR, FUNERAL SERMON, xxii. 125.

Marriage, in its purity, may stand with the strictest rules of holiness, ii. 100.
Holily entered into when the parties take one another out of God's
hands, ii. 163 ; when the directions of God's word are observed as to
the choice of parties, *ib.* ; as to consent of parents, 164 ; as to gain-
ing one another by warrantable, yea, religious ways, *ib.* ; as to clearing up our right and title by Christ, *ib.* ; as to the end, 165 ; God's
providence to be owned in, *ib.* ; to enter into, holily, a necessary duty,
166 ; in entering on, we are to ask his leave, 169 ; his direction, 170 ;
his blessing, *ib.* ; advice to persons entering into, *ib.* ; that God be no
loser, *ib.* ; that he be a gainer, 171.
The apostle Paul's comparison of the law to, xii. 104.

Mary, the Virgin, Romanists pray more to, than to God, iii. 99.

Masters, the choice of, is the great business which belongeth to our duty, xi.
309 ; in the choice we are guided by considerations of right and
interest, 310 ; the two, are sinful self and holy God, *ib.* ; no man
can serve both, 311 ; by nature all of us are servants of sin, grace
maketh us servants of God, 312 ; both sorts of servants receive wages
suitable and proportionable to the work they have done, 314 ; considerations to choose God's service, *ib.* ; and to continue therein, 315.
Two, divide the world between them, sin and God, xii. 248 ; both services are entered into by consent, *ib.* ; sin a usurper, and our enemy
as well as God's, 249 ; hence our duty to yield up ourselves to the
Lord, *ib.* ; with hearty and full consent of will, 250 ; out of a deep
sense of his love and mercy, *ib.* ; with grief and shame that his right
hath been so long detained from him, *ib.* ; the resolution must be
full and entire, *ib.* ; to submit ourselves both to his disposing and
commanding will, 251.

Matches, three must be made ere the conscience can have solid rest and quiet,
iv. 123 ; God and man must be brought together, *ib.* ; justice and
mercy must be brought together, 124 ; comfort and duty must be
brought together, 126.

Matheo Langi, Archbishop of Salzburg, on the reformation of the Catholic
church, xiii. 221.

Mean condition, they that fear God may be reduced to, viii. 490 ; that they
may know their happiness is not in this world, *ib.* ; to cut off the
visions of the flesh and the fuel of their lust, 491 ; that they may
be sensible of God's displeasure against their sins, *ib.* ; that they may
learn to live upon the promises, and exercise suffering graces, 492 ;
that God may convince his enemies that there is a people who serve
him disinterestedly, *ib.* ; that his glory may be more seen in their
deliverance, *ib.*

Meanness and want of outward pomp and splendour, the great prejudice against the entertainment of Christ and the things of his kingdom, iii. 223 ; yet is by the special appointment of God, 228 ;
willingly taken up by him in his birth, and life, and manner of
appearing among men, 229 ; his meanness a great mercy to mankind,
231.

Means, none can avail without God's blessing, i. 276.

Ministry of reconciliation, ministers are 'ambassadors for Christ' to reconcile us to God, xiii. 290 ; the nature of their office explained, *ib.* ; the value and authority of it, 291 ; the credit and respect due to their message, *ib.* ; the manner how their office is to be executed, 293 ; with love and sweetness, meekness and patience, *ib.* ; the matter or message about which they are sent, reconciliation to God through Christ, *ib.* ; exhortation to sinners to become reconciled to God, 295 ; the n·essity of it, *ib.* ; God's condescension in it, 301 ; the value and worth of the privilege, 302 ; the benefits depending on it, 303 ; the great dishonour done to God in refusing it, *ib.* ; exhortation to christians to become yet more reconciled to God, 304 ; persuasives to, *ib.*

Miracles done in one age for confirmation of the true religion should suffice for after ages, i. 298 ; why not necessary now, 299.

Popish, reasons for rejecting, iii. 67.

Are extraordinary works, iii. 71 ; their author God, either immediately or mediately, *ib.* ; their end to confirm some truth, *ib.* ; Christ's, necessary to confirm his person and office, 72 ; and sufficient, *ib.* ; ceased when the faith of Christ was sufficiently confirmed, 73 ; suspicion attaches to those who pretend to revive, *ib.* ; in attestation of false doctrines, are lying wonders, 74 ; such are those of Popery, *ib.* ; seven points in Popery sought to be confirmed by, *ib.* ; pilgrimages, prayers for the dead, purgatory, invocation of saints, adoration of images, of the host, the primacy of the Pope, 75.

Wrought in Christ's name, were wrought by power, but ended in mercy, iv. 453.

Are a solemn confirmation, or letters-patent brought from heaven, to authorise any person or doctrine, x. 441 ; not necessary now, because the same doctrine and rule is continued to us without change, 442 ; are sufficiently attested to us, 443.

Mirth, the christian's, should be thanksgiving, xix. 209.

Miscarriages, real or supposed, of christians, the shame of, redounds to God and religion itself, vi. 413.

Of some members, the whole body not to be condemned for, x. 349.

Miseries sweet or bitter according as we reckon them, iv. 22 ; not to be judged by sense, *ib.* ; but by supernatural light, *ib.* ; and on supernatural grounds, *ib.*

MISERY, MAN'S IMPOTENCY TO HELP HIMSELF OUT OF, v. 473.

Misery, the common burden of the sons of Adam, xix. 126 ; virtuous good men more miserable than others from their temper and the state of the world, *ib.* ; of all good men, christians most, *ib.* ; to induce men to lead a godly life, motives are necessary which are greater than the temptations of the world, 127 ; Christ hath promised a happiness that will countervail all these afflictions, *ib.* ; this happiness is at the general resurrection, or Christ's coming to judgment, 128 ; christians of all men most miserable, not in respect of their inward enjoyments, but their outward estate, 131.

Mission of Christ is by the Father, x. 462 ; includes the designation of the person, 463 ; his qualification for the work, *ib.* ; his authority and power, 467 ; end of, *ib.*

Missionaries to the heathen, may they, without tempting God, ask of him the gift of miracles ? i. 299.

Mockers and scoffers, their prevalence in the last days, v. 323 ; usually the worst of sinners, *ib.*

Monasteries, &c., Popish, so many sties of filthiness, v. 275.

Morality, partial, is injurious to the law and opposite to the gospel, ii. 54.
MORALS BEFORE RITUALS, ii. 5.
Morality, the best human, defective, vi. 85.
More, Sir Thomas, his prayer, i. 294.
Morning our golden time for prayer, and should not be neglected from sluggishness, whatever dispensation there be for weakness, ix. 70; shown by the example of Christ and his saints, *ib.*; because whenever we have strong affections to anything, we make it our morning work, be it good or bad, *ib.*; it is the choicest time of the day, and therefore should be allotted to the most serious and necessary employment, 71; it is profitable to begin the day with God, *ib.*; it will be some recompense for the time lost in sleeping, 72.
Mortal, what sins the Papists reckon, iv. 103; none but such as are not mortified, 104.
Mortification consists not in a bare abstinence and retreat from temptations, but in a spirit fortified against them, ii. 98.
A fruit of faith, ii. 149; concerneth our lusts, as self-denial our interests, *ib.*
Impatience of the doctrine of, ii. 230; arises from sottish atheism and unbelief, *ib.*; from libertinism, 231; from the passionateness of carnal affections, 232.
Must go before quickening, vi. 389.
And vivification inseparable, xi. 231.
Of sin, what it is not, xii. 56; pagan mortification, *ib.*; Popish and superstitious mortification, *ib.*; mortification of the hypocrite, 57; what mortification is, 58; passive, *ib.*; active, 59; general and particular, *ib.*; privative and positive, 60; ordinary and extraordinary, *ib.*; why christians must mortify the deeds of the body, 61; with respect to Christ, *ib.*; with respect to sin, 62; in regard of grace received, 63; enforcements to the exercise of this duty, 65.
Of sin, we and the Spirit must concur in, xii. 72; the manner of this co-operation, *ib.*; the Spirit the principal agent in this work, *ib.*; yet we must charge ourselves with the duty, 73; we must use the means which tend to, *ib.*; in mortification the Spirit worketh in us as a spirit of light, life, and love, 74; the necessity of the Spirit's concurrence and operation in us, 76; from the state of the sinner, *ib.*; the honour of our Redeemer requireth it, 77; the necessity of our co-operation, 78; that God may apply himself to us in our way, *ib.*; that we may meet with God in his way, *ib.*; exhortation to mortification of the deeds of the body, 79; means whereby we may attain it, 90.
The guard of sincerity, xiii. 136.
The influence of faith upon, xv. 72.
Mortifying of sin, motives to, xi. 180.
Moses and Elias really present at the transfiguration, i. 358; why these two, *ib.*; appeared in their own bodies, 360.
'Prophet like unto,' could only be Christ, i. 365.
Dispute about his body, v. 241; different explanations of, 242.
Mourning a necessary duty, iv. 374; befitteth this life rather than rejoicing, 375; some special seasons and occasions of, *ib.*; God looketh not after the outward expressions of, but the humble heart, 377.
Bitterly, even for other men's sins, the duty and property of a godly man, viii. 421; a matter of duty lying upon all christians, 422; though it lies upon all, it chiefly concerns public persons, *ib.*; tears not absolutely necessary for the expression of this grief and tender-

Name and title of God hath been made known by degrees, xi. 132; fully in the gospel, *ib.*; none but Christ can discover, 133.

Of Christ, how it is glorified in us by suffering, xx. 327.

Narrowness of the way engageth believers to the exercise of care, iii. 307; to a great deal of pains and sorrow, *ib.*; to a great deal of self-denial, *ib.*

Nathan, his innocent and pious mistake, xviii. 62.

Natural light chiefly reacheth to duties of the second table, i. 26.

Men bound to pray and perform duties, vi. 241.

Nature, divine, of which christians are partakers, not the essence of God, but his communicable excellencies, ii. 214; considered as begun, increased, and perfected, 217.

Can discover a God, and a reason that he should be worshipped, but not such a worship as is proper to him, ii. 371.

Light of, antecedently to any external revelation, will sufficiently convince of the being of God, and our dependence on him, iii. 22.

Whatever is good in, is from God, iii. 174.

Our, horrid defilment and depravation of, iv. 117.

They that plead for the power of, shut out the use of prayer, vi. 370.

Makes us sensible of the evil of trouble; grace, of the evil of sin, viii. 368.

New, is the product of the Holy Ghost, xi. 405; is a spirit of love and power, and a sound mind, *ib.*; answering to the nature of God, whom we apprehend under the notions of wisdom and goodness and power, 406; it belongeth to Christ to give, 408; given by the gospel, 409.

Light of, sufficient for the condemnation of those who have not the gospel, xx. 246.

A kind of election within the sphere of, xx. 291.

Nearness of God to his people, ix. 102; not in regard of his essence, for so he is everywhere present, *ib.*; nor in regard of his general providence and common sustentation, 103; but his friendly and gracious presence, *ib.*; his visible presence in his ordinances, *ib.*; distinction between a state of, and acts of, 104; grounds of, 106; his covenant with them, *ib.*; our union with Christ, *ib.*; the inhabitation of the Spirit, 107; the mutual love between God and them, *ib.*; result of God's readiness to hear our prayers, *ib.*; our converse with God in holy duties, 108; and in a course of holiness, 109; brought about by Christ's merit, *ib.*; and by our change of heart, 110.

Necessaries of life, daily bread, daily pardon, daily strength, i. 230.

Necessities of christians, Satan takes advantage of, for temptations, i. 273; tempteth to unlawful means to supply our wants, *ib.*; to question our adoption, 274; to distrust God's providence, *ib.*

Lead us to the promises, the promises to Christ, Christ to God, vi. 449.

Necessity a time for duty, v. 102.

Of mankind, the deep, xi. 420; met by Christ's incarnation, 423; and his passion, 427.

Negatives not to be rested in, vi. 37.

Neglect, voluntary and allowed, of any portion of the law, makes us guilty of the violation of the whole law, iv. 215.

Of God will keep us out of heaven not less than profaneness, viii. 186.

Neighbour, scripture requires us to love, as ourselves, iv. 207 ; who ? 208 ; every one to whom we may be helpful *ib.* ; more especially those who dwell by us, and first our wife, then our children, &c., *ib.* ; spiritual, *ib.* ; what love ? 209 ; as ourselves in manner, not in measure, *ib.* ; to mind the good of others, *ib.* ; as truly, though not as much, as our own, 210.

New creature, orderliness of, ii. 241 ; is the wisest creature on this side heaven, 263.

What it is to be, xiii. 232 ; implies such a change wrought in us that we are other men and women than we were before, as if another soul came to dwell in our body, *ib.* ; this change must amount to a new creation, *ib.* ; some changes which do not go so far, *ib.* ; no change amounteth to the new creation which does not introduce the life and likeness of God, 234 ; why called a new creation, 235 ; how we are united to Christ in the new creation, 236 ; how the new creation floweth from our union with Christ, *ib.* ; the necessity of it, 237 ; how ill they can make out their interest in Christ that are not sensible of any change wrought in them, 239 ; the new creation the work of God and the effect of the Spirit, 241 ; this appeareth from the state of the person renewed, *ib.* ; the nature of the work, 242 ; its connection with reconciliation, 243 ; and the effect of it, 244 ; all things belonging to the new creation are ascribed by scripture to God, 245 ; the difference between the natural man and the new creature, 247; cautions against abuse of this doctrine, 248 ; it is not in vain to press people to become new creatures, 249 ; the true use to be made of the doctrine, 250 ; God the author of, as reconciled to us in Christ, xiii. 251.

New Testament testimonies to the divinity and humanity of Christ, i. 478.

Night a special occasion for meditation on holy things, ix. 82 ; on account of its solitude and silence, *ib.*

Niobe, the christian, xvii. 217.

No Excuse against a Speedy Obeying Christ's Call, ii. 121.

Not to be Offended in Christ the Ready Way to Blessedness, ii. 79.

Nullifidians, the doctrine of the, disproved, xvii. 428.

Oath, to bind ourselves by, to God and the duty we owe to him, concerns us sometimes, viii. 81 ; lawfulness of, appears from God's injunction, *ib.* ; and from the practice of the saints, *ib.* ; convenient to answer God's love and condescension to us in the covenant, 82 ; to testify our affection to his service, *ib.* ; very profitable because of our backwardness, *ib.* ; our fickleness and inconstancy, 83 ; our laziness, 84 ; should be used in a matter lawful, *ib.* ; and in a matter weighty, necessary, and acceptable to God, 85 ; must be religiously performed and observed, 86 ; the same motives which inclined us to make, should persuade us to keep, 87 ; our oath a further aggravation of our sin, *ib.* ; God hath ever been a severe avenger of breach of covenants, *ib.* ; should be often revived and renewed, 88 ; because we are apt to forget, and have not a lively sense of a thing long since done, *ib.* ; this forgetfulness an occasion of many and great troubles, 89 ; when to be renewed; *ib.* ; when we stand in need of some special favour from God, *ib.* ; after some special mercy, *ib.* ; when the state of religion is collapsed, either around us or within us, *ib.* ; when we are to draw nigh to God in the use of the seals of the new covenant, *ib.* See *Covenanting*.

Oppression, a very grievous evil, often deprecated by the people of God, viii.
259; is an abuse of power to unjust and uncharitable actions,
ib.; the oppressors are the proud, mighty, rich, great men, at least
by comparison with those whom they oppress, *ib.*; a grievous evil
in itself, *ib.*; odious to God, as being a perversion of the ends of
his providence, *ib.*; offensive to his people, and burdensome to
them, 260; is both theft and murder, *ib.*; aggravated when God's
servants are oppressed for religion, *ib.*; most of all when power and
advantage is fetched from any ordinance of God to commit it, *ib.*;
dissuasion from, 261.

Deliverance from, a blessing to be sought from God in prayer, viii.
399; we have liberty to ask temporal things, *ib.*; our spiritual
welfare is concerned in such temporal deliverances, that we may
serve God without impediment, 400; the glory of God is concerned, *ib.*; prayer engageth us to constancy, 401; seeking deliverance at the hands of God doth ease the heart of a great deal of
trouble, *ib.*; not to be asked in the first place, as our main blessing, 403; must be asked with submission, *ib.*; with the end that
God may be glorified, 404; in faith, that God can deliver, and will
in due time, when it is good for us, *ib.*; deliverance should quicken
and encourage us in God's service, 406.

Ordinances, their purity an honour to God, of great profit to the church,
and a rejoicing to God's people, i. 109.

Merit of Christ doth reach, that by them grace may be conveyed, and
sin mortified and subdued in us, ii. 209.

Their end to stir up love to God, ii. 245.

Simple plainness of, an obstacle to men's believing, iii. 224; administered by weak men, *ib.*

They who deny that they are useful to believers are ignorant of the
nature of grace, which always, after a taste, longeth for more, iv.
129; are ignorant of the intent and end of the word, which is not
only to beget us, but to make the saints perfect, *ib.*; are ignorant
of the state of their own hearts, 130.

They that would have grace must have recourse to, ix. 391.

God's people have a great value and esteem of, xviii. 147; by
a spiritual instinct, *ib.*; from experience, 148; from necessity, 149;
from utility and profit, *ib.*; esteem them above all other things, 150.

Others, to do to, as we would have them do to us, a sure and a full rule, ii.
370; Severus had it written in his palace, and engraved in golden
letters in the courts of justice, *ib.*; considered negatively, 371;
positively, 374; objections answered, 377; ground and equity of,
378; in what sense the law and the prophets, 379.

Our, force of, in 'Our Father,' i. 54; to comfort us in the sense of our interest in God, *ib.*; to mind us of the common interest of all the saints
in the same God, 55.

Pains, Christ not only bore, for our sakes, but those that we should have
endured, or at least equivalent to what we should have borne, if
we had suffered for sin, iii. 261.

Papacy, its wickedness marks it out as the man of sin, iii. 31.

Why not immediately destroyed, iii. 60; God hath uses for it, *ib.*; to
scourge his people for their sins, *ib.*; to try his people, *ib.*; to cure
our divisions, 61; to keep up a remembrance of his mercies, *ib.*;
its pomp and height about A.D. 1500, *ib.*

no other but Christ can procure this benefit, 274 ; the necessity of faith that it may be applied to us, 277 ; the use of baptism in respect of, 180.

Pardoning mercy the ground and foundation of all our hope and comfort in our restoration after distresses, xv. 438 ; reasons of this, *ib.* ; is the chief glory of God, 441 ; the excellency of the christian religion above all others in this respect, 445 ; the effect this should have on us, 446.

Parents should seek blessings for their children, xiv. 391 ; are guilty of more sin than they are aware of in depriving their children of the privilege of baptism, 393 ; should strive to keep up religion in their families by the education of their children, 394.

Their duty lieth greatly in providing meet callings for their children, xiv. 423.

Exhorted to bring up their children for God, xviii. 93.

Parliament exhorted to endeavour after unity, v. 404.

Paschal lamb prefigured the person of Christ, xviii. 477 ; his death on the cross, *ib.* ; the fruits and benefits of his sacrifice, 480.

Passing from death to life, what it is, xxi. 114 ; love of the brethren a sure sign of, 119.

Passions, great and excessive inconvenience of, i. 373.

Patience, threefold, ii. 248 ; bearing, *ib.* ; waiting, *ib.* ; working, 249 ; its influence upon religion, 252.

In running the race set before us, needed because of the length of the race, ii. 420 ; the impediments, *ib.* ; the discouragements from the spectators, 421.

Of Christ under oppression, iii. 337.

A grace of excellent use and value, iv. 33.

Christian, is a submission of the whole soul to the will of God, iv. 419 ; the judgment subscribeth, then the will accepteth, then the affections are restrained, and anger and sorrow brought under the restraint of the word, *ib.* ; progress of, *ib.* ; the soul seeth God in the suffering, God acting with sovereignty, sovereignty modified and mitigated in the dispensation of it with justice, mercy, and faithfulness, *ib.*

Persuaded by the example of the saints, iv. 426.

Of God, in not taking a full revenge of his creatures till the last day, x. 86.

Creation teacheth us a lesson in, xii. 181.

The fruit of hope, as hope is of faith, xii. 222; is of a threefold character—bearing, waiting, and working, *ib.*

And comfort of the scriptures, a higher thing than what is learnt by the institutions of philosophy, xix. 12.

A contrasted endurance of painful evils, xx. 203 ; under trials, is a manifestation of faith, 204.

And constancy under troubles, the honour done to Christ by, xx. 327.

Patriarchs had the same kind of faith that we have, xiii. 374.

Paul, commending himself to the Corinthians, furnishes an occasion of offence to the vainglorious, xiii. 100 ; his answer and defence, *ib.*

Valued the glory of God above that personal contentment and happiness that should come to him by his own salvation, xiii. 137.

Though an eminent christian, groaned under the relics of corruption, xiii. 172.

Pope, his universal bishopric impossible as to matter of fact, sacrilegious as to matter of right, vi. 308.

Popedom, its rise, i. 462.

Popery, to be detested, as of the devil, iii. 70.

    Cause to fear a return of, iii. 84.

    Absurdity of its errors, iii. 89; adoration of images, *ib.*; invocation of saints, *ib.*; works of supererogation, *ib.*; obstinacy with which they cleave to them, 90; given over to believe a lie, 91; why so many learned men continue in, 92.

    Its ways and errors damnable, iii. 97; they live in wilful disobedience to God, *ib.*; deprive the people of the means of salvation, 98.

Popish and heathen idolatry little different, v. 254.

Portion, God alone is the godly man's, vii. 107; a good portion, *ib.*; one that he has an interest in and a title to, 109; a proper and suitable good, 110; sufficient, 111; satisfying, 112; and delightful, 113.

Poverty and meanness of condition not disgraceful, iii. 231; should not be irksome to us, 232.

Power, omnipotent, can save to the utmost, infinite love can pardon to the utmost, if we can believe, iv. 54.

    God's, the great trouble of the soul ariseth from unbelief of, v. 363.

    God's, is his liberty and sufficiency to do whatever he may will, vii. 414.

    That goes along with the word, viii. 340; to humble and terrify, *ib.*; to convert and transform, 341; to comfort, 342; to confirm and strengthen, *ib.*

    Christ's, over all flesh, x. 130; is by grant and donation, *ib.*; if not God, he would not have been capable of such power, *ib.*; given to him as mediator, 131; not confined to the elect, *ib.*; not confined to the church and things merely spiritual, *ib.*

    One of God's greatest perfections, xiii. 434; in creation no attribute so eminent, *ib.*

    Of God necessary to bring us into a state of grace, xx. 286; to keep and maintain us in a state of grace, 287; sufficiency of, 288.

PRACTICAL COMMENTARY ON THE EPISTLE OF JAMES, iv. 1.

PRACTICAL COMMENTARY ON THE EPISTLE OF JUDE, v. i.

PRACTICAL EXPOSITION OF THE FIFTY-THIRD CHAPTER OF ISAIAH, iii. 187.

Practice, how much it exceeds speculation, viii. 24.

    Pleasure of, greater than of contemplation, xviii. 370; because practice giveth a more experimental knowledge, 371; the taste of things is kept up on our hearts by serious practice, *ib.*; every holy action is rewarded by peace of conscience, *ib.*; our title to the heavenly inheritance more clearly made out, *ib.*; our will is conformed to the will and law of God, *ib.*

Praise, christians more backward to, than to prayer, i. 76.

    Real (not merely verbal), is what God seeks, i. 78.

    And blessing God, distinction between, i. 244.

    The most effectual spiritual oratory or way of praying, i. 844; the noblest part of worship, 245,

    Every mercy received should lead us to, vi. 67; respecteth God's excellencies, as blessing or thanksgiving his benefits, *ib.*; to be with an upright heart, 69.

    Ought continually, frequently, and on all occasions, to be offered to God, viii. 111; a nobler duty than prayer, *ib.*

Praise, blessing God and giving thanks sometimes used promiscuously, but strictly blessing and thanks relateth to benefits received, praise to God's excellencies, ix. 191; faith and love must be at the bottom of, *ib.*; is an acknowledgment, by some outward expression, of the divine virtues, benefits, and perfections, *ib.*; the fruit of, is holiness, 192; is good and profitable, *ib.*; pleasant and delightful, *ib.*; comely and honourable, 193; should never cease, in respect of the preparation of the heart, *ib.*; should be for his word, 194; for the dispensation of his providence, fulfilling his promises to the faithful, and executing his threatenings on the wicked, 195; for favours, *ib.*; for afflictions, *ib.*; causes of backwardness to, 197; little love to God, *ib.*; neglect of observation, *ib.*

PRAYER, THE LORD'S, A PRACTICAL EXPOSITION OF, i. 1.

Prayer, the Lord's, analysis of, i. 3.

    Public, efficacy of, i. 8; private, encouragements to, from God's sight and God's reward, 9; how he openly rewards secret prayer, *ib.*

    Closet, a duty very necessary, i. 10; appears from God's precept, *ib.*; from Christ's example, *ib.*; from God's end in pouring out the Holy Ghost, 11; from the practice of the saints, 12; from our private necessities, *ib.*; very profitable, 13; conduceth much to enlargement of heart, *ib.*; makes way for secret manifestations of love on God's part, *ib.*; is a mighty solace and support in affliction, *ib.*; is a great trial of sincerity, faith, love, and obedience, 14; because of the great promises made to it, *ib.*

    Neglect of secret, a sin of omission, i. 14; omission of a duty which is very natural to the saints, 15; secret should in some respects be more prized than other prayer, 16; mischief which follows neglect of, 17.

    Private, excuses for neglecting, i. 19; want of time, *ib.*; want of a place, *ib.*; want of parts, *ib.*; exhortation to frequency in, 20; its seriousness, cautions, and warnings, 21.

    Ought to be simple and plain, i. 28; vocal, useful to bound our thoughts, warm our affections, and strengthen our faith, *ib.*

    Increases faith, love, and hope, i. 30; five abuses in, 31; idle and foolish loquacity, *ib.*; frothy eloquence and affected language, *ib.*; heartless speaking, *ib.*; mere outward vehemency and loud speech, 32; Popish repetition, and loose shreds of prayer often repeated, *ib.*; directions in, *ib.*; about our words, *ib.*; thoughts, 33; affections, 37.

    Affections proper in, i. 37; fervency, *ib.*; reverence, 38; confidence, *ib.*

    The Lord's, to be highly esteemed by christians, i. 39; though we are not tied to it as a form, yet it may be humbly used, *ib.*; preface to, 40.

    Incumbent as a duty on natural men, and yet they cannot discharge it, i. 49; duty with reference to, of those who do not know their adoption, 50.

    An act of the heart, not of the lips, i. 60.

    Lord's, contains four petitions for the bestowal of good, two for the removal of evil, i. 66.

    Is both an expression of a desire, and an implicit vow or solemn obligation that we take upon ourselves to prosecute what we ask, i. 66, 75.

    To be in love as well as in faith, i. 108.

    Is oftener from our memories than our consciences, and oftener from our consciences than our affections, i. 126.

increaseth, light increaseth, *ib.* ; as grace increaseth, their love to God increaseth, and so they hate sin more, *ib.* ; experience maketh them wise and provident, 90 ; they know more of the vanity of the world, *ib.* ; they are more acquainted with themselves, *ib.* ; by frequent communion with God they know more of God, and so more of themselves, 91 ; their work is now to look to the degree, *ib.*

Prolegomena to the commentary on James, iv. 8.

Promise, that it be immutable, three things necessary, iii. 152 ; that it be seriously and heartily made, *ib.* ; that the promiser continue in his purpose without change of mind, 153 ; that he is able to perform it, *ib.*

The accomplishment of one, confirms another, vi. 399.

Of mercy usually goeth before the bestowal of it, vii. 21 ; usually some time of delay between the promise and the fulfilment, *ib.* ; to try our faith, 22 ; our patience, *ib.* ; our love, 23 ; to enlarge our desires, *ib.*

Three things necessary that it may be certain and firm—that it be made seriously and heartily, with a purpose to perform it ; that the promiser continue in his purpose ; that he has the power to fulfil it, vii. 364 ; these concur in the promises of God, 365, 401.

Three things required in, viii. 263 ; *veritas,* sincerity, or truth in making, *ib* ; *fidelitas,* faithfulness in keeping, 264 ; *justitia,* righteousness in giving to him to whom the promise is made what the promise has made his, *ib.* See *Righteousness,* God's promise, &c.

Promises, God's, their sufficiency and stability, i. 312.

How they make us partakers of a divine nature, ii. 216 ; from their drift, 220 ; their matter, *ib.* ; their conditions or terms, 221 ; the power which accompanies them, *ib.*

Particular application of general, is necessary, vi. 404.

There are in the word of God, that we may believe, and others because we do believe ; to faith and for faith, vii. 23.

Of scripture, comforting in affliction, vii. 34 ; particularly of pardon of sin, *ib.* ; of eternal life, *ib.* ; concerning our temporal estate, 35.

To be made much of, vii. 202.

The children of God make more of, than others do, because they value the blessings promised, and believe that they shall be fulfilled, vii. 361.

God may suspend the fulfilment of, not because he is unwilling to give, but because he will have us better prepared to receive, vii. 365 ; to awaken fervency of prayer, and that the blessing may be more earnestly desired and more highly valued, 366 ; to prove and exercise our faith, *ib.* ; that patience may have its perfect work, *ib.* ; because the frame of his providence requires it, *ib.*

Some have been made to one generation and fulfilled to another, vii. 408 ; the same common, have been fulfilled to the faithful in all ages, *ib.*

God's, motives to take, for our heritage, viii. 144 ; every man hath some heritage, a chief good, *ib.* ; this is a portion which will go along with us wherever we go, *ib.* ; all other things will never satisfy, 145 ; this heritage sanctifies all our heritages, *ib.* ; it is a good sign of adoption, *ib.* ; this is a peculiar heritage, and always goes along with the favour of God, *ib.* ; they that refuse this heritage, the Lord's vengeance will seize upon them, *ib.*

Sacraments, a solemn means of our communion with the death of Christ, xi. 163. See *Communion,* &c.

And sacrifice, difference between, xiii. 444.

Sacrifice of Christ, its value commended by the dignity of his person, the greatness of his suffering, and the merit of his obedience, i. 431.

Every christian is, ii. 223; mortification is the salt wherewith it must be salted, 226.

Of Christ, the only true satisfactory and expiatory sacrifice for sin, iii. 387; because it was of God's own ordaining, *ib.*; other sacrifices but types of it, *ib.*; no other thing could be satisfactory and expiatory, *ib.*; it complied with God's design of discovering the glory of the Trinity, his love to the souls of men, and the Spirit's efficacy, 388; and of magnifying his justice and displeasure against sin, *ib.*

Instituted because of sin, xi. 427; the victims were substituted for the offender, and died for him, *ib.*; the offerings presented to God in our stead were consumed and destroyed, *ib.*; effects of, respect God, *ib.*; or sin, 428; or the sinner, *ib.*

Of Cain and Abel, the occasion of, xiii. 437; the warrant of, 439; wherein lay the difference between, 442.

Christ's death hath the true notion and full virtue of, xviii. 79; the new covenant made and confirmed by virtue of this, 80.

Christ's, accepted of God, xix. 182; the greatness of his sufferings, *ib.*; from the dignity of his person, *ib.*; the merit of his obedience, *ib.*; God hath himself declared it, 183; by his resurrection, *ib.*

Sacrifices, what was figured in the old, must be spiritually performed in the duty of prayer and praise, viii. 109; brokenness of heart, *ib.*; eyeing of the Redeemer, *ib.*; renewing of the covenant, 110.

Legal, were glasses to represent their misery, and the debt contracted by sin, xviii. 81; were figures of the mercy of God and the merit of Christ, 82; were obligations to duty, *ib.*

Sad, reproof of those who are always, x. 359; makes unfit for duty, darkeneth the ways of God, and brings a scandal upon Christ's spiritual kingdom, 360.

SAINT'S TRIUMPH OVER DEATH, ii. 439.

Saints, a praying people, i. 12.

Their privileges and benefits in the world to come, i. 374; freedom from all evil, *ib.*; enjoyment of all good, 375; their glorified bodies, *ib.*

We must be here, or we shall never be hereafter, v. 33.

In what sense they shall judge the world, v. 293.

Cannot give grace, ix. 383; have not a sufficiency for themselves and us too, *ib.*; have no power to transfuse and put over their righteousness to another, 384; nor authority and commission to do so, *ib.*

Permitted so often to fall that they may stand the firmer, x. 337.

Of all places and ages make but one perfect body, xi. 72.

They only are acquainted with the operations of the Spirit, xii. 254; they only are fit to converse with God in prayer, *ib.*

All believers are or ought to be, xix. 194; some are so only by external dedication and profession, *ib.*; others by internal regeneration, 195.

Blessedness of in the resurrection is complete felicity in body and soul, xx. 64; why the body shows the felicity, *ib.*; because the man cannot be happy till the body be raised, *ib.*; the body had its share of the work, and shall have of the reward, 65; the estate of those who die will not be worse than that of those who are changed, *ib.* ; in the heavenly state there are objects which only the bodily senses can discern, *ib.* ; as Christ's body is in heaven, so shall those of his people be, *ib.* ; felicity of the soul in the vision of God and the likeness of God, *ib.* ; perfection of justification, adoption, and redemption, 66 ; means of attaining, *ib.* ; holiness, dying to sin, and living to God, 67 ; sufferings, 68 ; rather than fail of, we must submit to any means which God hath appointed, 69.

Saints, their examples set before us for our imitation, xx. 110 ; those who lived in former ages, *ib.* ; their examples suited to persons of all degrees, and for all christian ends, 111 ; show that there is nothing impossible in our duty, and nothing so difficult but can be overcome by Christ's help, *ib.* ; confirm by experience the truth and reality of our hopes, 112 ; those now living, *ib.* ; they are in our eye, *ib.* ; greater provocation in their examples, 113 ; their circumstances are more like our own, *ib.* ; how to be imitated, *ib.* ; how far, 114 ; why, 115.

In glory, all have the same felicity in substance, but not in degree, xx. 233.

Glory reserved for, at the day of judgment, xx. 265 ; absolution pronounced by the judge on the throne, *ib.* ; a participation of judicial power, *ib.* ; Christ's public owning of them before God and his angels, 266 ; in the immortality, charity, and spirituality of their bodies, 267 ; the full satisfaction of their souls, *ib.*

And believers, identical, xx. 271.

Salt, wherewith the christian or a sacrifice is salted, is the grace of the Holy Spirit, by which sin is subdued and prevented, ii. 226 ; fitness of the comparison, *ib.* ; necessity of, 228.

Salting with fire and with salt, what it means, ii. 222.

Salvation, what it is, ii. 152 ; what the right of believers is to, 153 ; what the faith is that giveth a title to, 154.

Beginning and first cause of, the mere love of God, ii. 340.

Every well of, hath its proper stream, iii. 353

Business of man's, transacted by way of covenant between God and Christ, iii. 376.

Of sinners, Jesus Christ taketh an infinite contentment and satisfaction in, iii. 408 ; pleased and entertained himself in the thought of it before the world was, *ib.* ; the end and aim of his coming into the world, 409 ; his rejoicing in heaven to see the work thrive, *ib.* ; shall be his triumph and his joy when he cometh to judge the world, *ib.* ; nature of this satisfaction, *ib.*

We are not only to take care of our own, but of that of others, iv. 474.

None but Christ, iv. 479 ; none can be saved by him but those that know him and believe in him, *ib.* ; and that according to the tenor of the scriptures, *ib.* ; lesser differences in and about the doctrine of the scriptures, though consistent with the main tenor of salvation, yet if held up out of bye-ends, or against conscience, are damnable, *ib.* ; gross negligence, or not taking pains to know better, is equivalent to reluctation or standing out against light, 480.

Course of, first rise and spring in election, breaketh out in effectual calling, floweth down in the channels of faith and holiness, till it lose itself in the ocean of everlasting glory, v. 18.

Sermons, the actual profit we get from, is when we deal seriously with God about what we have heard, i. 18.

Servant of God or Christ, different applications of the term in scripture, v. 10 ; any kind of subserviency to God's will and secret counsels, or instrumentality in the execution of his decrees ; so Cyrus and Nebuchadnezzar, *ib.* ; noteth a pious care to perform God's revealed will ; so christian masters are said to have God for their master, *ib.* ; designation to any public office for God's glory, as magistrates, Old Testament priests, New Testament ministers, *ib.* ; especially the prophets and apostles, *ib.* ; Christ himself, because of his office of mediator, *ib.*

sanctification, *ib.*; justification considered with respect to the fault, the guilt, and the punishment, 51; whether all sins are forgiven at once, 53; the extent of the privilege, *ib.*; what the blood of Christ doth as the meritorious cause, 54; whence it hath its cleansing power, 56; the persons who receive this benefit, 58.

Sincerity, a kind of perfection, iv. 205.

Singing of psalms, a duty of the gospel, iv. 441; scruples about, *ib.*
Psalms, a godly exercise, xvi. 157.

Sinlessness, question of the possibility of, in this life, merely curious, and of no use and profit, iv. 275; of particular actions may be possible, *ib.*

Sinners, misery of impenitent and unpardoned, i. 175.
God may choose the worst of, iv. 267.

Sinning, many several ways of, iii. 304; by reason of the activeness of man's spirit, *ib.*; through diversity of constitution, *ib.*; from different businesses and occasions in the world, 305; custom and education, *ib.*; company and example, *ib.*
None absolutely good and exempted from, iv. 277; sins of the best are many, 298.

Sin-offering usually called sin, iii. 369.

Sins, God may blot out of his book, when he doth not blot them out of our consciences, i. 179; do not bring eternal death on pardoned persons, but may occasion temporal troubles, 180.
Of particular persons often bring mischief on the whole community, i. 188.
All mortal and damnable, i. 137.
Renewed, need new pardon, i. 426.
Not mortified are mortal, ii. 451.
Not all equal; all damning, not all alike damning, iv. 213.
Whether any are so foul in their nature that a child of God cannot fall into them, iv. 276; some gross corruptions very contrary to grace, into these they may fall, though very rarely and seldom, *ib.*; other sins extremely contrary to nature itself, into which a renewed man cannot fall, *ib.*
Seldom go alone, iv. 335; wantonness goes with drunkenness, envy with covetousness, &c., *ib.*
Degenerate human nature doth not only practise, but glory in, iv. 395; of ignorance, are sins, though more remissible, 396; of knowledge are most dangerous, *ib.*; of omission, as well as of commission, aggravated by knowledge, 398.
Often the cause of sickness, iv. 455.
Multitude of, doth not hinder our pardon or conversion, iv. 481.
Incident to sharp and tedious afflictions, vii. 375; impatience and murmuring against God, *ib.*; a spirit of revenge against the instruments of our trouble, *ib.*; using indirect means for our relief, 376; desponding and distrustful thoughts of God, 377; questioning our interest in God merely because of the cross, *ib.*; not only despairing, but atheistical thoughts, *ib.*; considerations to preserve us from, 378; we make our condition so much the worse if we fall into sin because of trouble, *ib.*; a sincere love to God will make us adhere to him when he seemeth to deal most hardly with us, *ib.*; by forgetting God's precepts we put away comfort from us, *ib.*; afflictions rightly imposed will make us remember God's precepts rather than forget them, 379.

very dishonourable and derogatory to Christ, 432 ; a dishonour to our profession, *ib.* ; very prejudicial, 433 ; very unreasonable, *ib.*

Sorrow, God's children oftentimes lie under the exercise of such deep and pressing, as is not incident to other men, vi. 265 ; their burdens are greater, *ib.* ; their sense is greater, 266 ; their exercise is greater, 267.

Immoderate, and uncomely dejection of spirit checked by consideration of God's faithfulness, vii. 278.

Soul, all other things must be hazarded for the saving of, ii. 141 ; only faith will make us do this, *ib.*

Blessedness of the saint's, in heaven, ii. 466 ; perfection of knowledge, *ib.* ; complete love, 467 ; complete union with, and fruition of, God, *ib.*

Its diseases greater than those of the body, as being seated in the nobler part, as a cut in the body is worse than a rent in the clothes, iii. 286.

Travail of Christ's, the affliction of his whole man, but chiefly of his inward man, iii. 401 ; suffered in his reputation, 402 ; in every part of his body, and through every sense, *ib.* ; consummated in his painful, shameful, and accursed death, *ib.* ; in his soul, 403 ; his desertion, *ib.* ; the apprehension of his Father's wrath, 404.

Salvation of, a christian's main care, iv. 151.

God must be served with, as well as with the body, ix. 228 ; because God hath a right to both, as he made both, *ib.* ; because soul-service is suitable to his nature, 229 ; because the soul is the principal thing, *ib.* ; is *fons actionum ad extra,* *ib.* ; *terminus actionum ad intra,* 230 ; it is hearty soul-service that will bear weight in the balance of the gospel, *ib.*

Is with Christ presently after death, xi. 94.

At death, is sanctified and purified from all imperfections, and brought into the sight and presence of God, xii. 15 ; at the resurrection, shall assume its body again, *ib.*

That it is distinct from the body appeareth from scripture, reason, and experience, xiii. 27 ; that it is not only distinct from the body, but can exercise its operations apart from it, and that the souls of the saints actually do so, proved from scripture, 29 ; at death the soul immediately appears in the presence of the Lord, *ib.*

Of man is a spirit, xix. 62 ; immediately framed by God, 63 ; returneth at death to God as judge, *ib.* ; its immortality, *ib.* ; proved from scripture, 64 ; from reason, 68.

Soundness of heart is opposed to the form of godliness, vii. 340 ; and to the sudden pangs and hasty motions of temporaries, *ib.* ; is such a receiving of the word into the heart that it is rooted there, and diffuseth its influence for the seasoning of every affection, 341 ; requires an enlightened understanding, 342 ; an awakened conscience, *ib.* ; a rightly-disposed will, 343 ; the affections purged and quickened, *ib.* ; value of, shown by the respect God hath to it, *ib.* ; and the evil it freeth us from, 344 ; directions to attain, 348.

Sovereignty of God modified and mitigated in the dispensation of it with infinite justice, ii. 337 ; great faithfulness, 338 ; great wisdom, *ib.* ; much love, *ib.*

Of Christ over his church is superadded to the sovereignty of God, the Father, Son, and Holy Ghost, as creator, xix. 458 ; is comfortable and beneficial to us, 459.

Sparing, sordid, a sure sign of a worldly heart, iv. 403.

272; these are continued and increased, *ib.*; there is a concurrence of God to the act, *ib.*; is needful for duty, *ib.*; for suffering, 273; for conflict, *ib.*; is wholly of God, *ib.*

Strictness, reproof of those who scoff at, xix. 354; not inconsistent with christian liberty, 355.

Striving, none crowned without, yet not for, iv. 75.

Study is like the winter sun, which shineth, but warmeth not; meditation is like blowing up the fire, when we do not mind the blaze, but the heat, vi. 140.

    Of religion, and the grounds of it, indispensable, vi. 294; the providence of God doth necessitate, *ib.*; sad consequences of erring, *ib.*; if we light upon a good way without search and choice, it is but a happy mistake, when we have no sufficient evidence, *ib.*; truth has a greater force upon the heart when we see the grounds and reasons of it, i. 295.

Stumbling, not light, but love, keepeth from, ix. 214; of God, *ib.*; of the law of God, *ib.*; of the brethren, 215; by this love the love of the world and its prosperity is much abated, *ib.*

Subjection of the church to Christ founded upon his authority, xix. 458; consisteth of willing and hearty consent to become his subjects, 459; and actual obedience, *ib.*; is willing, 460; thankful, *ib.*; constant, 461; reverential, *ib.*; universal and unlimited, 462.

Submission to God, as to the choice of instruments for promoting his glory, required, i. 77; and as to the ways in which it is to be promoted, *ib.*; to God, what it is, iv. 358; subjection to God's will, of the whole man to God's whole law, *ib.*; humble addresses, *ib.*; referring ourselves to the disposal of God's providence, *ib.*; must be performed sincerely, *ib.*; freely, *ib.*; faithfully, 359; considerations to urge this duty upon the soul, *ib.*; the necessity of it, *ib.*; the nobleness of it, *ib.*; the utility and benefit of it, *ib.*

    To providence, a fruit of faith, ii. 150.

    To God's will before the event a notable piece of faith; after the event, is patience, ii. 331.

    To God's will is not insensibility, ii. 335; but a work of the judgment, *ib.*; and of the will, *ib.*; grounds of, 336.

    To the will of God, we must pray and wait with, viii. 257; for the mercy itself, in what kind we shall have it, 258; for the time, *ib.*; for the ways and means, *ib.*

    To authority, ecclesiastical, civil, or economical, a duty, xix. 432; to be in love, *ib.*; in the fear of God, *ib.*

Substance (ὑπόστασις), meaning of the word, xiii. 324.

Success, not too much stress to be laid on, iii. 246.

Suffering and doing, which is the greater, xiii. 334.

    The greatest, to be chosen before the least sin, xix. 355.

Sufferings of Christ, inward, iii. 267; the assaults of spiritual wicked-ness, *ib.*; the desertion of God the Father, *ib.*; the impressions of his Father's wrath, *ib.*; suffered to free us from the wrath which he endured, 268; to satisfy for our sins that he had taken upon him, *ib.*

    Of Christ at his death, many and bitter, iii. 274.

    Of Christ laid on him by ordination and appointment of God the Father, iii. 370; he chose Christ's person, and designated and deputed him to the office of mediator, *ib.*; bestowed him upon us, 371; determined all his sufferings, *ib.*; not only foreknew and permitted, but concur-

special sin of the age, *ib.*; because it seemeth so small a sin, 171 ; because it is usually the hypocrite's sin, *ib.* ; because there is such a quick intercourse between the tongue and the heart, and the tongue is the best discovery of it, *ib.* ; bridling of, is restraint of lying, swearing, cursing, railing, ribaldry, 172.

Tongue, to be able to bridle, an argument of some growth and happy progress in grace, iv. 278 ; how to be done, 293.

Evil, is like a fire (James iii. 6), iv. 286 ; for the heat of it, *ib.* ; the danger of it, 287 ; the scorching, *ib.* ; kindled from hell, *ib.* ; evils of, of large and universal interest, diffusing themselves into all conditions and estates of life, 288.

Sins of, xviii. 389 ; lying, *ib.* ; railing, 390 ; ribaldry, *ib.* ; self-boasting, *ib.* ; cursing and swearing, *ib.* ; scorning and deriding at the power of godliness, 391 ; idle discourse and foolish garrulity, *ib.*

Is our glory, xix. 202 ; because thereby we can express the conceptions of our minds for the good of mankind, *ib.* ; and to the glory of God, 203 ; sins of, 204 ; filthy speaking, *ib.* ; foolish speaking, 205 ; jesting, 206.

Tradition, unwritten, hath no evidence of its certainty, iii. 25.

Doctrine of christianity is necessarily, iii. 127.

No rule of faith, v. 494 ; yet not all to be rejected, 498.

TRADITIONS, UNWRITTEN, SCRIPTURES SUFFICIENT WITHOUT, v. 485.

Traditions, either human or divine, iii. 123 ; unwritten not of authority now, 129 ; all not to be rejected, 134.

Trajan's testimony to the early christians (Tertullian), xiii. 383.

TRANSFIGURATION, CHRIST'S TEMPTATION AND, i. 255.

TRANSFIGURATION OF CHRIST, i. 337.

Transfiguration of Christ a solemn confirmation of his person and office, i. 337 ; a pledge of our glorious estate, *ib.* ; witnesses of, why three, why those three, 338 ; mountain of, supposed to be Tabor, *ib.* ; preceded by prayer, 339.

Of Christ, a necessary and solemn act of his mediation and manifestation to the world, i. 354 ; how his body, when transfigured, differed from his body at other times, *ib.* ; and how from his glorified body, 355 ; ends of, to show what Christ was, *ib.* ; what he should be, 356 ; and what we shall be, *ib.*

The voice from heaven Christ's instalment in his mediatory office, and showed his fitness for it, i. 392.

The disciples' fear and astonishment, i. 402 ; their comfortable and gracious recovery by Christ, 408 ; event and issue of, 410.

Transgressors, Christ reckoned amongst, especially in his death and sufferings, iii. 477 ; by wicked men, *ib.* ; by godly men, *ib.* ; by God, *ib.*

Treasure in heaven,' what it is, xvi. 481.

Tree of life, what it was to Adam, xxii. 16.

Trial, why God makes, of his people, iv. 30 ; not for his own information, but that we may know ourselves, *ib.* ; to convince the world by their constancy, *ib.* ; with a respect to the day of judgment, 31.

Trials, God's people are not to seek, but to submit to, when they come upon them, i. 204.

The common lot of the saints, xiv. 355 ; sometimes to discover their weakness, sometimes to manifest their glory, *ib.* ; are sent to prove their sincerity, faith, patience, and humility, 356 ; our obedience, contempt of earthly things, and our dependence and trust in God, 357 ; seeing we must have trials, we should look for and prepare

ceived wounds in the house of her friends, *ib.* ; when professors grow
worldly, *ib.* ; when they come, should not be thought strange, 370.

TRUE CIRCUMCISION, DESCRIPTION OF THE, ii. 23.

True nobility is to have a holy kindred, xiv. 394.

Trust a part of faith, ii. 351 ; respects all Christ's offices, *ib.* ; is practical, 352.

In God, an exercise of faith, whereby looking upon God in Christ
through the promises, we depend upon him for whatever we stand
in need of, and so are encouraged to go on cheerfully in the ways
wherein he hath appointed us to walk, vi. 449 ; how we ought to
depend on him for temporal supplies, 450 ; not to set him a task
to provide meat for our hearts, *ib.* ; not to be faithless and full of
cares about outward supplies, 451 ; cannot be absolutely confident
of particular success in temporal things, *ib.* ; must commit ourselves
to God's power, and refer ourselves to God's will, *ib.* ; our duty,
452 ; benefits of, 453 ; marks of, 455.

In God binds him to his promises, vii. 23 ; for his own honour, *ib.* ;
with condescension to his people, 24 ; with respect to their enemies,
ib. ; may be pleaded in prayer, *ib.*

In God, what it is to trust ourselves in the hands of the Almighty,
xxii. 23 ; how it is expressed and recommended to us in Ps. xci. 1,
26 ; how necessary a duty for all christians, 30.

Trusting God, utility and profit of, xviii. 59 ; grounds of, *ib.* ; to be against
carnal reason, 60 ; and carnal affection, *ib.* ; upon his gospel assurance, *ib.*

Truth, the good of the understanding, iii. 19.

Love of, what not to receive, iii. 79 ; in order to this love, the truth and
doctrine of Christ must be made known, *ib.* ; it is not committed
by bare weakness of understanding, 80 ; truth may be received in
the light of it while not in the love of it, *ib.* ; this love must not be
a slight affection, 81 ; just punishment of those who receive not
love of the truth, 83.

Constancy in the profession of, requires conviction and assurance of
the grounds of it, iv. 58.

Plain enough to those who wish to know, difficult enough to harden
others to their ruin, iv. 107.

Pretences of, are a disadvantage, arguing a conviction of the, and yet
a refusal of it, iv. 232.

Must not be violated for peace's sake, lest while we make peace with
men we make a breach with God, iv. 316.

Good to know in its frame, iv. 351.

Honoured by a bold and resolute defence of it, v. 113 ; all should contend for, 119 ; private christians, *ib.* ; magistrates, 120 ; ministers,
121.

The perfection of a rational creature, v. 130.

The good of the understanding, vi. 130.

The way of, to be chosen on the evidence of reason, vi. 310 ; of scripture, 311 ; and of the Spirit, *ib.*

God's, the instrument of sanctification, x. 418 ; God's way of working
is by light, and in infusing grace he beginneth with the understanding, *ib.* ; it must be a true, and not a false light, 419 ; every true
light will not serve the turn ; it must be the light of the word, 420 ;
not every part of the truth worketh, but only the gospel, *ib.* ; the
gospel worketh not unless accompanied with the Spirit, 421 ; it

ib. ; because of God's express exclusion, *ib.* ; from the heinous nature
of the sin, 216; because unclean persons are not meet for heaven,
217; the exclusion so absolute and peremptory, that it admits no exception but that of sincere repentance, *ib.* ; if the children of God fall
into, they lose not their right, but their present fitness, 219.

Unction, extreme, of the Papists, is but a ridiculous hypocrisy, iv. 447.

    The saints have a special, from Christ, to enlighten and confirm them in
the truth of the gospel, xxii. 95; what this unction or anointing is,
ib. ; the author or fountain of it, 99; the benefit, ' Ye shall know all
things' (1 John ii. 20); how this is to be understood, *ib.* ; why this
anointing confirms us in the truths of the gospel, 101; what we should
do to get this unction, 103.

Understanding is the great wheel of the soul, and guide of the whole man,
iii. 423; all the great opposition to faith is from, *ib.*

    David begs for, again and again, vi. 256.

    Got by the precepts of the word is better than that gotten by long ex-
perience, viii. 16; it is more exact, *ib.* ; a more sure way of learning
wisdom, whereas experience is more uncertain, 17; a safer and a
cheaper way of learning, *ib.* ; the way by age and experience is long,
and so a man's younger age must be miserable and foolish, *ib.*

    Is vain, unless it lead to hatred of sin, viii. 63; he is made wise that
is made better, *ib.*

    Spiritual, necessity of, ix. 30; because of our ignorance and folly,
which is the cause of all our sin, *ib.* ; because knowledge is our cure,
ib.

Undertakings must all be referred to the will of God, iv. 393; measuring
all our actions by his revealed will, *ib.* ; undertaking any action more
comfortably when we see God in it, *ib.* ; not binding the counsels of
God in our desires and requests, *ib.* ; constantly asking his leave in
prayer, *ib.* ; still reserving the power of his providence.

Ungodliness, God being the first cause, ignorance is ungodliness, v. 136; and
want of dependence on him, 137; and not observing his providence,
ib. ; and not sanctifying the things we use and undertake by asking his
leave and blessing, 138; God being the chiefest good, it is ungodliness not to think often of him, *ib.* ; not to delight in communion with
him, 139; not to fear to offend him, *ib.* ; not to care to please him,
140.

    God being the supreme truth and authority, it is ungodliness not to
receive the counsels of his word with all regard and reverence, v. 140;
not to yield him reverence in worship, *ib.* ; not to give a willing subjection of our hearts and lives to his laws, 141; God being the
utmost end, it is ungodliness not to aim at his glory in all acts,
natural, moral, spiritual, *ib.*

    What is meant by, xvi. 75; what it is to deny ungodliness, 77; what
it is in itself, 78; negatively, in denying God his due honour, reverence, and obedience, *ib.* ; positively, in putting actual contempt and
scorn upon God, 88; cautions against, *ib.* ; means to avoid, 89.

Unification of the heart, v. 453.

Union, necessity, excellence, and utility of, ii. 73; seven uniting considerations, 74.

    Mystical, is of believers with Christ, the head by faith, with one another
by love, x. 323; moral, is of believers with one another, consisting
of consent in doctrine, *ib.* ; and a mutual agreement and concord of
affection, *ib.* ; the end of Christ's incarnation, 324; no one thing so

Victory, Christ's, over sin, death, and the law, ii. 443 ; is imputed to us, *ib.* ; the benefit is imparted and applied to us, 444.

The christian's, not to be measured by prosperity or adversity, but by his adherence to God, vii. 156.

Of faith, the true believer is more than conqueror over the trials and tribulations of the world, xii. 393 ; the author or cause of the victory is Christ working through the Holy Spirit, *ib.* ; the nature of the victory explained, *ib.* ; the ends or things we contend for, 394 ; how we are more than conquerors, 396 ; who they are that will be more than conquerors, *ib.* ; reasons why we are more than conquerors, 397 ; persuasions to get such a degree of faith, love, and patience as will make us more than conquerors over the world, 403.

Of Christ over Satan is by his incarnation, xviii. 19 ; by his passion, or death on the cross, 20 ; by his resurrection and ascension, *ib.* ; by his sitting at the right hand of God, *ib.* ; by his secret and invisible providence, *ib.*

Violence, none in Christ, in spirit, words, or practice, iii. 366.

Virgins, christians are called, for the purity of their faith, ix. 321 ; of their worship, 322 ; of their conversation, *ib.*

Foolish, do not represent members of a church corrupt in worship, discipline or doctrine, ix. 323 ; nor scandalous members of a pure church, *ib.* ; nor only those that have a false or counterfeit profession, *ib.* ; but those who had a common, though not a saving, work in their hearts, *ib.* See *Common* work.

Virtue cannot be supported without the thought of a world to come, iii. 7.

Vision of Christ, in what it consists, xx. 460 ; is either ocular or mental, *ib.* ; three things are necessary to—a prepared faculty, a suitable object, and the conjunction of these, 462 ; the season when we shall enjoy this, 466.

Volition and velleity, difference of, vi. 50.

Waiting for the coming of Christ would much quicken us to repentance, ii. 251 ; engageth to holiness, and putteth life into obedience, *ib.* ; would produce a more heavenly temper and conversation, *ib.*

Implies an earnest expectation of what is to come, and a patient submission to God for the present, xii. 187.

Walking with God, what it implies, xiv. 52.

With God, in what it consists, xv. 405 ; reasons enforcing this duty, 409.

Wander, readiness to, men are the more sensible of, the more experience they have of the ways of God, vi. 96 ; through a large sense of duty, *ib.* ; and greater experience of difficulties and dangers, 97.

Wantonness, how the grace of God may be turned into, v. 49.

War, in a wicked man's heart, between him and his conscience, iv. 326 ; between conviction and corruption, 326 ; between corruption and corruption, *ib.*

Wars, whether any are lawful, iv. 327 ; nothing in scripture expressly against, *ib.* ; seemeth to be somewhat in the letter of scripture for, 328 ; may be proved lawful by such reasons and consequences as do well suit with the analogy of faith and the intent of the scriptures, *ib.* ; so little in scripture about it, because nature is so prone to, 329 ; conditions to lawfulness of, *ib.* ; a good cause, good authority, a right end, a right way of conducting, *ib.*

Watchfulness needed against occasions of sin, x. 398 ; and privy distempers of heart, 399.

Watchfulness, omission of, xi. 286; when we grow bolder with sin, and the temptations and occasions of it, *ib.*; when we make a small matter of those corruptions which were once so grievous and intolerable, 287; when we content ourselves with the customary use of holy duties, *ib.*; when we neglect the state of our hearts, *ib.*; spring and rise of, in the soul, from faith, 289; fear, *ib.*; love, 290; is never out of season, *ib.*; must be against Satan, 291; the world, *ib.*; the flesh, 292; more particularly the object is our thoughts, 293; occasions, 294; all appearance of evil, *ib.*; to prevent the sin itself, *ib.*; the mischief of heinous or presumptuous sins, 295; evil customs, 296; darling sins, 297.

Necessity of continual, xx. 82; the course of temptation may be altered, *ib.*; corruptions are sometimes strangely disguised, *ib.*; there is danger after suffering, *ib.*; when there seemeth to be least danger, there is often most cause of fear, *ib.*; when conscience is asleep, a child of God may fall into grievous sins, *ib.*

Watching is made up of prudence and diligence, ix. 413; with respect to our present state and safety, 414; for the avoiding of evil, *ib.*; for the performance of our duties, 416; *unto* prayer, *in* prayer, *after* prayer, *ib.*; with respect to our future state, that we may be ready to meet Christ at his coming, 417; consisteth in a deep and lively sense of Christ's appearing, *ib.*; in preparation, 418; and that speedy, *ib.*; serious and thorough, 419; constant and daily, 420; reasons to move us to, 421.

Way, every man naturally turneth to his own, iii. 308; implieth a defect or want of guidance, 309; a following the dictates of our own corrupt minds, *ib.*; and a fulfilling the desire of a corrupt will, 310; our own way not the right way to please God, 311; or to do good to ourselves, 313; cautions against our own way, *ib.*

Ways of God, undeserved censures cast upon, yet at length wisdom found in, ii. 101.

And laws of God, the more others despise, the more should a gracious heart love and esteem, viii. 308; because the ways of God are still the same they were before, *ib.*; God expects more from gracious hearts, 309; the good and bad do exercise and keep one another in breath and vigour, 310; unless our love be exercised at such a time, it will not hold out against so great a trial, *ib.*; because it is very acceptable to God, and a note of sincerity, to increase in zeal when others desert him, 311.

Of God, the privilege and duty of those whose hearts are set upon, to go from strength to strength, xviii. 317; reasons, 318; that we may recover what we have lost, *ib.*; to preserve what we have, *ib.*; to attain to what is promised, *ib.*; to perform what is required, 319; to answer the patterns set before us, *ib.*; to answer our many experiences, *ib.*; to answer the care and cost that God hath been at with us and for us, 320; motives, 322.

In which God and Christ are glorified when the work of faith is fulfilled with power, xx. 324; passively and actively, *ib.*; in the heart, *ib.*; with the tongue, 325; in our lives, *ib.*; by fixing this glory as the end of our lives, *ib.*; by doing such things as best suit with this end, 326; by our patience and constancy under troubles and persecutions, 327; by open confession and praise, 328; in deeds many ways, *ib.*

Weakness, God pardoneth much, where he findeth anything of grace and sincerity, iv. 268.

God's right, *ib.* ; our own incapacity, *ib.* ; the benefit that accrueth to us, 130.

Will of God, motives to a more tender regard of, i. 130 ; his absolute authority to command, *ib.* ; the equity of what he hath commanded, *ib.* ; to be given up to our own will a great judgment, 131 ; to be subject to, the truest liberty, *ib.* ; he who hath a heart bent to, hath the clearest knowledge of the mind of God, *ib.* ; God will surely punish violations of, 132 ; directions to do, *ib.* ; there must be some solemn time of resigning our wills to him, *ib.* ; and that without bound or reservation, 133 ; make great conscience of special things concerning which God has more expressly given charge, *ib.* ; be willing to obey God at whatever cost, 134 ; do not disobey him for whatever profit, *ib.*

Mistakes about doing, i. 134 ; pretending to do it in the general, but sticking at it when it comes to particulars, *ib.* ; commending and approving, but not practising, *ib.* ; having high thoughts of it, under temporary impulsions, without serious choice and invincible resolution, 135 ; being urged to do God's will by a seeming awe on the conscience, while yet the heart is averse from God, *ib.* ; an idle wish that we were brought under the power of it, *ib.* ; halving the will of God, 136 ; loathness to know the will of God, 137.

God's intended, is either secret or declared, ii. 330.

A twofold, as a twofold nature, in Christ, ii. 333.

Of God, disposing, demands absolute submission, iii. 144 ; governing, requires obedience, *ib.*

God's, is the supreme reason of all things, vi. 43.

Our own, is the proudest enemy Christ hath out of hell, i. 122 ; more corrupted than the understanding, *ib.*

Winning of Christ is getting an interest in him and his benefits, xx. 36 ; ransom from the wrath of God, 37 ; the favour of God and comfortable access to him, *ib.* ; restoration of the image of God, *ib.* ; supply of all wants, 38 ; hope of eternal life, *ib.* ; excellence of, above all other gain, *ib.* ; is most comfortable, universal, everlasting, and sanctifying, *ib.* ; in order to, must use the means, 40 ; submit to his terms, *ib.* ; trust in him that is true, *ib.*

WISDOM IS JUSTIFIED OF HER CHILDREN, ii. 93.

Wisdom means the doctrine of the gospel, ii. 94 ; children of, professors of the gospel, *ib.*

Justified more by works than a verbal plea, ii. 102.

And prudence shown by God in the dispensation of grace by Christ, ii. 257 ; as to the purchase and impetration of grace by the incarnation and death of his son, *ib.* ; as to the publication of it in the gospel or covenant of grace, 259 ; in the application of grace to particular believers, 262.

Needed for the right management of affliction, iv. 39 ; to discern God's end in it, *ib.* ; to know the nature of it, whether to fear or destroy, 40 ; to find out our duty, *ib.* ; to moderate the violence of our own passions, *ib.* ; must be sought of God, *ib.*

And knowlege do well together, the one to inform, the other to direct, iv. 299 ; true, endeth in a good conversation, 300; the more true the more meekness, *ib.*

True, is pure and clean, iv. 310 ; in heart and life, *ib.* ; from error and sin, 311 ; in word and deed, *ib.* ; evangelically and morally, 312 ; in inward frames and outward administrations, *ib.* ; from real defilements and defilements in appearance, 313.

them, *ib.* ; to depend upon God for the moderating of them and deliverance from them, *ib.* ; shows the experience of God's people under
the cross, *ib.* ; teaches that God governs all things for the good of
his people, *ib.*

Word of God abideth for ever in respect of its obligation and authority, vii.
461 ; in its fruits, *ib.*; eternal life is in it, 462 ; God's people have a
great love to, 463 ; it deserves this love in respect of its author, *ib.* ;
because of its matter, 464 ; recommended by its truth, *ib.* ; its goodness, 466 ; its profoundness, 468 ; because of its use, 469 ; the saints
readily yield this love, 471 ; because their hearts are suited to it, *ib.* ;
because they have tasted its goodness, *ib.* ; love of, will wean us
from sinful delights, 472 ; will make our hearts stable and upright
with God, 473 ; will give us a clearer understanding in the mysteries of godliness, *ib.* ; directions to get this love, 474 ; signs of it,
476.

He that would keep, must stand at a great distance, in heart and practice, from all sin, viii. 26 ; a christian must do both, *ib.* ; and both
with the whole heart, *ib.* ; the one required in order to the other, 27 ;
avoiding evil first in order, *ib.*

Of God, called a light, as it shows us the right way to our desired end,
viii. 65 ; as it convinceth of errors and mistakes, both in judgment
and practice, 66 ; by way of prevention, *ib.* ; of humiliation and
reproof, *ib.* ; in regard of comfort, *ib.* ; in outward darkness, *ib.* ; in
spiritual troubles, 67 ; types of, *ib.* ; the pillar of fire, *ib.* ; the lamp
of the sanctuary, *ib.* ; natural men have a sense of, and therefore fear,
68 ; godly men find a great deal of comfort and satisfaction from,
ib. ; those who go against, do sensibly miscarry, *ib.* ; is like its
author, ' God is light,' 69 ; those by whom it was given were holy
men, 70 ; God's end in giving, 71 ; that heavenly doctrine might be
kept free from corruption, *ib.* ; that it might be read of all ages and
sexes, 72 ; for converting of men, or leaving them without excuse,
ib. ; to be a rule of faith and manners, by which all doctrines are to
be tried, *ib.* ; is a full direction, *ib.* See *Scriptures,* clearness of.

We ought not only to love, but to love above all worldly things whatever, viii. 315 ; from the worth of it, and the reward and benefits
that are gotten by studying and obeying it, 316 ; because, if
it be not preferred before earthly things, it is not received with any
profit and good effect, 317 ; unless we love it above riches, we
cannot possess riches without a snare, *ib.* ; because, where grace
is planted in the heart and prevaileth, the desire of wealth is mortified, and worldly lust denied, 318 ; signs of such an esteem and
affection to the word of God, 319.

Of God, wonderful, viii. 333 ; in itself, *ib.* ; in its effects, *ib.* See
Testimonies, God's.

Of God, purity of, viii. 478 ; pure in itself, because it is a holy rule,
ib. ; as it maketh us pure if we diligently attend to it, *ib.* ; an appointed instrument by which the Spirit works in purifying our hearts,
ib. ; a fit instrument for this end, 479 ; as containing pure precepts,
ib. ; pure examples and patterns, 480 ; offering great helps to purity,
ib. ; excellent encouragements and motives from the rewards promised to the pure, 481 ; and terrible threatenings to the impure,
482.

Of God, love of, viii. 482 ; not an outward receiving, or a loose owning of it as the word of God, *ib.* ; not a bare approbation of its purity

fulness, 432 ; must be renounced when sinful in themselves or when
they cannot be kept and enjoyed without sin, 433 ; the influence
of faith upon this renunciation, 434.

Worldly lusts, what they are, xvi. 91 ; how they are to be denied, 96 ; the
difficulty of denying them, 98 ; how grace teaches us to deny them,
100 ; how unseemly and unsuitable they are to our condition, 101 ;
reproof of those that do not deny, but feed and serve worldly lusts,
103 ; exhortation and arguments to a denial of, 105.

World's duration, in comparison with eternity, short, iv. 423.

Worm that never dieth, means the anguish of conscience ; fire that is not
quenched, the anger of God, ii. 222.

That never dieth, fitly representeth the gnawings of conscience, v. 225.

Worship, to suit with the nature of God, must be spiritual and holy, not
pompous and theatrical, i. 34 ; of many is flat atheism, *ib.*

God to be sanctified in, i. 87.

The great end of, not so much the relief of man as the honour of God,
i. 244 ; praise the noblest part of, 245.

Implieth an act of the judgment, an act of the will, and an external act
of the body, i. 316 ; due to God, 317 ; and to God alone, 318 ; cannot be given to any creature without idolatry, *ib.* ; from its nature,
as a profession of dependence and subjection, cannot be terminated
on any object but God, 319 ; to give to the creature, is without
command, promise, or example, and therefore without faith, *ib.*; is
against the express command of God, the threatening of scripture,
and the examples recorded in the word, 320.

Heart, most seen in love and trust, i. 321.

To rest in outward duties of, a mark of pharisaism, ii. 12.

Internal, ii. 24 ; external, 25 ; reasons for, 26 ; reproof of those who
neglect, 27 ; of those who perform it by halves, 28 ; of those who do
not worship in the spirit, 29.

Controversies about, have ever been, are, and, for aught we can see, ever
will be, vi. 290.

Must be done out of conscience and with respect to the institution, xiii.
440.

Carnal men may join with the people of God in external duties of, xiii.
445 ; yet in the performance there is a sensible and manifest difference, 452 ; why it is so, and wherein the difference consists, *ib.* ;
this sensible difference ariseth from the influence and efficacy of faith,
465 ; why faith occasions this difference between worship and worship, 466.

Natural conscience and custom will put men upon the duties of, xiii.
446 ; vainglory and secular advantage two carnal ends from which
men act in such duties, 447 ; a bare performance of the outward
duties of, not enough, 448 ; notes by which we may discern the
working of natural conscience in the duties of religion, 450 ; wherein
lies the difference between the worship of the godly and the carnal,
453 ; this difference the effect of faith, 466.

Cases of conscience—(1.) Whether it be not a mere natural act to perform
duty with an eye to punishments and rewards ? xiii. 457 ; (2.) Whether
the children of God may not be surprised with perfunctory deadness,
and wicked men by high impulses be raised to extraordinary quickness and zeal in duties of worship ? 461 ; (3.) Whether the children of
God may not sometimes reflect upon a carnal end in the duties of
worship, and how far this is a note of insincerity ? 464.

and his institutions pure, 470 ; his servants free from injury and
oppression, 471 ; its acts with respect to these objects, *ib.* ; quickens
us to our duty, and makes us publicly active for God, *ib.* ; maketh us
spare no cost, yea, judgeth that best done for God which costs us
most, *ib.* ; vents itself by holy grief and anger when any of these are
violated, 472 ; must be accompanied with knowledge and discretion,
ib. ; must be mingled with compassion, that, as we mind the glory of
God, so we may pity deluded souls, 473 ; must be constant, 474 ; we
must seek for great and pure, if we have any love to God, his laws,
and his ways, 475 ; notes by which it may be discerned, 476.

Zeal, true, not seen so much in fighting with antiquated errors, as in being
established in the present truth, xi. 122.

    Carnal men count the zealousness of God's servants to be madness,
evidenced from scripture, xiii. 111 ; what it is in christianity which
is thus reckoned, *ib.* ; why it is so, 112 ; reasons showing how justly
this crimination might be retorted on the carnal world, 114.

    In good works a note of God's people and a fruit of Christ's pur-
chase, xvi. 275 ; what good works are, *ib.* ; the kinds of them, *ib.* ;
the requisites of a good work, 278 ; what it is to be zealous of good
works, 279 ; the place of zeal with respect to good works, 280 ; exhortation, 283.

INDEX OF TEXTS.

INDEX OF TEXTS.

Exodus.

chap. ver.	vol. page
23. 20–23	1. 289
— 20–22	13. 259*
— 20–22	14. 461
24. 8	22. 107
27. 20, 21	8. 67
28. 3	14. 236
— 35	19. 25
29. 9	19. 94
30. 12–15	16. 251
— 20, 21	19. 97
31. 3	14. 235
32.	21. 141
— 1	9. 240
— 7	7. 447
— 10	4. 465
32. 17	1. 44
— 25	12. 462
33. 12	21. 181
— 15	20. 258
— 18	14. 144
34. 5, 6	5. 57
— 5, 7	9. 465
— 6	6. 441
— 6, 7	21. 468
— 7	14. 9
— 13	16. 89
— 21	22. 91

Leviticus.

chap. ver.	vol. page
1. 9	19. 182
2. 14	16. 413
6. 5	16. 147
9. 24	21. 98
10. 3	5. 444
— 3	13. 132
— 3	15. 429
— 3	17. 443
— 9	16. 132
— 19	2. 432
13. 27–46	11. 271
14. 5, 6	11. 200
15. 4, 17	5. 359
16. 2	21. 186
— 6, 7, 10	1. 480
— 14	3. 492
— 21, 22	19. 187
17. 3, 4, 7	5. 252
18. 25	12. 182
19. 6	4. 380
— 15	18. 410
— 16	6. 126
— 17	19. 107
19. 17	21. 124
— 18	21. 87
— 33, 34	2. 372
23. 42, 43	14. 265
25. 23	5. 51
— 23	10. 309
— 25	16. 251
— 25, 26	18. 432
26. 25	20. 259
— 41	2. 335
— 41	15. 250

Numbers.

chap. ver.	vol. page
1. 52, 53	19. 96
4. 18–20	19. 96
6. 12	6. 314
— 12	14. 281
10. 9	15. 19
11. 12	9. 383
— 21, 22	14. 372
— 29	1. 80
— 29	13. 138
12. 3	16. 390
14. 9	22. 23
— 11	5. 181
— 11	21. 393
15. 38, 39	13. 397
16. 3	5. 272
— 6	12. 150
— 31	12. 163
— 32	12. 164
17. 12, 13	19. 97
— 17, 18	21. 186
20.	16. 388
— 12	21. 218
21. 8	17. 453
— 9	19. 33
22. 8–19	1. 135
23. 8	12. 332
— 8, 10	18. 42
— 9	13. 153
— 10	9. 291
— 10	13. 458
— 10	14. 290
— 19	16. 299
— 19, 20	18. 43
30. 2	8. 86
31. 16	18. 43
32. 23	14. 65
33. 23	21. 183
33. 42, 43	17. 459
35. 15	16. 335

Deuteronomy.

chap. ver.	vol. page
2. 3	5. 390
— 30	17. 227
3. 27	16. 393
4. 5, 6	6. 346
— 5, 6	19. 347
— 6	6. 261
— 23	18. 84
— 23, 24	19. 349
— 29	14. 162
5. 23	1. 59
— 29	6. 471
— 29	11. 313
— 29	17. 233
— 29	19. 151
— 29	22. 47
6. 5	6. 27
— 5	13. 169
— 5	15. 278
— 6, 7	8. 165
— 7	18. 93
— 16	1. 287
— 24	15. 398
7. 7, 8	2. 341
8. 2, 11	18. 46
— 3	1. 272
— 18	15. 88
9. 4	16. 46
10. 12	5. 75
— 12	15. 400
— 12	18. 144
— 12	20. 505
— 12–15	21. 466
— 16, 17	17. 201
— 20	1. 314
12. 30	14. 138
13. 3	14. 361
15. 7	21. 145
— 10	16. 478
— 11	21. 146
18. 8, 9	5. 260
— 10–12	17. 359
— 15	13. 288
— 15–19	1. 481
19.	16. 334
20. 7	19. 488
— 30	13. 156
21. 15, 16	21. 123
— 23	17. 460
22. 4	4. 476
23. 14	9. 111
24. 18, 19	19. 253
25. 2, 3	22. 34

Job.

Proverbs.

Matthew.

chap.	ver.	vol.	page
5.	29, 30	16.	73
—	29, 30	17.	50
—	29, 30	20.	72
—	32	12.	124
—	43, 44	19.	110
—	44	7.	375
—	44	19.	262
—	44	19.	23
—	44	21.	92
—	44, 45	19.	170
—	44, 45	21.	84
—	45	3.	488
—	45	15.	421
—	46	15.	293
—	46	19.	21
—	46, 47	16.	461
—	46, 47	18.	308
—	48	15.	398
—	48	20.	83
6.	1	16.	481
—	1, 2	21.	146
—	2	5.	30
—	2	18.	298
—	2	18.	469
—	2	19.	152
—	2-16	14.	92
—	3	12.	198
—	4	12.	118
—	6	9.	67
—	6	9.	240
—	6	18.	153
—	7	12.	240
—	11	15.	93
—	11	16.	160
—	11	17.	494
—	12	2.	188
—	12	13.	269
—	13	17.	404
—	14, 15	1.	184
—	19, 20	15.	84
—	19, 20	15.	418
—	19, 20	16.	481
—	19-21	2.	141
—	19-21	12.	330
—	20	12.	492
—	20, 21	13.	36
—	20, 21	18.	316
—	20, 21	21.	261
—	21	8.	392
—	21	13.	342
—	21	15.	85
—	21	15.	377

Matthew.

chap.	ver.	vol.	page
6.	22	4.	286
—	22	18.	152
—	22	20.	100
—	24	11.	268
—	24	11.	311
—	24	15.	280
—	24	16.	421
—	24	17.	19
—	24	20.	106
—	24	20.	124
—	24	20.	144
—	24	21.	369
—	24, 33	18.	190
—	25	6.	253
—	25	16.	142
—	25	19.	75
—	25	22.	25
—	25, 26	20.	145
—	25, 26	18.	451
—	25, 32	6.	453
—	26	16.	142
—	27	15.	101
—	27	16.	142
—	28-30	7.	189
—	29	16.	139
—	30	18.	177
—	31, 32	14.	238
—	31, 34	16.	140
—	32	7.	332
—	32	12.	248
—	32	13.	411
—	32	15.	492
—	32	16.	141
—	32	18.	71
—	32	20.	369
—	32	22.	24
—	33	1.	380
—	33	5.	53
—	33	8.	359
—	33	12.	333
—	33	12.	340
—	33	13.	7
—	33	13.	213
—	33	14.	218
—	33	14.	223
—	33	14.	447
—	33	15.	85
—	33	15.	99
—	33	15.	276
—	33	15.	403
—	33	16.	125
—	33	16.	142

Matthew.

chap.	ver.	vol.	page
6.	33	16.	411
—	33	18.	70
—	33	18.	301
—	33	19.	212
—	33	20.	19
—	33	20.	105
—	33	20.	135
—	33	20.	508
—	33	21.	257
—	34	16.	114
—	34	19.	360
—	37	15.	237
7.	1, 6	19.	121
—	3	15.	262
—	3-5	19.	123
—	6	21.	403
—	7	17.	159
—	7	18.	68
—	7	21.	262
—	7, 8	21.	194
—	9-11	12.	408
—	11	14.	146
—	12	15.	289
—	12	16.	149
—	12	19.	269
—	12	20.	277
—	14	12.	223
—	14	17.	63
—	14	22.	15
—	16	5.	280
—	16-18	19.	307
—	17	1.	46
—	20-22	6.	19
—	21	15.	160
—	21	16.	484
—	21	19.	452
—	21	21.	371
—	21-23	16.	17
—	22	13.	34
—	22	13.	92
—	22	18.	281
—	22, 23	10.	64
—	22, 23	16.	268
—	22, 23	21.	290
—	22, 23	21.	297
—	23	15.	484
—	26, 27	15.	171
8.	2	1.	249
—	2	15.	69
—	2	17.	91
—	2	17.	164
—	2	20.	488

Matthew.

1 Peter.

2 F

1 John

1 John.

INDEX OF PRINCIPAL TEXTS

Matthew.

chap. ver.		vol.	page
9. 13	...	2.	5
11. 6	...	2.	79
— 7–9	...	15.	487
— 18, 19	...	2.	93
15. 7, 8	...	5.	443
16. 24	...	15.	179
17. 1	...	1.	337
— 2	...	1.	347
— 3	...	1.	358
— 4	...	1.	370
— 5	...	1.	382
— 6–8	...	1.	402
19. 30	...	22.	41
22. 11–13	...	16.	11
— 14	...	20.	353
25. 1, 2	...	9.	319
— 3, 4	...	9.	331
— 5	...	9.	348
— 5, 6	...	9.	360
— 7, 8	...	9.	371
— 9	...	9.	383
— 10	...	9.	392
— 11, 12	...	9.	404
— 13	...	9.	413
— 14, 15	...	9.	423
— 16–18	...	9.	434
— 19–23	...	9.	447
— 24, 25	...	9.	461
— 26, 27	...	9.	470
— 28, 29	...	9.	482
— 30	...	10.	3
— 31–33	...	10.	14
— 34	...	10.	45
— 35, 36	...	10.	56
— 37–40	...	10.	66
— 41	...	10.	77
— 46	...	10.	100
27. 46	...	2.	264

Mark.

chap. ver.		vol.	page
2. 17	...	18.	3
3. 5	...	17.	191
4. 24	...	18.	420
7. 37	...	20.	364
9. 49	...	2.	222
10. 17	...	16.	409
— 18	...	16.	421
— 19	...	16.	433
— 20	...	16.	444
— 21	...	16.	456
— 22	...	17.	13
— 23	...	17.	24

Mark.

chap. ver.		vol.	page
10. 24	...	17.	36
— 25	...	17.	48
— 26	...	17.	59

Luke.

chap. ver.		vol.	page
2. 52	...	18.	116
9. 28	...	1.	337
— 29	...	1.	347
— 30, 31	...	1.	358
— 32, 33	...	1.	370
— 57–62	...	2.	113
12. 48	...	16.	363
16. 25	...	18.	295
— 30, 31	...	17.	353
17. 32	...	15.	369
19. 10	...	18.	155
— 14	...	18.	104
22. 20	...	15.	475
— 31, 32	...	17.	395
23. 34	...	19.	14

John.

chap. ver.		vol.	page
1. 29	...	18.	475
3. 14, 15	...	17.	453
— 16	...	2.	340
— 33	...	15.	379
8. 56	...	17.	167
13. 8	...	15.	450
14. 1	...	16.	345
17. 1	...	10.	109
— 2	...	10.	125
— 3	...	10.	139
— 4	...	10.	169
— 5	...	10.	185
— 6	...	10.	195
— 7	...	10.	218
— 8	...	10.	226
— 9	...	10.	241
— 10	...	10.	255
— 11	...	10.	269
— 12	...	10.	334
— 13	...	10.	352
— 14	...	10.	363
— 15	...	10.	389
— 16	...	10.	403
— 17	...	10.	411
— 18	...	10.	461
— 19	...	11.	3
— 20	...	11.	15
— 21	...	11.	23
— 22	...	11.	54
— 23	...	11.	62

John.

chap. ver.		vol.	page
17. 24	...	11.	89
— 25	...	11.	114
— 26	...	11.	131
18. 11	...	19.	3
19. 30	...	19.	29
— 34–37	...	22.	33

Acts.

chap. ver.		vol.	page
2. 38	...	5.	461
3. 26	...	2.	201
7. 55, 56	...	22.	70
10. 34, 35	...	18.	405
17. 30, 31	...	16.	397
21. 14	...	2.	327
24. 14–16	...	17.	419
— 25	...	18.	357

Romans.

chap. ver.		vol.	page
1. 29, 30	...	2.	275
2. 7	...	19.	145
4. 18–21	...	17.	179
5. 6	...	5.	475
6. 1, 2	...	11.	153
— 3	...	11.	162
— 4	...	11.	171
— 5	...	11.	181
— 6	...	11.	191
— 7	...	11.	201
— 8	...	11.	211
— 9, 10	...	11.	220
— 11	...	11.	228
— 12	...	11.	236
— 13	...	11.	246
— 14	...	11.	256
— 15	...	11.	299
— 16	...	11.	307
— 17	...	11.	317
— 18, 19	...	11.	327
— 20	...	11.	336
— 21	...	11.	343
— 22	...	11.	352
— 23	...	11.	370
8. 1	...	11.	385
— 2	...	11.	395
— 3	...	11.	420
— 4	...	11.	430
— 5	...	11.	438
— 6	...	11.	459
— 7	...	11.	469
— 8	...	11.	478
— 9	...	11.	484
— 10	...	12.	11

THE END.

*9 7 8 1 5 8 9 6 0 3 5 1 6 *